Jesus
The King and His Kingdom

Jesus
The King and His Kingdom

by
GEORGE WESLEY BUCHANAN

MERCER

MUP

All books published by Mercer University Press are produced
on acid-free paper that exceeds the minimum standards set by the
National Historical Publications and Records Commission.

Library of Congress Cataloging in Publication Data:

Buchanan, George Wesley
Jesus, the King and his kingdom

Abbreviations: p. xiii
Includes index
1. Jesus Christ—Historicity.
2. Kingdom of God.
3. Jesus Christ—Parables.
I. Title.
BT303.2.B82   1983   232.9'08   83-24939
ISBN 0-86554-072-1 (alk. paper)

Contents

To Professor William Reuben Farmer

Abbreviations

Allen	*ICC Matthew*	Allen, W. C. *A Critical and Exegetical Commentary on the Gospel According to St. Matthew* (New York, 1913; Edinburgh, 1965).
Aristotle	*Rhetoric*	Aristotle, *The Art of Rhetoric.*
Augstein	*Jesus*	Augstein, R., *Jesus the Son of Man*, tr. H. Young (New York, 1977).
Bailey	*Poet*	Bailey, K. E., *The Poet and the Peasant* (Grand Rapids, 1976).
Brown	*Birth*	Brown, R. E., *The Birth of the Messiah* (Garden City, 1977).
GWB	*Consequences*	GWB, *The Consequences of the Covenant* (Leiden, 1970).
	Revelation	GWB, *Revelation and Redemption.*
Bultmann	*History*	Bultmann, R., *The History of the Synoptic Tradition*, tr. J. Marsh (New York, 1962).
	"Study"	Bultmann, R., "The Study of the Synoptic Gospels," *Form Criticism*, tr. F. C. Grant (New York, c1962).
	Theology	Bultmann, R., *Theology of the New Testament*, tr. K. Grobel (New York, 1951) I.

Meyer	*Matthew*	Meyer, N. A. W., *Critical and Exegetical Hand-Book to the Gospel of Matthew*, tr. P. Christie (New York, 1884).
Montgomery	*ICC Daniel*	Montgomery, J. A., *A Critical and Exegetical Commentary on the Book of Daniel* (New York, 1927).
Morgenstern	*Antecedents*	Morgenstern, J., *Some Significant Antecedents of Christianity* (Leiden, 1966).
	"Calendar"	Morgenstern, J., "The Calendar of the Book of Jubilees, its Origins and its Character," *VT* 5 (1955): 34-76.
Perrin	*Rediscovering*	Perrin, N., *Rediscovering the Teaching of Jesus* (New York, c1967).
Plummer	*ICC Luke*	Plummer, A., *A Critical and Exegetical Commentary on the Gospel according to Luke* (Edinburgh, 1969).
	Matthew	Plummer, A., *An Exegetical Commentary on the Gospel according to St. Matthew* (London, 1909).
Sayre	*Cynics*	Sayre, F., *The Greek Cynics* (Baltimore, 1948).
Schniewind	*Matthäus*	Schniewind, J., *Das Evangelium nach Matthäus* (Göttingen, 1950).
Schweitzer	*Quest*	Schweitzer, A., *The Quest of the Historical Jesus*, tr. W. Montgomery (London, 1956).
Soiron	*Bergpredigt*	Soiron, T., *Die bergpredigt Jesu: Forgeschichtliche Exegetische und Theologische Erklärung* (Frieburg, 1941).
Strecker	"Makarismen"	Strecker, G., "Die Makarismen der Bergpredigt," *NTS* 17 (1971): 255-75.
Taylor	*Formation*	Taylor, V., *The Formation of the Gospel Tradition* (London, 1949).
Vermes	*Jesus*	Vermes, G., *Jesus the Jew* (London, 1973).

Preface

My interest in the historical Jesus began in Sunday school, but it was not until Dr. Ernest W. Saunders taught a course, "The Life and Teachings of Jesus," at Garrett-Evangelical Theological Seminary that I began to realize the problems involved in learning details about the life of this important person. I continued as a skeptic, from the historiographical point of view, while studying form criticism under the guidance of Dr. Henry Cadbury, Dr. Vincent Taylor, and Dr. Morton Smith at Drew University. It was Dr. William R. Farmer, director of my Ph.D. program, who encouraged me to think the quest of the historical Jesus might be a fruitful endeavor. He also introduced me to *The Groundwork of the Gospels*, by R. O. P. Taylor (Oxford, 1946), from which I began work on the chreia as a literary form. It is to Professor Farmer that I dedicate this book in appreciation for his inspiration and guidance.

Jewish linguistic and literary backgrounds for this study were strengthened with the support of Horowitz and Scheuer fellowships to study at Hebrew Union College-Jewish Institute of Religion, Cincinnati, Ohio, 1957-

1960, and a Hebrew Union College Biblical and Archaeological School fellowship for study at Jerusalem, 1966-1967. With the aid of a Bollingen grant, I spent the summer of 1957 in Nablus, Jordan, participating in an archaeological excavation and visiting with Jordanians. An Association of Theological Schools grant enabled me to discover the northern boundaries of the promised land during the summer of 1966. Conversations with Syrians and Lebanese not only helped me to understand better the geography of the Near East but also increased my knowledge of Near Eastern customs. This was further increased during the summer of 1973. The summer of 1972 I spent in linguistic studies in Jerusalem, and the year 1973-1974 found me in Jerusalem translating theological, apocalyptic, and poetic documents composed from the time of Bar Kokhba until the end of the Crusades. I spent the summer of 1968 in Göttingen, West Germany, learning the scholarly reaction to H. S. Reimarus in the eighteenth century.

Twenty-one years of teaching theological students has also helped to clarify my understanding of the historical Jesus. An Association of Theological Schools grant, together with the Claremont-Society of Biblical Literature Fellowship, enabled me to spend the entire year, 1980-1981, at the Institute for Antiquity and Christianity, Claremont, California, preparing this manuscript for publication. This undisturbed period, with access to Claremont Graduate Schools' libraries and the Institute for Antiquity and Christianity's word processor, was a very fruitful time for the development of this manuscript. I am exceedingly grateful to all of the agencies that have provided me with opportunities for the kind of research needed to understand the historical Jesus.

From one to three chapters of this book have been read at some stage in its development by Professors William R. Farmer, Ronald Hock, Marvin Meyer, James M. Robinson, and Morton Smith. Their suggestions have all been helpful, but they are not responsible for the contents of the book. The administration and faculty of Wesley Theological Seminary where I have taught for more than twenty years must also be exonerated from any criticism that might come to this book. I accept responsibility for all ideas in the book that have not been acknowledged as having come from some other source. I also assume responsibility for all translations of biblical and other texts quoted in the manuscript that are not documented otherwise. I have deliberately rendered most passages in a rather ''wooden'' fashion that is intended to disclose the grammatical form of the language that was translated. This is particularly true of those passages which illustrate literary forms.

Chapter one, "The Kingdom of God," is an update of chapter two in *The Consequences of the Covenant* (Leiden: E. J. Brill, 1970). Chapter five, "Monasticism and Economic Classes," is principally composed of two articles published earlier: (1) "Jesus and the Upper Class," *Novum Testamentum* 7 (1964):195-209, and (2) "Jesus and other Monks of New Testament Times," *Religion in Life* 48 (1979):135-42. The discussion on Johannine miracles in chapter nine is taken from a previously published article, "The Samaritan Origin of the Gospel of John," J. Neusner, ed., *Religions in Antiquity* (Leiden: E. J. Brill, 1970) 149-75. A part of chapter three was summarized and published in an earlier form as "Chreias in the New Testament," J. Delobel, ed., *Logia: The Sayings of Jesus* (Leuven, 1983) 501-505. I appreciate the permission that has been granted by the various publishers involved to use these materials again in this book.

My cousin, Ms. A. Lucille Loudenback, has read the entire manuscript for clarity and comprehensibility and has made good suggestions for its improvement. My wife, Harlene, has read the manuscript several times and has made many suggestions for improvement of sentence structure, style, and grammar. More than that, she has been my constant encouragement and emotional support, not only in this project, but in all my research. I am grateful to all of my students, colleagues, relatives, and friends who have stimulated and assisted in this research.

An
Introductory
Note

Inasmuch as many have set their hands to organize narratives about the things that have been fulfilled in our midst, just as those who were eyewitnesses and servants of the word have handed down to us by tradition, it seemed [proper] also to me, having followed all things carefully for some time, to write an orderly account for you . . . so that you may know the [degree of] confidence [that is justified] concerning the things you have been taught (Lk 1:1-4).

In the first draft of this book, I had a separate chapter listing and appraising the works of other scholars from the time of Reimarus in the eighteenth century until our day. This had required a certain amount of selection and omission, as the summarizing judgments required by space limitations seemed inadequate and sometimes necessarily unfair. Since I was already faced with a problem of length, not wanting to produce another book that was too expensive for anyone to buy and read, I omitted that chapter. I reasoned that others[1] have done this work very well and anyone who chooses can read other surveys and analyses of previous scholars. Furthermore, I much prefer analyzing historical data to passing judgment on other scholars. Since, however, I sometimes lead the readers across minefields of scholarly objection, I tried to show in footnotes and appendices the views of other scholars on the subjects discussed. Later, in the interests of space, the three appendices were omitted, since two of them have been published in an earlier form.[2] Analyses of other scholars in footnotes are by no means complete because I have endeavored not to raise any unnecessary smoke screens. The major emphasis here is not the views of others but the data needed to make decisions. This book represents the results of twenty-five years of searching, collecting, sorting, and organizing materials that I think are relevant to learning that which can be known of the historical Jesus.

As a Christian, I have found honest analysis of what is known about the historical Jesus as difficult as most Christians do. Like other Christians, I have theological and ethical opinions as well as historical judgments. It seems to me, however, that one of the basic reasons Christians have not satisfactorily come to grips with research about the historical Jesus has been our inability to separate theological from historical judgments and to be objective enough to reach accurate conclusions, even if they do not please us. It does not seem helpful to any religion to evade truth, whether that truth is at first comfortable or not. It is preferable *first* to face the facts as closely as we can and then to decide the ethical and religious issues that follow with clearer vision than would otherwise be possible. Therefore I have tried to examine the historical Jesus with the same objectivity that a historian would expect to apply to the historical Socrates, Diogenes, or Rabbi Johanan ben

---

[1]For the response of German scholarship and church leadership to H. S. Reimarus, see GWB, "Introduction," H. S. Reimarus, *The Goal of Jesus and his Disciples* (Leiden, 1970) 1-32. For nineteenth century scholarship, see A. Schweitzer, *The Quest of the Historical Jesus,* tr. W. Montgomery (New York, c1968). For twentieth century scholarship, see J. M. Robinson, *A New Quest of the Historical Jesus* (Naperville, c1959); W. G. Kümmel, "Ein Jahrzehnt Jesusforschung (1965-1975)," *Theologische Rundschau* 40 (1975):289-336; and P. Merkley, "New Quests for Old: An Historian's Observation on a Bad Bargain," *CJT* 16 (1970):203-18.

[2]For an analysis of the Son of man in Daniel, Enoch, and the gospels, see GWB, *To the Hebrews* (Garden City, 1972) 38-51. For an analysis of the Beatitudes in the Gospel of Matthew, see GWB, "The Matthaean Beatitudes," W. R. Farmer, ed., *New Synoptic Studies* (Macon GA: Mercer University Press, 1983).

Zakkai, searching in every way possible to gain access to facts and find ways of testing the data for accuracy.

According to Francis Bacon, ''It is the true office of history to represent the events themselves together with the counsels, and to leave the observations and conclusions thereupon to the liberty and faculty of every man's judgment.'' I not only want to leave the situation open for ''every man's judgment,'' but also to every woman's, assuming that all readers are capable of reaching legitimate conclusions if they have access to the data. Data can be slanted, however, simply by the inclusion and exclusion of information. I have tried to protect the reader from this eventuality whenever possible by presenting all the information necessary for reaching a conclusion. For instance, in testing literary forms, I have included *all* the literary forms called chreias (some transliterate the plural as *chreiai*) and parables in the gospels. In situations where this amount of data seems to be an obstacle to anyone except technical scholars I have summarized the content of an argument in the text and referred to details in earlier publications, so that those who wish may stop at that point, look up the earlier article and read it. Others may continue the chapter without interruption.

One of the omitted appendices included an English translation of a large collection of chreias published by F. W. A. Mullach, "De Diogene Cynico," *Fragmenta Philosophorum Graecorum* in three volumes (Darmstadt, 1968) 2:295-330. *All* of the chreias in that collection were used for analysis here. Those who wish may check the Greek text of Mullach. There may be others, however, who want to check the English translation of these chreias, organized according to subject matter. Such people as these may send me a large envelope with enough postage to mail twenty-two pages, and I will send them this list free of charge. It is not my desire to withhold from readers data that has been used for conclusions drawn here.

I try to appraise the degree of confidence that the conclusion holds in relationship to the data presented, allowing alternate points of view that are also justified. I assume that many will accept the alternate conclusions, especially book reviewers. Those who do, of course, will have better bases for their own conclusions than they would have had if they had not considered the information presented here. One of the purposes of the book is not just to defend one point of view but to stimulate further interest in honest analysis and continuing research. The search for truth is more important than one definite set of conclusions.

In addition to studying Greek and Latin writings, anyone who wishes to understand the life, times, and teachings of Jesus must learn as much as possible about the surrounding literature—both Jewish and Christian—from the times before, during, and after Jesus lived. No one can master this extensive body of literature perfectly, but, like others, I have tried to control as much as I could. The first place in this study belongs to the New Testament. In the second place there is the pre-New Testament literature, including the Hebrew Bible (the "Old Testament" for Christians), most of the apocrypha and pseudepigrapha (intertestamental literature), the works of Philo, and the Dead Sea Scrolls. Contemporary with New Testament literature are Second Baruch, Fourth Ezra, the works of Josephus, and probably some of the apostolic fathers. Some of the targumin may have been written before, during, or after the composition of the New Testament. In post-New Testament times one finds most of the apostolic fathers, The Ante-Nicene and Post-Nicene fathers, The Tannaitic literature, and all of the rest of the medieval Jewish literature.

Most Christian readers know something about all this except for the rabbinic literature. Very few New Testament scholars are familiar with rabbinic literature and even fewer understand legitimate ways to use this literature for improving their understanding of the New Testament.[3] Therefore I will briefly survey rabbinic literature.

Scholars are not agreed on the dates when the targumim originated. Some hold that they were all written in pre-Christian times, whereas others say they were composed as late as the third or fourth centuries A.D. References to targum passages are indicated by a capital letter to indicate the name of the targum, the abbreviation "targ," and the Old Testament passage translated. For example, NTarg Deut 6:1 means Neophyti Targum on Deut 6:1. The targumim are more or less free translations of the Hebrew Bible. They are useful, because they show how Jews understood the Scripture sometime during the period between the first two pre-Christian centuries and the third or fourth centuries A.D.

The Tannaitic literature includes the Mishnah, at least the parts of the Tosephta that are parallel to the Mishnah, and the Tannaitic Midrashim. The

---

[3]For a more extensive and better documented presentation, see GWB, "The Use of Rabbinic Literature for New Testament Research," *Biblical Theology Bulletin* 7 (1977):110-22. That essay was earlier delivered to a plenary session of the Hudson Bay region of the Society for Biblical Literature at the University of Pennsylvania.

Mishnah is an extensive collection of Jewish Laws, organized according to their subject matter. They are documented according to chapter and verse, just as biblical references are. For example San 4:2 refers to Mishnah Sanhedrin chapter 4, verse 2. There is a synoptic relationship between parts of the Mishnah and parts of the Tosephta. The Tosephta is a larger collection than the Mishnah, and scholars disagree about whether the Tosephta passages that are unique were added later or were laws the Mishnah omitted. The letter *T* distinguishes Tosephta passages from Mishnah passages. TSan 4:2-3, for instance, means Tosephta chapter 4, verse 2 and 3.

The Tannaitic midrashim include Mekilta, Sifre, and Sifra. Mekilta is a commentary on parts of the book of Exodus and is documented according to subheading, chapter, and verse. Thus Mek, *Bahodesh* 9:65-68 means Mekilta, chapter 9, verses 65-68. Sifre is a commentary on parts of Numbers and Deuteronomy. It is documented according to the Old Testament passage on which the comment has been made was well as the number of its paragraph and the page on which it is found. Thus SDeut 33:6; #347; 144a means Sifre on Deuteronomy 33:6, paragraph 347, page 144a. Some rabbinic literature is numbered according to its *daf*. A *daf* is a sheet of paper with two pages. These pages are noted either *a* or *b*. Some sheets have two columns per page. Therefore each *daf* has four columns, numbered a-d. The above Sifre reference to 144a means *daf* 144, column a. Sifra is a verse-by-verse commentary on the complete book of Leviticus. It has been divided into several degrees of subheadings that cannot be abbreviated easily. Therefore, only one of these is given, together with the Old Testament passage involved and the page number. Thus SLev 12:5, *Tazria'* 58d means Sifra on Leviticus 12:5, subheading *Tazria'*, *daf* 58, column d. Tannaitic literature competes with the targumim for the earliest place in rabbinic literature. No one is quite sure when these documents were written or when the laws they contain were composed, but they are roughly dated between A.D. 70 and 225.

The Talmud is a commentary by later rabbis on the Mishnah and is documented according to column. San 97a means Babylonian Talmud *daf* 97, column a. The Jerusalem Talmud is distinguished by the initial letter *J*. Therefore JKidd 59d means Jerusalem Talmud on Mishnah Kiddushin, *daf* 59, column d. These were composed sometime between A.D. 225 and 1000. There are numerous other smaller commentaries, collections of sermons, hymns, poems, and letters also belonging to the middle ages.

Some scholars date rabbinic passages according to the rabbi to whom quotations have been attributed, but this is not valid. Rabbinic scholars have not yet worked critically enough on these texts to know whether a saying attributed to an early rabbi was really first said by that rabbi or whether some later rabbi attributed his own or someone else's saying to him. Some sayings have been attributed to two different rabbis of different periods.

Some scholars also admit that some rabbinic sayings are reported in documents that belong to late medieval Judaism, but they affirm without evidence that, "of course," they represent "very early" traditions, and therefore presume that they were sources for New Testamen authors. It is true that there are old traditions in some of these late documents, but that cannot be presumed. Their primitive status must be established point by point, and sometimes this can be done.

Rene Bloch,[4] for example, found a traditional story which announced the birth of Moses to Pharaoh in the following documents: Jerusalem Targum, The Chronicle of Moses, Sefer Ha-Yasher, Yalkut Shimoni, Sefer Ha-Zikhronot, San 101a, Sotah 12b, Rashi's Commentary on Exodus, Pirke Rabbi Eliezer, Tanhuma, and Exodus Rabbah. Some of these documents are very late, but she also found the same story in Josephus, *Antiquities*, which was composed in the first century A.D. This means some form of this tradition was early enough to have been used by the synoptic gospel writers. If, by further study, it could be shown that the story in an early datable source, such as Philo or Josephus, was a commentary on a source found in one of the late medieval works, it might then be presumed that the tradition contained in this late document represented a tradition earlier than the works of Philo or Josephus, but this has not been shown in many rabbinic passages.

McNamara has found some cases in which the New Testament author has quoted a reference which does not agree exactly with either the Masoretic text or the Septuagint, but instead follows a text of some targum passage.[5] In these instances, it may be supposed that at least these passages of the targum involved were composed earlier than their quotations in the New

---

[4]R. Bloch, "Note Methodologique pour L'Etude de la Literature Rabbinique," *RSR* 43 (1955):121-27.

[5]M. McNamara, *The New Testament and the Palestinian Targum to the Pentateuch* (Rome, 1966) 70-81.

Testament. There are still more cases where the same tradition occurs both in the New Testament and one of the targumim alone. In these cases it is reasonable to assume that the tradition involved is at least as old as these two documents.

Sometimes a targum will contain a prediction about some historic character which was not fulfilled by history. In these cases, it seems that the prediction was written down before the outcome was known.[6]

When all of these examples are totaled, they constitute only a very, very small percentage of the entire body of rabbinic material. Therefore rabbinic literature is not very useful for showing sources for New Testament literature. It is useful, however, for other purposes, and it is these other purposes that are important for the research done on this book.

Anyone who has read copiously in the Old Testament, New Testament, apocryphal writings, church fathers, the works of Philo and Josephus, the Dead Sea Scrolls, and rabbinic literature becomes convinced of the tenacity by which early Judaism and Christianity held to traditions. Surprisingly, many of these traditions cut across all sorts of sectarian boundaries. It is quite common for an Essene practice not only to be found in Tannaitic literature but also in mediaeval Karaitic sources and in so-called "Christian Gnostic" works. Customs, laws, teachings, and practices that are reported in the Old Testament, New Testament, apocrypha, pseudepigrapha, Dead Sea Scrolls, church fathers, and rabbinic literature do not prove that there is any kind of a literary dependence of one of these documents on any other. It just means that several sects at different periods of history were familiar with the same practice. If, however, these various accounts are collected and compared, there is often more detail in some than in others which simply allude to the practice without describing it or defining its significance. The more definitive reports can then be used to clarify some of those which are less complete. That is a practice which I have employed here. When references are given from various documents in relationship to a New Testament text, this does not imply that I think either that Jesus had read a source quoted by some late rabbinic document or that the New Testament author involved had used rabbinic literature. It just means that the New Testament passage involved was not unique. It belonged to a tradition that was used both by early Christians and Jews. For example, the gospels report that Je-

---

[6]P. Kahle, *The Cairo Geniza* (Oxford, 1959) 202-203.

sus was in conflict with other Jews about Sabbath practices, without detailing what all of the rules were governing the Sabbath. The rules which Jesus could have read, however, are spelled out in the Pentateuch, and other Old Testament documents, such as the works of Jeremiah or Nehemiah, show how these laws were applied. Detailed implications are also given, showing sometimes differing interpretations, in the Damascus Document, the Mishnah, Tosephta, and both Talmuds. When these are all consulted, the researcher has a good idea of the atmosphere against which the conflicts in the New Testament took place, without claiming any dependence of the New Testament on any of the documents involved.

Readers may, and reviewers certainly will, judge for themselves the extent to which I have used these rabbinic materials fairly.

Procedurally, this book begins with a comparison of the political situation in the Near East today with that of the Near East two thousand years ago. These insights, then, are applied to the concept ''the Kingdom of God'' or ''the Kingdom of Heaven'' that was central to Jesus' mission. Chapter two is dedicated to the task of evaluating basic literary forms to learn how these forms, used in the gospels, as well as other ancient literature, can be tested and used with confidence in appraising the reliability of the teachings of Jesus reflected in these forms. The basic form examined is the *chreia*, which is defined, illustrated, and tested in many ways and in many different contexts. Chapters three, four, six, and seven examine the teachings of Jesus that are included in chreias and parables under the same content headings. In chapters three and four the question is raised concerning the relationship of Jesus to the upper-income classes of Jews of his day and monastic responsibilities. Because this is also considered in other chapters, chapter five analyzes the possibility that Jesus had once come from a very wealthy family and had later joined a monastic movement. Chapter seven also summarizes the content of chapters three through seven and considers how the person reflected in these chapters could have become the leader of the church that was organized in his name. Chapter eight examines some Near Eastern concepts about time and the way some Jews appropriated these points of view for understanding their own position in God's predestined plan. Their understanding of history and the proper use of scripture was responsible for the rules by which they anticipated the future and also reconstructed unknown history in the past. Chapter nine shows how some of these rules were applied by the church in composing unknown periods in the life of the historical Jesus. Some final conclusions are given here, suggesting some possible factors that might have been at work in the organization of the early church.

Since this entire volume represents historical research that involves analysis, deduction, and conjecture of situations and events, based on incomplete data, the conclusions cannot be absolute. They are, nonetheless, offered for consideration, together with the facts and logic upon which they are based. This is the place where the book ends. The place where it begins, however, is in the next chapter which starts with well-known Near Eastern reports from daily newspapers and television announcements.

CHAPTER ONE

The Kingdom of God

Introduction

Jesus and Modern Christians. There has been a great demand on the part of Christians for historians to point out for them what can be known of the Jesus of history, but this demand has not come unqualified. Researchers must "discover" a historical Jesus who never made a mistake, was never involved in politics, and was two thousand years ahead of his time. Furthermore, Christians have not been willing to settle for partial knowledge about Jesus the way we do about all other historical figures. Some of us demand all the words that Jesus himself ever spoke or nothing. The reply scholars have given this demand for information is, "Nothing can be known of the historical Jesus." Such limitations make it impossible for historians to examine the data fairly. Dogmatic limitations safely remove Jesus from the realm of history that can be analyzed.

But Jesus was a human being who lived in history, where people live, become parts of their environments, and make human mistakes; so it is possible to learn something about him from a historical point of view, in just the way other people have been studied by historians. The validity or nonvalidity of creedal statements or religious beliefs cannot be examined at all from a historical point of view. These all lie outside the framework of study of the historical Jesus.

Jesus and History. In human terms, there was a man, nearly two thousand years ago, named Jesus, a Jew, who lived in Palestine. He was called a "messiah,"[1] which meant "anointed king"; "Son of God,"[2] which is a title for a king; "Son of man,"[3] which is a mythical title for a king; and he was given the title "king" itself. This naturally suggests that the person to whom these titles have been applied was somehow related to politics, even though many scholars have been adamant in insisting that this was not so. Furthermore, the central focus of Jesus' message indicates that he was very much interested in a kingdom that Jews might enter.[4]

---

[1]S. Mowinckel, *He That Cometh*, tr. G. W. Anderson (New York, c1954) 123, said ideas related to Israel's kings were also associated with messiahs. The only difference is that the Messiah belongs to the future and the king, to the present. The messianic expectations began with Israel's hope of national restoration (p. 157). Mowinckel considered such zealot-like pretenders as Hezekiah (San 98b, 99a), Menahem, Judas the Galilean, Theudas, and Simon bar Kokhba (pp. 284-85) to have been messiahs. Although R. Bultmann, *Jesus and the Word*, tr. L. P. Smith and E. H. Lantero (New York, c1958), 9, did not think Jesus considered himself to have been a messiah, Bultmann thought zealot generals were messiahs (pp. 21-22). Mowinckel thought that in spite of all attempts at idealization, "the Messiah and his kingdom remained this-worldly in character" (p. 321; see also p. 62). See also G. H. Dalman, *The Words of Jesus*, tr. D. M. Kay (Edinburgh, 1902) 273; and I. Engnell, *Studies in the Divine Kingship in the Ancient Near East* (Oxford, 1967) 80. E. E. Jensen, "The First Century Controversy over Jesus as a Revolutionary Figure," *JBL* 60 (1941):261, listed more than seventeen leaders of insurrection in the first century.

[2]There seems little a priori reason for thinking that Jesus would not have been called "Son of God" before Easter. Contra Käsemann, "The Problem of the Historical Jesus," *Essays on New Testament Themes* (Naperville, c1964) 31. Since kings were sometimes called sons of God and Jesus was a pretender to the throne, being called "Son of God" is not "a far higher status" than messiah as S. G. F. Brandon, *Jesus and the Zealots* (Manchester, 1967) 7, thought. See further Engnell, *Divine Kingship*, 31-35, 80; H. Gressmann, *Der Messias* (Göttingen, 1919) 28, 37, 39; and H. J. Kraus, *Die Königherrschaft Gottes im Alten Testament* (Tübingen, 1951) 69-70.

[3]"Son of man" is a mythical name for king. Judas the Maccabee apparently was the one in Dan 7 who was "like a Son of man," because that title was given to the first leader of the "saints of the Most High," namely the Jews after the temple had been cleansed. In Daniel, Enoch, and the gospels, a "Son of man" is always shown acting like a king. See further GWB, *To the Hebrews*, 38-51.

[4]For an analysis of the ways scholars have reasoned around the logical conclusion the data suggests—that the Kingdom of God is the promised land free from foreign rule, see

There is as much or more valid data for studying about the historical Jesus than about the historical Socrates,[5] Rabbi Johanan ben ben Zakkai, or many other comparably ancient figures in history. We know the period of history in which Jesus lived and the geographical territory with which he was familiar. There are early written reports about him and many of his teachings have apparently survived. There are other reliable records of political, religious, and social conditions of Palestine at the time Jesus is reported to have lived. If we do not expect to recover a biography from cradle to grave but are willing to learn only as much as the information shows, then we can learn something about the Jesus of history. We will begin by considering the kind of politics that was customary in Palestine two thousand years ago and its relationship to Jewish religion at that time.

Near Eastern Monarchies

Problems in Thought-Form. Even though Americans have become accustomed to democracy, separation of church and state, racial desegregation, human rights, and many other precious concepts, these have come to our civilization rather recently, and many of them were opposed by leaders of the Christian churches and Judaism. Coexistence as equals among peoples of other religions has not been traditionally a Jewish or Christian principle.[6] For thousands of years both Jews and Christians have fought wars to prove that they were the chosen people, segregated from the heathen, and they have used political and military force to suppress one another and others of different convictions. A brief review of our history will remind us that we have a long tradition of religious movements, like the Crusades, the Spanish Inquisition, the Wars of Religion, and activities like those of the Ku Klux Klan, the Irish Republican Army, and the Jewish Defense League that are both political and religious. We have only to read or listen to the news to learn that separation of religion and politics is far from a reality in the Near East, even today.

GWB, *The Consequences of the Covenant* (Leiden, 1970) 43-55. For a demonstration of the ways scholars have evaded futuristic eschatology, see R. H. Hiers, *The Kingdom of God in the Synoptic Tradition* (Gainesville, 1970) 6-21.

[5]A. Schweitzer, *The Quest of the Historical Jesus*, tr. W. Montgomery (New York, 1975) 6.

[6]See R. D. Morrison, "Human Rights, Critical Philosophy, and Black Theology," *The A.M.E. Zion Quarterly Review* 92 (1980):20-29.

Current Near Eastern History. Since study about Jesus in history involves an attempt to define the term "Kingdom of God," which had its origin in the Near East, we can prepare for this endeavor by studying very briefly the recent religious/political movements in the Near East. In Iran, for example, there was for many years the very strong ruler, the Shah, who governed the Iranians with a firm hand. This was possible because of materials and directions he had received from superpowers, like the U.S.A. Almost unknown to the United States, the Shah was zealously resisted by conservative religious factions in his country who were sowing seeds of revolution. He evicted from his country people like Ayatollah Khomeini and Bani Sadr, but the Ayatollah continued to be held as a messianic figure in the minds of loyal Iranian adherents of the religion of Islam, who religiously believed that the Ayatollah was chosen by God to deliver them from bondage to the Shah and his foreign supporters. They were not trying to establish a Western democracy. They only wanted a religious monarchy and they were driven by religious convictions to sabotage the Shah at every possible point, until they had enough power to evict him.

Then the Imam Khomeini, an Islamic messiah, made his *parousia*. The secret movement became public. What had been told before in secret was then shouted from the housetops. Although there are some differences between a Persian monarchy of two thousand years ago and an Iranian religious monarchy today, there is more similarity between an Iranian religious monarchy today and a Near Eastern religious monarchy of two thousand years ago than between a Near Eastern monarchy of two thousand years ago and an American democracy of today. The Shah was more like Herod the Great than President Reagan. A messiah, who was trying to become a king in Palestine two thousand years ago under the rule of Herod Antipas, would have had to use methods more like those employed by Menachem Begin, Ayatollah Khomeini, or Yasir Arafat than those used by Ronald Reagan, Edward Kennedy, or John Anderson.

It is normal for Americans to think of some things as belonging to the realm of "religion" and others to the realm of "politics." There are sacred and secular divisions of life and we work hard to keep them separated. This is only a recent heritage, however, forced upon us by our American situation. At the expense of the American Indian, people from many countries, languages, and religions settled here and were forced to get along together for reasons of economics and security, without forcing one another to change religions. Most of us have come to like it this way and forget that this tradition is less than three hundred years old!

But the cultural and religious roots of most Americans go back to Palestine where religion and politics were identical. People paid their income tax and their church pledges by the same tithes. We have only to examine our theological language to realize that it had its origin in a national religion: words like kingdom, king, Lord, apostle, worship, prayer, judge, judgment, law, righteousness, and unrighteousness are terms belonging to the court. Words like treasury of merits, debts, redemption, and forgiveness originated in a finance system. Words like hosts (troops), armor, swords, spears, cavalry, salvation, helmets, and fortress come from a military organization. The most popular attribute given to this God was to call him the God of armies (צבאות). He saved his people and gave them "rest" by overpowering enemies of the faithful and providing them security within desirable borders. War was religious. Laws were religious. Sex was religious. There was no "secular" area within the believing community. Even the area outside, the world of foreigners, was religious. It belonged to pagan gods and their worshipers.

With this introduction, we will begin to examine the data available to us for analyzing the concept "Kingdom of God," as it would have been used in Jesus' time in Palestine.

Kingdom in the Old Testament

Word Usage. Words do not always mean what an outsider would expect. For instance, after the sixties in the U.S.A. the word "hippy" no longer meant someone with big hips and most Americans are not able to explain why the word "hippy" was given to the group of people who were so designated. After the election of 1972, the word "Watergate" did not mean just a place on the Potomac River bank where the Marine band played every week and where there were some nice apartment buildings and offices. Words sometimes change, so their meaning must be determined in relationship to the time and place in which they were used. A person who wants to be understood in the U.S.A., using words like "hippy" and "Watergate," must learn what other people mean by these words and use them in that manner.

To learn what the word "Kingdom of God" meant in Jesus' time, we must study the use of the term "kingdom" and its related expressions as they were used in literature closely allied to the New Testament. This involves the Old Testament, the Dead Sea Scrolls, and the *Wars of the Jews* by Josephus.

The Kingdom of God. Carmignac has examined all of the terms related to a king in the Old Testament, the Dead Sea Scrolls, and Rabbinic literature.[7] He has shown that the terms ממלכה, מלוכה, מלכות can all be used to mean rule, royal, or kingdom. In Aramaic, only the one term, מלכו, or מלכותא, is used for all of these meanings. The same is true of the Greek βασιλεία which, depending on its context, means rule, royal, or kingdom. This has given many apologetic scholars an excuse for rendering every occurrence of βασιλεία to mean rule, regardless of context, and to interpret away all the obvious political implications associated with this political term. Josephus, in *The Wars of the Jews*, for instance, used the term βασιλεία twenty-eight times referring in some way to the authority of those who were kings, aspired to be kings, or had the honors of kings. These should probably be rendered ''royalty,'' ''reign,'' or ''ruling authority.''[8]

There are an additional fourteen instances that could make sense understood as principally related either to the office of a king or to the country of a king,[9] so it is difficult to know whether they should be rendered ''royal government'' or ''kingdom.''[10] There are an additional forty-seven instances in which βασιλεία refers to a territory ruled by a king. It is something that could be inherited (*BJ* 1.40, 454, 612), wasted (1.91), plundered (7.251), bargained for (1.259), from which lands could be detached (1.362; 2.97, 215, 217, 223, 247, 252, 362). It could be great (1.458) or small (1.395), annexed (1.396, 398), include locations (1.407), have cities and plains (1.417, 423), have limits (1.474). It could be visited (1.513), administered (1.669), be identified, territorially, as Agrippa's kingdom (2.481, 483; 3.37, 56, 443, 445, 541; 7.97), or the Kingdom of the Jews (7.301). (See also *BJ* 1.98, 457, 461, 490, 514, 518, 576, 634, 637; 2.25, 32; 7.228, 235, 251.)

---

[7] J. Carmignac, *Le Mirage de l'Eschatologie* (Paris, 1979) 13-22.

[8] Josephus, *BJ* 1.74, 111, 131, 203, 248, 285, 322, 370, 401, 479, 483, 503, 507, 561, 587, 623, 631, 665; 2.20, 26, 27-28, 60, 89, 182, 220, 285; 5.409; 7.44.

[9] *BJ* 1.70, 72, 107, 120, 317, 392, 434, 521, 525, 558; 2.34-35, 93, 94, 102.

[10] Note the difficulty Carmignac (note 7) had in deciding which rendering should be given for each use of βασιλεία in the New Testament.

It is not always certain which emphasis should be given to the Greek word, but there is little danger of its being misunderstood. If it is royal, it includes the crown, robes, or honors pertaining to a certain king who rules a certain kingdom. If it is a kingdom, it is a territory of a certain king who rules at that time. The same is true of terms used in the Old Testament related to the Kingdom of God. Whether it is called "The Rule of God" or "The Kingdom of God" it is assumed that God is in charge, but the geographical territory involved is also identified and should not be ignored.[11]

When David was prohibited from building a temple for the Lord, Nathan said the Lord promised that he would raise up one of David's sons to establish his kingdom (מלוכתו, 1 Chron 17:11). This son would build the Lord's house (ביתי) and be confirmed in the Lord's kingdom (מלכותי) for the age (1 Chron 17:12-14). Nathan said that God would be Solomon's father, and Solomon would be the son of God (1 Chron 17:13; 22:10). This means that the kingdom that then belonged to the Lord also was ruled by Solomon as king of the United Kingdom of Israel and Judah. Solomon sat "on the throne of the Kingdom of the Lord (מלכות יהוה) over Israel" (1 Chron 28:5). At the outset, this seems to mean that anyone who was king over Israel would be both Son of God and ruler over the Kingdom of the Lord,[12] an epithet which is very similar to the "Kingdom of God." Because most New Testament scholars do not reason this way, however, the subject will be examined further.

When David was confident that his kingdom was secure for his posterity, he said, "Yours is the kingdom, O Lord" (יהוה הממלכה, 1 Chron 29:11), meaning the United Kingdom. After the ten tribes had seceded from the union, Abijah tried to reunite the tribes. When he was within shouting distance of the North Israelites, the Chronicler reported him as saying, "Are you not aware that the Lord God of Israel gave the kingdom to David over Israel for the age? to him and to his sons [confirmed by] a covenant of salt? . . . and now you are saying that you will establish yourselves in place

---

[11]Contra J. Jeremias, *New Testament Theology*, tr. J. Bowden (New York, c1971) 98; and H. E. Tödt, *The Son of Man in the Synoptic Tradition*, tr. D. M. Barton (Philadelphia, c1965) 26. The latter referred to it as "the coming universal reign of God which means the end of the world as a whole." What a joyful anticipation!

[12]This is the usual meaning of the title "Son of God" in ancient Near Eastern countries. See GWB, *Consequences*, 57, and W. W. Hallo and W. K. Simpson, *The Ancient Near East* (New York, 1971) 175.

of the Kingdom of the Lord (ממלכה יהוה) through the sons of David!'' (2 Chron 13:5, 8). From the Chronicler's point of view, the only acceptable ruler over the Lord's kingdom, that is, the territory ruled by the Lord, was one of the sons of David, ruling from Jerusalem. Even if the word ''kingdom'' here were instead translated ''rule'' it would still involve the same rulers over the United Kingdom, so that the conviction was that only those from the Davidic dynasty had the right to sit on the throne in Israel during the ''rule of God,'' just as would be the case if this were called the ''Kingdom of God.''

The Book of Obadiah is a vengeful poem whose author looked forward to the day of the Lord (יום יהוה, Obad 15) when the nations that had injured Judah would be punished. At that time, Mount Zion would be restored to a center of political power (Obad 21) and the southern kingdoms would unite in burning Edom like stubble (Obad 17-18). At that time the Kingdom would be the Lord's (והיתה ליהוה המלוכה, Obad 21). This seems to imply that the kingdom or ''rule'' would be the Lord's only when Jews were ruling the country with their own king from Jerusalem. This is the way some rabbis understood the system.[13]

Windisch[14] made an extensive study of the expressions in the New Testament that meant ''entering'' in relationship to the Kingdom of God or the Kingdom of Heaven. He found that the expression ''enter the Kingdom of Heaven'' was closely allied with ''inheriting the Kingdom of Heaven'' and ''entering into life.''[15] There is no similar equivalent in the Rabbinic literature, but Windisch found its counterpart in the Old Testament and in apocalyptic literature. In the Old Testament, the elect entered into the promised land, the land of Canaan, and the holy city. Those who entered the land of Canaan also had life and inherited the land.[16] There were also a few references in relationship to the congregation of Israel or the congregation of worshipers. Those without the proper qualifications were forbidden to enter

---

[13]Bereshit Rabbati 74; *Shin* from the ''Complete Alphabet of Rabbi Akiba''; SDeut 32:10; Yalkut 1.408 to Vayakhel; also 2 Bar 75:8; 4 Ezra 9:6-9.

[14]H. Windisch, ''Die Sprüche vom Eingehen in das Reich Gottes,'' *NTW* 27 (1928):163-89.

[15]Ibid., 167.

[16]Ibid., 177.

the congregation.[17] He concluded that "the whole complex of ideas appears much more strongly anchored in the Old Testament than one usually thinks."[18]

Old Testament Translation. Although the Hebrew Bible in Jesus' time was generally considered by Jews to be the source for all ethics and politics, most scholars, who know that the Kingdom of the Lord meant the Kingdom of Israel as governed by the leadership of one of the descendants of David, still insist that in New Testament times the expressions, "Kingdom of God" or "Kingdom of Heaven," had nothing to do with political rule over a geographical territory, but only God's ruling activity in general, over all mankind and the world.[19] Once the emphasis was placed on God's ruling, scholars could say God ruled over all the world and all peoples. This unity of God's rule removed the provincialism of a nationalistic religion. God's oneness, however, did not mean universalism to many Jews of New Testament times. Josephus said the zealots who fought the war against Rome (A.D. 66-70) fought for the national freedom on the conviction that God alone was Lord (*BJ* 2.119-66; *Ant* 12.171-73; 17.11-25). The conflict between scholarly practice and historical probabilities makes it necessary to examine literature that is closer to the New Testament in origin than the Hebrew Bible is in order to learn New Testament concepts. One of these sources is the targumic literature.

The word, targum, means "translation" and it is a translation of the Hebrew Bible into Aramaic at a time when Aramaic was the most popular language of the Jews. At Sabbath services one person read the scripture to the congregation in Hebrew and a translator (*meturgaman*) translated it freely in terms the people could understand, frequently paraphrasing and sometimes adding explanatory interpretations. Since these were used in Jesus' day, it would seem reasonable to assume that these translators would interpret Hebrew terms in the way they were normally understood at that

---

[17]Ibid., 184.

[18]Ibid., 187.

[19]P. Billerbeck, *Das Evangelium nach Matthäus* (Munich, 1956) 1:178-79, 418-19, et al. Although some earlier scholars had been interpreting the relevant terms "rule" of God rather than "Kingdom of God," it was G. H. Dalman, *The Words of Jesus*, (Edinburgh, 1902) 92-139, who popularized this view and gave it scholarly appeal. Few have analyzed his material enough to realize that he never made a convincing case. He only repeated his claim many times and translated the passages to his satisfaction.

time. These do not support the popular view that the Kingdom of God was unrelated to a geographic territory and a political ruler. For example, the translation for "Thus shall descend the Lord of armies to fight on Mount Zion," is "Thus shall be revealed the Kingdom of the Lord of armies" (מלכותא דיהוה צבאות, Targ Isa 31:4). Zechariah's prophecy that "The Lord will become King (והיה יהוה למלך) over all the land" was translated, "The Kingdom of the Lord will be revealed" (ותתגלי מלכותא דיי, Targ Zech 14:9). Not only would this Kingdom of the Lord be *revealed* (Targ Isa 24:23; 31:4; 40:9; 52:7; Obad 21; Micah 4:7; Zeph 3:8; Zech 14:9), but it is one that would *come*[20] or draw near.[21]

Those who think this is still an abstract divine rule should note further that this kingdom was also called *the* kingdom (מלכותא) and identified with the kingdom of the house of David, established on the holy mountain of Israel (Targ Ezek 17:22-23; Amos 9:11). It was to be revealed in Jerusalem or on Mount Zion (Targ Isa 24:23; 31:4; 40:9; Micah 4:7, 8; Ezek 17:23). The feet that were to bring good news to Zion would travel over the mountains of the Land of Israel (Targ Isa 52:7). When the captive sons of Israel who were in France, Spain, and Rome returned to Mount Zion, then the Kingdom of the Lord would be revealed over all those who dwelled in the land [of Israel] (Targ Obad 21). This kingdom was not just called the Kingdom of the Lord; it was also called "The Kingdom of your God" (היך מלכותא דאל) which would be revealed or set up so that people could see it when the report of good news was brought to the congregation of Zion (Targ Isa 52:7) or to Jerusalem and the cities of the house of Judah (Targ Isa 40:9). The Kingdom of the Lord would be revealed to "a powerful people in Mount Zion, from then and until the age [to come]." "The Kingdom is destined to come" to "the Messiah of Israel" (ואת משיחא דישראל) as well as to the congregation of Zion or Jerusalem (Targ Micah 4:7-8). Jews were promised that they would "see the kingdom of their Messiah (במלכות משחיהון) and multiply sons and daughters" (Targ Isa 53:10).

---

[20] עתידא מלכותא וייתי למיתי שולטנא Targ. Micah 4:8. J. Jeremias, *New Testament Theology*, 33, erroneously followed M. Burrows, "Thy Kingdom Come," *JBL* 74 (1955):1-8, and was followed by N. Perrin, *The Kingdom of God in the Teaching of Jesus* (Philadelphia, c1963) 57, in holding that the expression "Kingdom come" or "reach" is nowhere found in Jewish literature outside the New Testament. For other examples see 2 Bar 44:12 and Tanhuma 3:28b. See also GWB, *Consequences*, 67.

[21] לקרבא מלכותא , Targ Zeph 3:8.

It seems obvious that the entity which Targumic Jews were expecting, which they called "the Kingdom of God," "the Kingdom of the Lord," "the Kingdom of the Messiah," or "the Kingdom of the house of David," was to come to Jerusalem when the diaspora Jews returned to Zion. Enemies of the Jews were to be punished (Targ Zeph 3:8) and messengers would travel over the mountains of Israel to bring the good news of salvation to the congregation of Zion. These were all future expectations that applied to the promised land restored to Jews under the leadership of a Davidic king whether the crucial word be rendered "rule" or "kingdom." This king would be the Messiah and he would rule over a powerful nation from Jerusalem. Those who wrote the targumim thought that when the Kingdom of the Lord came, Palestine would be restored to Jewish control under a Davidic king.

Klaus Koch[22] agrees that the targumic interpretation of "the Kingdom of God" is a monarchy, but he thought that "the kingdom of Heaven" mentioned in rabbinic sources had nothing to do with the political aspirations of the Jews who composed the targumim.[23] His misinterpretation at this point will require further demonstration.

The Kingdom and Rome. Rabbis believed that the land of Israel, the temple, and the kingdom of David were all given conditionally. If Jews were faithful, these would be given; if not, they would be withheld (Mekilta, *Amalek* 4:132-43). The Kingdom of God required the establishment of all three. There were seven things that were hidden from people: "(1) the day of death; (2) the day of comfort; (3) the depths of judgment; (4) no one knows in what he can profit; (5) no one knows what is in the mind of his fellow; (6) the kingdom of the house of David—how long until it is restored to its place; and (7) this guilty kingdom—how long until it is uprooted?" (Mekilta *Vayassa'* 6:61-64). The day of comfort would come when the Kingdom of God was revealed, the kingdom of the house of David ruled from Jerusalem, and Rome was displaced. These things would happen all at once. The depth of judgment referred to the amount of guilt stored against Israel that had to be paid before these hidden things could be revealed.

Rabbi Eleazar asked, "How long will it be until the name of these people is destroyed? At the time when idolatry will be uprooted and its idol

---

[22]K. Koch, "Offenbaren Wird Sich Das Reich Gottes," *NTS* 25 (1979):158-65.

[23]Ibid., p. 159.

worshipers; then the Lord will be the only God in the world; and his kingdom (מלכותו) will be for the age and for ages of ages" (Mekilta, *Amalek*
2:159-63). R. Judah in the name of R. Samuel, commenting on Isa 66:2,
said, "Whenever the Israelites are in exile, the Kingdom of Heaven is not
at peace, and the nations of the earth dwell

	in serenity, but whenever the
"Upon whom shall I look?	Israelites are redeemed, the
Upon the humble and *quiet*	Kingdom of Heaven is *at peace*
	and the nations of the earth
man who *trembles*	*tremble*.
at my words" (LXX Isa 66:2).	Hence, 'The Lord reigns! Let the peo-
	ples *tremble*' " (Midr Ps 99:1).

Jews thought that whenever God's kingdom would appear, God would
rise up from his royal throne and punish the Gentiles and destroy their idols.
Then Israel would be happy. She would "mount up on the necks and wings
of the eagle [Rome] and they [the Romans] will be ended."[24] Israel believed
she was destined to judge the nations and rule the whole earth (Jub 32:19;
Wis 3:8). The poet who confessed that the Lord was King and that the
"Kingdom of our God (ἡ βασιλεία τοῦ θεοῦ ἡμῶν) was forever over
the Gentiles in judgment" (Ps Sol 17:1, 4) also reminded the Lord that the
Lord had chosen David to be king over Israel (Ps Sol 17:5) and urged the
Lord to raise up for his chosen people their king, the son of David (Ps Sol
14:23). The establishment of a Davidic king over Israel would involve shat-
tering the unrighteous rulers (Ps Sol 17:24), rescuing Jerusalem from the
nations (Ps Sol 17:25), and gathering together the saints at Jerusalem after
it had been cleansed and made holy (Ps Sol 17:28, 32, 34). The heathen
nations would then be subject to this Davidic king (Ps Sol 17:32), who
would be the anointed of the Lord (Ps Sol 17:36) even though the Lord himself would be King at the same time. The Sibyl anticipated the time when
God would establish his kingdom over people (SO 3:666-668). Then those
to whom he had made promises (namely Israel) would become prosperous
and happy (SO 3:669-671) and people would bring gifts and frankincense
to the temple of the great God, which would become the only temple in the
world for future generations to know (SO 3:669-676). First Rome would
gain control over Egypt so that Gentile political forces would all be con-

---

[24]Assump Mos 10:1-8. A reflection on Deut 32:11 and Isa 40:31.

centrated in one country. "Then the greatest kingdom of the immortal king will appear" (SO 3:46-48). The Messiah would come and Rome would be demolished in the judgment of the eternal God, the mighty King (SO 3:55-104).

The Yoke of the Kingdom. As part of their daily prayers, Jews accepted the yoke of the Kingdom of Heaven (עול מלכות שמים, Ber 2:2, 5; 14b-15a; 16a; 21a). Koch[25] said this prayer had nothing to do with Jewish expectation of a Kingdom of God established as a political kingdom with its capital city at Jerusalem. Nevertheless, the same Jews who read and heard the targumim spoken in their synagogues looked forward to the establishment of a Kingdom of Heaven in peace, while the nations of the earth trembled (Mid Ps 99:1). They also recited the Eighteen Benedictions and Amram's Kaddish. It seems very unlikely that these Jews had one meaning for the Kingdom of Heaven when they read the targumim and a radically different one in mind when they took upon themselves the yoke of the Kingdom of Heaven.

Rabbis said that the one who separated himself from sin (meaning that he observed regulations such as dietary rules) took upon himself the Kingdom of Heaven. Those who refused to isolate themselves in this way from the heathen, would then belong to Nebuchadnezzar and his fellows, rather than the Lord (Sifra Lev 20:26; 93b). This means Jews in the diaspora could have allegiance to only one government—either they mingled with the Gentiles and became real citizens of the country in which they lived, or they kept themselves segregated from the Gentiles and remained loyal citizens to the unrealized Kingdom of Heaven. Some adapted one way and some another. The recital of the *Shema'* with its accompanying prayers, was the Jewish oath of allegiance. Jews believed that "every Israelite who lived in the land of Israel accepted the yoke of the Kingdom of Heaven, and every Israelite who left the land was as if he were worshiping idols. So it was with David when he left the land to live near Philistia. He said, 'Cursed be those before the Lord, for they have excluded me today from becoming a citizen in the inheritance of the Lord, saying, "Go, worship other gods!" ' " (Sifra Lev 25:38; 109c). Rabbi Akiba said the Israelite who accepted the prohibition against taking interest from his fellow Jews accepted the yoke of Heaven but if he charged interest to his brother, he classified himself with Gentiles by rejecting the yoke of Heaven (Sifra Lev 25:38; 109c).

---

[25]Koch, "Offenbarung," 159.

Rabbis interpreted SS 2:12 as follows: *"The time of singing has come near* (הגיע). The time of the foreskin (or Gentile) has come near that it may be cut off; the time of the Canaanites has come near that they may be cut off; the time of the land of Israel has come near that it may be apportioned to Israel. . . . *The time of singing has come near.* The time of the foreskin (or Gentile) has come near that it may be cut off; the time of the wicked has come that they may be broken, as it is said, *The Lord has broken the rod of the wicked* (Isa 14:5). The time has come near for the Babylonians to be destroyed; the time of the temple has come near that it may be rebuilt. . . . The time of the Kingdom of the Cuthians (Christians)[26] has come near that it may be destroyed; the time of the Kingdom of Heaven has come near that it may be revealed (הגיע זמנה מלכות שמים שתגלה), as it is said, *and the Lord will become King over all the land* (Zech 14:9) and *the voice of the turtle is heard in our land* (SS 1:12). What is this? This is the voice of the king messiah who proclaims and says, *How beautiful upon the mountains are the feet of the one who publishes good news"* (Isa 52:7; SSR 2:13; *Pesikta Rabbati* 15, 75a).

This means that when the Kingdom of Heaven came all of the other conditions mentioned in this text would come with it. Jews who accepted the yoke of the Kingdom of Heaven with all of its risks and responsibilities would be rewarded with prosperity and privilege of citizenship when the Kingdom of Heaven came. Those who accepted the yoke of the Kingdom of Heaven provided a subversive force against any "wicked kingdom" that controlled Palestine. This does not show, as Koch believed, that the Kingdom of Heaven is at all distinct from the Kingdom of God, the Kingdom of the Lord, the Kingdom of the Messiah, or the Kingdom of the house of David. Even if that distinction were allowed, it would have to be explained in such a way that the aspirations for the Kingdom of Heaven involved an equally fervent yearning for Palestine to be restored to Jewish control. The meanings would be so close that the term "Kingdom of Heaven" could be used as a code word for the restoration of the promised land, whatever meaning were given to it. Jewish eschatological expectations were the same whether they were praying or interpreting scripture. In *The Book of Zerubbabel*, in a passage where Jellinek's text reads, "The Kingdom will be the

---

[26]So A. Feldman, *The Parables and Similes of the Rabbis* (Cambridge, 1927) 55 n.1.

Lord's'' (Obad 1:21), the Bodleian text of the same passage reads, "The Kingdom will be Israel's'' (Obad 1:21; BZ 7:11-12).

Since the term "Heaven" is frequently used to mean "God," it is not surprising to learn that "The Kingdom of Heaven" is the same as "The Kingdom of God." The eschatological expectations associated with the one are the same as those associated with the other. Whether the expression, or one related to it, is found in the OT, the targumim, Tannaitic midrashim, or later rabbinic literature, whether the term be translated "Kingdom" or "Rule" of God or of Heaven, the effect is the same. It takes place when the promised land is under Jewish control. It should not be surprising, then, to learn that the same expression, when used in the NT had the same meaning, even though the majority of NT scholars refuse to accept that conclusion.

Kingdom in the New Testament

Introduction. In contexts similar to those in Amram's Kaddish, the targumim, the OT, Tannaitic midrashim, Pseudepigrapha, and other rabbinic literature, the terms "Kingdom," "Kingdom of God," "Kingdom of Heaven," and "Kingdom of my Father" appear in the NT. No attempt will be made at this time to determine which, if any, of these expressions reflects the opinions and teachings of Jesus. It is enough to show that these terms have the same meaning in the NT as they have in other Jewish literature.[27]

Use of Scripture in the New Testament. One of the ways early Jews and Christians proved their arguments was to quote scripture that was generally accepted as authoritatively the word of God. Arguments built around biblical passages are called midrashim. One example of the way Jews and Christians argued, using texts, is the following passage from Acts 13:33-38: "It is written in the second Psalm, *My son are you; today I bore you* (Ps 2:7). Because he raised him from the dead, no longer about to return to corruption, he spoke as follows: *I will give you the holy and faithful things of David* (Isa 55:3). Wherefore, it also says in another Psalm, *You will not let your holy one see corruption* (Ps 16:10). Now, on the one hand, *David*, after he had served the counsel of God in his own generation, *fell asleep*, was laid *with his fathers* (1 Kgs 2:10), and *saw corruption* (Ps 16:10). But, on the other hand, the one whom God raised up saw no corruption. There-

---

[27]Schweitzer, *Quest*, 368, held that Jesus had the same eschatological expectations as late Judaism. He thought, however, that, since these were apocalyptic, they were not also nationalistic. They were only supernatural and transcendental.

fore, let it be known to you, men, brothers, that because of this man, to you
is announced the forgiveness of sins.''

All by itself, this argument is not sound. What does all this reasoning
about seeing corruption or being God's son have to do with obtaining forgiveness of sins? Since, however, the author quoted from Isa 55, he presumed that the reader would know the rest of the chapter and take into
account Isa 55:7, which the author of Acts did not quote:

> Let the wicked forsake his way,
> and the unrighteous man his thoughts
> let him return to the Lord
> that he may have mercy upon him
> and to our God, for he will abundantly pardon.

Therefore, the argument ran from the proof that Jesus was God's son and
also the son of David to identify him with the holy and faithful things of
David. Because the Lord's holy one would not see corruption, either David
or his son would not see corruption. David died and saw corruption, so the
scripture did not apply to him. Therefore, it refers to Jesus as the holy one
or the holy and faithful things of David mentioned in Isa 55:3. That same
scripture, however, goes on to promise that those who forsake their wicked
ways and return to the Lord can receive the forgiveness of sins (Isa 55:7).
Twentieth-century Americans may not accept this kind of logic, but it was
accepted in New Testament times as valid, so those who want to understand
the meaning of the New Testament must realize what the authors meant
when they used scriptures.

In the references related to the "Kingdom of God" or the "Kingdom
of Heaven," OT quotations will be identified and quoted along with the NT
scripture so that the reader can recognize the allusions. Even so, the reader
will often need to read the wider context of OT scripture to learn the basic
message that the author of the NT scripture understood. The background
for the Beatitudes, for instance, is Second Isaiah and some Psalms that
teach nonviolence which can support the passive suffering servant eschatology of Second Isaiah.[28] The Psalms involved are 37 (LXX 36) and 73.
The Isaiah chapters that receive direct attention are 57, 61, and 66.

---

[28]See GWB, *Consequences*, 1-41, for an account of active and passive eschatology and
ethics. See also K. Stendahl, "Hate, Non-retaliation, and Love 1QS x.17-20 and Rom
12:19-21," *HTR* 55 (1962):343-55.

When Nebuchadnezzar conquered Judah, he took the wealthiest, the best leaders, and the most intelligent Jews with him to Babylon, so that they would not lead an insurrectionist movement back in Judah. In Babylon, these Jews were apparently well treated and soon became prominent leaders. One of them (Nehemiah) became "cupbearer for the king," a title for an important government official. Because these Jews were removed from the promised land, just as their forefathers had been in Egypt, they identified themselves with the Hebrews in Egypt when they were receiving their worst treatment. They called themselves "poor," "mourners," "captives," "servants," and other similar names. They were allowed to return to the land later because they had enough influence and control in Babylon to negotiate with Cyrus of Persia, with whom they cooperated to enable him to conquer Babylon. But this is not the *theological* interpretation they gave for their release.

Theologically, they believed that their nonresistant suffering in Babylon had paid their indebtedness to the heavenly treasury of merits. In fact, they had paid *double* for all their sins, as Jeremiah (16:18) had said they would have to do. They had been mourning for Zion all the time they were in Babylon; the comfort they wanted was permission to return to the promised land. Since their nonresistant mourning had been rewarded by restoration of the land, Jews in New Testament times believed that they should practice the same behavior, so that God would restore the land again. Although they then lived in Palestine, they considered themselves to be "captives" of the Romans who dominated the land. The temple was controlled by the Romans, so they could not perform undefiled services that the law required. While some Jews were zealously trying to recover the land by military conquest and rebellion, others were attempting to cancel Israel's indebtedness to the treasury of merits by turning the other cheek, walking the second mile, mourning for Zion, and meekly accepting the domination of Rome.

An author who believed in passive suffering as the correct methodology for regaining the land prepared the Beatitudes, which he based on passages from Second Isaiah and others from a complementary Psalm 37. Ps 37 encourages the reader not to be disturbed by the apparent success of evildoers. In the long run, the evildoers would be punished and the righteous would be rewarded. Peaceful ones would receive salvation from the Lord (37-39); the wicked would be cut off, but the righteous who blessed the Lord would have children who would be a blessing (22, 26). It was the meek and the poor who would inherit the land (9, 11, 29, 34) and enjoy great peace (11). Noting that the other Psalms promised that God would be good to Israel when Jews had pure hearts (Ps 73:1) and that pure hearts were required of the priests who should conduct worship services in the temple (Ps 24:3-4), the author of the Beatitudes wove these themes into a unified literary unit based on the promises of the Old Testament which were conditional upon Jews being nonresistant, meek, humble, persecuted, and pure of heart.

PROMISE	CONDITIONS	REWARDS
Blessed are	the poor in spirit	for the Kingdom of Heaven is theirs.
Blessed are	those who mourn	for they will be comforted.
Blessed are	the meek	for they will inherit the land.
Blessed are	those who hunger and thirst for vindication	for they will be satisfied.
Blessed are	the merciful	for they will receive mercy.
Blessed are	the pure in heart	for they will see God.
Blessed are	the peacemakers	for they will be called God's sons.
Blessed are	those who are persecuted for the sake of justice	for the Kingdom of Heaven is theirs.

The concluding Beatitude has the same promise as the beginning one. This is a typical Semitic way of forming a literary unit. It is called an *inclusion*. It is clear here that all of the blessings are promised to the same group of people—the nonresisters, who are labeled "poor in spirit," "mourners," "meek," "those who yearn ardently for vindication," "the merciful," "the pure in heart," "the peacemakers."

Not only are the qualifications of the beneficiaries of the blessings identical, but the rewards promised are those promised in the OT—they would be "comforted," as Jews would be when the land is restored; they would inherit the land; they would be vindicated in their trial against Rome; they would receive mercy as Jews were promised by the restoration of the land; the temple would be cleansed and reestablished by authentic priests who had clean hands and pure hearts; they would be called God's children. When all of this happened, they would also be in possession of the Kingdom of Heaven, so it is clear what the author expected when he used the term "Kingdom of Heaven." It was something Jews would receive with the restoration of the promised land under Jewish control, as it was in the time of David and of the Hasmoneans. So obvious was the meaning of the Beatitudes in the early church that the Latin text of the *Didache* 3:7-8 said the meek would inherit the holy land (*sanctam terram*).[29]

The following dialogue is from the *Apocalypse of Paul*: ''I said, 'Lord, what is this?' Then he said to me, 'This is *the land of the meek* (ἡ γῆ τῶν πραίων), or do you not know that it is written, ''Blessed are the meek, because they will inherit the land''?' ''[30]

Jesus and the Kingdom

Exodus Typology. Deut 1:35-39: ''[May all these unexpressed curses come upon me] if anyone of these men (אנשים) of this evil generation will see the good land which I have sworn to give your fathers . . . but your children (טפכם), who you said would become plunder, and your teenagers (בניכם), who do not this day know good and evil (that is, the minors), will enter there, and to them I will give it, and they will inherit it.''[31]

When the spies returned from searching out the promised land, they brought back a bad report. They said it would be impossible for the Hebrews to take over such a strong people as those who then dwelled in the land. Moses understood that this showed their lack of faith. They had tempted the Lord in not accepting his promises. Therefore the adults, who were responsible for their decision, would not receive the promise. Not one of their generation would see the promised land, except Caleb and Joshua, who brought back a minority report. Nonetheless, God's promise would not be withdrawn. The minors, who were not legally responsible for these decisions, would enter the land, and theirs would be the land that later became the kingdom. Far from becoming plunder, the children would be the ones who would inherit that land. Jesus knew of this scripture before he confronted the following problem:

''Then little children were brought to him, so that he might lay his hands on them and pray. But the disciples rebuked them. Then Jesus said, 'Let the children come to me, and do not prevent them, for of such as these is the Kingdom of Heaven' '' (Matt 19:13-14).

---

[29]J. P. Audet, *La Didache* (Paris, 1958) 132-37, 144.

[30]For a more extensive defense of this interpretation of the Beatitudes, see GWB, ''The Matthaean Beatitudes,'' W. R. Farmer, ed., *New Synoptic Studies* (Macon, 1983).

[31]See GWB, *Consequences*, pp. 173-82 GWB, ''The Old Testament Meaning of the Knowledge of Good and Evil,'' *JBL* 75 (1956):114-20.

Typologically, Jesus seems to have thought his generation was reliving the exodus from Egypt. He and his generation of Jews were "at the border of the land," and the adults were pushing the children away, as if they were "plunder." Jesus reminded them that in Moses' day the adults were too stiff-necked to enter the land of Canaan. There were probably those of Jesus' day, as well, who doubted the possibility that the Romans could ever be driven out of the land. Those who were tempting the Lord by their lack of faith would not receive the kingdom, but the younger generation, like the wilderness generation, would still receive the Kingdom of Heaven, an expression which he seems to have used as a code term for the same territory as that which the spies of old had examined before they brought back their report.

Exodus Miracles. "Aaron reached out his hand with his wand; he struck the dust of the ground, and gnats appeared on man and beast—all the dust of the land became gnats in all of the land of Egypt. The magicians did the same with their secret arts to produce gnats, but they could not. There were gnats on both man and beast. Then the magicians said to Pharaoh, *It is the finger of God*, but Pharaoh's heart was hardened, just as the Lord had said" (Exod 8:12-15).

This is the historical background that prompted Jesus to respond as he did in the following situation: "Some of them said, 'It is by means of Beelzebul, the chief of demons, that he casts out demons.' Others, tempting, asked for a sign from Heaven from him. Knowing their thoughts, he said to them, ' . . . if *it is* by *the finger of God* that I cast out demons, then the Kingdom of God has reached you' "(Lk 11:15, 16, 20; Matt 12:28).[32]

Here again appears exodus typology. When his authority for performing miracles was challenged, Jesus compared his miracles to those performed by Moses and Aaron in Egypt. When the plagues of Egypt came, that which followed was the exodus and the opportunity to enter the promised land. The miracles Jesus performed should have prompted Jews to realize that God was at work again to free his people from their foreign oppressors. The Kingdom of God was right upon them. The importance of the plagues of Egypt is that they weakened Egypt so that the Hebrews could escape. This

---

[32]Matt 12:28 has changed "finger" to "spirit" to conform to his entire theme on Isa 42:1-4. See O. L. Cope, *St. Matthew, A Scribe Trained for the Kingdom of Heaven* (Washington, 1976) 32-39.

was a very crucial step toward gaining control of the land of Canaan. After the miracles, Jews asked Jesus for a ''sign from Heaven,'' when he had just given them one. Like the Hebrews at the edge of the promised land, these Pharisees were tempting the Lord. His miracles, like the plagues of Egypt, showed that he was performing no ordinary magic. This was ''the finger of God.''

This is one of the passages ''realized eschatologists'' use to insist that Jesus believed the Kingdom of God had already come. They argue that since the verb ''has reached'' (ἔφθασεν), is in the past tense, the Kingdom cannot, therefore, be in the future. Hiers,[33] however, has argued that this verse, like all synoptic expressions of eschatological expectation, really shows an expectation for a future coming of the Kingdom. He held that the casting out of demons always precedes the coming of the Kingdom, so the Kingdom would come later. This expression means the same as many others, ''The Kingdom of God has come near.''

Perrin[34] claimed that this certainly is one of the authentic sayings of Jesus, on the basis of dissimilarity. Nowhere, he argued, in Jewish or later Christian literature is the word ''come'' ever associated with the Kingdom of God. Perrin and Jeremias were both in error in thinking this word never appears in Jewish literature. Both scholars were aware of Targ Micah 4:8: ''The Kingdom is destined to come (למיתי).'' Still, looking for uniqueness in the verb ''come,'' Jeremias insisted that this passage did not count because it was not a finite verb! The following passages, however, refer to the expectation in finite verbs: Baruch expected the new age would come (*'ate'*, 2 Bar 44:12); R. Tanhuma (3:28b) spoke of ''a time to be redeemed, which has come'' (שבאתה).[35] On the basis of Perrin's arguments, this verse is far from being ''established beyond a reasonable doubt.''[36] He was still further afield from this verse's typological context when he said its meaning was that these events ''in the ministry of Jesus are nothing less than *an ex-*

---

[33]Hiers, *Kingdom*, 30-35.

[34]N. Perrin, *Rediscovering the Teaching of Jesus* (New York, c1967) 63-64; and *The Kingdom of God in the Teaching of Jesus*, 57-59. Also see Jeremias, *New Testament Theology*, 33.

[35]GWB, *Consequences*, 67.

[36]Perrin, *Rediscovering* 65.

perience of the Kingdom of God.''[37] Jeremias said that to say the Kingdom of God had come near was the same as saying, ''God is near.''[38] Chilton attempted to prove this claim of Jeremias through the targumim.[39] By showing the Masoretic text and the targum passages, he made the equation that ''The Kingdom of the Lord'' = God. Some of his examples are:

> MT—''and the Lord will be king upon all the earth.''
> Tg—''and *the Kingdom* of the Lord will be *revealed* upon all the *dwellers of* the earth'' (Zech 14:9).[40]

According to Chilton's logic, the phrase ''will be king upon all the earth'' = ''will be revealed upon all the dwellers of the earth.'' The word ''king'' in the first passage, however, parallels part of the word ''kingdom'' in the second. The Lord's becoming *king* is what happens when the Lord's *kingdom* is revealed. The whole of the MT passage was translated by the entire passage in the targum. The same is true of the following example Chilton gave:

> MT—''and the kingdom will be the Lord's.''
> Tg—''and *the Kingdom of* the Lord will be *revealed upon all the dwellers of the earth*.'' (Obad 21).[41]

Chilton correctly observed, ''the practical equation between God's kingdom and Jerusalem's autonomy is underlined in the last clause. . . . '' He reached his conclusion, however, in the next sentence, without any supporting justification: ''Such a limited kingdom conception is not that of the New Testament, and it even disagrees with Tg Zechariah 14:9.''[42] The idea that the Kingdom of God = God, is wishful thinking and it makes no sense, even as a euphemism.

Hiers was correct in holding that this verse demands a future expectation, but there is a better reason for thinking that than any he suggested. Since this was clearly a typology of the events of the exodus, the miracles of Jesus are equivalent to the plagues. The plagues preceded the crossing

---

[37]Ibid., 67.

[38]Jeremias, *New Testament Theology*, 102.

[39]B. Chilton, ''Regnum dei deus est,'' *SJT* 31 (1978):261-70.

[40]Ibid., 265.

[41]Ibid.

[42]Ibid., 269-70.

of the sea and the wilderness experiences before the entrance into Canaan. Therefore the miracles of Jesus revealed the same "finger of God" which marked the beginning of the end, but not the completion. It took a while after the plagues had begun before the escape from the Egyptians, and it would, correspondingly, take a while for the promised land to be transferred from Roman to Jewish administration, but things were beginning to happen.

Like other eschatologists, Jesus was optimistic that the time schedule could be shortened. On the basis of his conviction that the time was short, Jesus preached, "Repent for the Kingdom of Heaven has drawn near" ἤγγικεν = הגיע, Matt 4:17; 10:7; Mk 1:15; Lk 9:2). This also reflects an Exodus type. According to the rabbis (Mekilta, *Beshallah* 1:93-96, 106-107), when the Israelites were ready to leave Egypt, Moses took a gold tablet on which the Tetragrammaton had been carved, threw it into the Nile and said, "Joseph, son of Jacob, the oath which the holy One blessed be He swore to Abraham, our father, that he would redeem his sons, is ready to be fulfilled" (הגיע) R. Isaac used the same verb to say the time of the Kingdom of Heaven had come near (הגיע, SSR 2:13; PR 15,75a). The time was still future, but it was so close that the Israelites were getting ready to leave that night! When Jesus said the Kingdom of Heaven had come near, he meant the Son of man was just about to come into his glory, which was a typological and mythical way of saying that the Messiah was just about to be enthroned at Jerusalem. He may have thought it would take as many as three and a half years before the enthronement, as in Daniel. Under oath, he said that there were some standing around him at that time who would live to see the Son of man coming into his kingdom (Matt 16:28; Lk 9:27).

At the last Supper, Jesus told his disciples that this was the last Passover he would celebrate with them before the Kingdom came. This meant he expected the kingdom to come before the next Passover when he would drink the fruit of the vine with them again, this time in the Kingdom of his Father (Matt 26:29; see Lk 22:15-18). This does not mean he expected that both he and they would die and be in heaven within a year, but that the Kingdom would have come by then, and he would be sitting on his glorious throne in Jerusalem. They also would then be governing the twelve tribes of Israel.[43]

---

[43]E. Linnemann, *Jesus of the Parables*, tr. J. Sturdy (New York, c1966) 37, said Jesus and John differed from the apocalyptists in that apocalyptists calculated whereas these simply announced that the time was up. How did they know that if they had not first calculated, studied signs, etc.?

The Homecoming. Isa 49:8, 12: "Thus says the Lord, 'In a time of favor I have answered you, in a day of salvation I have helped you; I have kept you and given you as a covenant to the people, to establish the land, to apportion the desolate heritages . . . look, these shall come from afar, and look! these from the North and *from the West*, and *from the land of Syene* [in the East] . . . for the Lord has comforted his people.' "

Isa 59:19-20: " 'So they shall fear the name of the Lord *from the West*, and his glory *from the rising of the sun* [in the East], . . . and he will come to Zion as Redeemer to those in Jacob who turn from transgression,' says the Lord."

On the basis of Deuteronomy, both Jeremiah and Ezekiel had promised that the Lord would reject his people from the promised land, but he would not leave them outside forever. Whenever they had paid double for all their sins, he would comfort his people and bring them back from the diaspora where they had been sent. In Babylon a poet believed that the sins had been paid off, double, and the Jews were just about to return to the promised land from every country where they then lived. When they actually returned, however, it was not nearly as rosy as Second Isaiah had promised. There was a lot of rebuilding to do. The Babylonians had taken the most prestigious people to Babylon, so that they could lead no independence movement in Palestine. This means that the craftsmen, farmers, unskilled laborers, and other lower-class people were left. When the wealthy, well-educated Jews from Babylonia returned, they wanted nothing to do with these local lower-class Jews, whom they styled as "people of the land," comparing them, disparagingly, to the Canaanites whom Joshua found in the land when he began his conquest.

Jesus seems to have visualized a similar situation when the Kingdom of Heaven came again. After he had witnessed the faith of the centurion, apparently a Jew in the Roman army who lived outside the boundaries of the promised land,[44] he said, "I tell you truly that I have not found such

---

[44]Contra P. D. Meyer, "The Gentile Mission in Q," *JBL* 89 (1970):405-17. Josephus told of Jewish officers in the Roman army who became revolutionary officers in the Jewish war against Rome. One of them, Silas the Babylonian, deserted from the army of King Agrippa to become an officer in the Jewish rebellion (*BJ* 2.520). Simon from Perea had also been a royal officer before the rebellion (*BJ* 2.57). Earlier, Pitelaus, who had been second in command with the troops at Jerusalem, deserted to Aristobulus when the latter escaped from Rome to regain his kingdom (*BJ* 1.171-172).

faith in Israel, but I say to you, many [others] will come *from the East and from the West*, and they will recline at a banquet with Abraham, Isaac, and Jacob in the Kingdom of Heaven, but the citizens of the Kingdom will be cast out into outer darkness'' (Matt 8:11-12; see also Lk 13:28-29).

Citing quotations from Second Isaiah, Jesus was apparently comparing his situation, typologically, with the previous restoration. He knew that there were faithful Jews in the diaspora, in addition to this Jewish centurion. He had also found many hard-headed Jews in Israel. When the diaspora Jews came to Palestine, they would show such leadership and commitment that they would displace the local Jews. So this would mean that Israel had the same meaning as the Kingdom of Heaven. This is the most logical explanation for the event in light of the passage quoted from Isaiah.

The End of the Greek Age. Dan 12:1-7: ''In that time Michael the great general who stands over the sons of your people will appear, and there will be a time of suffering such as has not been from the establishment of the nation [Israel] until that time. At that time your people will escape—all who are found written in the Book of Life. Many of those who sleep in the dust of the ground will jump up, some to life of the age (לחיי עולם = εἰς ζωὴν αἰώνιον) and others to reproach and rejection of the age [to come] (עולם [הבא] = αἰώνιον [τὸν ἐρχόμενον]). Then the instructors *will shine like the sun* in the firmament and *the righteous* of the congregation (הרבים = τῶν πολλῶν like the stars for the age and until the time of the end לעולם ועד = εξ τοὺς αἰῶνος καὶ ἔτι). Now you, Daniel, cover the words, and seal the book, until the time of the end (עד עת קץ = ἕως καιροῦ συντελείας).''

This was prophecy written after the fact by a pro-Hasmonean who had interpreted the Hasmonean victory over the Greeks as God's predestined deliverance in fulfillment of Jeremiah's prophecy.[45] The important three-and-a-half-year period between the end of the Greek age and the beginning of the Jewish age [to come] was a time of divine judgment during which Judas led Jewish troops against Antiochus IV Epiphanes. It took roughly three to three and a half years of intensive fighting from the time Antiochus defiled the temple until it was cleansed and rededicated (*BJ* 1.32). This was the turn of the ages, later called the birth pangs of the Messiah. It was only a matter of time after that until the Maccabean kingdom came and the

---

[45]Jer 47.

Greeks were driven out of the promised land. Many Jews in NT times believed that God was just about to drive the Romans out in the same way. This
would be the end of the Roman age and the beginning of the Kingdom of
God. That is what the listening Jews heard when Jesus said, *"At the end of
the age* (συντελεία τοῦ αἰῶνος) *the righteous will shine like the sun* in
the kingdom of their Father" (Matt 13:41, 43). They would also correctly
have understood Jesus to have meant by "the kingdom of their Father" the
same kingdom the Hasmoneans recovered at the end of the Greek age.[46]

The National Prayer. A very popular prayer was composed sometime
after construction had begun on Herod's temple (ca. 20 B.C.) and before the
temple was destroyed (A.D. 70) which expressed Jewish longings for the
restoration of the nation under Jewish control: "May his *kingdom* reign in
your lifetimes and in your days and in the days of all the house of Israel,
quickly and soon. Amen. . . . May the prayers and petitions of all Israel be
accepted before their *Father who is in heaven.* . . . May the One who makes
peace in his high places make peace over all Israel. . . . May his great *name
be* magnified and *sanctified* in the age which he is destined to renew, raise
the dead, rebuild the city of Jerusalem, complete the temple, uproot foreign
worship from the land and restore the holy worship of *Heaven* in its place.
May his Kingdom rule. May he cause his redemption to spring forth, and
may he hasten the consummation of the Kingdom of his Messiah, in your
lifetimes and in your days and in the lifetimes of the whole house of Israel,
quickly and soon. Amen."[47]

Jeremias correctly held that the Kaddish was the background of thought
and aspiration for the Lord's prayer. He also claimed correctly that this was
an eschatological prayer, employing enthronement themes.[48] He did not use
the earliest form of the Kaddish, however, that employed all of these clearly
nationalistic aspirations—driving out the Romans, cleansing the temple,
restoring true worship in Jerusalem, and establishing the kingdom of the
Messiah. Therefore, he thought the kingdom meant simply "God." To say,

---

[46]S. G. F. Brandon, *Jesus and the Zealots*, 7, said ". . . there can be no doubt that Jesus
looked forward to the achievement of an apocalyptic situation that necessarily involved the
elimination of the Roman government in Judaea."

[47]See GWB, *To the Hebrews* (Garden City, c1972) 38-51, and GWB, *Revelation*, 268-
69.

[48]Jeremias, *New Testament Theology*, 198.

"The Kingdom of God has come near," said Jeremias, is the same as saying, "God is near."[49] The Jews who prayed the Kaddish were asking for something less abstract. They were praying for a kingdom they could see in their lifetimes—a kingdom that would be *theirs*. They wanted it to come soon. When it came, foreign worship would be uprooted and the Messiah would rule. Peace would come to Israel, secure within its own borders. Jesus also taught his disciples to pray:

Our *Father, the One in the heavens,*
may your *name* be *sanctified.*
may your *Kingdom* come,
may your will be done,
as in *heaven*, also on the land (Matt 6:9-10).

It seems strange, indeed, for Jesus to have taught his disciples a prayer that was standard Jewish liturgy, pleading for the Kingdom to come and not to have meant anything like that which other Jews meant when they offered the same prayer. Had he done this, he would surely have confused his disciples whom he was trying to lead. There is not one word of explanation indicating that, although he was striving for something that involved the same terms that other Jews held uppermost in their minds, he had goals that were completely different from theirs. Since there is not, it is reasonable to think that he and they had the same goals. They wanted the Kingdom of Heaven to come. This involved getting rid of the Romans.[50] There were two possible ways of doing this: (1) leading a long, drawn-out military movement, like that led by Joshua and Judas the Maccabee, or (2) paying double for all their sins like the Jews in Babylon, who were readmitted to the land after Cyrus of Persia took care of the military demands, leaving the Jews free to return without a battle. The Lord's prayer asks that the latter be the case:

Lead us not into the test,
[probably means war with Rome],
but deliver us from evil.
[probably means Roman rule].

---

[49]Ibid., 102.

[50]G. Bornkamm, *Jesus of Nazareth*, tr. I. and F. McLuskey (London, c1960) 137, thought that because the Lord's prayer is not as explicit as the Kaddish, it is therefore nonpolitical.

The Political Monarchy. Jesus' own disciples understood the Kingdom of God as a name or code word for a distinctly political monarchy in which Jesus as king would have chief counselors around him. James and John applied for some of these key positions (Matt 20:20-23), and Jesus did not say there would be no such advisors or that his Kingdom was only a spiritual entity.

In fact, he told the twelve that they would have special governing responsibilities, each one ruling over one of the twelve tribes of Israel when the Son of man was enthroned (Matt 19:28). He promised them many material rewards when his administration was installed. The twelve had invested heavily in his campaign, but "to the victors belong the spoils," and when the Kingdom came, they would receive many times more things than they had given up (Matt 19:28; Mk 10:37; Lk 22:29). It would take some ardently committed Jews to bring this about. The rich who would not give up all their wealth would not make it (Matt 19:16-25). Those whose righteousness was no greater than that of the Pharisees, who gave only their tithes, would not qualify (Matt 5:20). If they invested everything they had to bring about the Kingdom, they would be amply rewarded when the Kingdom came (Matt 6:33; Lk 12:31). There was more involved in acquiring the Kingdom than simply addressing their leader as "Lord," the way most subjects addressed a king (Matt 4:21). They had to do the will of Jesus' heavenly Father which meant supporting his campaign.

After Jesus had spent his entire public life urging people to get behind a serious campaign to initiate the Kingdom of Heaven and had been crucified by the Romans as an insurrectionist, there were some on the way to Emmaus who had followed his actions and teachings. They were disappointed because they had believed he was going to redeem Israel (Lk 24:19-20). Why did they associate his teachings about the Kingdom of Heaven with redeeming Israel? Probably because he had also identified the Kingdom of Heaven with Israel as Jews had done before him and after this time.[51] If he had meant something else, he would have had to say so, or he would have been misunderstood.

In a period when there were strong nationalistic feelings, and, when almost every year there was at least one guerrilla encounter with Rome in an

---

[51]Contra R. Bultmann, *Jesus and the Word*, 107, who said, "Undoubtedly his expectation of the imminent coming of the Kingdom of God excluded the question of practical regulations for nation and state from the centre of his thought."

attempt to evict the Romans from Jewish territory, it would have been difficult for a leader to have been very popular in Palestine who in no way had been sympathetic to the feelings of other Jews. But he did have a strong following of people who believed he would redeem Israel, sit on his glorious throne, and rule over the promised land. This is what they thought was involved in receiving the Kingdom of God. He spoke of nothing so often as the Kingdom of God or of Heaven.[52] Was he deliberately trying to deceive his fellow Jews into thinking he was sympathetic with their movement and wanted to lead it, but really had something else in mind? There is no evidence to indicate that he was. There are two passages that are frequently quoted to show that Jesus was not interested in politics when he spoke of the monarchy of God. They are as follows:

Not of this World. When Jesus was reported to have said, ''My Kingdom is not of this world'' (Jn 18:36), he did not mean that it was in heaven. In the Gospel of John all people are divided into two groups: (1) those of the world and (2) those not of the world. Those not of the world included Jesus and his followers who believed in him. They lived on the earth. They were not in heaven, but they were not the heathen. They belonged to ''the church'' in contrast to ''the world.'' ''The world'' included all the pagans and those who refused to believe in him. This was the negative word in the Fourth Gospel, so it would have been out of character for Jesus in this gospel to have been reported as leading a kingdom of ''the world,'' but this is not in conflict with a political theory of a kingdom.

In Your Midst. ''When he had been asked by the Pharisee when the Kingdom of God would come, he answered them and said, 'The Kingdom of God will not come with observation, and they will not say, ''Look here! or there!'' Look, the Kingdom of God is in your midst.' '' (Lk 17:20-21).

Hiers[53] has argued strongly that this is a future expectation and does not mean that the Kingdom had already arrived. He claimed that these verses belong to a larger context, which continues in verse 23 to say, ''And they will say. . . . '' Since that is future, and the illustration also says, ''Look

---

[52]Eusebius, reporting events of his own day, said Christians in Melitene and Syria tried to take possession of the empire (*HE* 8.vi.8). In the same book, Eusebius reported Martyrs ''of the Kingdom of Christ'' who had proclaimed the heavenly kingdom of Christ (τὴν οὐρ-άνιον τοῦ Χριστοῦ βασιλέως). These movements to acquire the ''heavenly'' kingdom finally led to the support of Constantine's conquest of Rome.

[53]Hiers, *Kingdom*, 22-29.

there and here'' (Lk 17:23), this all belongs to the one unit that was composed at one time. Hiers failed to notice that Lk 17:20-21 is a chreia, a literary form defined by the Greek rhetoricians as one formed to preserve
sayings of their teachers. All the context existing today is that which is provided by the structure of the chreia itself. The larger structure given to the
chreia by the Lukan editor is not original to the context in which the statement was made. Therefore we will try to imagine the kind of context in
which this saying would make sense and attempt to understand its possible
meaning.

The topic of discussion is the Kingdom of God and how it might come
to the Jews in Palestine at a time when they were under Roman domination.
It seems obvious that Israel could not have independence unless something
happened to overthrow Rome. There are two ways in which a revolution can
be successful within a country. Since it begins among a minority, resisters
cannot lead a sudden military movement to overthrow the government in power
unless they can obtain outside aid from some strong nation that is an enemy
of the ruling power. This happened when the Maccabees got support from
the Romans to overthrow the Syrian Greeks (*BJ* 1.38, 48) and to George
Washington when he got help from the French to fight the English. When
this help is not available, the revolutionary party must then undermine the
ruling party with sabotage and fifth columnist activity, getting their members
into positions of power in the ruling party and weakening it from within.
This is the way Moses led the Hebrews out of Egypt. This is the way Esther,
Daniel, and Nehemiah functioned. Allowing for the legendary character of
some of these heroes and heroines, their methodology reflects the ideal of
the people and has influenced Jews and Christians in political activity for
hundreds of years. It would be strange if there were no counterparts of these
figures in NT times.

While the Shah ruled Iran, there was a kingdom of the followers of
Khomeini forming quietly within Iran. During that time, no one could point
his finger and say, ''Look, here is Khomeini's kingdom!'' But it was in the
midst of Iran and it did finally come into being. In a political resistance
movement, as one expects who is in quest of a kingdom, such a response
as the one Jesus gave to the Pharisees seems fitting, and it had more content
than the implication of a divine inner experience or mystic feeling of security. The only way people can ''experience'' a kingdom is to get control
of one, and this is what Jesus and his followers were trying to do.

The titles attributed to Jesus were those appropriate for a king.[54] The kingdom he was trying to obtain was the kind of kingdom all other kings rule. It was mythologically called the Kingdom of God or the Kingdom of Heaven, but Jews of New Testament times knew that this kingdom would come into being only when the Romans were expelled from Palestine and their own king sat on the throne, ruling from Jerusalem. There are several parables attributed to Jesus that reflect the kind of underground movement that would be necessary to acquire such a political kingdom as this. Those parables will be considered here as valid teachings of Jesus. The next chapter will examine some literary forms necessary for establishing that validity for some points of view Jesus is reported to have taught.

---

[54]See further H. Frankfort, *Kingship and the Gods*, (Chicago, c1958); and R. E. Pike, *Republican Rome* (New York, 1966) 92. For the title, "Son of man" see GWB, *To the Hebrews*, 38-51.

CHAPTER TWO

Rhetoricians, Philosophers, and Literary Forms

Introduction

There were Greek rhetoricians long before the time of Aristotle (4th B.C.), and they continued at least until the eleventh century A.D. Rhetoricians were those who trained lawyers and other public orators. At least from the time of Theon (1-2nd A.D.) to the time of Doxapatres (11th A.D.), these teachers used a literary form, called a *chreia* (χρεία), in their training program. Students were taught both to recognize chreias and to use them in argument. For purposes of training it was necessary to define these literary units sharply, and fortunately, many books of instructions have been preserved that were prepared by rhetoricians. The definitions of chreias that were prepared by rhetoricians are helpful for anyone interested in the literature or history of the period involved.

The synoptic gospels are part of the literature composed during the time of the rhetoricians, and since these gospels also contain chreias, it seems normal to use what the rhetoricians taught for understanding the literature of the gospels. The first step will be to explain the chreia as clearly as possible, giving illustrations and examples. The next step will be to try to discover the origin of chreias, their preservation and use in the earliest times, and the reliability of the philosophers, historians, and rhetoricians who preserved them. Finally chreias will be applied and tested on early Jewish and Christian literature.

Chreias Defined and Illustrated

Rhetoricians. A papyrus fragment, now in a museum in Florence, Italy, contains a definition of a chreia, apparently part of a student's assignment: "What is a chreia (χρία)? It is a reminiscence (ἀπομνημόνευμα), [that is] succinct, about a character, whom it credits. Why is a chreia a reminiscence? Because it is remembered that it may be told. Why is it succinct? Because if it were extended, many times it would be a narrative or something else. Why is it about a character? Because many times without a character reference a succinct reminiscence is a maxim (γνώμη) or something else. Why is it called a chreia? Because of its usefulness."[2] This definition was also well-known by teachers of rhetoric. One such teacher was Theon (1-2d A.D.): "A chreia is brief statement or action attributed aptly to a definite character or [something] corresponding to a character. A maxim and a reminiscence are [forms] like it, for every maxim [that is] brief and attributed to a particular character makes a chreia, and the reminiscence also is

---

[1]This seems to be a misspelling. The word is usually spelled χρεία. *Papiri Greci e Latine* 1, Firenze, 1912, no. 85. Its plural in Greek is χρεῖαι. The Anglicized plural is "chreias," just as the Anglicized plural of parable is parables. Dr. William R. Farmer first introduced me to chreias in R. O. P. Taylor's book, *The Groundwork of the Gospels* (Oxford, 1946). See also Taylor's "Form Criticism in the First Centuries," *ET* 55 (1944):218-20. I also read the definitions of M. Dibelius, *From Tradition to Gospel*, tr. B. L. Woolf (London, 1934) and H. A. Fischel, "Studies in Cynicism and the Ancient Near East: The Transformation of *chreia*," *Religions in Antiquity*, ed. J. Neusner (Leiden, 1968), pp. 372-411, but I quickly decided that both were operating on false assumptions, so I began to work seriously with L. Spengel, *Rhetores Graeci* in 3 vols. (Leipsig, 1856). The works of H. Rabe, *Rhetores Graeci* (Leipsig, 1926) and C. Walz, *Rhetores Graeci* (Stuttgart, 1834-36) are still better, but Spengel's volumes were more easily available to me and they are adequate. In the Fall semester, 1980, I attended the chreia seminar at the Institute for Antiquity and Christianity, Claremont, California, which had been in existence more than a year. This provided me an opportunity to improve my Greek, test some of my theories, and gain access to more library materials on chreias. Particularly helpful to me was Dr. Ronald Hock, Associate Professor of Religion at the University of Southern California and a member of the chreia seminar. He directed me to sources, checked my translations in this chapter, and read this entire chapter twice, making helpful suggestions for its improvement.

[2]*Papiri Greci e Latine* 1, no. 85.

an action or word useful for life. The maxim, however, differs from the chreia in the following ways: (1) the chreia is certainly attributed to a particular person, the maxim is certainly not; (2) the chreia is sometimes a statement about a general matter and sometimes, a particular matter, but the maxim is only a statement about something general; (3) the chreia is sometimes something witty, having nothing useful for life, whereas the maxim is always [concerned] for things that are useful for life; and (4) the chreia may be either an action or a statement, whereas the maxim is a statement only.

"The reminiscence is distinguished from the chreia in two ways: (1) the chreia is brief, but the reminiscence is sometimes expanded, and (2) the chreia is attributed to a certain character, whereas the reminiscence is told for itself (καθ' ἑατό). It is called 'chreia' [useful] *par excellence* because it, more than others, is useful for life in many ways, just as although there are many poets, we customarily call Homer alone *par excellence* 'the poet.' "[3] Although rhetoricians repeatedly explain that the name, chreia, originated from its usefulness, it was distinguished also from the proverb because it was not always useful. Without really knowing how the literary form got its name, rhetoricians probably deduced it from the etymology of the word.

According to Hermogenes (2nd A.D.), "A chreia is a reminiscence of some statement or action or a combination of the two, briefly told, usually for the sake of something useful."[4] "The chreia differs from the reminiscence, especially in length. The reminiscence might be quite extensive, but the chreia must be brief. Furthermore, the chreia is attributed to a definite character, but the reminiscence is told for itself. [The chreia] differs from the maxim in that the maxim is told in a bare statement, whereas many times the chreia [is told] in question and answer. Again the chreia deals also with actions, but the maxim with statements only. Furthermore, the chreia contains the character who speaks [or acts], whereas the maxim is told without a character."[5]

---

[3]Theon, "Progymnasmata," L. Spengel, 2.v. p. 97,3-10.

[4]Hermogenes, "Progymnasmata," Spengel, 2.iii, p. 5.25-27.

[5]Ibid.,2.iii, p. 6,5-15, accepting the reading of Hugo Rabe, "Homilies on Aphthonius," *Rhetores Graeci*, 10, p. 6.15-7.6, to include "speaks" in the last line. For similar definitions, see Aphthonius, "Progymnasmata," Spengel, Ibid., 2.iii, p. 23.1-5, and Nicolaus, "Progymnasmata," Spengel, Ibid. 3.iii, p. 459.24-26.

Clarification and Illustration. The rhetoricians were consistent in their understanding of the definition of the chreia. The requirements were as follows: (1)it is always concise; (2) the speaker is identified; (3) the statement or action is always given; and (4) the content is various. It can either be witty or beneficial for life, or it might even be a meaningful action without words. These distinctions were made in relationship to reminiscences and maxims. Responsive chreias and some assertive chreias give the person or situation that prompted the speaker to speak. The illustrations given in chreias by the rhetoricians enable us to sharpen the definition still more. There are hundreds of chreias in classical Greek literature. Only a few are listed as examples by the rhetoricians. For all except the simplest assertive chreias, the examples chosen by the rhetoricians consist of one or two sentences only and begin with an aorist participle, a genitive absolute, or both. Of the sayings recorded by historians and philosophers that appear to be chreias, at least ninety-five percent also follow this grammatical pattern. None of the definitions includes grammatical or stylistic qualifications, but the tendency was to write Greek literary forms in good literary Greek, and rhetoricians, naturally, chose good literary examples for use in teaching. Few units that otherwise seem to be chreias employ finite verbs rather than participles. Illustrations of both forms will be shown. In the illustrations to follow, the aorist participles are translated so that their force is evident, and the participles are italicized to make their function still more obvious:

Having seen an undisciplined youth, Diogenes chided the instructor, saying, "Why are you teaching such things?"[6]

Having been advised by his friends to build up resources, Alexander, king of the Macedonians, said, "But these things did not help even Croesus."[7]

Having heard that her son had claimed to be [the son] of Zeus, Olympias, the mother of Alexander, said, "Will that boy never stop accusing me to Hera?"[8]

Having been asked where the muses dwell, Plato said, "In the souls of those who have been educated."[9]

---

[6]Aphthonius, "Progymnasmata," Spengel 2.iii, p. 23.11-13.

[7]Theon, "Progymnasmata," Spengel 2.v, p. 100.4-6.

[8]Nicolaus, "Progymnasmata," Spengel 3.iii, p. 460.26-29.

[9]Ibid.

Having been asked where the boundaries of Sparta were, a Lacedaemonian pointed to his spear.[10]

Having been asked if anyone who does anything wrong escapes the notice of the gods, Pittacus of Mitylene replied, "Not even one contemplating [doing wrong]."[11]

One of his pupils, Apollodorus, *having said* to him, "The Athenians have unjustly condemned you to death," Socrates, the philosopher, laughed and said, "But would you prefer [that they condemned me] justly?"[12]

His sandals *having been stolen*, Damon, the lame gymnasium teacher, said, "May they fit the thief!"[13]

These chreias were all attributed to recognized teachers, scholars, or kings, with two exceptions—Olympias, the mother of a king, and an unspecified Spartan. An action, such as the Lacedaemonian, pointing to his spear, had the effect of a sharp, oral answer. Most were assertive chreias in which the situation was given which prompted the speaker to speak. Others were responsive chreias. In all cases the speaker was identified. Without the character identification and the situation or question which prompted the character to speak, the quotation might be a proverb or a reminiscence. The major characteristics of these and most classical Greek responsive chreias and assertive chreias introduced by a situation that prompted the character to speak are:

(1) The speaker or actor is identified (sometimes only as "a Lacedaemonian").

(2) The situation is given which prompted the speaker to speak.

(3) The statement made or the action taken is reported.

(4) The whole unit is very brief.

In grammatical structure, not all chreias have the preceding form. Some assertive chreias begin with something like, "Isocrates, the sophist, used to say . . . ,"[14] indicating that this was typical and probably had been said many times. Others include the following:

---

[10] Ibid., p. 460.20-21.

[11] Theon, "Progymnasmata," Spengel 2.v, p. 97.30-32.

[12] Ibid., pp. 99.30-100.1.

[13] Ibid., p. 100.6-9.

[14] Theon, "Progymnasmata," Spengel 2.v, p. 102.1-3.

Someone said Diogenes was stupid (mindless). He responded, "I am not stupid (mindless), but I do not have the same mind as you" (Mullach, 11).[15]

Diogenes once asked Plato for three dried figs from his bag. When he sent two bushels, [Diogenes] said, "Thus also when he is asked one [question] he answers ten thousand" (Mullach, 51).

[Diogenes] was begging from a miser who was very slow at giving. He said, "I am begging for food—not for burial" (Mullach, 192).

Since none of the definitions prevents these from being considered chreias, we will consider them as such, noting that all chreia forms, whether assertive or responsive, were tightly confined by definition to brevity. They were never extended into dialogues, as Dibelius claimed. Dibelius, ignoring the definition that required them to be succinct, said, "The terse style of the 'Chria' tolerates many extensions without spoiling its form."[16] Dibelius erroneously included as chreias some of the debates recorded by Xenophon, such as the following quotation:

Of another who said the drinking water at his home was [too] warm: "Then," he said, "when you want warm water in which to wash, it will be ready for you," "But," he said, "it is [too] cold for washing."

He asked, "Then, are your servants distressed when they drink it and also wash with it?"

"No," he said, "but I surely have been surprised how willingly they use it for both [of these] purposes."

"Which is warmer to drink, " he asked, "the water at your place or that at Asclepius?"

"That at Asclepius," he answered.

"Which," he asked, "is colder to wash in, that at your house or that at Amphiaraus?"

"That at Amphiaraus," he replied.

---

[15]The number is from the list of apophthegmata on Diogenes prepared by F. W. A. Mullach, "De Diogene Cynico," *Fragmenta Philosophorum Graecorum* in 3 vols. (Darmstadt, 1968), 2:295-330. This is far from a perfect list. There are chreias in Diogenes Laertius's collection that are not included here. This has the benefit of being an extensive list, so it can be used objectively. No additions or subtractions have been made.

[16]M. Dibelius, *From Tradition to Gospel*, tr. B. L. Woolf (Greenwood, S.C., n.d.), p. 155.

"Consider, then," he said, "that you run the risk of being more difficult to please than servants and invalids."[17]

This unit is not a chreia but a reminiscence. The American given here is for the Greek used in Xenophon's title that is normally rendered "Memorabilia." Doxapatres, in his commentary, gave an illustration about as long as this unit to show that it was a reminiscence and *not* a chreia, because it failed to meet the qualification of being succinct.[18]

The Greek rhetoricians, however, were more constrained in their definitions. They instructed their pupils in the homiletic art of expanding chreias, but they did not say that the resulting midrash, sermon, or narrative, would still be a chreia. "Why is [a chreia] succinct? Because if it were extended, many times it would be a narrative or something else."[19]

Problems. The definitions provided by the rhetoricians are amazingly consistent when one considers the length of time that elapsed from the time of Theon (1-2nd A.D.) to Doxapatres (11th A.D.). There is a problem, nevertheless, concerning the exact meaning of Theon's definition: "A chreia is a concise statement or action which is aptly attributed (ἀναφερομένη) to some specific character or [something] corresponding to (ἀναλογοῦν) a character."[20] Does the word "attribute" mean they were fictitiously composed and attributed to historical characters? Does the term "character" (πρόσωπον), like the Latin equivalent, *persona*, simply mean a character in a play?[21] Or, does the term "specific character" mean a definite, histor-

---

[17]Xenophon, *Memorabilia*, 3.xiii.3.

[18]Doxapatres, "Homilies on Aphthonius," Walz 2.iii, p. 250. H. A. Fischel, "Studies in Cynicism," p. 402, erroneously classified chreias in four different forms: "1. terse (usually not more than two sentences); 2. full (but without any superfluous detail); 3. elaborate (diatribic-rhetorically enlarged; 4. composite (several *chreiae* combine to form a new item.)"

[19]*Papiri Greci e Latine* 1, no. 85. For a later commentary on this point, see Doxapatres, "Homilies on Aphthonius," Walz 2.iii, pp. 248.30-249.31.

[20]Theon, "Progymnasmata," Spengel 2.v, p. 96, 19-22.

[21]At the time I left the Claremont Chreia Seminar, many members of the group were basically convinced that chreias were fictitiously created by rhetoricians. They held that the phrase in Theon's definition, "attributed aptly," meant rhetoricians invented or found sayings they, themselves, needed for their arguments and attributed them aptly to some ancient philosopher, like Diogenes, Alexander, or Socrates. At that time, however, no member of that seminar had seen Doxapatres' interpretation of the phrase, "attributed aptly," to mean attributing the chreia to the right character.

ical person? Doxapatres, in his commentary on the chreia about Diogenes and a youth said ''the youth'' was not the ''character'' in the chreia, but Diogenes was.[22] What does the word ἀναλογοῦν mean as it is used here? There may be an intentional distinction made between a definite character, like Plato, Diogenes, or Crates, and something that corresponds to a character, like ''a certain Lacedaemonian.'' Whatever Theon meant by it, later rhetoricians did not consider it a necessary qualification, so they neither accepted nor continued it.

There were rhetoricians long before the time of Aristotle (4th B.C.). Aristotle wrote extensively on logic, attitudes, and techniques necessary for rhetoric, but he did not mention chreias as literary forms.[23]

Fact or Fiction

Did these rhetoricians find chreias included among the collections of sayings of great men that were already available to them, or did they make up sharp sayings and attribute them aptly to historical figures of the past? Should chreias be considered historical data or historical fiction?

Hypothetically, any historical writing may have been forged or altered by later writers and chreias are not exempt from human possibilities. In testing this likelihood, the first step will be to consider the seriousness with which rhetoricians and other historians of antiquity understood their responsibility in composing or recording history. One of the late rhetoricians, Doxapatres, commenting on the definition found in the works of an earlier rhetorician, Aphthonius, said, ''The expression, *attributed to some character,* teaches us through the definition as we attempt to discover first who is the one who has spoken here, to attribute the chreia to him and not, perhaps, if Plato said it to say that Isocrates or someone else said it.''[24] Doxapatres gave an example to illustrate the point he had in mind: If someone like Aphthonius had quoted Hesiod, the rhetor was not free to say Aphthonius said it. He must attribute it to Hesiod, as Aphthonius did. To do otherwise would be to attribute something to some character inappropriately (οὐκ εὐστόχως).[25] Historians, like Diogenes Laertius, frequently noted

---

[22]Doxapatres, ''Homilies on Aphthonius,'' Walz 2.iiif., p. 258.18-21.

[23]See Aristotle, *The Art of Rhetoric* and *Rhetoric to Alexander.*

[24]Doxapatres, ''Homilies on Aphthonius,'' Walz 2.iii, p. 251.1-5.

[25]Ibid., p. 251.5-12.

that the same chreia had been attributed to two different philosophers, so, like Doxapatres, in fairness alerted readers to both of the possibilities.

Historians and Chreias

Because of the uncertain implication of terms like "attributed" and "corresponding to," the definitions of chreias are somewhat uncertain, and the rhetoricians did not tell how these units of literature came into existence. Did the rhetoricians compose them and attribute them to ancient leaders in whatever way they considered appropriate? Did they sharply define for purposes of instruction literary units that had been preserved for many years before their time? Were chreias carefully composed near the time of the events and statements reported? Although absolute answers cannot be obtained to all of these questions, some of the following information will be gathered upon which to base conjectures: (1) How did the early historians who used chreias obtain their data? How early were their sources? What kind of sources did they have? (2) How did ancient teachers teach? (3) In a test case, how coherent were the sayings attributed to one philosopher? (4) How carefully did scribes preserve messages of chreias after they had been composed? The first step will be to consider one historian who has reported hundreds of chreias, Diogenes Laertius.

Diogenes Laertius. Diogenes Laertius seems to have belonged to the third century A.D. although this is not certain. What is certain is that he examined many written sources before he wrote his *Lives and Opinions of Eminent Philosophers*. For example, in a brief narration of the life of Empedocles (ca. 2,200 Greek words), Laertius mentioned the names of twenty additional authors whose works he had studied and compared.[26] In his life of Diogenes the Cynic, Laertius referred to the works of Antisthenes, Sotion, and Sosicrates, who wrote in the first half of the second century B.C.; also Theophrastus (ca. 372-287 B.C.), Apollonius (ca. 295-215 B.C. Menippus of Gadara (3d, B.C.), Satyrus of Smyrna (fl. 200 B.C.), and Favorinus (1-2nd A.D.).[27] Of course, Laertius may have obtained this data

---

[26]Hippobatus, Timaeus, Hermippus, Eratosthenes, Aristotle, Apollodorus, Heraclides, Satyrus, Favorinus, Telauges, Neanthes, Empedocles, Theophrastus, Alcidamas, Hironymous, Aristippus, Xanthon, Timon, Diodorus, and Demetrius.

[27]The dates for these authors are taken from W. Schmidt and O. Stahlin, *Wilhelm von Christs Geschichte der Griechischen Litteratur* (München, 1913), 7.ii.1 and 2. In proper sequence, the pages are: 7.ii.1, pp. 85, 49, 60-61, 140, 90, 83, and 7.ii.2, pp. 600-601.

completely from secondary sources, but the fact that he intended contemporaries to think he used them implies that they existed in his day and could have been consulted. Historians, then, who lived and wrote during the time of rhetoricians who used chreias in their instructions, were not dependent upon the compositions of the rhetoricians. They had at their disposal sources that had been written hundreds of years before, as did the rhetoricians themselves. Some of these were collections of chreias.

In his work on Crates of Thebes, who flourished in 326 B.C., Laertius claimed to have consulted a collection of chreias written down by the famous Zeno of Citium (333-261 B.C.) (6.91). These materials had evidently been reported orally or written down and then collected in less than seventy-five years after the events reported—not by rhetoricians, like Theon, Nicolaus, Aphthonius, or Doxapatres. The philosopher to whom Laertius credited the most chreias was Diogenes the Cynic (404-323 B.C.). Some of Laertius's sources for these chreias are collections of chreias preserved by Metrocles (ca. 300 B.C.) and Hecato of Rhodes (ca. 100 B.C.) (6.32-33). Hecato evidently had more than one book of chreias, because Laertius referred to his "first book" (Ἑχάτων ἐν τῷ πρώτῳ Χρειῶν). Laertius also said he consulted the chreias of Hecato to compose his work on Antisthenes (ca. 446-366) (6.4), Metrocles (6:95), and Cleanthes (7.172). "The Wiener Diogenes Papyrus," belonging to the first half of the first century B.C., has many of the same chreias as those preserved by Laertius. This is an independent testimony to the reliability of Laertius's sources.[28] The care which Diogenes Laertius had taken to acknowledge his sources of information at least shows he was conscious of this existing body of source material and he might even have consulted it the way he said. It is unlikely that he attributed to these early historians collections of chreias that had been composed by his contemporaries who were rhetoricians. Diogenes Laertius referred to the numerous chreias he credited to Bion (3rd B.C.) as "reminiscences" (ἀπομνήματα) and useful or "chreia-like" sayings (ἀποφθέγματα χρειώδη) (D.L. 4.47).

When disciples of philosophers wrote histories about their teachers, they did not simply list chreias, as Zeno, Metrocles, and Hecato apparently did. Instead, they told of events in greater detail, evidently based on chreias or told in ways that could easily be reduced to chreia form. These are "rem-

---

[28]D. R. Dudley, *A History of Cynicism* (London, 1937) 123.

iniscences'' or ''memorabilia.'' Examples of this are Xenophon, *Memorabilia* and Lucian, *Demonax*. Chreias seemed to have been shorthand accounts for easy collections and memorization.

Aristotle. Diogenes Laertius also recorded a chreia, attributed to Aristotle, that employed the word ''chreia'': ''When Diogenes was giving him [Aristotle] dried figs, he [Aristotle] realized that if he [Aristotle] did not take them, he [Diogenes] had a carefully prepared chreia (χρεία). After he had accepted them, [Aristotle] said, 'With the chreia, Diogenes also lost the dried figs' '' (5.18). The word ''chreia'' here seems to mean something like a sharp retort, ''perfect squelch,'' or ''sizzling comment.'' Since many chreias contain, as the preserved quotations, sharp insults, the literary form may have acquired its name from the kind of retorts which these units were famous for preserving. If this is so, the rhetoricians did not know it, because they explained the term on the basis of the etymology of the Greek word.

Although Aristotle has not commented on the chreia as a literary form which rhetoricians should study and use as a base for literary compositions, he seems to have known the word ''chreia,'' and authors who lived in the period of the great classical Greek philosophers wrote books of chreias, so the literary form was known long before the time of Theon. The rhetoricians whose definitions are preserved evidently used and defined literary forms that were already available to them.

Teaching Methods

The teaching career of Diogenes, the Cynic, evidently involved teaching the children of Xeniades. Diogenes taught these children everything from good manners to philosophy. This included athletics, diet, wearing apparel, and academic study. Teachers in those days taught everything that pupils needed for life. Early philosophers, like the later rabbis, expected their students to imitate them in every walk of life. This required students to observe everything their teacher did and said, whether personal or social. Diogenes trained the children of Xeniades to memorize many passages from poets and historians, *as well as the writings of Diogenes himself,* according to Diogenes Laertius (6:31). He drilled them in many shortcuts (σύντομον) necessary to obtain a good memory. This may have involved reducing events and quotations to chreia form for easy memorization. Some of these writings of Diogenes that could be memorized may have been the statements now preserved in chreias.

Students of those Greek philosophers took notes of their teachers' lessons. One of Zeno's students, Cleanthes, was reportedly so poor that he could not afford paper, but he wrote Zeno's lectures down on shoulder blade bones of cattle and on ostraca (D.L. 7.174). There are no extensive writings preserved that are attributed to Zeno such as there are for other philosophers. This may be a circumstantially caused situation. Antigonus provided Zeno with secretaries to record his lectures (D.L. 7.36), so it was not necessary for Zeno to teach shorthand organization for memory in order to get his teachings recorded the way Diogenes and Cleanthes did. When a certain Hegesias asked Diogenes to lend him some of his writings, Diogenes called him a simpleton for wanting to settle for written lectures when he could hear the lecture for himself (D.L. 6.48). Nevertheless, Diogenes had written lectures which he could have shown Hegesias, had he chosen to do so.

Philosophers of the classical Greek period wrote books, and those books were sold and read (D.L. 7.32). Some of these were books of chreias, so there is very little reason for thinking their teachings were not recorded early in chreia form. Diogenes, for example, is quoted in chreias several times as responding to something with an appropriate quote from Homer. It is not necessary to presume that these were all created by the later rhetoricians and attributed falsely to Diogenes. Diogenes taught his students to memorize poetry (D.L. 6.31). One of these students, Crates, became especially fond of Homer's poetry (D.L. 6.84). Instances in which Diogenes quoted Homer appropriately might have been recorded in students' notebooks, along with other sayings of Diogenes, written down in the form of chreias, and later collected by such authors as Zeno, Hecato, and Metrocles. This has not been proved, but since these scholars did collect chreias about philosophers, it seems more likely that those collected were accurately attributed to the correct author and preserved for hundreds of years than to suppose that the later rhetoricians created these chreias fictitiously.

A plausible explanation for the way chreias that are attributed to Diogenes came into existence may be found in Diogenes' classes. There he probably retold the situations reported in his chreias. His lectures may have included many illustrations of experience he had had outside of class in his association with others. Perhaps his skill in retelling those and in training students to take them in short-hand for memorization accounts for the creation of chreias attributed to Diogenes. The chreias attributed to Greek philosophers include the kind of information students were expected to learn from and about their teachers in order to practice their ways of life and to defend their points of view. One hundred ninety-four of these chreias attributed to the fourth century B.C. Cynic, Diogenes, have been collected by Mullach.[29]. These can be classified into coherent categories.

An Analysis of Scholarly Opinion

Gerhard. The most extensive work on chreia literature related to Diogenes among the classical scholars was prepared by Gerhard.[30] Gerhard held that after Diogenes there developed two groups of Cynics, the hedonistic and the antihedonistic. He further conjectured that these sects composed chreias in conflict with one another and attributed them to Diogenes, arguing that this accounts for the large number of chreias attributed to this one philosopher. He said these conflicts were reflected in the following areas: (1) The first was religion. There were the Cynics that believed in the gods, even though not the popular gods, and there were the contrasting Cynics who were blasphemous in their scorn of religion. Gerhard gave no chreias to illustrate this point.[31] (2) Some materials show Diogenes scorning glory, but one chreia pictured Plato ridiculing Diogenes for enjoying the pity that he was getting (D.L. 6.41). (3) With reference to wealth, Diogenes responded to Alexander the Great that his only need was for Alexander to stop standing in the sun, but he also said the most wretched thing in the world was a destitute old man.[32] (4) Diogenes was reported to have lived on black bread and to have scorned the rich food of royal and wealthy people.[33] But he was also shown discarding black bread to replace it with white bread. More than that, some chreias show him saying that wise men ate all kinds of food. (5) At one time he was reported to have refused to drink wine lest it destroy him, but at another time he was seen drinking in a tavern.[34] (6) On the one hand he said a beautiful harlot was poisoned honey, but he also was shown masturbating in the market place. Gerhard concluded that

---

[29]Mullach has numbered his units from 1 to 301. All that seem to be chreias are considered here, and the number given is to document the unit according to Mullach's list.

[30]Gerhard, *Phoinix von Kolophon* (Berlin, 1909) and "Zur legende von Kyniker Diogenes," *Archiv für Religionswissenschaft* 15 (1912), pp. 388-408.7

[31]Gerhard, "Zur legende," pp. 395-408.

[32]Ibid., pp. 396-98.

[33]Ibid., pp. 400-01. See also pp. 403-04.

[34]Ibid.

these contradictory acts could not apply to the same person. Therefore they must have been invented by later Cynics.

Although Gerhard's conjecture is a reasonable theory to consider, and other scholars have accepted it almost uncritically,[35] there are some problems involved: (1) Gerhard was not carefully form critical. Some of his arguments depend on nonchreia narratives. (2) He has arbitrarily attributed to Diogenes at least one narrative which his source identified only as "a certain Cynic."[36] (3)Some of his illustrations do not clearly represent the side on which Gerhard has placed them. (4) Gerhard's illustrations of chreias that he thought were either anti- or prohedonistic represent about ten percent of the chreias attributed to Diogenes. (5) Gerhard admitted that the entire collection of chreias attributed to Diogenes could not be divided into prohedonistic and antihedonistic categories. (6) There are other ways to explain some, if not all, of Gerhard's arguments. Gerhard sometimes used material attributed either to Antisthenes or Crates to define true Cynicism against which he contrasted some of the chreias attributed to Diogenes. (7) Gerhard himself considered his study to be preliminary rather than definitive. For these reasons this case needs to be reexamined.

Von Fritz. One of the most skeptical of the critics was K. von Fritz.[37] Von Fritz examined the problem of Diogenes from a source-critical point of view. He worked from four basic sources: (1) the work of Diogenes Laertius;[38] (2) the apocryphal letters of Diogenes;[39] (3) the writings of Dio Chrysostom;[40] and (4) other writers—Epictetus, Maximus of Tyre, and Caesar Julian.[41] Von Fritz thought Laertius's work was so badly organized that someone else must have found the loose pages of a manuscript and put it

---

[35]Such as D. R. Dudley, *A History of Cynicism* (London, 1937) and F. Sayre, *The Greek Cynics* (Baltimore, 1948).

[36]Gregory of Nazianzen, *MPG* 37, 698.250-258. This also is not a chreia.

[37]K. von Fritz, *Quellen-untersuchungen zu Leben und Philosophie des Diogenes von Sinope* (Leipzig, 1926), *Philologus,* Supplementband 18, heft 2.

[38]Ibid., pp. 1-63.

[39]Ibid., pp. 63-71.

[40]Ibid., pp. 71-90.

[41]Ibid., pp. 90-97.

together without trying to discover its original plan of organization.[42] None-theless, Laertius is the best source for Diogenes studies. There were three basic sources Von Fritz conjectured for this material: (1) paragraphs 20-24 and 70-73 are from one source; (2) paragraphs 25-69 consist of anecdotes from many sources; and (3) paragraphs 74-81 were composed by Laertius himself.[43] Of these, the most important part is the central section. Here, Von Fritz found a few chreias with textual problems for which he offered corrections. He suspected some scribal miscopying. He thought the "Sale of Diogenes" was a heroic legend composed by Menippus. He did not ap-praise the chreias as literary units, but it is clear that these are the literary forms he doubted least.

Von Fritz thought there was little value to discourses of Dio Chrysos-tom. Some of these discourses show acquaintance with chreias reported by Laertius, but they are no longer in chreia form. Von Fritz is probably correct in holding that these orations were partially used by Dio to get ancient au-thority for his own political positions which he did not dare to express pub-licly. If this is so, Dio would not have been the first or last to exploit history in this way. Neither would he have been the first or last to expand chreias into complete orations. Von Fritz also doubted some of the legends Laertius reported about the death of Diogenes. They cannot all have been correct. It seems probable that Diogenes died wrapped in his cloak, and someone found him that way. No one knew the cause of his death, and there was no coroner to diagnose the case, so different guesses arose. These postmortem judgments, of course, were not written down in chreia form, attributed to Diogenes. Von Fritz found two lists of works attributed to Diogenes that were not identical. Therefore he suspected that both were forgeries.[44] Right or wrong, the works are no longer extant, so it makes little difference.

Von Fritz observed that there were many anecdotes attributed to Di-ogenes but few to Antisthenes.[45] This made him suspect that later philos-ophers took some of Antisthenes' anecdotes and attributed them to Diogenes. Because chreias were often listed without names when they all

---

[42]Ibid., p. 4.

[43]Ibid., pp. 12-13.

[44]Ibid., pp. 55-59.

[45]Ibid., p. 83.

belonged to one person, it is possible to have confused a few that began, "He used to say . . .," but that would not account for a general transfer, intentionally made, as Von Fritz thought. Perhaps Antisthenes did not teach exactly the way Diogenes did. Because of his shorthand method of instructing students to preserve notes and memorize teachings, Diogenes enabled his students to preserve large numbers of his teachings in a way Antisthenes may not have done. Von Fritz also presumed that some of the sayings attributed both to Diogenes and Bion were originally said by Bion and not Diogenes.[46] Dudley, however, held that Bion used sayings he had already found in earlier sources, some of which came from Diogenes, rather than the other way around.[47]

Dudley and Sayre. Two later scholars, who were dependent both on Gerhard and Von Fritz were D. R. Dudley and F. Sayre.[48] When Sayre wrote about Diogenes, he took each opportunity to interpret sayings attributed to Diogenes in such a way as to give them a negative meaning. Sayre did not like Cynics. Dudley, on the other hand, was inclined to interpret these same sayings positively, but both scholars based their interpretations of Diogenes on chreias attributed to him. Both agreed with Von Fritz that there were many legends created around Diogenes, and, partly because of this, they presumed that the collection of chreias now extant is really an accumulation that has snowballed, mostly having been added by later philosophers.[49] Dudley and Sayre agreed with Von Fritz that the story of the Sale of Diogenes was fictitious.[50] Sayre also believed the stories about Diogenes' death and tombstone were legendary.[51] He thought that the hero named Diogenes in Menippus's fiction was not originally intended to be Diogenes of Sinope at all.[52] Sayre and Dudley both called the works of Menippus "romances."[53] Sayre even quoted Dio Chrysostom to prove that some stories at-

---

[46]Ibid., p. 42.

[47]Dudley, *History*, p. 68.

[48]See note 35.

[49]Dudley, *History*, p. 19.

[50]Dudley, *History*,, p. 18, and Sayre, *Cynics*, pp. 72-75.

[51]Sayre, Ibid., pp. 4-5.

[52]Ibib., p. 69.

[53]Dudley, *History*, p. 24, and Sayre, *Cynics*, p 69.

tributed to Diogenes were legendary.[54] Sayre believed Diogenes must have confronted Alexander-the Great sometime, perhaps in about the manner described in the chreia, but he assumed Cynics added more legends about Diogenes in relationship to kings.[55] There also developed legends about the origin of the name "dog" and legends about Diogenes' death.[56]

Dudley followed Von Fritz[57] in considering Diogenes Laertius the best source for historical data about Diogenes. It was on the basis of the chreias that Dudley reconstructed his picture of Diogenes, even though he did not acknowledge that fact. Dudley also noticed some similarities between the teaching methods Laertius ascribed to Diogenes and the educational methods that were generally approved by many of Diogenes' contemporaries in the educational profession. Therefore, Dudley held, Laertius "fastened on Diogenes" the methods used in Diogenes' day.[58] This is an application of the faulty criterion of dissimilarity that has also been misapplied in NT study. Apparently Dudley supposed that Diogenes would have been unique; he would not have taught like his contemporaries! But why not? Most teachers learn from earlier teachers. If some of Diogenes' chreias are the same as those also attributed to Antisthenes, on the one hand, and Bion on the other, what is surprising about that? Most people are surprised to find a Bultmannian student with an anti-Bultmannian view or a Barthian who is critical of Karl Barth. This logic should also apply to historical study. Similarities among teachings of students and teachers do not prove falsification, as Von Fritz, Dudley, and Sayre all suppose.

Sayre did not know the difference between a chreia and any other apophthegm,[59] but he believed these sayings attributed to Diogenes came from many sources. "But," he said, "it is probable that many others were fresh inventions."[60] The only evidence he gave for this conclusion was his belief that many sayings were "non-Cynic and even anti-Cynic." This same

---

[54]Sayre, *Cynics*, p. 72.

[55]Ibid., pp. 71-73.

[56]Ibid., pp. 74-75.

[57]Dudley, *History*, pp. 18, 54.

[58]Ibid., p. 88.

[59]Sayre, *Cynics*, p. 76.

[60]Ibid., p. 78.

logic, if applied to Martin Luther, would discount all of Luther's writings that contradict some dogma held by later Lutheran churches. Neither Luther nor Diogenes was limited in his days to the views of any group that was later organized in his name.

The work of these classical critics is not infallible. Rather than accept their judgments uncritically, NT scholars should reexamine the problem. The chreias preserved by Laertius, Mullach, and others are available for study. These should be compared to the way other ancients preserved chreias, and legends about Diogenes should be compared with the way other legends were formed. The same form-critical method should be applied to the letters attributed to Diogenes before final conclusions are reached. Some of that work is done in this chapter.

Diogenes was a Cynic philosopher and a teacher of ethics who considered all aspects of life a necessary part of philosophy and teaching; therefore, chreias attributed to him reflect many areas of his experiences. These chreias can be categorized under such headings as: education, ethics, philosophy, values, health, wealth and poverty, insults, religion and superstition, human nature, and personal references. Many of the chreias could easily be placed under more than one category. For example, many of Diogenes' comments dealing with education or ethics are also insults. Some of his comments on health and values are also philosophical. There is no obvious reason why anyone thought some of them were brilliant enough to save. For instance, there does not seem to be anything extraordinary about telling a runaway slave, sitting on a well curb, to be careful not to fall in— that seems to be good advice for anyone sitting on a well curb. Why would anyone falsely create such a report and attribute it to anyone?

Gerhard seemed to think that some of the chreias attributed to Diogenes were in direct contradiction, but that is not obvious enough to conjecture their creation or preservation by two different schools with different points of view, as Gerhard has supposed.[61] To be able to discern which chreias are legitimate and which ones have been created by others, the historian would have to understand the comprehensive viewpoints of Diogenes and of other philosophers or students, and such material does not exist. Even the skeptical scholars base their outlines of the life of Diogenes on the chreias collected about him and the history written by Diogenes Laertius.

---

[61]Gerhard, "Zur legende," pp. 388-408, esp. pp. 390 and 406.

These chreias of Diogenes seem to be the kind that would be collected by pupils who were trained to take notes of lectures and prepare them for easy memorization, as Diogenes trained them to do. At one time, some of his students may have been members of his own household where he had been assigned the responsibility of instructing them in all necessary education for personal living and functioning in society. There seems to have been no secret about the fact that Diogenes was once a civil officer who was involved in some illegal activity and had to flee from his community. Scholars question the report that he became a slave in a wealthy man's household. Even if this has been grossly exaggerated, Diogenes may have been a teacher of this rich man's children, without being slave. From the time of his flight to the time of his begging and teaching, a great transformation took place in his life. No one knows how many years were involved in this change. He lived to be an old man and these chreias reflect various times in his life after his teaching began.

The early collections of chreias formed by and about philosophers support the likelihood that these units were composed early. The fact that some chreias seem very much like units attributed to other philosophers or that two chreias seem very similar should not be surprising. Students learned from their teachers and they sometimes continued to teach the things they learned. Therefore different students may correctly have heard the same teachings, one from Antisthenes, for example, and another from Diogenes, Crates, or Bion. The fact that Diogenes Laertius clearly cited more than one collection of chreias about the same person allows the possibility of duplicate reporting. All of this supports the belief that these chreias were formed at a stage much earlier than the time of Theon, Hermogenes, and other rhetoricians who defined them carefully for training in rhetoric. The next step will be to examine the care with which rhetoricians themselves preserved chreias once they were in their possession.

If rhetoricians had really created chreias fictitiously, without any concern for historical truth, then it is strange that they copied them at all. Why not just compose new ones for each generation or for each teacher? There are ways to test whether rhetoricians were primarily copyists or creative fiction writers. We have collections as early as Theon and Hermogenes, who were no later than the second century A.D. and the commentator, Doxapatres, who flourished in the eleventh century, A.D. Doxapatres, who had access to the works of Hermogenes, Nicolaus, and Aphthonius, has also reported the following eighteen chreias that are the same as those reported by

Theon. These are placed, side by side, so that they may be compared. As much as is possible in English, their grammatical differences and content differences in Greek are shown, although these are much more evident in Greek.

From Theon to Doxapatres

THEON	DOXAPATRES
When Olympias found out that her son, Alexander, declared himself [the son] of Zeus, she said, "Will this one not stop accusing me to Hera?" (99.23-26).[62]	When Olympias, the mother of Alexander, heard that her son said he was [the son] of Zeus, she said, "Will the young man not stop slandering me to Hera?" (247.20-23).[63]
When Pythagoras, the philosopher, had been asked how long the life of man was, he went up on the roof and peeked over briefly (99.6-8).	When Pythagoras had been asked how long the life of man would be, he appeared briefly and then hid (251.28-29).
A certain Lacedemonian, when someone asked him where the Lacedemonians held the boundaries of the land, pointed to his spear (99.9-10).	When the Lacedemonian had been asked where the boundaries of Sparta were, after he extended his spear and pointed, he said, "There" (251.30-252.1).
When Alexander, the king of Macedon, stood over Diogenes, while he was sleeping, he said, "It is not good for a counsellor to sleep all night long" (Il. 2.24), and Diogenes answered, "To whom the people turn and who has so many cares!" (Il. 2.25) (98.23-27).	When Alexander stood over Diogenes, sleeping, he said, "It is not good for a counsellor to sleep all night long" (254.5-6).[64]
Plato, the philosopher, said branches of virtue grew with sweat and labor (100.12-13).	Plato used to say the branches of virtue grew with sweat and labor (254.12-13).
Isocrates, the rhetor, used to say his well-developed disciples were children of the gods (101.14-16).	Isocrates said his well-developed disciples were children of gods (256.11-12).

---

[62]All of the references to Theon's column are page and line numbers in Spengel 2.

[63]All of the references to Doxapatres' column are page and line numbers to Walz 2.

[64]Doxapatres (254.1-10) said this might not qualify as a chreia. He may have meant that it was not the complete double chreia that was familiar. Nevertheless, without the second quotation, it would qualify as a chreia.

When Diogenes, the Cynic philosopher, saw a wealthy, uninstructed youth, he said "This one is silver-plated filth" (ὕπος) (97.20-21).

When Diogenes saw a wealthy, uninstructed person, he said, "This man is silver-plated horse" (ἵππος) (256.16-17).[65]

When Pitticus, the Mitylenian, was asked if anyone did something wrong would the gods overlook it, he said, "No, not even thinking [wrong]" (97.30-32).

When Pitticus, the Mitylenian, was asked if anyone did something evil would the gods overlook it, he said, "Not even thinking [evil]" (256.25-27).

When Socrates had been asked if the king of Persia seemed happy to him, he said, "I cannot say, for I do not even know how he stands on education" (98.9-12).

When Socrates had been asked if the king of Persia seemed happy to him, he said he did not know, for he did even know how he stood on education (257.4-6).

Once when Diogenes was eating breakfast in the marketplace, and he had invited Plato to the breakfast, [Plato] said, "How pleasant would be your unpretentiousness, Diogenes, if it were not so pretentious!" (98.14-17).

Once when Diogenes was eating breakfast and he had invited Plato to be present at the breakfast, Plato said, "How pleasant your unpretentiousness would be, Diogenes, if it were not so pretentious!" (257.10-13).

When Diogenes, the Cynic philosopher, saw a child, living on junk food, he struck the teacher with his staff (98.32-99.2).

When Diogenes saw a cannibalistic child, he struck the teacher (257.18-19).

Bion, the sophist, used to say the love of money is the mother city of all evil (99.18-19).

Bias [said] the love of money is the mother city of all evil (257.29-30).[66]

Isocrates, the rhetor, counselled his acquaintances to honor their teachers before their parents, because, "Those have become causes of life only, but the teachers have become the causes of living nobly" (99.20-23).

Isocrates counselled his acquaintances to show greater honor to their teachers than to their parents, holding, "Those are the causes of life, but these are the causes of living well" (258.2-5).

When Alexander, the king of Macedon, was counselled by his friends to build up resources, he said, "But these things did not benefit even Croesus" (100.4-6).

When Alexander was counselled by his friends to build up resources, he said, "They did not benefit even Croesus" (258.11-13).

---

[65]This seems to be a scribal error. Compare the Greek with the parallel chreia of Theon.

[66]Some scribe has confused Bion and Bias, who were different philosophers.

When Diogenes, the Cynic philosopher, saw a youth, the son of an adulterer, throwing stones into the marketplace, he said, "Stop, child, lest you hit your father without knowing it" (100.30-101.1)!

When Diogenes saw a youth who was the son of an adulterer, throwing a stone into the crowd, he said, "Will you not stop, boy, lest you hit your father without knowing it" (258.18-20)?

When Alexander, the king of the Macedonians, had been asked by someone where he kept his treasures, he said, "In these," pointing to his friends (100.9-11).

When Alexander had been asked where he kept his treasures, he pointed to his friends (259.10-12).

When Theano, the Pythagorean feminine philosopher, was asked by someone how long after [intercourse with] a man a woman is undefiled to attend the Thesmophorian [celebrations], she said, "From her own husband, immediately; from someone else's, never (98.3-7).

When Theano, the Pythagorean feminine philosopher, was asked how long after [intercourse] with a man is a woman undefiled to attend the Thesmophorean [celebrations], she said, "From her own husband, immediately; from someone else's, never (256.28-257.1).

Damon, the gymnasium instructor, having both feet crippled, when his sandals were stolen, he said, "May they fit the thief" (100.7-9).

Damon. For this one was crippled, and after he had lost his sandals, he said, "May they fit the feet of the thief" (258.14-16).

Evaluation

The variations between these two editions of the same chreias are not important enough to make any historical, factual difference. The variants are consistent. Doxapatres' chreias are almost always shorter than Theon's.[67] Some are not direct quotations as Theon's are. The qualifying identifications of the character of the chreia, which were usually given in Theon's chreias, were regularly omitted in Doxapatres' chreias. Nonetheless, the message of the units was clear in either collection. There would be greater variance among most newspaper accounts of the same event given in the twentieth century. Nevertheless, historians would consider newspaper reports that differ a great deal in length and style to be valid historical data.

There were hundreds of chreias circulating in published collections at the time these rhetoricians were preparing their teaching materials, but the

---

[67]This is contrary to the relationship of editors to their texts upheld by the Markan priorists who say the editor always expands and improves the text. This is apparently not an infallible rule. See further GWB, "Has the Griesbach Hypothesis Been Falsified?" *JBL* 93 (1974):550-72.

rhetoricians did not use hundreds of them. They limited themselves to a few select ones which they shared and used in their training programs. Had they been very creative and had a tendency to compose messages to attribute to these ancient philosophers, the reader would expect there to be many different chreias attributed by different rhetoricians to the same historical character. These, then, would be incoherent among themselves, because different rhetoricians would have different imaginations and rhetorical needs. But this is not the way it happened.

Instead of being authors of historical fiction, these rhetoricians seem, instead, to have been careful scribes who copied one another's work with a great deal of exactness, showing very slight differences in their definitions of what constitutes a literary unit, such as a chreia, or in their editions of chreias. If there was a great deal of forgery and fictitious composition, it would have been done in the Greek classical period before the time of Theon and the gospel writers. This is enough positive evidence on the chreia as a Greek literary form to provide confidence in its use as a literary form in NT *times*. It is not enough, however, to qualify it for use in NT *study*. The NT did not originate from classical Greek communities. It came into existence in relationship to communities that were basically Jewish in a Greek-speaking Roman world. Therefore, the literature has certain Jewish peculiarities that have to be taken into consideration by anyone who wishes to understand its meaning. The next step in this study, then, will be to examine a few literary units taken from rabbinic and NT literature in comparison with the chreias found in classical Greek literature.

Chreias and Jewish Literature

Assertive Chreias. There are numerous assertive chreias in *The Sayings of the Fathers* alone. Only a few of them will be given here:

> Jose ben Johanan of Jerusalem said, "Let your house be opened wide; let poor people be your household; and do not speak much with your wife" (1:5).
>
> Shammai said, "Make your Torah a fixed duty; say little and do much; and greet everyone with a cheerful look on your face" (1:15).
>
> Rabbi Tarfon said, "The day is short; the work is extensive; the laborers are slow; the wages are high; and the master of the house is urgent" (2:19).
>
> Rabbi Hanina ben Dosa said, "Everyone whose fear of sin precedes his wisdom, his wisdom endures; and everyone whose wisdom precedes his fear of sin, his wisdom does not endure" (3:12).

Rabbi Judah said, "Be careful in teaching, because every error in teaching amounts to sin" (4:16).

Rabbi Jannai said, "It is not in our hands [to justify] either the prosperity of the wicked or the punishment of the righteous" (4:19).

Responsive Chreias. There are not many responsive chreias in rabbinic literature, but three of the following are attributed to Rabban Gamaliel, and a fourth, to Rabbi Nehoniah:

It once happened (מעשה) that Rabban Gamaliel recited (שקרא) [the Shema'] on the first night of his marriage. His disciples said to him, "Did you not teach us, Rabbi, that a bridegroom is exempt from reciting the Shema' on the first night?" He said to them, "I will not listen to you to reject from me the Kingdom of Heaven, even for one hour" (Ber 2:5).

[Rabban Gamaliel] bathed the first night after his wife died. His disciples said to him, "Did you not teach us, Rabbi, that a mourner is prohibited from bathing?" He said to them, "I am not like all other men; I am weak" (Ber 2:6).

When [Rabban Gamaliel's] slave, Tabi, died (כשמת), he accepted condolences for him. His disciples said to him, "Did you not tell us, Rabbi, that we do not accept condolences for slaves?" He said to them, "My slave, Tabi, was not like all other slaves. He was *kasher*" (Ber 2:7).

Rabbi Nehoniah ben ha-Kanah used to pray, (היה מתפלל) when he entered the house of study and when he went out, a short prayer. They said to him, "What a place is this for prayer?" He said to them, "When entering, I pray that I will not get off the track [in the halakah]; upon departure, I give thanks for my lot" (Ber 4:2).

These seem to meet the four standard qualifications for a responsive chreia: (1) the situation is given in which someone prompts the speaker to speak; (2) the character is identified; (3) the response of the character is given; and (4) the entire unit is succinct. There is also no obvious incoherence among the three chreias attributed to one rabbi, as they seem to fit the same personality.

These literary forms differ somewhat from classical Greek chreias. First of all, they are not as succinct, and secondly, they do not follow the typical Greek style of beginning with an aorist participle or a genitive absolute construction. Most of them begin with a clause, employing a finite verb. One exception is the fourth illustration which begins with a periphrastic participle, "was praying." It is not possible, however, to transfer the peculiarities of good Greek style into Semitic, or even Latin, style and maintain all the details of grammar. For example, the following is a classical Greek chreia: "Diogenes, the Cynic philosopher, *having seen* (ειδοντες) a boy misbehaving, struck the teacher with his rod."[68] A Latin translation of this, rendered into English, is as follows: "Diogenes, *when he saw* (*cum vidisset*) a boy acting indecently, he struck the teacher with a stick"[69] The aorist participle, "having seen," which is a part of a genitive absolute in Greek, was rendered by an adverb and a finite verb in Latin "when he saw." Latin has no perfect (Latin equivalent for aorist in Greek) participle or genitive absolute, so even when a very rigorous and literalistic translation of the Greek chreia is made into Latin, it has to change with translation. This is even more the case when Greek is translated into a Semitic language. This can be shown by comparing the Greek NT with the Syriac NT. Sometimes the Syriac NT will reflect good Greek style, as in Matt 13:10-11:

GREEK	SYRIAC
The disciples *having come to* him, said, "Why in parables do you speak to them? *Having answered*, he *said*, "To you it is given to know the mysteries of the Kingdom of Heaven, but to those it is not given."	*Came to* his disciples and saying to him, "Why in parables are you speaking with them?" He, then, *answered* and *said*[70] to them, "To you it is given to know the mysteries of the Kingdom of Heaven, but to those it is not given."

Even the Greek reflects the Semitic, "it is given," to mean "God has given," but otherwise the Greek has aorist participles where the Syriac has finite verbs. In the following example, the periphrastic imperfect in the Greek is almost a wooden rendering of some Semitic language, like the Syriac. Other expressions are typically Semitic and woodenly rendered in the Greek. This is confirmed by the Syriac.

GREEK	SYRIAC
except for *a word of indecency* (Matt 5:1).	except for *a word of indecency*

---

[68]Theon, "Progymnasmata," Spengel 2.v, p. 102.16-18.

[69]Priscian, "De Usus," H. Keil, *Grammatici Latini* 3 (Hildesheim, 1961), pp. 431.35-432.1.

[70]Rabbis said wherever it is mentioned that someone "answered and said" that person spoke in the holy language [Hebrew] and through the Holy Spirit (EcclesR 7:2.4).

The Pharisees *were fasting* (Mk 2:18). *and he went to the other side* of the sea (Mk 5:1).

The Pharisees *were fasting and he went to the other side* of the sea

and he went out from there, *and he comes* (Matt 13:54 has *having come*; Mk 6:1).

and he went and he comes

This means that chreias in the NT cannot be restricted to the narrow limitations of typical, classical Greek chreias. Part of them may be translations from some Semitic language; others may have originated among Jews who spoke a "Yiddish" type of Greek; still others may occur in classical Greek form. It is not the style but the definition that determines whether a literary unit in the Greek NT is a chreia or not. Once this allowance is made for local talent, it is possible to find many chreias, not only in the NT, but in the writings of the church fathers. The NT chreias will be examined under topical categories in some of the next chapters, but here we will show the way one chreia was utilized over a period of several centuries. The character of this chreia was a certain John, called the elder, apostle, disciple, evangelist, or saint.

John and Cerinthus. "Once the apostle John entered a bath house in order to wash himself, but when he learned that Cerinthus was inside, he left the place, fled through the door, and would not remain under the same roof with him, but urged each one with him, saying, 'Let us flee, lest the bath house collapse, since Cerinthus, the enemy of the truth, is inside!' " (Eusebius, *DE* 3.39,6, on the authority of Polycarp, d. A.D. 156).

This is an assertive chreia prompted by a situation: (1) The situation that prompted the character to speak is given; (2)the character is identified; (3) the message of the character is quoted; and (4) the entire message is brief. When Eusebius repeated the same chreia, he made some modifications, still leaving it in the following chreia form:

"John, the disciple of the Lord, when he went to wash himself in Ephesus, after he saw Cerinthus inside, ran out of the bath house without washing, but called out, 'Let us flee, lest even the bath house collapse, since Cerinthus, the enemy of truth, is inside!' " (*DE* 4.6, ca. A.D. 320).

Eusebius improved the chreia style by abbreviating the context but keeping the message itself reliable. The next version was composed more than a hundred years later (ca. A.D. 447).

"This one, as they say, saw the divine John, the evangelist, washing himself, for it happened because of ill health that he used the bath house.

'Let us flee,' he said, 'from here, lest because of Cerinthus, the bath house fall in and we share [the destruction]' '' (Theodoret of Cyr, *Eccl. Hist.* 2.3).

Theodoret both abbreviated the chreia and varied it, even the quotation, but he retained the sense of the event in his periphrastic way. The exact chreia was preserved still better by Timothy, presbyter of Constantinople, who wrote nearly three centuries after Eusebius (A.D. 600) and was probably dependent upon him.

"They said that also Saint Polycarp said that when washing himself in a bath house, the evangelist John, having learned that also Cerinthus was washing himself, left the place and fled, warning those with him, 'Let us flee, lest the bath house collapse, since Cerinthus, the enemy of truth, is inside' '' (*de recept. haer.* 28 c-29A).

Paulus, in the eleventh century, still preserved the same chreia, making the kind of changes, stylistically, that would not destroy its message.

"When it was necessary, the apostle John used a bath house, but when he found out as he was about to enter that Cerinthus was inside, he jumped up and left through the door as quickly as possible, not considering it right to be with him under the same roof. He explained also to those with him, saying, 'Let us flee, lest the bath house collapse on us, since Cerinthus, the enemy of truth, is inside' '' (*de haer. libell.* 4).

At the same time this chreia was circulating and being copied, while retaining its chreia form over a period of more than nine hundred years, it was also expanded into a homily, preserved by Epiphanius (ca. A.D. 376).

"(24.1) Again the *same John,* while preaching in Asia, tells of an amazing event, composed as a lesson of truth. For, although he observed a very admirable way of life in conformity with apostolic trustworthiness— he never even bathed completely—[but on the occasion], he was required by the Holy Spirit to *proceed to the bath house,* saying, 'Take for me the [way] to the bath house,' (2) and while those with him were surprised, he went to the bathing place itself, and, as he came to the man who customarily holds the garments of those who are washing themselves, he asked who was inside the bath house. (3) Now the guardian, who regularly looks after the clothing (for in gymnasiums this is a job by which some earn their living), said to Saint John that *Ebion was inside.* (4) Then *John immediately* understood the direction of the Holy Spirit and why he had been summoned to go to the bath house, so, I said, as a memorial, so he could leave for us the hypothesis of truth, because there are some servants of Christ and apostles and some of the same truth, but there are [also] certain vessels of evil and gates of Hades which must not overpower the Rock and holy church of God, constructed upon it. (5) *At once he became troubled and* wailed quietly, so that everyone could hear as a testimony, he presented a spotless teaching: *'Hurry, brothers,' he said, 'let us leave here, lest the bath house collapse and bury us with Ebion, who is inside the bath house, because of his impiety.'* (6) Let us not be surprised at hearing that Ebion had encountered John, for the blessed John lived a long life, continuing up to the rule of Trajan, (7) but it is clear to everyone that all the apostles considered the faith of Ebion to be alien to their own preaching'' (*anacephalaiosis* 30.24,1-7).

Epiphanius apparently confused Cerinthus with the head of the Ebionite sect, whom he believed to be Ebion. This confusion was understandable as Cerinthus and the Ebionites were both Jewish Christians. Epiphanius communicated the basic message of the chreia with much expansion in terms of explanation, clarification, and added comment on related subjects. The final result is no longer a chreia because the narrative is not brief—a primary requirement for a chreia.

Rhetoricians expected chreias to lose their form when they were developed into homilies, but that did not prevent their continued independent existence as chreias. Hermogenes gave directions for developing homilies from chreias. Using a chreia associated with Isocrates, which includes the quotation about instruction, ''The root is bitter, but the fruit is sweet,'' Hermogenes gave the steps necessary for development of the chreia into ''something else,'' namely a homily: (1) First, the homiletician should praise the speaker briefly. In his case, this was Isocrates. (2) The thesis of the chreia should be presented. This did not mean just to quote the saying but to expand and clarify it. (3) The third step should praise the speaker who said this further, telling what a wise man he was, etc. (4) He should then develop the cause the chreia exemplifies, in this case, mentioning that the greatest deeds love to be accomplished by labor. Of course, the accomplishment brings with it necessary pain. (5) The interpreter should next attack the subject from the opposite direction. He should note that incidental deeds do not require much labor and the end has no great pleasure. The opposite, however, is true of great deeds. (6) After that, the interpreter should illustrate the chreia from an analogy or parable. Here he might tell about farmers who have to labor on the land before they can harvest the fruits. (7) It is also good to give an illustration. For instance, after Demosthenes had worked hard at many things, he later received many crowns and public proclamations. The speaker might also apply to this the case of Hesiod, who said, "The gods have set sweat in front of virtue," and another poet said, "The gods sell us everything good for labor." (8) Finally, the interpreter should set forth an exhortation that it is to the benefit of the hearer to be convinced by the arguments of the speaker.[71]

Anyone studying this list could think of ways of reducing the number: The encomium of point one could be combined with the praise of point three to make one point. The thesis of the chreia could be presented and developed in one step, rather than two as Hermogenes suggested (two and four). All of the illustrations could be put under one classification instead of two (six and seven). Nevertheless, these are basic points to be considered in developing any text, and Epiphanius evidently used some of them in his interpretation of the chreia: (1) He praised John, telling of his admirable way of life, leading by the Holy Spirit, and called his saying "a spotless teaching." He did this in two places, the way Hermogenes recommended. (2) He used the chreia. (3) He developed the cause the chreia exemplified, expanding on John's asceticism and Ebion's wickedness. (4) Finally, he concluded that John was in agreement with all the apostles in his resistance to Ebion, implying that hearers should also resist Ebion.

Some of the same methods of development of texts can be illustrated from similar commentaries on chreias within the gospels themselves, but the main purpose of this study has been to show that Christians, like Greek rhetoricians and historians, used and preserved chreias over a long period of time. Approximately the same length of time that elapsed between Theon and Doxapatres elapsed between Polycarp and Paulus. Just as Doxapatres faithfully preserved the chreias also found in the works of Theon, so also Paulus preserved faithfully the chreias found in the works of Polycarp. Various interpreters along the way also used and modified the chreias, but messages were preserved. Even though one person might develop the chreia into a homily, the chreia continued to be preserved in its own form for later generations. This does not imply that any of the versions of the chreia about John preserve his identical words, but they give a true teaching about the kind of person John was and how he felt about the Jewish Christians. The same is true of chreias quoted by Doxapatres. The scribes—whether Greek rhetoricians, Jewish rabbis, or Christian leaders—seemed to have been very

---

[71]Hermogenes, "Progymnasmata," Spengel 2.iii, pp. 6.19-7.10.

conscientious in their respect for basic messages of speakers. This is also reflected in the gospels.

When the narratives common to Matthew, Mark, and Luke are compared, there is a great deal of similarity of order, but wide variation of exact wording. In the teaching material common to Matthew and Luke, however, there is a great deal of variance in order, each gospel writer putting the teachings wherever he wanted in his work, but there is close agreement in actual wording, since the gospel writers were not careless with the quotations entrusted to them.

Conclusions

This chapter began with an introduction to the Greek rhetoricians of the first to the eleventh centuries A.D. and the literary form, chreia, which they defined. Although they defined chreia very carefully and in great detail, it was not clear at the outset exactly what these definitions meant or how or when they originated. Since they used terms like "character," they might also have considered their characters just as playwrights do, as roles to be developed. They might have attributed to ancient leaders messages they, themselves, composed from their own needs and imaginations. In order to answer these questions, it was necessary to examine the relationship between historians and rhetoricians and to evaluate their methods of instruction and use of materials.

The philosophers involved were also studied—their methods of teaching, the books they wrote, their relationship to their students, and their expectations from their students. Because the philosophers—men like Socrates, Aristotle, Plato, Diogenes, Crates, and others—were related to one another, some as contemporaries and others as teachers or students, there was a continuation of teachings, with some philosophers publishing books of chreias that they had collected in relationship to earlier philosophers. Students were trained in copying the works of teachers in such a way that they could memorize them readily—taking shortcuts in memorization. These philosophical gems that were memorized probably provided the situation that made chreias necessary as a literary form. In the days of the philosophers chreias were used to preserve teachings that philosophers wanted students to learn. There are good reasons to think Greek philosophers preserved chreias rather than distorted them, but early Greek philosophers were more creative than later rhetoricians. If chreias were forged or misrepresented, it was more likely to have been done in pre-New Testament times than later.

By the time of the later rhetoricians, like Theon, Hermogenes, and Nicolaus, a few of the same chreias were selected for repeated use as vehicles for training students in speech and debate. Not only did this study show that there were needs, methods of education, ways of preservation, and collections of chreias, but the examples cited in the case of those chreias which are attributed to Diogenes seemed strikingly coherent. It would take a great deal of credulity to believe that rhetoricians who lived five hundred to one thousand years later would have composed all of these and attributed them fictitiously to earlier philosophers without disclosing any of their own points of view or historical situations. Since there are so many hundreds of chreias, it would take a farfetched imagination to suppose that these were all composed by later noncreative rhetoricians, and then, these same rhetoricians would employ only a few of their own compositions. To make the skepticism still greater, it would be necessary to notice that the few chreias used by rhetoricians were used by nearly all of them, one borrowing chreias from the other just as they had borrowed definitions from one another. This was shown by comparing the chreias recorded by Doxapatres with those of Theon, about nine hundred years earlier. The same proved true when a chreia from the Christian tradition was compared over a period of nine hundred years.

Some readers may think the discourse and amount of illustration in this chapter is excessive. When the author becomes selective in his or her illustrations, however, there is always the conscious or unconscious temptation to slant the selection to support the case presented. An attempt was made here to let the reader see enough data to pass his or her own judgment. Any way the evidence is organized, it points to care in composition and preservation of such historical materials as these—not in the composition of historical fiction.

An examination of the grammatical details of the Greek chreia as compared with later Jewish and Christian chreias revealed that the grammatical style of the chreia was not a necessary part of the definition—that which is typically good Greek style is not necessarily good or even possible style in Latin, Hebrew, Aramaic, or Syriac. In the NT, where there is a mixture of Semitic and Greek influences, chreias can be found which fit either the classical pattern of the aorist participle and/or the genitive absolute—one sentence construction—whereas others employ finite verbs with adverbs or else use present participles or periphrastic imperfect verbs. The main points of identification are those disclosed by the definitions of the rhetoricians: (1)brevity; (2) identification of the character; (3) the message attributed to the character; and (4) in the case of the responsive chreias and some assertive chreias the situation or person that prompted the character to speak is given.

This chapter has not attempted to show that there were no editorial modifications made in the preservation of chreias. Neither has it indicated that all chreias contain the exact words of the character. Acknowledging a normal amount of intentional or accidental distortion, an amazing amount of tradition is evident behind the custom of preserving sayings faithfully, especially in NT times and later. There does not appear to be any literary form so well designed both to record and to preserve quotations in context as a chreia. This shorthand method of preservation does not demand exact wording as poetry does, but it requires the basic idea to be recorded. It would take a great deal of evidence to prove the contrary—to demonstrate that the chreia was designed and used primarily for creating fiction. This would require more than being able to imagine a situation in which a rhetorician or his student might invent quotations and attribute them to ancient philosophers in chreia form. Skeptics will have to show that chreias have *actually* been invented by later students in a considerable number of instances. It would not be enough proof to show a few different names associated with the same chreia or a variation of textual readings. The examination made here indicates that tradition favors integrity rather than fiction in preparing and preserving chreias.

Technicalities related to chreias will be considered in the examples given in the next several chapters which include the units in the gospels that are believed to be chreias. These will also be tested for reliability in other ways in relationship to teachings of Jesus in the parables. The next chapter will examine those chreias and parables that picture Jesus on the campaign trail, recruiting disciples.

CHAPTER THREE

Campaigning
Under Pressure

Literary Forms Applied

Methods of Testing. The two best-known form critics of the twentieth century were Martin Dibelius and Rudolf Bultmann, although both worked with inadequate forms. Bultmann considered the basic form for gospel research to be the *apophthegm.*[1] There are thousands of *apophthegmata* preserved in Greek literature and in the records of the early church.[2] These forms, however, are very general, ranging in size from one sentence to one large paragraph. There are no special stylistic requirements, so a narrative, a dialogue, or a chreia may also be an apophthegm, so long as it includes one or more sayings of some person. Dibelius was correct in saying that it

---

[1]Bultmann, *History,* pp. 11-69, and "Study," pp. 39-46.

[2]For these see F. C. Babbitt, (tr. and ed.), *Plutarch's Moralia* 3 (Cambridge, 1968); Migne, *Patr. Gr.* 65.71-440; Migne, *Patr. Lat.* 73.855-1022; 74.381-394. For a description of these and a careful analysis of all these texts, see W. Bousset, *Apophthegmata Studien zur Geschichte des ältesten Mönchtums* (Tübingen, 1923).

was not very definitive.[3] Dibelius, however, did no better. Instead of relying on some literary form used in antiquity, he conjectured a distinctive form, which he called a "paradigm," the invention of which he attributed to these unliterary disciples. Since he also believed Mark was the earliest gospel he found the data for this conjecture only in that gospel, in which he identified the following units as *paradigmata*.[4]

The Healing of the Paralytic .... Mark ii.1ff.
The Question of Fasting .... Mark ii.18f.
The Rubbing of the Ears of Corn .... Mark ii.23ff.
The Healing of the Withered Hand .... Mark iii.1ff.
The Relatives of Jesus .... Mark iii.20f.
Blessing the Children .... Mark x.13ff.
The Tribute Money .... Mark xii.13ff.
The Anointing in Bethany .... Mark xiv.3ff.

In these paradigms, the teaching of Jesus is the center of interest.[5] They are brief in scope and provide Jesus the opportunity to make some pronouncement.[6] The context is given in a very brief space. With only eight units upon which to base our knowledge of the historical Jesus, it is not surprising that many scholars did not get very enthusiastic about the possibilities based on this kind of form criticism. This is further weakened by the fact that no ancient literary artist defined these literary forms. They were entirely conjectured in the twentieth century. Dibelius also knew of the chreia which rhetoricians had carefully defined, but Dibelius held that the chreia allowed for many extensions without losing its form, so he confused the chreias with the reminiscences of Xenophon. The result of this logic was to think of the chreia as a literary unit no more precise than the apophthegm.

The advantage of beginning with the chreia, unimpeded by the faulty analyses of Dibelius, is that it is a definite literary form that was known and defined in antiquity. It was not conjectured in the twentieth century. It is well defined so it is not necessary to confuse it with a reminiscence, a

---

[3]M. Dibelius, *Tradition*, pp. 151-52.

[4]Ibid., p. 43.

[5]Ibid., p. 42.

[6]Ibid., p. 80. From this clue, V. Taylor, *The Formation of the Gospel Tradition* (London, 1949), pp. 71-82, called them "pronouncement stories."

maxim, or an extended narrative. It was used before, during, and after NT times, not only by Greek philosophers, church fathers, rabbis, and rhetoricians, but also by the gospel writers themselves and their predecessors. It is to those that we now turn attention.

It cannot be assumed offhand that all of the chreias contained in the gospels preserve the very words of Jesus. That was not presumed by ancient historians and rhetoricians. They understood chreias to preserve the basic messages which scribes and interpreters tried to use faithfully. Chreias will, however, provide a basis for testing. Rhetoricians and church fathers used chreias in their formation of other, secondary literature, and since the gospel writers were also editors and authors of literature, they also expanded chreias in legitimate ways to convey the message in a way that seemed best to them.

This means that the chreias in the gospels are sometimes woven into other narratives and cannot always be extracted again with perfect confidence. So many chreias were used by the gospel writers, however, that there are several about which there is little question. These will be examined here and tested in three ways: (1) They will be compared with one another for subject matter to see how coherent they are. Are they contradictory? Could one person have said all these things? (2) Does their content presuppose a period of history later than the time when Jesus lived? (3) Is there any geographical content which indicates an area where Jesus never traveled? Any one of these might prove that these chreias had not been reliably composed on the basis of Jesus' own teaching. The historian who tries to uncover the historical Jesus is on the defensive. Scholars have shown that parts of the gospels contain material attributed to Jesus that presumed a later date and therefore could not have been said by him, so it is apparent that some of the sayings attributed to Jesus were probably added by the later church. To suggest that any sayings attributed to Jesus are genuine, then, it is necessary to show a high degree of probability that they were not instead composed by the church itself. An examination of chreias may provide a means for beginning to separate the teachings of Jesus from those added by the later church.

Chreias and Parables. Chreias were literary forms that the ancients composed to preserve the messages of specific great leaders. Parables were not believed to contain quotations of historical personalities. The *dramatis personae* of parables were not identifiable persons but general figures like "a sower," "a merchant," "a shepherd," "a king," or "a certain man in a certain city.'' Rhetoricians said they might even be constructed around senseless objects or dumb beasts, as many of Aesop's fables were.[7] Parables differed from paradigms in that paradigms were taken from history, whereas parables were not.[8] A similitude is like a parable except that it enables the listener both to hear and to see the intended figure. It is therefore more distinct.[9] Bultmann judged all the gospel parables to be similitudes. He may be correct but no such distinction will be made here. A distinction will be made, however, that the Greek rhetoricians did not make. They considered simple analogies to be parables. The parable was any word or group of words that were laid alongside others for (1) amplification, (2) reflection, or (3) clarity.[10] Not all gospel analogies will be considered here, only the more extensive ones. These are analogies that resemble the parables reported in rabbinic literature more than any parable considered by the Greek rhetoricians.[11] Jewish and NT parables are more like Greek fables than Greek parables. Rabbinic parables frequently begin, ''To what can this be compared?'' Then follows something like, ''to a king of flesh and blood . . . למה הדבר דומה? למלך בשר ודם.'' That which is compared does not simply resemble a ''king of flesh and blood,'' but a situation in which a king of flesh and blood does such and such. The whole narrative about the king or some other subject is the parable which is laid alongside something needing amplification, reflection, or clarity.

Speakers and teachers used parables, but the parables were not constructed around particular teachers themselves as chreias were. Speakers and readers both knew parables were intended to illustrate, not narrate, or

---

[7]Apsinot, ''The Art of Rhetoric,'' Spengel, *Rhetores* 1.viii, p. 372.29-31.

[8]Minoukianus, ''Concerning Proof,'' Ibid., 1.i, pp. 418.28-419.11. The term ''paradigm'' here is used to mean ''example,'' and not any kind of technical literary form.

[9]Ibid., 1.ii, p. 419.2-11.

[10]Polybius Sardianus, ''Concerning Illustration,'' Spengel, ibid., 3. p. 106.15-23.

[11]Yoshihiro Sakaguchi has collected more than three hundred rabbinic parables that are very similar to those in the NT. When he has completed his collection and has classified the various parables in various ways, his research will be useful to NT students to compare with the parables attributed to Jesus. P. Fiebig, *Altjüdische Gleichnisse und die Gleichnisse Jesu* (Tübingen, 1904), in response to Jülicher, showed the similarity of NT parables to rabbinic parables. He concluded that gospel parables differed from rabbinic parables in content only—not in form. See also D. Flusser, *Die rabbinischen Gleichnisse und der Gleichniserzähler Jesus* (Las Vegas, c1981).

report on history or existing persons. The early form critics turned their attention to parables. Taylor believed the essence of the parable was that it suggested analogy or a spiritual truth. The details of the story were secondary.[12] Taylor agreed with Dibelius that the parables had been preserved with great fidelity. Jesus may have used and adapted some parables that were familiar at his time, but this does not rob them of their reliability or originality.[13] Bultmann followed Jülicher in distinguishing the parable from the similitude. The parable, he said, did not bring two sets of facts together, but rather transposed them into a story.[14] This is not according to the rhetoricians. The similitude, Bultmann said, was a strong Jewish traditional form marked by its conciseness of narrative and its inclusion of no more persons than were necessary to make the point. There are succinct parables, to be sure, like the precious pearl (Matt 13:45-46), but there are also extensive ones, like the sheep and the goats (Matt 25:31-46) and the prodigal son (Lk 15:12-32).

Parables and similitudes were units that could be taken from one context and placed in another to give them different meanings. They were sometimes supplied new introductions and sometimes expanded by commentary or interpretation.[15] Because of their adaptability, Bultmann said that the original meaning of many similitudes could no longer be recovered.[16] Part of Bultmann's skepticism about parables is that many of them are centered around the Kingdom of God which, he held, was not thought of as a human community either by Jesus or the early church.[17] He said parables and similitudes were so common in the Judaism of Jesus' day that Jesus probably created these stories as others did; but the church may also have added parables from the Jewish tradition to the sayings of Jesus—sayings that did not originate with Jesus, and whose reliability consequently is dubious.[18]

---

[12]Taylor, *Formation*, p. 101.

[13]Ibid., pp. 104-05.

[14]Bultmann, "Study," p. 174.

[15]Ibid., pp. 166-98.

[16]Ibid., p. 199.

[17]Ibid., p. 200.

[18]Ibid., p. 203.

Jewish and Christian parables were not composed as ends in themselves. They were composed for the purpose of illustrating something else. When someone wanted to communicate some message that needed an illustration he composed a parable which would illustrate the point whether or not it was completely reasonable as a fact in history. For example, Rabbi Shimon ben Yohai was once asked by his disciples: ''Why did the manna not come down to Israel once a year?'' He replied, ''I shall give a parable: 'This may be compared to a king of flesh and blood[19] who had one son, whose maintenance he provided once a year. [This meant that the son] would visit his father only once a year, [to receive his allowance]. Thereupon, [the king] provided for his maintenance day by day, so that [the son] would call upon him every day.' The same is true of Israel. One who had four or five children would worry, saying, 'Maybe no manna will come down, tomorrow, and all will die of hunger.' Thus they were found to turn their attention [day by day] to their Father in Heaven'' (Yoma 76a; for another example, see Men 104b).

It is not reasonable to assume that a king would give his son money only once a year, as an annual allowance. Neither is it reasonable to think that a king's son would come to see his father only when he needed money, but since manna came down every day and could not be stored up for a year, the rabbi composed a parable explaining why it happened this way rather than some other. He was not trying to teach how kings manage their household affairs or domestic discipline.

After David had seduced Bathsheba and had her husband Uriah killed, Nathan came to David to ask his judgment about a situation: '' 'In a certain city there were two men, one was rich and the other, poor. The rich man had numerous flocks and herds, but the poor man had only one little ewe lamb, which he had purchased. It grew up with him and his children. It ate from his food and drank from his cup. It used to lie in his bosom. It was like a daughter to him. Now a traveler came to the rich man as a guest. He was not willing to take one of his own flock or herd to prepare for the traveler who came to him, but he took the poor man's lamb and prepared it for the man who had come to him.' David became very angry against the man and said to Nathan, 'By the life of the Lord, the man who did this deserves to

---

[19]This expression frequently means a Gentile king in contrast to a messiah of Israel. See Midr. Ps 21:2.

die, and he will restore the lamb fourfold, because he did this and because he had no pity.' Nathan said to David, 'You are the man!' '' (2 Sam 12:1-7). This parable is very dramatic, pointed, and effective. Part of the reason we know its effectiveness, however, is that we have it in the context in which it occurred.

In the parables of Jesus, however, the context which prompted Jesus to tell the parable is not always given, and even if it is, it may now be displaced. In order to be quite certain of the teaching intended by each parable, however, it would be necessary to know what question Jesus was answering, what point he was illustrating and clarifying by the parable. This is one of the questions twentieth-century Bible students are asking, rather than knowing. The content of each parable will have to be used to deduce the question, and that will not always be done accurately. The situation would be much worse, however, if there were not three items that come to our aid: (1) the meanings of some parables are disclosed through scripture and/or Jewish tradition mentioned in the parable; (2) there are many parables, so that they may be compared to one another; and (3) there are also many chreias whose content is inherent in the structure and whose content can be understood fairly well. Therefore, it is proper to assume that some of the same conditions apply to the parables as to the chreias that have been attributed to the same person. This is especially true in that the content of the parables seems to be coherent with the content of the chreias, but this will not be assumed in advance.

Since Jesus reportedly told many parables, those attributed to him will be studied here in comparison with chreias for subject matter and made the objects of the same tests applied to the chreias. This will enable us to determine if the confidence of Taylor and Dibelius or the skepticism of Bultmann about parables is justified. The tests applied here would not have occurred to the form critics who were previously mentioned because all of them believed the earliest forms occurred only in Mark and there were at most eight of these. This is not enough to form a valid basis from which to test other materials for coherence of subject matter. Since this study is made only for the purpose of determining the teachings of the historical Jesus, it does not make any difference when a parable was composed originally or what its original meaning was. The real question is whether or not Jesus used these parables, and if so, what he meant by them at that time. The content of the parables will disclose the message he chose to communicate, if they can be established as authentic. This is not the conclusion reached, but the question to be examined.

After all the apparent chreias and parables of Jesus recorded in the synoptic gospels have been collected, they can be classed under general headings, but these are not very sharp and frequently overlap. Different scholars would probably choose different headings and a different number of headings, but the categories must be the kind that represent the subjects one person might have considered important and about which he might have spoken. One of the topic headings chosen is "Campaigning under Pressure," because all of the chreias and parables in this category stressed, among other things, urgency, seriousness, crisis situations, haste, importance of decision, great demands, and other similar pressures related to the task to which Jesus had dedicated himself as he recruited, instructed, organized, and directed the movement to which he was committed.

Examples of Pressure

The King in Hiding. "One scribe, approaching, said to him, 'Teacher, I will follow you wherever you go,' but Jesus responded, 'The foxes have holes, and the birds of the heaven, tents, but the Son of man has nowhere to lay his head' " (Matt 8:19-20; Lk 9:57-58).

This unit is a responsive chreia. It is succinct, containing only enough context to provide a setting for Jesus' response. It was attributed to a particular person, Jesus, but the questioner was not identified. This is normal. Doxapatres said there can be only one character in a chreia. The anonymous person that prompts the speaker to speak was not called a character.[20]

The expression "one scribe" is an apparent Semiticism. Some translators have rendered it, "One, a scribe."[21] Luke's reading does not show the problem, because the word, "scribe," is not in the text. Otherwise, Luke's statement varies somewhat from Matthew's, but the quotation from Jesus is the same.

As Wellhausen said, the man who approached Jesus was at the time no disciple.[22] While Jesus was recruiting followers, the man volunteered. M'Neile said he thought the man was willing to follow Jesus only to his res-

---

[20] Doxapatres, "Homilies on Apthonius," Walz 2.iii, p. 252.9-11.

[21] Allen, *ICC Matt*, p. 82; Meyer, *Matthew*, p. 182.

[22] J. Wellhausen, *Das Evangelium Matthei* (Berlin, 1914), p. 37.

idence, assuming that he had one.[23] The man addressed Jesus as "teacher." This does not mean that Jesus could not also have been a messiah or military organizer and leader. Judas and Mattathias, the leaders of a resistance movement whose students cut down the Roman eagle which Herod had erected over the great gate, were called *sophists*. They and their students were killed for insurrection (*BJ* 1.648-655). Judas the Galilean, who incited a revolt at the time of Archelaus, was called a *sophist* (*BJ* 2.117-118). One of the generals who led the war against Rome was Menahem, who wore royal robes and was called a *sophist* (*BJ* 2.444-445). These were men who organized and led military movements. Nonetheless, each of these scholars would have been rightly called, "teacher." Jesus was also a teacher who did not spend all of his time in the classroom, but was recruiting followers when this scribe volunteered to join the movement.

Jesus' answer would have discouraged any but the most courageous. Although the volunteer seemed willing, Jesus warned him that the Son of man was not yet on his throne. His followers, like Jesus, would have to live a fugitive existence. Jesus' response was a little like the quotation from Tiberius Graccus when speaking in behalf of the poor in Italy: "The wild beasts of Italy have dwelling places and holes, and each has its own place of escape, but for those who fight and die for Italy, there is air and light, but nothing else" (Plutarch, *Tib. Gracc.* 9.4-5).

M'Neile, Meyer, and Plummer[24] all observed that "nests" is not the best translation of κατασκηνώσεις. The word really means "encampments" and usually applied to tents used for soldiers engaged in battle. The Greek word for "nest" is νεσσεία, νεσσία, or νοσσία.[25] This word occurs several times in the OT, rendering the Hebrew קן.[26] It is only twice rendered by something that does not mean "nest," and in both cases it is used metaphorically to mean either the temple (rendered "dwelling," LXX

---

[23]M'Neile, *Matthew*, p. 109.

[24]Ibid., p. 109.

Meyer, *Matthew*, p. 183.

A. Plummer, *A Critical and Exegetical Commentary on the Gospel according to Luke* (Edinburgh, c1969), p. 266.

[25]See Liddell and Scott. Also *Arrian's Discourse of Epictetus* 3.xxiv.6.

[26]Num 24:21; Deut 22:6; 32:11; Job 29:18; 39:27; Prov 27:8; Isa 16:2.

Obad 3), or a secure military installation (rendered "fortress," LXX Jer
30:16). In no case is the Hebrew "nest" rendered by the Greek "encamp-
ment." Although Jesus referred to the dwelling places for birds, he seems
really to have been talking about quarters for troops. Birds were equipped
for their outdoor dwelling, but Jesus had neither a cot nor a military tent.
The Maccabean guerrillas had found cover and protection in the caves in the
mountains—the same kind of protection as foxes found in their holes; but
the Son of man still did not have caves at his disposal. Those interested in
the movement Jesus was leading were put under extreme pressure. They had
either to sacrifice a great deal or withdraw.

M'Neile, Schniewind, and Zahn[27] all thought "Son of man" meant
simply "man" or "mankind," but Schniewind said that he was the man
from heaven who will be the judge of the world. Zahn said he was a man
like no other man. Allen and Meyer[28] correctly held that "Son of man" here
means "Messiah" or "Christ." This is not only true here, but wherever the
name occurs in relationship to Jesus it is a mythical term that has the historical meaning of a Jewish messiah or king over Jews in Palestine.[29] Because this was a mythical term that sounded rather harmless, it could be
used openly, without any fear that the Romans would suspect that the "Son
of man" was engaged in leading an insurrectionist movement, the way they
would if he were called messiah or king. This makes it easier to understand
the situation that existed in Palestine when Jesus was recruiting followers
without adequate quarters or equipment. Many guerrilla leaders begin this
way. Although designated by his followers as a messiah or king, he was not
yet at the point of dwelling securely in a palace. Those who wanted to have
chief seats in the new kingdom would have a lot to sacrifice first, helping
him with his campaign. The same kind of pressure is present in the next
literary unit.

---

[27]M'Neile, *Matthew*, p. 109.

J. Schniewind, *Das Evangelium nach Matthäus* (Göttingen, 1950), pp. 113-14.

T. Zahn, *Das Evangelium des Matthäus* (Leipzig, 1910), pp. 351-61.

[28]Allen, *ICC Matthew*, p. 82.

Meyer, *Matthew*, p. 184.

[29]GWB, *Hebrews*, pp. 38-51.

The Living and the Dead. "Another of the disciples said to him, 'Lord, permit me first to go away and bury my father'; but Jesus replied, 'Follow me, and let the dead bury their own dead' " (Matt 8:21-22).

"Then he said to another, 'Follow me!' He responded, 'Permit me first to go away and bury my father.' He said to him, 'Let the dead bury their own dead, but you, after you have gone away, announce the Kingdom of God' " (Lk 9:59-60).[30]

These are both chreias. Each is attributed to a particular person, Jesus. Each is terse, including only enough context to provide a basis for the response. Each contains the statement of the teacher which is succinct and sharp. Luke's version is a "double chreia" because the important line is a response to a response. It is not likely that these refer to different recruits on different occasions, but there are enough differences between them to suggest that they came from different lines of tradition and were composed by different listeners, who separately recorded the incident in different chreias. Matthew's is more succinct, but Luke's is stylistically artistic because the answer has picked up the word "go away" in the objection and used it also in the response. The absence of the word "Jesus" in Luke's version provides no problem. It is evident from lists of chreias attributed to Diogenes and others that collectors of chreias regularly substituted the pronoun for the proper name when it was evident from the context that the character was the same in all instances.

It is normal for Matthew to give two examples, apparently to fulfill the requirement that it takes two or three witnesses to make a case valid (Deut 19:15; Matt 18:16). Here there are two chreias in parallel relationship in the Gospel of Matthew (Matt 8:19-20, 21-22). They evidently did not happen at the same time and the same place, but the Matthaean editor either found them together or put them together from different sources. One was a scribe and the other a disciple, although it appears as if the person was really a

---

[30]E. Linnemann, *Jesus of the Parables*, tr. J. Sturdy (New York, c1966), p. 103, asked, "But what has this literal following, this wandering after Jesus on the highways of Palestine, to do with the Kingdom of God? How is this the way to seize the unique opportunity of its nearness? This remains hidden from us. The texts are ciphers whose meaning we cannot read." This is true of those who see no relationship between the Kingdom of God and the promised land.

recruit who was not yet a disciple or a follower. Meyer, Plummer, and Zahn[31] are all mistaken in thinking that the man's father was actually dead at that time and had not yet been buried. Allen[32] suggested that this might be a proverbial saying, meaning, "Cut yourself adrift from the past when matters of present interest call for your whole attention." If the father had already died, as these scholars assumed, then the man would have been at home in a defiled state taking care of the burial. This does not seem to be the real situation involved.

The disciple was probably not asking simply for a few days' leave. One of the commandments required children to honor their parents (Exod 20:12; Deut 5:19), which meant providing food, shelter, and clean garments for the parents in their old age (Mekilta, *Bahodesh* 8:1-40). If the disciple in question should leave his family at once, possibly contributing all of his material possessions to the communal society to which he was considering membership, it would force him to neglect his father in his old age, breaking one of the commandments in the process. If he could just wait until his father had died, and he had given him a proper burial, he would be free to contribute the rest of his money to the group and follow with a clear conscience. In answering that the "dead" could bury their own dead, Jesus was not implying that corpses could bury corpses, but covenantal communities who considered themselves the only true elect of God also described existence in their community as "life," and existence outside of their community as "death."[33] If the disciple followed Jesus, he would then be alive. If he did not, he would instead be "dead" as were his father and other relatives who were not following Jesus. These "dead" should be left to care for one another. Although those who kept the commandment to honor their parents were promised in the Torah that because they did this they would be rewarded by living long in the land, Jesus said here that those who chose to honor their parents instead of following him were dead already. The exclusive brotherhoods in which life was considered possible had no responsi-

---

[31]Meyer, *Matthew,* p. 186.

Plummer, *ICC Luke,* p. 260.

T. Zahn, *Das Evangelium des Lucas,* (Leipzig, 1920), p. 350.

[32]Allen, *ICC Matthew,* p. 82.

[33]GWB, *Consequences,* pp. 110-49.

bility for non-followers, even if they were parents. The urgency of the situation required at least temporary abandonment of some of the commandments. This was the same kind of "Torah expediency" ethics as the Hasmoneans applied to fighting on the Sabbath. It was thought better to break one commandment in order to get control of the land so that all of the commandments could be observed than to be destroyed trying to keep one commandment meticulously (1 Macc 2:40-42).

Prepared to Plow. "Also another said, 'I will follow you, Lord, but first let me put my house in order.' Then Jesus said, 'No one who puts his hand to the plow and looks back is well-set for the Kingdom of God' " (Lk 9:61-62).

This unit is succinct, providing only enough context to justify the saying. The volunteer in Luke's preceding chreia was not identified. Luke may have found both chreias in a single source since they are so similar, stylistically. They also vary stylistically from those in Matthew's gospel. They are coherent from the standpoint of content and are also coherent with the chreia studied in Matthew's gospel—both are involved with situations where Jesus was confronting volunteers to both of whom he made very stringent demands. In the earlier chreia the term "go away" was employed in both parts of the unit; in this chreia the thought of getting things organized or well-set was used in both parts. The response itself might have been a common proverb or maxim originally. Pliny said that a plowman who did not bend attentively over his work would have a crooked furrow.[34] If so, the saying has now been put into chreia form and therefore is no longer a proverb. The Greek rhetoricians said that this was frequently done.

Jesus seems here to have imitated Elijah's response to Elisha's request when invited to be his disciple (1 Kgs 19:19-21). Elisha was plowing when Elijah put his own mantle on Elisha's shoulders. Elisha said he would follow Elijah, but he wanted first to go back and say farewell to his family. It is not absolutely clear whether he was granted permission or not. It seems that he butchered his oxen right there, held a feast for his friends, and then followed Elijah without going back to say farewell. It can also be understood, however, that this feast was the way Elisha said farewell. Whichever way it was for Elijah, Jesus' action was to reject the request. His program

---

[34]Pliny, *N. H.* xviii.19, 49.

was then on the move. Those who wanted to follow him had to do so immediately.

The figure presented is that of a plow following oxen in a rocky field. If the driver did not keep his mind on the work immediately before him, his plow would soon jump out of the furrow because it was not "well-set." Then the driver, like the plow, would not be well-set. Jesus could not allow people to join his ranks who had their minds partly on something else.

The Widow's Commitment. "When he looked up he saw the rich people putting their gifts into the treasury, and he saw one poor widow, putting her two mites, and he said, 'I tell you for a fact that this poor woman gave more than all [the rest]' " (Lk 21:1-3; Mk 12:41-44).

This unit qualifies as a chreia whose spokesman was identified only in context. It is slightly expanded and interpreted in Mark. The chreia itself does not explain why Jesus thought that this widow gave more than all the rest. It certainly was not mathematically true, but the following interpretation is probably correct. Consistent with other chreias, this pictures Jesus approving complete dedication and commitment. The demand that people give all that they have is not evident here, but when it was done, he approved.

The Fallen Temple. "Now when Jesus left, he went away from the temple, and his disciples came to show him the buildings of the temple. He said to them in response, 'Do you not see all these things? Truly, I tell you, there will not be left here one stone upon another which will not be broken down' " (Matt 24:1-3).

"Now as he was coming out of the temple, one of his disciples said to him, 'Teacher, see what kind of stones and what kind of buildings!' Then Jesus said to him, 'Do you see these great buildings? Not one stone will be left here on another that will not be broken down' " (Mk 13:1-4).

"Now some were saying concerning the temple that it was decorated with beautiful stones and foundations. He said, 'These things which you see—the days will come when not one stone will be left upon another here, that will not be broken down' " (Lk 21:5-7).

All three examples are preserved in chreia form. They are succinct; the teacher, Jesus, is identified; the context is given which prompted the teacher to speak; and that response which he gave is quoted. The quotation is nearly the same in all three chreias, although the structure, which holds the quotation in chreia form, varies from text to text. These may have come from separate collections and have been composed by different authors, but that is not required to allow for the variants. In all three gospels, this chreia is used as the main text upon which a whole discussion is based. It was normal for authors and orators to develop chreias like this into homilies.

Modern commentators almost universally fail to comment on this chreia. They begin with the commentary that starts with the following verse in all cases. Using methods developed by the rhetoricians, someone in the later church developed a lengthy narrative about signs that mark the end of the Roman age and the beginning of the new age of Jewish independence. Much of this commentary is based on the mythical report of events that occurred during the three-and-one-half-year period between the defilement and the rededication of the temple in the Hasmonean Revolt. This commentator or these commentators understood that when Jesus prophesied the destruction of the temple, he was talking about this as part of the general conflict that would be necessary before the Romans could be driven out and the temple restored in purified form.

With no more evidence than that given in the chreia, the conjectured basis for his prediction can only be tentative and never certain. Like members of the community at Qumran, Jesus may have been offended by the corruption and defilement that took place in the temple under Roman rule. He may have thought, based on Ezekiel's prophecy (Ezek 4 and 5), that this could never be simply cleansed as Judas had done nearly two hundred years earlier. Ezekiel's prophecy would be fulfilled; there would be a siege against Jerusalem and against the temple.

Whatever the understood meaning of the chreia, the statement of Jesus is coherent with the other chreias quoted here. Anyone recruiting very intensely dedicated followers for the Kingdom of God, reporting that he lacked the ''encampments'' that birds had, and holes, like foxes, could, without contradiction, speak of the destruction of the temple. There is no need that these chreias should have been composed after the fall of Jerusalem, even though some parts of the commentary may have been.

The Blessed Do God's Will. ''It happened while he was saying these things a certain woman from the crowd raised her voice and said to him, 'Blessed is the womb which bore you and the breasts which nursed you.' But he replied, 'Rather blessed are those who hear the word of God and keep it.' '' (Lk 11:27-28).

The context of this unit is a little longer than some, giving the situation which prompted the woman to speak as well as Jesus' answer. This is called a double chreia.[35] Jesus was identified by context, and his saying was brief and astute. Partially quoting from Exod 24:7, the response of the Israelites to the demands of the commandments, when Moses came down from Mount Sinai, was, "We will keep [the commandments,] and we will hear (obey)" (Mekilta, *Bahodesh* 5:80). The pressure is evident in Jesus' unwillingness to accept a compliment, either for himself or his mother. Instead he reminded those around him of the one thing that was important—doing God's will. Doing God's will, of course, meant following Jesus and this seemed the most important thing to be considered. All other things were subordinated.

It was ordinarily considered proper to bless the Messiah. One of the rabbinic blessings is as follows: "Blessed be the hour in which the Messiah was created; blessed be the womb from which he came; blessed be the generation that sees him; blessed be the eye that is worthy to see him" (pesikta Rabbati 149a). The response attributed to Jesus is not a proverb which might have been placed on the lips of many teachers in various periods and locations. There was a local incident which prompted this distinctive saying, although it is no longer certain just when this event occurred in Jesus' travels. Once the discussion was reduced to a chreia, it could be inserted into any part of a narrative. The context that is reliable is that which is included in the chreia. It seems reasonable to believe that a person who was as demanding as Jesus is shown in the previous chreia might also say something like this. It reflects the seriousness with which he understood his leadership program. A similar statement is contained in a literary unit that once may have been a chreia. It now is expanded internally to break this form. The conjectured additions have been put in brackets.

The Adopted Family. "While he was still speaking to the crowds, look, his mother and brothers were standing outside, seeking to speak to him. [Someone said to him, 'Look! your mother and brothers stand outside, seeking to speak to you.'] He, replying, said to the one who was speaking to him, 'Who is my mother, and who are my brothers?' Then, extending his hand to his disciples, he said, 'Look! my mother and my brothers, for whoever does the will of my Father in heaven is my brother, sister, and mother' " (Matt 12:46-50).

---

[35]Theon, "Progymnasmata," Spengel, *Rhetores* 2.v, p. 98.20-27. Dibelius, *Tradition*, p. 162, called this a Chria.

This is a mixed sayings and action chreia. It is not certain whether the original chreia had this last verse, "For whoever does the will of God . . ." or whether the chreia ended just before that, having the statement, "Look! my mother and my brothers," as the punch line. It is possible that the last line was an interpretive editor's addition. It is evident that there has been some editorial expansion to this chreia, because the verse, "Someone said to him, 'Look! your mother and brothers stand outside, seeking to speak to you,' " has been omitted by several of the important texts. The Gospel of Thomas has a similar teaching attributed to Jesus.

"Jesus said, 'Whoever does not hate his father and his mother cannot be my disciple, and whoever does not hate his brothers and sisters and does not take up his cross in my way will not be worthy of me' " (Log. 55).

These teachings that ask followers to reject their families or that indicate that Jesus has rejected his family in favor of a brotherhood are monastic. Because of the urgency of the situation, followers are asked to give up everything in order to do God's will.

Herod's Threat. "In that very hour, certain Pharisees came, saying to him, 'Hurry and leave this place, because Herod wants to kill you.' Then he said to them, 'When *you* leave, tell that fox, "Look, I cast out demons and perform healings today and tomorrow, and on the third [day] I will be finished" ' " (Lk 13:31-32).

Dibelius[36] said this was a chreia which Luke composed, using a saying of Jesus. Bultmann[37] also considered it an apophthegm. Denaux[38] set out to prove Dibelius's point that Luke may have been the one who created the chreia. Presuming Q, he made a word study of the main words in the pericope and concluded that they are Lukan. He failed to notice, however, that the typically Lukan words he listed fell almost completely in verse 33, which he considered a part of the chreia. Dibelius also considered the unit to be Luke 13:32-33, but Bultmann correctly noted that verse 33 might be "an unattached saying." The rhetoricians said chreias must be succinct, but they could be expanded to create a narrative or something else. This seems to be the function, not only of verse 33, but also of verses 34 and 35.

---

[36]Dibelius, *Tradition,* pp. 162-63.

[37]Bultmann, *History,* p. 35.

[38]A. Denaux, "L'hypocrisie des Pharisiens et le Dessein de Dieu Analyse de Lc., 13, 31-33," F. Neirynck (ed.), *L'Evangile des Luc* (Belgique, c1973), pp. 245-85.

The editor put this chreia in the position he thought most suitable, then he added verse 33, in typically Lukan terminology, to explain further what Jesus meant by his statement on his way to Jerusalem. That provided the editor an excellent opportunity to conclude the chapter with the poem of Jesus' lament over Jerusalem in verses 34 and 35. Chreias, however, were circulated without any more context than the chreia itself provided. It was the editor who placed it on the way to Jerusalem in his own structure. This is a responsive chreia in which the situation that prompted Jesus to speak was the warning of the Pharisees that Jesus had better flee, because Herod was trying to capture and kill him. Jesus was identified only by the context in which the chreia had been placed. Divorced from its context, the "he" would need to be replaced by "Jesus" to be complete. When collectors assembled many chreias about one character, however, such as Diogenes or Isocrates, they usually replaced the personal name with "he" or "the same man," since the name of the character had been given earlier. The statement Jesus made was quoted and the whole unit is succinct.

Jesus had evidently been working under pressure. While he was recruiting disciples and performing the necessary miracles expected of a messiah, he was being threatened by the state. Jesus responded that he was too far along to be stopped. The sharpness of the response was partly contained in the word, "leave." The Pharisees told him to leave (πορεύου); Jesus answered, "When *you* leave (πορευθέντες)." This is reminiscent of Amos's repartee with Amaziah. Amaziah said, "Go! (לֵךְ) Flee to the land of Judah" (Amos 7:12), and Amos responded, "But the Lord said to me, 'Go! (לֵךְ) Prophesy to my people Israel' " (Amos 7:15).

Denaux argued that the Pharisees had inaccurately informed Jesus of Herod's intentions and desires. Since they were enemies of Jesus, they were trying to disrupt his program.[39] This is not necessarily so. It may have been early or late in his campaign. The fact that Jesus had been closely allied with John the Baptist who had been killed by Herod for insurrection, followed further by the fact that Jesus was finally also killed by the Romans, suggests that Jesus' movements to continue John's program would have been held under careful surveillance by Herod. A warning by the Pharisees might have been intended to be helpful. In other chreias Jesus was observed recruiting volunteers while he was inadequately equipped for the program

---

[39]Denaux, Ibid., p. 385.

he needed to carry out, implying that he was living a rather fugitive existence. His response to the Pharisees seems to mean that he would keep on‑
doing what he was doing, day after day, until he was finished. No one, including Herod, would be able to stop him.[40]

The Voice of the Stones. "Now certain of the Pharisees from the crowd
said to him, 'Teacher, warn your disciples.' But he, replying, said, 'I tell
you, if these keep still, the stones will cry out' " (Lk 19:39-40).

Dibelius[41] called this a chreia, but thought Luke had composed it,
based on a saying of Jesus. Bultmann called it an apophthegm and correctly
observed that the saying of Jesus, apart from its context, could never have
survived.[42] Bultmann also preferred the Matthaean account of "children"
to Luke's "disciples," but Matthew's form is simply a part of a longer narrative. If Matthew had once received this in chreia form, he destroyed the
form to compose a narrative. In its Lukan form, this is a chreia. There is
enough context to show what prompted the respondent to speak. Only in the
greater context is the identity of the respondent identified. The quotation is
given and the unit is succinct.

The Pharisees were people who took the law seriously and tried to keep
peace. Their conflict with Jesus may have been partly because they feared
that he would cause another uprising among the people that would prompt
the Romans to get out their troops—as they had before—who would kill
many Jews, but accomplish nothing positive so far as Jewish independence
was concerned. Their attempts to warn Jesus of Herod's interest and their
efforts to keep the movement quiet may have been a humane desire to avoid
conflict with the Romans. Their addressing Jesus as "teacher" did not necessarily have a negative connotation, as Plummer suggested.[43] Being a
teacher in Judaism was a position of honor; it did not have to mean "only a
teacher." Teachers were also messianic pretenders and leaders of revolutionary movements in Judaism in NT times. Of course, the other possibility
that Plummer suggested, namely, that they were Jesus' enemies and wanted

---

[40]For the expression, "today and tomorrow, and on the third day," see Denaux, Ibid.,
pp. 279-81.

[41]Dibelius, *Tradition,* p. 162.

[42]Bultmann, *History,* p. 34.

[43]Plummer, *ICC Luke,* p. 449.

to weaken his movement for their own selfish reasons is possible. Since this is a chreia, there is no certainty that Luke placed it in his gospel at the point in Jesus' activity where it originated. It may not originally have been an account of incidents related to Jesus' entry into Jerusalem. It could have happened at any time the Pharisees felt threatened or anxious about the consequences of Jesus' movement. Whenever that was, it means that Jesus had at that time enough of a following to have aroused public attention and to have attracted the interest of Herod.

Judging from the response of Jesus, the Pharisees' warning to Jesus was that his disciples *keep still,* because Jesus' response indicated that he surely was not going to make them keep still. He evidently was so certain that God approved of his actions that he did not think anything under the sun could stop his movement. God would make it succeed. This is coherent with other chreias that reflected Jesus' enthusiasm and action under pressure. The fact that Jesus thought Herod, rather than he, should be afraid, and that he did not feel any need to keep his movement quiet, apparently indicates that he had a strong movement going by the time these repartees took place. This makes no sense for a nonpolitical, philosophical mission.

Weeping Women. "A great crowd of people followed him and women who mourned and lamented for him. Jesus turned and said to them, 'Daughters of Jerusalem, do not weep for me, but weep instead for yourselves' " (Lk 23:27-28).

This is clearly a chreia. It is brief; the respondent is identified; the answer given was prompted by the action of the women. Dibelius did not discuss this passage in relationship to chreias, but only in relationship to the passion. Bultmann considered this passage, plus verses 29-31, to be an apophthegm. He supposed that it was composed at the same time as the material around it. He did not presume that it was imaginary.[44] It is true that the *Sitz im Leben* seems most likely to have been at the cross, when weeping would have been most normal. It is difficult to imagine any other time in Jesus' ministry when his movement was so seriously threatened that women would have needed to weep for him, but hypothetically that would have been possible. Once chreias had been written down, later editors were free to place them in their literature wherever they chose. Wherever and when-

---

[44]Bultmann, *History,* p. 37.

ever this originated, it reflects a tense, urgent situation under pressure at a time when Jesus' movement seemed to be a failure.

Expanded Chreias

The chreias given above are preserved in their pure chreia form. Since chreias were literary units to be used by preachers or editors, they were often interpreted by following statements or illustrations. Sometimes the statement alone was preserved and the context was omitted. Sometimes the chreia was expanded internally for interpretive purposes. Often the only form preserved is an expanded chreia or a statement that has been separated from its context in a chreia. In these cases it is possible only to conjecture that the statement once belonged to a chreia or that the expanded chreia was once unexpanded. There is no certainty about these conjectures. In the synoptic gospels, sometimes one gospel preserved the chreia in its pure form, but another varied it in some way. The instances in which this occurs under the topic "Campaign Pressures" are as follows:

Fishers of Men. "While he was *walking along* the Sea of Galilee, *he* saw *two brothers,* Simon, called Peter, and Andrew, *his* brother, casting the nets into the sea, for they were fishermen. Then he said to them, 'Come after me, and I will make you fishers of men' " (Matt 4:18-19).

"While he was *going along* the Sea of Galilee, he saw Simon and Andrew, the brother *of Simon,* throwing their nets into the sea, for they were fishermen. Then *Jesus* said to them, 'Come after me, and I will make you *become* fishers of men' " (Mk 1:16-17).

This is a chreia in both gospels. The wording varies slightly, as the italics show, but such variance is normal among the chreias. The shorthand method of preservation did not concentrate on details of wording—just the basic message. Each example is brief with enough context to inspire the response given and the assertion is provided. Since the response is to a situation rather than to a person, they are assertive chreias. The context which prompted the response is somewhat longer than many chreias, but these are probably inherent parts of the original chreia, since all of this is necessary to prepare the reader for the point of Jesus' asking these fishers to become fishers of men.

The call of James and John (Matt 4:21-22) was similar but not in chreia form. The succinct description of Levi's call (Lk 5:27) is very similar in form to a chreia, but the simple command, "Follow me," is not related to his vocation of collecting taxes in the very sharp way fishers of men is related to fishers. Therefore it is probably not a chreia because it is not sharp and astute as well as terse. Dibelius considered Matt 4:18-19 to be a legend with no more material for the author than the names of the disciples and the line about the fishers of men.[45] Bultmann, on the other hand, considered Mk 1:16-20 to be an apophthegm, saying that there is just as much reason to assume a unitary conception from its start as to assume that it was later reedited to become this way.[46]

It is not very likely that the historical situation was as spontaneous as the chreia describes. Jesus probably interviewed these brothers at length. Part of his recruitment speech involved changing their vocation from fishers to fishers of men. The disciples, then, summarized the invitation in the form of a chreia, such as still exists in Matthew and Mark. Most chreias have been formed in ways like this. The goal is to summarize the context and quote the words of the speaker as closely as possible. Teachers, like Diogenes who expected his students to memorize important parts of his teachings, may have learned to teach in sharp, succinct ways that could easily be made into chreias. Jesus may have done the same, but this is not a prerequisite for either. The students may have been taught, methodologically, how to summarize and put things in chreia form. This may have been what Diogenes Laertius meant when he said Diogenes taught his students "shortcuts" in memorization (D.L. 6:31).

Schniewind[47] said these brothers were invited to become "servants of the word." Meyer[48] said Jesus was inviting these brothers to become disciples which probably involved winning over souls for themselves or others. The expression, "Come after me," means, "Become my disciples," but that was not all that was involved in the call. Meyer said they would be involved in winning souls, but the context does not indicate anything as passive as that. Souls were probably not separated from the men involved. Jesus was out recruiting followers, which probably had the same metaphorical meaning as "fishing." Those who were called to be "fishers of men" were expected to recruit still more men into the program. Matthew, at least, also understood it in this way, because he pictured them going out

---

[45]Dibelius, *Tradition*, pp. 112-13.

[46]Bultmann, *History*, p. 28.

[47]Schniewind, *History*, p. 35.

[48]Meyer, *Matthew*, p. 105.

to all Israel, announcing that the Kingdom of Heaven was very near (Matt 10:7). This was not just a pleasant thought. When it was heard, the announcers would be rejected many times; this would cause family members to become mortal enemies. The work was to be done in the "dark," in secret, but later, when the Kingdom came, all would become known. This kind of fishing did not promise peace but a sword. In the day of judgment, just before the Kingdom was inaugurated, those cities that rejected these fishermen would suffer more serious punishment than Sodom and Gomorrah which were utterly destroyed. This does not sound like a Sunday school picnic, but a political, military maneuver (Matt 10:1-37).

The story of the recruitment of the two brothers, reported in Matthew and Mark in a chreia, was told much more extensively in Luke's account (Lk 5:1-10). It began with Jesus and the crowd standing along the shore of Genesaret. He saw two boats in which there were fishermen, one of whom was Simon. Andrew was not mentioned. Luke may have altered the story to omit Andrew who was evidently not nearly as important as the other three. The Matthaean chreia was composed before that material was known. Jesus got into the boat of Simon and taught the crowd from the boat. Then he commanded Simon to let out his nets. Reluctantly, Simon consented and caught a netful of fish. After Simon's confession, Jesus told him and his partners, James and John, that he would make them become fishers of men. This seems to be a narrative which has expanded the chreia to include the call of James and John as well as Simon and to include the miracle of the large catch of fish, but it began and ended like the chreia in Matthew and Mark. It seems to have been developed from the chreia of Matthew and Mark just the way Epiphanius's homily was developed from the chreia about John and Cerinthus at the bath house.

Harvest and Laborers. ''When he had seen the crowds, he had compassion on them, because they were *scattered and torn like sheep that had no shepherd* (1 Kings 22:17). Then he said to his disciples, 'The harvest is great, but the laborers are few' '' (Matt 9:36-37).

This is a chreia in which the speaker made an assertion, prompted by the situation itself. The speaker was only identified by the general context. His response was quoted, and the whole unit is succinct. Therefore it is one of the two kinds of assertive chreias. The quotation from the OT was included by the disciples who created the chreia to preserve Jesus' statement. In that passage Micah prophesied that this would happen if Israel and the Syrians went to war against Ramoth-gilead. The war was undertaken and the king of Israel was killed, leaving the army without a leader.[49] The disciples who composed this chreia thought Jesus, while pondering over a leaderless group of Jews in Palestine, declared that the harvest was great, but the laborers were few. This was evidently a commentary on his situation after he had begun recruiting. It may have been after he had spent a good deal of effort recruiting and still was short of assistants to help him lead the program.

This chreia in Matthew was modified by Luke and worked into his story of the commissioning of the seventy to go out and recruit more laborers into the harvest.

"After this the Lord appointed seventy others and sent them out in twos before his face to every city and place where he, himself, was about to go. Then he said to them, 'On the one hand, *the harvest is great, but* on the other hand, *the laborers are few.* Therefore, pray that the Lord of the harvest will send out laborers into his harvest. Go! Look, I am sending you out as sheep in the midst of wolves . . .' " (Lk 10:1-20).

Straight Gate. "A certain man said to him, '[Would you tell me] if those who are saved are few?' Then he said to them, 'Struggle to enter through the straight gate, because many, I tell you will seek to enter, but will not be able' " (Lk 13:23-24).

This unit has a brief context, including a question which prompted the respondent to answer briefly in a poetic way. Jesus was identified as the respondent only in the general context. The saying is consistent with Jesus' severe demands given to would-be followers. The word "save" in the OT was used two hundred forty-four times to refer to national deliverances, usually in war; ninety-two times for deliverances of individuals from prison, illness, injury, and so forth; and fourteen times for those with proper qualifications such as the patient or righteous ones. In the Greek mystery cults, those saved were members of the cult. Those mentioned in the chreia as saved may have been the ones qualified for membership in the new nation—perhaps those who either survived the conflict with Rome and had qualified for citizenship in the new kingdom or had been killed in battle fighting for independence and would be raised, after the Gentiles had been driven out, to live the rest of their lives in the promised land, free from for-

---

[49]T. W. Manson, *The Servant Messiah* (Cambridge, 1966), p 70: "What Jesus saw on the shore of the lake was a Maccabean host with Judas Maccabaeus."

eign rule. Plummer[50] correctly observed that Jesus did not directly answer the question and say whether many or few would be saved. He said many would try to enter and would not succeed, perhaps implying that only a few would be saved. Dibelius[51] allowed that this is a chreia, but he presumed that Luke created it by adding only the introductory question to material he gleaned from the Sermon on the Mount. The editors studied in the last chapter appeared to have copied all of their chreias rather than having created them. It seems likely that Luke did the same. Bultmann[52] classified this as an eschatological discourse which Luke composed from "all sorts of pieces," and Bultmann thought it was rather clumsily done.

This Lukan chreia is somehow related to the following poetic account in the Sermon on the Mount, regardless of the authorship of the chreia:

Enter through the straight gate,
because broad and spacious is the way
that leads to destruction,
and many are those who enter through it,
because straight is the gate, and narrow is the way
that leads to life
and few are the ones who find it.   (Matt 7:13-14)

It is not certain which way the dependency lies. Greeks composed poems from chreias.[53] They also quoted poetry in chreias, but not poetry composed by the character involved. For instance, Diogenes quoted Homer in chreias but chreias are not preserved that parallel Diogenes' poems. In these quotations attributed to Jesus, someone may have composed a chreia based on this poetry which the author took to be the words of Jesus and therefore legitimate data for chreia composition. If so, there is not yet any apparent instance in the material studied from Greek historians, rhetoricians, or church fathers in which this was one of the customary ways of composing chreias. The other possibility is that Matthew composed poetry, using several chreias, among which was the one recorded by Luke. This seems to be the most likely possibility, but it is not certain.

---

[50]Plummer, *ICC Luke*, p. 346.

[51]Dibelius, *Tradition*, p. 162.

[52]Bultmann, *History*, p. 130.

[53]For examples see D. R. Dudley, *A History of Cynicism* (London, 1937), pp. 113-14.

The picture here is based on the two-ways doctrine of Prov 2-7[54] in which the wicked woman characterized the Gentile. The way to her house was to be avoided and the student was warned to stay with the bride of his youth, meaning he should hold fast to his traditional Jewish faith. In Palestinian NT times, the wide way probably pictured the stone-paved roads that led to Rome. The narrow way may have been some path that led up the mountainside to a small monastery with a narrow door. A few monks finally arrived there; otherwise it was isolated. For the monks, however, their doctrine taught them that here alone was the covenant really kept; here alone was life; all others were dead. Therefore, it was well worth the struggle. Those who would enter this monastery would understand the severe demands Jesus made on those new recruits who volunteered to follow him.

Rejecting Families. "Great crowds gathered to him, and he turned and said to them, 'If anyone comes to me and does not hate his father and mother, wife and children, brothers and sisters, and yet even his own soul (ψυχήν), he cannot be my disciple' " (Lk 14:25-26).

The speaker was identified only by the general context as Jesus. The situation was given and the assertion was made. The entire unit is succinct. Therefore, this is an assertive chreia. The point made was clear—to be a follower of Jesus, a person must break all family ties and become part of the celibate order. This probably reduced the "great crowds" to a very few zealous followers. "Hating" in this context probably does not refer to any specifically hostile feeling, but it meant rejection and isolation. The one who joined a communal brotherhood contributed all of his money to the group, called "brothers" or "the poor." He gave up all responsibilities to his family which meant that he would no longer honor his parents if they were still alive. All that he had went to the community, which, in turn, provided for him. Giving up his "soul" in "the world" may have meant giving up his identity and status in "the world"—family, occupation, normal place and position in society, and so forth. Only by doing this could he gain his soul by becoming a celibate member in the covenant community of which Jesus was the leader. This was similar to the demands made of other communal orders, such as the Essenes and the community governed by the "Community Rule" (1QS). The pressure here is the intensity of the need and the seriousness of the cause that required a great price for discipleship.

---

[54]GWB, "Midrašim Pre-Tannaítes," *RB* 72 (1965):227-39.

This chreia is coherent with other recruitment chreias that confronted volunteers with high demands for permission to follow Jesus.

In Matthew the same basic teaching is recorded, but not in a chreia form.

> He who loves father and mother more than me
> is not worthy of me
> he who loves son or daughter more than me
> is not worthy of me
> he who does not take up his cross and follow me
> is not worthy of me.
> He who finds his soul will lose it,
> and he who loses his soul for my sake
> will find it.   (Matt 10:37-39).

This is another case in which either Luke has summarized the poetic passage in Matthew and put it into chreia form by adding a general introduction to give it a context, or Matthew composed a poem based on a chreia. The latter seems more likely.

There are many indications that Jesus advocated celibacy. He told his disciples to call no man "father" on earth. Their only father was in heaven and they were all brothers (Matt 23:9-10). He never referred to Mary as his mother, but called her "woman" (Jn 2:4; 19:26). He held that his disciples were his mother and brothers (Matt 12:46-49). He told the Sadducees that in the resurrection there would be neither marriage nor giving in marriage, but all would be like the angels in heaven who are celibate (Mk 12:18-25). Jesus' disciples were those who had left all—houses, parents, brothers, sisters, children, and fields—to follow Jesus (Matt 19:27-29), professing at least temporary celibacy. Therefore, this teaching is coherent with many others attributed to Jesus.

Summary on Chreias Studied. These chreias pictured Jesus on the campaign trail, recruiting followers who would leave all they had, contribute their wealth to the group that called itself "the poor," and accept all the hardships necessary to acquire the Kingdom of God. The demands were consistently rigorous: disciples would have no place to lay their heads; they could not wait until they had satisfactorily settled their family responsibilities; they could not put their hand to the plow and look back. As their movement progressed, the temple at Jerusalem would be destroyed. Only those who did God's will (that is, followed Jesus) would be blessed. The movement could not be deterred because Herod seemed to pose a threat, neither could the disciples be expected to keep still in order to avoid a confrontation with Rome. Fishermen were asked to leave their nets and come fish for men. Laborers were urgently needed in this program, but that did not prompt Jesus to lower the standards. Only those who entered the straight gate would be saved. When women wept, Jesus told them to weep for themselves. These chreias pictured the same kind of person throughout. He had a purpose which he considered the most important in the world, and he used extreme pressure to recruit others to enter into the task required to bring about its fulfillment. Those who followed him had to commit themselves absolutely to Jesus' goal of acquiring the Kingdom of Heaven. We will now examine some parables which seem to teach something similar.

Parables on Pressure

The Returning Spirit. "When an unclean spirit goes out from the man, it goes through waterless places seeking rest, and it does not find [it]. Then it says, 'To my house I will return from which I have departed,' and when it has come and finds [it] empty, swept, and put in order, then it goes and brings along with it seven other spirits more evil than itself, and after they have entered they will dwell there. Then the last condition of that man is worse than the first. Thus also it will be with this evil generation" (Matt 12:43-45; Lk 11:24-26).

This parable, hypothetically, could be applied to many possible situations. Cope[55] has shown how the author who organized the structure of Matthew used this parable to strengthen his whole argument against the Pharisees and "this generation," whereas Luke used it differently. Demons, unclean spirits, the devil, and Satan constituted the evil forces that caused people to be ill, to have erroneous points of view, to sin, or to suffer in any way. Anyone speaking in opposition to the demons or evil spirits could be applying his arguments to almost any evil he opposed. Since the gospel writers themselves organized the parables to express their own arguments, it is not fair to learn from the wider context the message of the parable for Jesus.

It is necessary to learn what question Jesus was being asked that prompted this parable, if we are going to be able to determine what his mes-

---

[55]O. Lamar Cope, *Matthew a Scribe Trained for the Kingdom of Heaven* (Washington, 1976), pp. 32-44.

sage was. Unfortunately, that information is no longer available. Therefore, it will be necessary to conjecture the most likely context on some other basis, understanding that this is circular reasoning. We will, then, end up with the message needed for our own argument just the way Matthew and Luke did. If we were to begin with different assumptions, we would obtain different results from this parable. What assumptions will start the process and why? It seems that the most nearly objective method would be to learn from the chreias already studied what Jesus was doing, what his goals and answers were, and from that, conjecture a similar situation for this parable. In the chreias just discussed, Jesus appeared on the campaign trail, urging people to leave everything they owned and had, follow him and prepare themselves to obtain the Kingdom of God. Therefore, it would seem likely that he told parables at this time and in the same occasions to argue his cases.

Given that assumption, the parable of the unclean spirit would apply to someone like the volunteer who was convinced of Jesus' program but wanted time to complete his responsibilities first, or the people who began to follow him until he told them they would have to accept a celibate way of life in order to be his disciples. Once they had rejected their former way of life, they should not hesitate to become active in Jesus' program. Otherwise they would soon drift back to the place they were before but with still more resistance to the movement underway to obtain the Kingdom of God. If, however, it was assumed that Jesus had just healed a person by driving out the demons, he might have been speaking of ways to retain good health, but the chreias did not picture Jesus teaching good health practices, primarily. If he healed people, it was so they could be admitted into the Kingdom of Heaven. The evil spirits Jesus was opposing were those that prevented the Kingdom of God from being inaugurated. This is consistent with the chreias discussed and also with the parables that follow in which the central item of Jesus' concern is given in the parables themselves.

The Hidden Treasure. ''The Kingdom of Heaven is like a treasure hidden in the field, which a man, when he found [it] hid [it], and from his joy goes and sells whatever he has and buys that field'' (Matt 13:44).

This is a very apt parable. Jesus compared a kingdom, which is a geographical territory ruled by a king, to a field with treasure hidden in it. When the kingdom is distorted to mean something else, the parable loses its force. Schniewind, for instance, tried to compare ''God's rule'' (*Gottes*

Herrschaft) to the field with a treasure in it.[56] In what way is governing activity compared to a field? Governing might be compared to teaching, fighting, shipping, or some other activity, but not a field. A person can buy a field with a treasure in it. Would Schniewind and others have us believe that we can buy God's services in the same way? Once the real estate transfer has been made, the purchaser knows that the Kingdom of Heaven is his. How can anyone know that God's rule is his or hers?

Derrett argued that there was a technically legal way in which a person might successfully find and keep the treasure, but the day laborer, who would have found the treasure, according to Derrett and Jeremias, probably would not have known that. Neither would he have had enough money to buy it. Even if he had, Derrett said, it "is hardly loving one's neighbor as oneself."[57] This, however, is concentrating too much on the validity of the parable itself without trying to find the intention of the parable.

In this parable the objects compared are given: the Kingdom of Heaven is the promised land which is like a field with a treasure in it. This is the place to begin. In code language, Jesus was telling his listeners the tremendous value of the promised land in the hands of God's chosen people. Once acquired, then, from this land Jews could mine minerals, obtain food, and acquire wealth that is not obvious to the person who just looks at the surface of the ground. Palestine has always been a highly valued territory. Great nations must cross this land bridge to communicate with one another from Egypt to Assyria, Syria, Persia, and all other Middle Eastern countries. Trade caravans had to cross this land, each one being taxed heavily for this passage. Large countries would pay heavily for permission to use it as a buffer state.

Neither the earlier Hebrews nor the later Jews ever acquired this land from a "neighbor," meaning a fellow covenanter. They took it by force from the Canannites and the Syrian Greeks. Once it was in their possession they defended it with military weapons. It was not a question of legality. According to the Canaanite law, the Hebrew invasion was not approved. Hasmoneans were not guilt-ridden because they had bargained too sharply with

---

[56]Schniewind, *Matthäus*, p. 173; also J. D. Kingsbury, *The Parables of Jesus in Matthew 13* (St. Louis, 1977), p. 116.

[57]J. D. M. Derrett, *Law in the New Testament* (London, c1970), pp. 4-14, Jeremias, *Parables*, p. 139.

the Syrian Greeks. Jews negotiated for the land once with Cyrus of Persia. At that time, they were in Babylonia and agreed to ''cooperate'' in various ways that would help Cyrus take Babylon on the condition that Jews would then be allowed to return under Persian support and finance. Once there, they began to build walls, so as to be able to retain the land, legally or otherwise.

Therefore, the parable of the treasure in the field is a very apt metaphor. There was no concern about neighborliness or business ethics. The person who recognized the treasure got the field by any method possible and then held on to it with all the forces at his or her disposal. With all that treasure, the purchaser could hire quite a sizeable police force to defend it.

This was parabolic language or riddle language. To those who knew the high value Jews placed on the promised land and their way of acquiring it, Jesus' language would be understood. The rest would think this was just a nice story. The sense of urgency, pressure, and high value placed on the Kingdom of God and the sacrifices necessary to acquire it is present both in this parable and also in the chreias studied. There is a consistent message throughout.

The Precious Pearl. ''Again the Kingdom of Heaven is like a merchant seeking choice pearls, and after he had found one very precious pearl, he went away and sold all that he had and bought it'' (Matt 13:45-46).

This has often been recognized as a ''twin'' to the parable of the treasure in a field. Glombitza observed that these parables are separated in the Gospel of Thomas, but, following Bultmann, concluded that Matthew has them together the way they were originally.[58] It is not certain whether Matthew has them correctly organized or not. They may have been told at the same situation, but at different times. Matthew organized his materials very well according to a well-planned structure,[59] putting teachings together, miracles together, apocalyptic material together, etc. Therefore, he may have got them from separate sources and put them together because of the

---

[58]O. Glombitza, ''Der Perlenkaufmann,'' *NTS* 7 (1961): 153-61, also followed Bultmann in thinking that the parable of the fish net belonged with both of these. Glombitza's interpretation of all three of these as offering salvation to all overlooks the social and political situation in which they were told. Wellhausen, *Matthei,* p. 70, also considered the forms in Matthew to be primary to those in the Gospel of Thomas.

[59] See Cope, *Matthew,* pp. 13-31, for an explanation of the way Matthew organized chapter 13.

similarity of form and message. Nonetheless, wherever or whenever Jesus told the parable of the pearl merchant, the message is the same as the parable of the treasure in the field. Both are compared to the same Kingdom of Heaven and both are used as analogies to express the very high value of that kingdom. Both indicate that there is no price too high to pay. The person who recognizes that it is the Kingdom of Heaven that can be acquired should give up everything he has to obtain it. This is precisely the message Jesus expressed in the chreias when he told people to leave families, jobs, and everything to which they were devoted and become his disciples. So far, there is no obvious incoherence in these teachings.

Counting the Cost. "Who among you, wanting to build a tower, will not first, after he has seated himself, count the cost [to see] if he has enough for the completion? Otherwise he might lay the foundation and not be able to finish. Then all those who observe will begin to mock him, saying, 'This man began to build and was not able to finish.' "

Or,

"What king, going out to engage in battle with another king will not first, after he has seated himself, hold counsel [to see] if he is able with ten thousand soldiers to resist the one coming against him with a hundred thousand? If he cannot, while he is still a great distance, he will send a gift of honor and ask terms of peace" (Lk 14:28-32).

Luke has these parables placed in a context showing the high price demanded for discipleship. This is coherent with the chreias that warned volunteers of the difficulties involved in this movement. The dead must bury their own dead and the one who puts his hand to the plow may not look back. Volunteers must leave their families and possessions and accept a celibate existence (Lk 14:25-26) to be one of Jesus' followers. Most scholars[60] think that this is the original context or at least one that is fair to the parables. These are twin parables that bear basically the same message, the only difference is that one deals with a private situation and the other with an international one. Both demand care and prudence. It is better to accept the

---

[60]Such as A. Schlatter, *Das Evangelium des Lukas* (Stuttgart, 1960), p. 344; M. J. Lagrange, *Evangile selon Saint Luc* (Paris, 1941), pp. 410-12. O. L. Cope, "Matthew 25:31-46 'The Sheep and the Goats,' " *NT* 11 (1969): 31-44, has correctly understood the teaching of the parable. His conclusion that Matthew wrote the parable as an indigenous part of Matt 24-25, however, does not follow. This editor artfully put together this and other parables in these chapters, but that does not require composition on his part.

situation as it is than to begin something that makes more demands than the person can bear. This is true of discipleship. It is also true in military science. The Hasmoneans frequently attacked forces that outnumbered them many times and were successful. Therefore, in terms of Jewish guerrilla tactics the ratio of one to ten would be one to take into consideration. Another possible context for this parable may have been at a time when Jesus was being urged on by his closest supporters to begin action. When would these things take place? When would Jesus bring his opposition movement out into the open? At such a time Jesus may have told this parable to indicate that there was some basis for reticence so long as the Son of man had no place to lay his head. For awhile, at least, they had better strengthen their forces and wait for a better opportunity.

The following judgment scene is important background for the next parable. After the ''beasts'' had all been described in succession, the little horn from the last beast, which represented Antiochus Epiphanes, king of the Greek empire (fourth beast) was speaking great things. Instead of describing in historical terms the way the Maccabees led the rebellion against the Greeks until Judas succeeded in recovering the temple area and rededicating the temple, the author of Daniel described the whole event mythologically, in theophanic terms, showing the clouds of heaven as God's presence. Judas's victory was explained in terms of his winning a case in court, the verdict decreed was that he should be appointed leader, ''like a Son of man,'' or like a king. The drama reads as follows:

I was watching until thrones were placed, and the
Ancient of Days was seated.
His clothing was white as snow, and the hair
of his head was like pure wool
his throne was flames of fire, and its wheels, burning
fire; a river of fire shot out and went out before him
thousands of thousands served him, and myriads
of myriads rose up before him [in deference].
The judgment was held, and the books were opened.
I was watching then, because of the strong arguments
which the horn was speaking [in defense].
I kept watching until the beast was slain, its body
destroyed and given to be burned.
The rest of the beasts—their ruling authority
was removed, but they continued to live
for a season and a time.
I was observing visions in the night:

Now, look! with the clouds of heavens came one like a
Son of man up to the Ancient of Days.
He was ushered in before him, and [the verdict
was that] to him was given the ruling authority,
the glory, and a kingdom.
All peoples, nations, and languages would serve him.
His ruling authority would rule to an age, which
would not be repealed,
and his kingdom [would be one] which would not
be destroyed.   (Dan 7:9-14)

To keep anyone from confusing this with prose narrative of historical
events, the poem was presented as a vision in which the characters, although somewhat bizarre, could easily be identified by those who knew the
history of the Hasmonean period. The beasts were kings of various nations
that had ruled Israel after the fall of Jerusalem in 586 B.C.. last of these
kings was Antiochus Epiphanes, ruler of the Greek kingdom of Syria. Antiochus was the defendant in the trial who was ordered by the Judge to be
slain and his body, burned. The plaintiff was ''one like a Son of man'' who
was vindicated by this court judgment. He was the one who led the Maccabean Revolt and was the first leader of the nation of Israel after the temple
was rededicated. The same trial that pronounced a death sentence on Antiochus Epiphanes also awarded Judas the authority to rule over the glorious
kingdom of Israel. This was a patriotic and theological interpretation of the
Maccabean victory. Since the Maccabean victory was celebrated every Hanukkah, the *dramatis personae* were well understood by Jesus' audience.
Sheep and Goats.

When the Son of man comes
in his glory, and all his messengers with him,
then he will sit on his glorious throne,
and all nations will be gathered before him
then he will separate them one from another,
just as a shepherd separates the sheep from the goats;
and he will place the sheep on his right,
but the goats on his left.
then the king will say to those at his right,
        'Come, blessed of my Father, inherit the Kingdom
        prepared for you from the foundation of the world.
        For I was hungry and you gave me [something] to eat,
        and I was thirsty and you quenched my thirst;

I was a stranger and you gave me hospitality, naked,
and you clothed me;
I was sick and you cared for me, in prison,
and you visited me.'
Then the righteous will answer him, saying,
'When did we see you sick or in prison,
and we came to you?'
Then, by reply, the king will say to them,
'Whatever you did to one of the least of my
brothers you did to me.'
Then he will say to those on his left,
'Leave me, you cursed, into eternal fire prepared
for the devil and his angels.
For I was hungry, and you gave me no[thing] to eat;
I was thirsty, and you did not quench my thirst;
I was a stranger, and you gave me no hospitality;
naked, and you did not clothe me,
sick and in prison, and you did not care for me.'
Then they will answer, saying,

'Lord, when did we see you hungry or thirsty or
a stranger or naked or sick or in prison, and
we did not minister to you?'
Then, by reply, he will say to them,

'Truly, I tell you,
whatever you did to one of
the least, you did to me.'
Then, these will go away to eternal punishment,
but the righteous into eternal life.   (Matt 25:31-46)

This poem is one of the most elaborate and extensive of the parables attributed to Jesus. It is a unified poem that cannot be reduced successfully, layer by layer, the way Robinson has conjectured.[61] It is too carefully formulated to have been composed on the spur of the moment. It appears to be a literary unit composed with the intention of using it again and again. This is a picture, like the poem in Dan 7, of a dramatic judgment scene after the battle. The difference is that the Son of man, in this scene, is also the judge who has his accompanying messengers. Whereas the divine judgment scene

---

[61]J. A. T. Robinson, "The 'Parable' of the Sheep and the Goats," *NTS* 2 (1956):225-37.

in Daniel pictures the Son of man as the plaintiff receiving his kingdom at the same time the saints of the Most High receive the kingdom, this scene pictures the Son of man after that judgment had taken place, determining who would be accepted as the saints of the Most High. The war was over; the Son of man had been enthroned as king; and then he was about to pass judgment on the people who had participated in the conflict in some way. This is a realistic picture.

After the final battle of a war, it was customary for the leading general to pass judgment on the fate of the participants. After the fall of Jerusalem, for instance, the Romans separated the surviving Jews and decided which should be killed, which were to be sent to slavery in Egypt, and which would be led in procession to Rome. Only Jews who were also Roman citizens were released (*BJ* 6.378-434). After that judgment had been carried out, Titus set up his judgment seat and passed judgment on those who had shown special valor during the war. These were given special medals, promotions, and financial awards (*BJ* 7.2-16). This is the kind of judgment scene the parable pictured.

The theme of this parable is "to the victors belong the spoils." This may have been a parable that Jesus told many times while he was recruiting those who would be trained to recruit others. These "fishers of men" would need hospitality and provision as they traveled through Palestine recruiting followers for this new movement. Therefore, Jesus had this carefully prepared parable to suggest to the people to whom his recruiters would return how it would be with his supporters and his adversaries in the Kingdom of Heaven. At a time later in his program it became evident that not all cities supported his program, so he promised them destruction on the day of judgment. These included his own home town of Capernaum and the neighboring towns of Chorazin and Bethsaida (Matt 11:20-24).[62]

When Judas the Maccabee, nearly two hundred years earlier, asked permission to pass through Emphron, people blocked the gates with stones. Judas laid siege to the city, took it, killed all males, burned the city, and then passed through, walking over the top of all the dead bodies in the road (*Ant.*

---

[62]Dodd said he failed to understand what this meant. It seemed to be expressed in terms of war and social upheaval, but why should Galilean cities be more destructively treated than Tyre and Sidon in the upcoming Roman war. Dodd did not see that Jesus was not saying *Roman* troops would punish these cities, but that *he* would. See C. H. Dodd, *The Parables of the Kingdom* (London, 1960), p. 82.

12.346-347). The parable of the "sheep and the goats" reflects similar possibilities for non-cooperating villages. The same kind of pressure and seriousness that was evident in the chreia dealing with recruitment is obvious here and seems to point to the same person in a similar situation.

It is unlikely that this parable was composed by the church after A.D. 70 or appropriated from Jewish materials attributed to Jesus at that time. After A.D. 70, all attempts at acquiring a kingdom had failed. There continued to be Jewish uprisings in other parts of the Roman Empire, but there was no longer much hope of overthrowing Rome. All the political, messianic pretenders had failed. It seems very unlikely that Christians would have composed new literature that falsely attributed to Jesus predictions like this that obviously were not fulfilled. It seems much more likely that it was actually delivered at an earlier time, when hopes of victory over Rome were still high. That was at the time Jesus lived.

The logic of considering action done to Jesus' recruiters is the legal concept of agency. A man's agent or apostle was legally identical with the man himself, as men and women are today in most court systems. In royal terms, a king's ambassadors had the same authority to negotiate in behalf of a king as the king himself. When the Ammonites thought David's messengers were really spies, they shaved off half the beards of each and cut off their garments at their hips and sent them away (2 Sam 10:1-5). This was like treating David himself this shameful way, so David sent Joab to conquer the Ammonites (2 Sam 10:6-14). Jesus indicated by this parable that he would consider the treatment of his ambassadors the same way.

The Satisfied Soul. "The field of a certain rich man was productive, and he pondered, saying to himself, 'What shall I do, because I have no place in which to gather my produce?' Then he said, 'I will do this: I will tear down my barns and build bigger [barns], and I will gather there all my wheat and goods. Then I will say to my soul, "Soul, you have many good things laid up for many years. Rest, eat, drink, and be merry." ' But God said to him, 'Fool, this night I will take your soul from you. Then whose will be the things you have prepared?' Thus [it will be for] the one who lays up treasures for himself and is not rich with reference to God" (Lk 12:16-21).

Jesus began recruiting followers when he had no supplies to arm or house his troops. This means he had to recruit finances at the same time he recruited leaders. To do this Jesus had to go where the money was. This is probably the reason Jesus mingled with the wealthy tax collectors and sinners. It was to such people as these that Jesus told this parable with the same seriousness and sense of urgency that he expressed when he confronted those who thought they were willing to follow him wherever he went. Those who would not leave everything to follow Jesus could at least give up their money to support the movement. Jesus reminded the rich that it was more important to have their wealth in the ''Treasury of merits,'' being rich with reference to God rather than to have their money invested in banks and produce. One who had taken pains to ''redeem'' himself from poverty but was not religiously solvent was not at all prepared for the future. In fact he was a fool.

This parable seems coherent with the chreias that were related to the urgency of Jesus' task of recruiting followers. There seems no reason to think any Christian at a later time composed this parable in Jesus' name.

Values that Last. ''A certain man was wealthy. He wore purple garments and fine linen, feasting sumptuously every day. A certain poor man, named Lazarus, was left at his gate, covered with sores and wanting to be filled from the things that fell from the rich man's table, but the dogs came and licked his sores. Now it happened that the poor man died and was taken by angels to Abraham's bosom. The wealthy man also died and was buried. In Hades, he lifted up his eyes, being in torment, and saw Abraham at a distance and Lazarus in his bosom. Then he cried out and said, 'Father Abraham, have mercy upon me, and send Lazarus to dip the tip of his finger in water and cool my tongue, because I am tortured by this flame.' Then Abraham said, 'Son, remember that you received your good things in your lifetime, and Lazarus, likewise, misfortunes; now he is comforted here; but you are tormented. Besides all of this, there is a great chasm between you and us, so that those who want to cross over from here to you cannot, nor can they cross from you to us.' Then he said, 'I ask you then, Father, that you send him to the house of my father, for I have five brothers, so that he may testify to them, so that they may not come to this place of torture.' Abraham said, 'They have Moses and the prophets. Let them hear them.' He answered, 'No, Father Abraham, but if someone from the dead will come to them, they will repent.' He said to him, 'If they will not listen to Moses and the prophets, they will not repent even if someone were to rise from the dead' '' (Lk 16:19-31).

This seems to be another parable designed to motivate wealthy tax collectors and other businessmen to give generously to the program Jesus had organized that called itself ''the poor.'' The picture of the ''dogs'' that licked Lazarus' sores probably meant that even Gentiles pitied Lazarus and cared for him in minor ways while Jews let him die of starvation and illness.[63] Originally, the parable may not have included the dialogue about the brothers. This may have been added to the parable later by Christians in conflict with Jews who had not become believers even after Jesus had been raised from the dead.[64]

The Thief at Night. ''Now, you may be sure that if that householder had known at which watch the thief would come, he would have guarded and would not have permitted his house to be pillaged. For this reason you also must be prepared, because the Son of man comes at a time when you do not think [likely]'' (Matt 24:42-44; Lk 12:39-40).

There were many things for a pretending king to consider before he took action to attack the ruling power directly. If this was a Jewish messiah, he would also have to study extensively to learn whether or not this was God's will. He would need to study the Book of Daniel, Second Isaiah, Zechariah, and Exodus to learn how things happened successfully in the past. What signs were there that resembled the conditions just before the Maccabean Revolt? What about the calendar? Had Jews been ''wandering in the wilderness'' for the last forty years? Or had they been in ''captivity'' four hundred and thirty years, as in Egypt? Had the temple been defiled as it had been by Antiochus Epiphanes? Were the Romans suffering from a great deal of internal conflict and change of leadership as Syria was at the time the Hasmoneans rebelled?

A good messiah would study these items carefully, but he would also have to watch for the exact moment to act when the international and local conditions were just right to promise success. Such a time as this seemed to have arrived to the three pretending kings of Israel when Archelaus left Jerusalem unattended while he went to Rome to obtain political control of his office. These three were Judas, Simon, and Athrongaeus (*BJ* 2.55-65). Each one probably considered himself to be the Son of man, destined to lead Israel to independence from Rome. Each had probably organized people ready to follow whenever the leader chose to fight. In the meantime,

---

[63]R. Dunkerky, ''Lazarus,'' *NTS* 5 (1958/59):321-27 held that there must be some relationship between the Lazarus of Lk 16:19, 31 and the Lazarus raised in Jn 11.

[64]O. Glombitza, ''Der Reiche Mann und der Arme Lazarus,'' *Nov* 12 (1970):166-80, thought the parable entirely reflects Jewish-Christian relationships after A.D. 70.

they all went about their normal routines, not telling anyone related to the government that they were preparing an insurrection. To followers such as these who were impatient to get underway, or at least to be told about how long they would have to wait, Jesus told this parable. They should not lose their zeal. Neither they nor Jesus could know just when they would be called upon to act, but whenever that time came, he needed followers who were prepared to respond at a moment's notice. This advice is consistent with the urgency of the chreias that made extreme demands on those who wanted to follow Jesus.

Left Out. "Whenever the householder arises and closes the door, you also will begin to stand outside and knock on the door, saying, 'Sir, open for us.' Then he will say in reply, 'I do not know from where you have come.' Then you will begin to say, 'We ate and drank in your presence, and you taught in our streets.' Then, speaking, he will say to you, 'I do not know from where you have come. Leave me, all [you] workers of iniquity.' There will be there weeping and gnashing of teeth, when you see Abraham, Isaac, and Jacob, and all the prophets in the Kingdom of God, but you cast out. And they will come from the East, from the West, from the North, and the South, and they will recline in the Kingdom of God, and Look! there are [people] of last [rank] who will be first and [people of] first rank who will be last" (Lk 13:25-30).

There seem to be two parables here that the editor combined into one. The first parable is about the householder who closed the door at a certain point, allowing no more admissions. The house is analogous to the Kingdom of Heaven, which, Jesus said, would be closed at some point so that all those who were slow joining ranks with Jesus may try unsuccessfully, after it is too late. The message here is one of urgency. People must act quickly; there is no time for taking care of a household first or any comparable demand.

The editorial note is the warning that there will be wailing and gnashing of teeth. Then follows the second parable about those diaspora Jews who come from foreign lands and take over the chief seats in the Kingdom of Heaven because the local Palestinian Jews have been too incompetent. This parable in Matthew has been appended to the story of the faithful centurion where it seems more appropriate (Matt 8:10-12). It looks as if Luke had access to Matthew's text and that he took Matthew's frequently used statement about wailing and gnashing of teeth from Matt 8:12 and used it here as a connecting sentence to attach the parable about diaspora Jews to a separate parable not found in Matthew.[65] The urgency here is directed to local Palestinian Jews to hurry and take over the required responsibilities of the movement before they should be edged out by Jews from foreign lands whose faithfulness would draw them to Palestine in the last days.

The Clever Steward. "Then he began to say to his disciples, 'A certain man was rich, who had a business manager. Now this [business manager] was reported to him as one who was acting carelessly with his funds. After he had summoned him [the business manager], he said to him, "What is this that I hear about you? Give an accounting of your work! For you may no longer act as business manager." The business manager said to himself, "What shall I do? For my employer is taking away the office of business manager from me. I am not strong enough to do manual labor, and I am ashamed to beg. I know what I will do so that when I am removed from the office of business management they will receive me into their homes." After he had invited each one of his employer's debtors, he said to the first, "How much do you owe my employer?" He answered, "A hundred measures of oil." He [the manager] said to him, "Take your bill; sit down and quickly write, 'Fifty.' " Then he said to the next, "How much do you owe?" He replied, "A hundred measures of wheat." [The manager] said to him, "Take your bill, and write, 'Eighty.' " Then the employer praised that crooked business manager, because he had acted wisely' " (Lk 16:1-18).

This parable has caused Christians a great deal of distress because it pictures Jesus in some way admiring a crooked businessman for his shrewd action in providing for himself at the expense of someone else.[66] Like many others, we will try to make sense out of this parable in the business world of Jesus' time. The business manager evidently worked for someone else engaged in loaning money at a very high interest. This was customary for Gentiles and Jews loaning to Gentiles. Jews were prohibited from taking interest from one another. In the Lukan context, this parable prompted the comment that the children of this age (i.e. Gentiles and Jewish minglers) were wiser than the children of light (Jews).

---

[65]Contra Perrin, *Rediscovering,* p. 161, who said, "There can be no doubt that Luke has, in this respect, the more primitive version of the story."

[66]Plummer, *ICC Luke,* p. 380.

In a country ruled by some outside power, there was not much feeling of need for ethical restraints in dealings with Romans or their Jewish agents in Palestine. Jews who compromised with Romans became tax collectors and held other public offices which were for them very profitable, but it required them to betray their own people and oppress them in various ways. Such people were called "harlots," "sinners," "children of darkness," "Gentiles," and other uncomplimentary titles. People who held these offices were considered "unrighteous," and if one of them should lose his position, there would be no Jews to provide for him. It had been a long tradition of Jews to look after one another so that no fellow Jew would be in desperate need. The person who chose to take advantage of opportunities to get rich by mingling with Gentiles realized that he was forfeiting the security and insurance that belonged to his heritage.

Suddenly confronted with the situation that he was about to lose his position, where then could he turn? Like Jacob fleeing from Laban or the prodigal son in desperation, the crooked business manager had to consider how he could get back into the family. While he still held office, he thought of all the Jews who owed his employer money. These were contacts he still had. If he worked it right, doors might be reopened for him. It is possible that this business manager had overcharged these debtors, anyway. It was not uncommon for tax collectors to add to the taxes Rome required. Josephus said Herod Agrippa once was forced to borrow money through an agent, Marsayas. Herod had to sign a bond for twenty thousand drachmae, although he received twenty-five hundred drachmae less. This may have been Marsayas' added interest (*Ant.* 18.157). If the business manager had done something like that, then, what could he lose in his plan? He was soon to be fired, anyway. After that happened, he would not be able to collect these excessive interests for himself. If he called in these Jews who owed his employer money and reduced their loans by the amount he himself had added for his own wealth, then his employer would receive as much as that for which he had bargained and the business manager would forfeit only the excess interest in exchange for good feeling and approval from his Jewish contacts.

It is also possible that he had awarded his Jewish contacts money that really belonged to his employer. This would have endeared him to his Jewish friends but it might not have gained for him also the praise of his employer. The business manager had evidently done something before this that won for him the disapproval of his employer. It might have been precisely this: he had charged excessive interests in order to line his own pocket. Had he quickly acted to correct this situation, he might recover his position thereby. Although the employer praised him, there is no indication that he reemployed him, as most scholars assume. The point of the parable was not how to get a position back but how to get reinstated into the Jewish community.

Jesus directed most of his parables to these rich tax collectors and sinners. He evidently was successful in persuading some of them to repent and become loyal nationalists, giving up all of their wealth to his movement and undertaking vows of poverty, celibacy, and obedience. While addressing these same wealthy people who mingled with Romans, Jesus may have used this parable to urge them to act quickly to amend their ways. If Rome were ever successfully driven off the land, where would they turn? They were not at that time beloved by other Jews so they had better act to gain readmittance into the Jewish community. Of course, the best thing to do would be to give up their positions and support the nationalistic movement. The second best possibility would be to use their positions to help the movement from behind the scenes. This would involve diverting Roman money into Jewish purses the way the Israelites did just before they left Egypt. Or, they could utilize their positions to strengthen the Jewish nationalist movement the way Moses or Nehemiah had done. They could also use their influence to provide better conditions for other Jews the way Esther and Daniel had done under foreign domination.

When tax collectors came to John the Baptist, repenting, John told them not to collect more taxes than they were required by their Roman overlords. Jewish soldiers in the Roman army were told not to rob other Jews by violence or false accusation and to be satisfied with the pay they received from Romans (Lk 3:12-14). This may have been precisely the advice the crooked businessman took when he saw that his position was threatened. The general message of this parable may have been to all Jews in similar positions, reminding them that all of their positions would be threatened if there was a revolution. Therefore, they had better make friends with loyal nationalist Jews, even if they were not sympathetic with the movement. It was the prudent thing to do. Thus understood, this parable exhibits the same kind of urgency and pressure that is apparent in the chreias and parables examined so far.

The next parable seems to have been patterned after the following parable in the OT:

Isaiah 5:1-7:

I will sing to my beloved a song of my beloved
with respect to his vineyard:
'My beloved had a vineyard on a very fertile hill.
he spaded it, removed the stones,
and planted it with vines.
He built a tower in the midst of it
and carved out a wine vat in it.
He expected it to produce grapes,
but it yielded wild grapes.
Now, you who dwell in Jerusalem, you man of Judah,
pass judgment between me and my vineyard.
What should be done still with my vineyard that I
have not done?
Why have I expected it to produce grapes
and it produced wild grapes?
Now I will inform you what I will do to my vineyard:
Remove its hedge, and it will be burned;
break down its wall, and it will be walked on.
I will make it a desolation: it will not be
pruned or cultivated
briars and thorns will grow up.
I will command the clouds
against rain falling on it,'
for the vineyard of the Lord of armies
is the house of Israel,
the man of Judah is his pleasant plant.
I expected justice, but there was bloodshed,
righteousness, but there was a scream

This is part of the OT background reflected in the following parable:

Landlords and Tenants. ''A man was a landlord, who planted a vineyard, surrounded it with a wall, dug a wine press in it, and built a tower.
Then he rented it out to tenants and went away. When the time of the harvest
approached, he sent his servants to the tenants to collect his rent. Then the
tenants seized the servants: some they whipped, some they killed, and others they stoned. Again he sent different servants, more than at first, and they
did the same to them. Afterwards, he sent to them his son, saying, 'They
will respect my son.' When the tenants saw the son, they said among themselves, 'This is the heir. Come, let us kill him, and we will have his inher-

itance.' Then they seized him, threw him out of the vineyard, and killed him. Now, when the master of that vineyard comes, what will he do to those tenants? They said to him, 'He will utterly destroy them, and he will rent out the vineyard to other tenants, who will give him his rent on time' " (Matt 21:33-34; Mk 12:1-11; Lk 20:9-18).

This parable is more complex than any other parable attributed to Jesus.[67] It is found, not only in all three synoptic gospels, but also in the Gospel of Thomas with some variations among these sources. It seems quite likely to have been originally patterned after the poem in Isa 5 which was a threat to Judah and Israel for their unfaithfulness. All of the gospels have included this parable in contexts that seem to interpret Jesus as the son who was rejected. This is undoubtedly the decision of the church after Jesus' crucifixion. Presuming that the parable is now out of context, but is basically the same as the way Jesus told it, we will try to conjecture its initial function in Jesus' time, admittedly with no sense of certainty.

This parable seems to warn against trying to take the law into one's own hands and taking by force more than was in the initial contract. Since Jesus was recruiting followers who were devoted, faithful, committed, and interested in participating in a political movement to acquire the Kingdom of God at the same time that there were many other zealotish movements being undertaken with the same goal in mind, it would not be surprising to find some of these "fishers of men" less patient than Jesus. Some would have urged Jesus to begin the revolution at every feast, prepared or not. Some may have even considered taking over Jesus' leadership position so that the action could go on in the way they wanted. Jesus probably needed to remind them that he alone was their Master and they were all just brothers. Jesus seemed not only pressing for commitment and showing impatience with those not ready to begin at once, but he also seemed to be waiting for a sign from God to tell him how to act and when. Others may not have been so patient and to have needed the teaching that improper action might not reap

---

[67]For an understanding of the social and economic situaton against which this parable was composed, see M. Hengel, "Das Gleichnis von den Weingartneren Mc 12:1-12 im Lichte der Zenopapyri und der rabbinischen Gleichnis," *ZNW* 59 (1968):1-39. Hengel concluded that this parable did not need a post A.D. 70 date. See also Darrett, *Law*, pp. 296-309; and J. E. and R. R. Newell, "The Parable of the Wicked Tenants," *Nov* 14 (1972):226-37, noted that Jesus did not criticize the goal of the tenants—only their methods (p. 236). It seems to have been directed against the zealots who were using force for land reform (*BJ* 2.426).

the intended results, but only final destruction and failure. There are other parables with this same basic teaching.

Trustworthy Servant.

Who, then, is the faithful and prudent servant whom his employer set over his household, so that he would give to [the other servants] their food at the proper time. Blessed is that servant who, when his employer comes, he will find him doing just that. I tell you under oath that he will appoint him as administrator over all his possessions. But if that wicked servant says to himself, 'My employer is held up,' and he begins to strike his fellow servants, and eats and drinks with drunkards,
the employer of that servant will come
on a day when he does not expect,
in an hour when he does not know.
Then he will cut him in two,
and place his share with the hypocrites.   (Matt 24:45-51)

This is another business management type of parable, which is another indication that Jesus was in communication with wealthy businessmen who understood what was involved in this kind of administration. Any manager of large business finds it necessary to delegate authority to subordinate officials. If he has been in business very long, he has had experience in trusting the wrong people with responsibility. The sooner he finds this to be the case, the less damage will be caused. On the other hand, when he finds a faithful administrator who is responsible even when he is not under observation, he will surely find a way to use his talents more fully. This will involve a promotion. The word rendered "servant" here has a wide possibility of meanings in Greek. A "servant" could have been almost anyone in a subordinate position. Context alone defines the person's role. A servant might have been a slave who did unskilled manual work, but he may instead have been a high ranking official, so long as he was still responsible to someone with higher authority. For instance, a king's ambassador or highest ranking general was a servant. In this parable, the employer seems to have been some person involved in business who had many employees working for him. The "servant" who would either have been faithful or wicked, was a supervisor or superintendent in charge of this particular unit.

Now the question arises, "Why did Jesus tell the parable?" Since the point of the story hinged on whether the "servant" was faithful or wicked, there may have been a time in his organization and recruiting when he had to entrust part of his management to subordinate officials, such as apostles.

When he first recruited these ''fishers of men'' the urgency of the program was evident. He was planning to recruit, organize, and act quickly because the time was fulfilled. As time went on, it may have required occasional pep talks to maintain this same peak of readiness. As eager as Jesus was to act, he had to wait for the opportune moment to strike. He needed a sign from Heaven to show him when to begin, so he could not assure his subordinate officials that this would all take place in two weeks or six months. He could only tell them to keep on doing what they were assigned to do and be ready when called. This administration parable was evidently one that they would have understood, and this makes sense against a program addressed to such people as tax collectors and other businessmen as these leaders had been before they followed Jesus. This is a slightly different emphasis from the other chreias and parables that were addressed to people being recruited and being told the extreme demands required. This parable seems to have been addressed to those who had already been recruited to remember their original contract and sense of urgency. The demands were still great and the consequences, extensive.

Talents. ''Watch, then, because you do not know the day nor the hour. For it is like a man who went on a journey. He called his servants and entrusted to them his possessions, to the one he gave five talents, to another, two, and to the third, one—each according to his ability. Then he went away on his journey. The one who had received five talents went at once, invested them and gained an additional five. Likewise, the [one who had received] two, gained an additional two. But the one who had received one went out and dug [a hole in] the ground and hid his master's silver. After a long time, the master of those servants comes and holds a reckoning with them. The one who had taken five talents came and brought an additional five talents, saying, 'Sir, you have given me five talents. Look, I have gained another five talents.' His master said to him, 'Well done, good and faithful servant. You have been faithful over a few things. I will set you over many. Enter into the joy of your master.' The one [who had taken] two talents said, 'Sir, you have given me two talents. Look, I have gained an additional two.' His master said to him, 'Well done, good and faithful servant. You have been faithful over a few things. I will set you over many. Enter into the joy of your master.' Then the one who had taken the one talent came and said, 'Sir, I knew you, that you are a hard man, harvesting where you have not sown and gathering where you have not scattered, and, since I was afraid, I went away and hid your talent in the ground. See, you have your own [talent].'

Then his master, in reply, said to him, 'Wicked and cowardly servant! You knew that I harvested where I have not sown and gathered where I have not scattered. Then you were obliged to give my silver to the money changers, and when I came I would have acquired my [silver] with interest. Take, then, the talent from him and give it to the one who has ten talents, for

> to the one who has [interest]
>> shall be given everything,
>> and he will abound,
> but to the one who has no [interest],
>> even that [capital] which he has
>> will be taken from him.   (Matt 25:13-20; Lk 19:12-27)

Derrett[68] correctly observed that in the investment business, it is much easier to double a large amount of money than a small amount. The one with the one talent would have had to work much harder than the one with the five talents and that was part of the problem. The one with one talent felt that he had been slighted, so he sabotaged the program, planning to teach his employer a lesson. The employer had not given him enough capital with which to work and it was not worth his own time and investment to take the risks involved for the small amount of possible profits he might receive. The technical problem of taking something from a person who has nothing seems illogical, all by itself. Here it means simply that the one who had not increased his investment was relieved of his capital.

Like the parable of the trustworthy servant, this parable deals with a personnel problem. Leaders who had once been businessmen and tax collectors would understand all of the implications involved. The difference between their previous occupation and their current responsibilities as subordinate officials in Jesus' campaign is that their positions in the empire had changed. At one time, *they* had been top leaders; now they had to take positions that seemed beneath their dignity. Jesus had to remind them of their former business logic in order to keep them using all their talents and skills. Jesus had once called them to give up a great deal to help recover the Kingdom of God. They had been willing then and the need was as great as ever. There was no time to deal with sabotage. Every single skill, every single coin, and every single moment was needed. The campaign pressures were still on, just as they were when these leaders had first responded.

---

[68]Darrett, *Law,* p. 26.

Watching and Waiting. ''The Kingdom of Heaven is like ten virgins, who took their lamps and went out to meet the bridegroom. Five of them were foolish and five were prudent. The foolish ones took the lamps, but they did not take oil with them. The wise ones took oil in their vessels with their lamps. As the time for the bridegroom to come was delayed, they all nodded and fell asleep. Then, in the middle of the night, a cry went out, 'Look! the bridegroom. Go out to meet him!' All those virgins arose and prepared their lamps. The foolish ones said to the prudent ones, 'Give us some of your oil, because our lamps have burned out.' The prudent ones said by reply, 'No. There may not be enough for the both of us. Instead, go to the market and buy your own.' While they were going to buy oil, the bridegroom came, and those who were ready went in with him to the wedding chamber, and the door was closed. Later on, the rest of the virgins came, saying, 'Sir, Sir, open for us!' But he, in reply, said, 'I tell you under oath, I do not know you' '' (Matt 25:1-12).

The details of a wedding ceremony in NT times against which this parable makes sense are no longer known. The virgins seem to have been waiting at night in the home of the bride to usher in the bridegroom, whereas it is assumed that most bridegrooms came to the homes of the brides' fathers and took the brides to their own homes. Virgins may have been on hand to secure the tokens of virginity to take to the father of the bride to prove that his daughter was a virgin at the time of the marriage (Deut 22:13-21; Isa 64:5; Sifre 117a:234-118a:240). This may be one of those parables in which the imagery of the wedding situation was strained a little to make the point that Jesus really wanted to get across. He really was not speaking of weddings, but of the Messiah in relationship to the coming of the Kingdom of Heaven. He had been conducting his entire campaign to obtain the kingdom. It was a very difficult undertaking and would involve overthrowing the Roman government which was the greatest military force in the world at that time. He was not only trying to arouse the support of contemporary Jews, but he wanted those already aroused to stand by in readiness for the time when action was required. The message of ''Watching and Waiting'' is basically the same as the one of ''The Trustworthy Servant.'' The imagery is different. In the latter parable, the delay for the employer seemed to be a long time, perhaps many weeks or months, and the servant was expected to have been carrying on his assigned duties all that time. ''Watching and Waiting'' pictures virgins staying up all night with lamps with the requirement that they be ready at any moment—during one night only. Mark has compressed these two parables into one, giving the nonsensical picture of a man going away for an indefinite period of time and expecting the servant to be ready when he returned, always awake and watching at any time of the day or night. The vocabulary of Mark's abbreviated version of these two parables (Mk 13:34-36) is almost entirely included in Matthew's version (Matt 24:45-25:12). Matthew's version is reasonable, even if we do not know all of the wedding customs involved. Both bear the same message, even though the time involved is different. Those who consider Mark to be the earliest gospel find this problem difficult to explain.

Both parables were probably addressed to leaders who had already been recruited and were being encouraged to be prepared for the time when the Messiah (Jesus) declared his plans openly and entered the Kingdom of Heaven with his closest associates.[69]

Unworthy Servants. "Which of you, having a servant, plowing or herding sheep, who, after he has come in from the field, will say to him, 'Quickly come and rest!'? Rather, will he not say to him, 'Prepare something for me to eat! Then after you have girded yourself, serve me until I have eaten and drunk. After this, you also may eat and drink.' He will not thank the servant because he has done that which he has been commanded, will he? Thus, also you, when you have done everything that has been commanded you, say, 'We are useless servants. We have done that which we were required to do' " (Lk 17:7-10).

Plummer[70] said, "There is no need to seek for explanations as to why Jesus speaks to 'the poor Apostles' as if they had slaves who ploughed for them." He concluded that this parable was not addressed to the apostles. Lagrange[71] thought it was, but reasoned that the apostles could have understood this logic without themselves ever having been wealthy enough to have had servants. It is not the context that suggests that this was initially addressed to the apostles. Gospel editors could place parables in any context they wanted. It is the content of the parable itself that suggests the audience. The parable was addressed to people who once had servants, but who were at the time servants themselves. They had responded to a call that

[69]E. Linnemann, *Jesus*, p. 126, presumed this parable was written by and for the early church.

[70]Plummer, *ICC Luke*, p. 401.

[71]Lagrange, *Evangile*, p. 495.

required them to leave their families and their businesses, give up all their wealth, and accept conditions that were similar to those of a monastery. They did as they were commanded. They submitted completely to the demands of the Kingdom of Heaven. Jesus had to remind them of the terms of their contract, however, from time to time. This was not an equal opportunity program. There was no labor union involved to see that laborers were not exploited. This was no democracy. Jesus recruited people to help him establish the Kingdom of Heaven. This was to be a monarchy.

It is sometimes difficult for people who have once been in management themselves to have to accept the role of the lowliest employee. Apostles sometimes argued about who were the greatest and who would have chief seats in the Kingdom of Heaven. When that happened, Jesus reminded them again of the terms of celibate orders (Matt 20:20-27; Lk 22:24-26; Mk 16:42-43; Matt 10:25-26). They were to accept the positions they were given; they were to do the work assigned; they were servants, not masters, disciples, not teachers (Matt 10:24-25); they should be contented with this lot. If they had always been contented, however, Jesus would not have needed to have told this parable.

The Parables

Other scholars, like Dodd and Jeremias[72] have believed that the parables of Jesus represent a particularly trustworthy tradition, although they have not been able to say why. Clarity, simplicity, and masterful construction do not guarantee authenticity. The parables discussed here, however, have been shown to be coherent with the chreias which were also tested for authenticity by their coherence. Most of the parables, like the chreias, pictured Jesus engaged in campaign activity. He was giving responses to questions that were later made into chreias. These disclosed him making great demands on would-be disciples. At the same time he told parables that justified the same kind of demands. It was like selling all you had to buy a precious pearl or a field with a treasure. You needed to count the cost before accepting these demands. Soon the judgment would come and those who participated in the campaign would be rewarded, while the resisters would be punished. Then, there were other parables directed to Jesus' own staff,

---

[72]Dodd, *Parables*, p. 11.
Jeremias, *Parables*, p. 12

arguing to convince them to accept subordinate positions with difficult terms and be prepared when they are called upon to act. These all belong to the pressures of recruiting and organizing a staff or a campaign. But these are not all. The coherent chreias have the most reasons for being considered authentic teachings of Jesus. The parables that are coherent with the chreias should be considered next. There are still other teachings, which are neither chreias nor parables, which are coherent with both of these. These should also be recognized, although not with the same confidence as chreias or parables. Because they are in no special literary form to make preservation easy, they may have been corrupted or invented by the later church, but, on the other hand, they may not have been. Even if they were, their inclusion for consideration will not distort the teachings of Jesus. Some of these teachings that belong to the category of ''Campaigning under Pressure'' are as follows:

After Jesus had recruited ''fishers of men,'' he sent them out to recruit others, placing them under the same pressure as he himself felt. They were to go in haste, not heavily burdened with luggage, going only to the lost sheep of the house of Israel (Matt 10:5-10). They should not loiter; if they were not received, but instead, driven out, they should flee to the next town, continually announcing the coming of the Kingdom of Heaven (Matt 10:7, 23). The standards of discipleship were continued as demanding as before: Anyone who loved his family more than Jesus was not worthy of following him (Matt 10:37-38; Lk 14:26-27). They were not expected to have completed their travels through all the Judaean and Galilean cities before the Kingdom would come (Matt 10:23).

When he was reminded that in the understood order of expectations, Elijah was thought to come first and then the Messiah, Jesus replied that Elijah had already come, implying that this had been John the Baptist. Therefore it was later than they thought. Jesus was the one who followed John and was himself the Messiah (Matt 17:11-13; Lk 9:11-13). So urgent was the situation that Jews would be better off to have their hands or feet cut off or their eyes plucked out and still be admitted into this life than to be perfectly formed but be excluded (Matt 18:7-9; Mk 9:43-47). Only those who were willing to deny themselves and take up their crosses could follow Jesus (Matt 16:24). Those who wanted to save their souls would lose them; those who gave up their souls for Jesus' sake would find them (Matt (16:25). The sick were brought out to Jesus to be healed; he left them to go into other cities to preach, so urgent was his mission (Mk 1:36-38). He warned that he had not come to send peace but a sword, just as he assured the volunteer that he had no place to lay his head (Matt 10:34-35). Not only would followers have to leave families, but this program would divide family loyalties. At one point in the recruitment program, these "fishers of men" were sent out without provision to recruit more followers; at a later time, they were told to sell even part of their garments and buy weapons (Lk 22:35-36).

Throughout this chapter, we have been analyzing chreias, parables, and other teachings coherent with them that belonged to a classification dealing with recruitment pressures. All these teachings picture a leader who was engaged in a serious campaign, recruiting very dedicated followers for whom there promised little immediate reward and on whom great demands would be made. He asked people to give up all their wealth, their families, and their possessions for this program. Those who had positions in the Roman government were asked to use these positions and influence for the benefit of the Jewish nation.

Jesus' program involved acquiring the Kingdom of Heaven. This acquisition was so important that no ethical demand should be allowed to stand in the way of its attainment. These sayings are so consistent in message and manner that it would seem very difficult for anyone else to have composed parts of them and added them later in Jesus' name. Some of the teachings were related chronologically to Herod Antipas (Matt 14:1), tetrarch of Judah at Jesus' time. These show Jesus in conflict with the Roman authority—a normal situation for a pretending king, trying to reestablish the Davidic kingdom which Herod ruled. Very few of these messages would make sense after A.D. 70, when hopes of liberation had been crushed.

Summary

Chreias. The purpose of this chapter was to examine the chreias and parables that were coherent under the topic "Campaigning under Pressure." The following units of material in the synoptic gospels fit the classification of chreia:

The King in Hiding .... Matt 8:19-20; Lk 9:57-58
The Living and the Dead .... Matt 8:21-22; Lk 9:59-60
Prepared to Plow .... Lk 9:61-62
The Widow's Commitment................ Lk 21:1-3; Mk 12:41-44
The Fallen Temple............. Matt 24:1-3; Mk 13:1-4; Lk 21:5-7
The Blessed Do God's Will........................... Lk 11:27-28
The Adopted Family.................................Matt 12:46-50

Herod's Threat .... Lk 13:31-32
The Voice of Stones .... Lk 19:39-40
Weeping Women .... Lk 23:27-28
Fishers of Men .... Matt 4:18-19; Mk 1:16-17
Harvest and Laborers .... Matt 9:36-37; Lk 10:1-20
Straight Gate .... Lk 13:23-24; Matt 7:13-14
Rejecting Families .... Lk 14:25-26.

Parables. The following parables that have been attributed to Jesus are coherent with the chreias above, which are also attributed to Jesus. The parables fall in two classes: (1) those supposedly told while recruiting followers and (2) those supposedly told to maintain discipline and preparedness among his leaders. These were both parts of the administration necessary to a new movement.

GROUP 1

The Returning Spirit .... Matt 12:43-45; Lk 11:24-26
The Hidden Treasure .... Matt 13:44
The Precious Pearl .... Matt 13:45-46
Counting the Cost .... Lk 14:28-32
Sheep and Goats .... Matt 25:31-46
The Satisfied Soul .... Lk 12:16-21
Values that Last .... Lk 16:19-31
The Thief at Night .... Matt 24:42-44; Lk 12:39-40
Left Out .... Lk 13:25-30

GROUP 2

The Clever Steward .... Lk 16:1-8
Landlords and Tenants ... Matt 21:33-43; Mk 12:1-11; Lk 20:9-18
The Trustworthy Servant .... Matt 24:45-51
Talents .... Matt 25:13-30; Lk 19:12-27
Watching and Waiting .... Matt 25:1-12
Unworthy Servants .... Lk 17:7-10.

The next chapter will show the teachings of Jesus in relationship to other sects of Judaism and his justification for his own actions.

CHAPTER FOUR

Liberty
and Law

Introduction

The last chapter showed Jesus as a person who was working intensely to recruit followers for his movement to acquire the Kingdom of Heaven. He was apparently working against time, because he would allow volunteers no time off before beginning. No matter how little time he had for his campaign, he still refused to take followers on conditions. Those who followed him had to leave their homes, families, occupations, and give up their wealth to be a part of his movement. He was apparently able to gain a following of disciples who were willing to pay the price required but incurred the problem of maintaining their enthusiasm after they had joined. This message was reflected both in the chreias and the parables, as well as the additional messages not preserved in either of these two forms. This chapter will examine the chreias, parables, and other teachings following the same system, but considering a different topic. There are a number of teachings in the synoptic gospels that show Jesus relaxing the law in some ways, even though he was more demanding than most in other ways. He was attacked, usually by the Pharisees, scribes, and chief priests, for breaking Sabbath rules and mingling with those Jews who mingled with the Romans. These were the tax collectors, who were called ''sinners'' because of their failure to observe all of the restrictive rules necessary to keep Jews segregated from Gentiles. Jesus, evidently, not only did the things of which he was accused, but he also defended this action. This will be clear in the following teachings.

Reform Chreias

The Sick Need the Physician. ''Now it happened, when he was reclining in the house, and look! many tax collectors and sinners had come and were reclining with Jesus and his disciples. When the Pharisees saw, they began to say to his disciples, 'Why does your teacher eat with tax collectors and sinners?' When he heard, he said, 'The healthy have no need for a physician, but those who are ill' '' (Matt 9:10-13; Mk 2:15-17; Lk 5:29-31).

This is clearly a chreia. The situation that prompted the speaker to respond is given; the speaker is identified; and his answer is quoted. This is a double responsive chreia because the punch line is a response to a prior statement. Mark's edition has exactly the same quotation from Jesus with the introduction slightly more detailed. Luke's version is still more variant and extensive, beginning by telling that it was Levi who prepared the feast in his own home. More details lead up to the punch line which varies from the other two versions in only one word: The word for ''healthy'' in Luke is a synonym for the word used in Matthew and Mark. Luke may have taken his chreia from another source, or he may have adapted the chreia used by Matthew and Mark to fit his context, as other editors of chreias did. Although Luke's version is placed between two other chreias, it seems too long to qualify as a ''succinct'' unit of literature as it is.

Neither Dibelius nor Bultmann has analyzed this passage from the standpoint of literary structure. Lohmeyer, M'Neile, and Meyer[1] all thought that this meal took place in Jesus' home at Capernaum, since Matt 9:1 shows that Jesus had a home there and this is in the same context. The context is placed by the editor, however, so the place of the meal cannot be determined in that way. It says only ''in the house.'' It would not be out of character for Jesus to have invited wealthy tax collectors and other wealthy

---

[1]E. Lohmeyer, *Das Evangelium des Matthäus (Göttingen, 1926)*, pp. *167, 171; A. H. M'Neile, the Gospel according to St. Matthew*, p. 118; Meyer, *Matthew*, p. 197.

Jewish businessmen to his home as part of his recruitment program. It is not likely that this discussion all took place at the meal. At the meal were Jesus, his disciples, and the tax collectors, so if Pharisees had been there, they too would have been sinning. The event probably occurred; the Pharisees heard about it afterward and complained to the disciples. Only after that did Jesus offer a response, perhaps not directly to the Pharisees but when he was alone with the disciples. The response given may have been a proverb which Jesus only applied to this situation. The gist of the answer assumes the accusation of the Pharisees is correct: Jesus did eat with these people and they were sinners; but Jesus was trying to provide them healing. The first point to consider here is the nature of the sickness and the second will deal with Jesus' plan for healing.

In many Jewish sects at Jesus' time, segregationistic hospitality practices were rigidly enforced.[2] After the temple was destroyed in 586 B.C. the priesthood could no longer function there to provide an undefiled place for the Lord to dwell. The best possible substitute was provided. Pious Jews tried to keep their own hearths as undefiled as the altar in the temple and themselves as undefiled as the priests in the temple. This means they kept Levitical purity laws and Pentateuchal dietary laws very carefully. Rigorous sects, like the Essenes and Pharisees, would eat only in another Jew's home of the same sect because they were the only ones they trusted to keep their houses free from all types of midras uncleanness, see that all the food served was *kasher* and had been properly tithed. Furthermore, these sects would not allow any other Jew to enter their homes who did not observe these very same rules. These orthodox Jews called qualified Jews "worthy." "Unworthy" Jews were called "people of the land," identifying them, typologically, with the unobservant Palestinian Jews whom the returning Jews from Babylon found in the land when they arrived there. The most rigorous of these sects lived in monasteries, were unmarried, lived communally, and used extreme measures to keep their monastery free from defilement. Jesus offended people like the Pharisees, not only by accepting invitations into the homes of Jews who did not observe these hospitality laws, but he may even have invited them into his own home. In the eyes of the Pharisees, this was a serious matter. These tax collectors were defiled, or sick, from a liturgical point of view, and their sickness was contagious.

---

[2]GWB, *Consequences*, pp. 238-81.

Jesus knew the rules as well as the Pharisees. He also considered these people sick, but he thought they could be healed. These people with whom Jesus mingled were called "sinners" and "harlots." Therefore, people often picture Jesus as if he had been somewhere on a "Skid Row" working with drunks and prostitutes. This is certainly a false picture. These "sinners" were only outcasts from a liturgical point of view. They were not social outcasts, except to societies where very rigid dietary laws were observed. These "sinners" were some of the wealthiest people in the land. They would have belonged to the best country clubs and attended the most elaborate social functions. They were also called "harlots," not because of any sexual promiscuity on their part, but because they mingled with the Gentiles and other defiled Jews in business and society. They were insultingly considered to be contemporary types of which the ancient prototypes were sacred prostitutes of the fertility cults. The insult was intended to imply that they were at least as bad as pagan sexual prostitutes.[3] These same Jews also called Gentiles who mingled with these Jews "dogs," thus identifying them, typologically, with the masculine prostitutes in ancient fertility cults. Because these Jews and Gentiles ate together and transacted business together, Pharisees implied that they cohabited. These "sinners" and "harlots" were the ancient counterparts of modern Reform Jews. Ancient Pharisees would also have called Jews in America who are members of Congress, Supreme Court justices, and managers of large businesses "sinners" and "harlots" for the same reason. Their business requires them to touch Gentiles and sometimes even to eat with them. Orthodox Jews today do not approve of this behavior, either, and they have insulting names for these upper class Jews. Good Pharisees would never have allowed such Jews in their homes or eaten with them in any home.

If Jesus had always entertained these wealthy Jews, Pharisees would have expected that of him and would have considered him just another "sinner" or "harlot." At one time, however, he was closely associated with John the Baptist; at which time, he probably observed dietary rules just as rigorously as John did. Just as the Hasmoneans decided that it was better to break the Sabbath and save the nation than to keep the Sabbath and lose their freedom, so Jesus seems to have reasoned that it was necessary for a successful movement to have the cooperation of these wealthy Jews in influ-

---

[3]Ibid., pp. 184-89.

ential Roman government positions. They also would have been good leaders and administrators. A later apocryphal document said Jesus selected his own apostles from the worst kind of sinners (ὄντας ὑπερ πᾶσαν ἁμαρτίαν ἀνομανωτέρους) (Epistle of Barnabas 5:9). This probably meant that the apostles, themselves, had formerly been tax collectors (like Levi) and other nonobservant "Reform" Jews. The accusations hurled at them by the Pharisees indicates that this was true. The Pharisees gave tithes, faithfully, but no more. These tithes went to the proper places, as they were assigned, but Jesus needed lots of money for an effective revolution against Rome, and this money would have had to come after tithes had been given. Where could he get it? It seemed necessary to persuade these wealthy Jews to give up their wealth and position and dedicate all of their leadership talents to an attempt to acquire the Kingdom of Heaven. It seems like good administration to go where the money and leadership talent are if they are the primary needs, but the Pharisees were religiously opposed to this. They frequently attacked Jesus for these social and business contacts. He was also attacked by the disciples of John the Baptist, as the next chreia shows.

No Fasting at a Wedding. ''Then the disciples of John approached him, saying, 'Why do we and the Pharisees fast, but your disciples do not fast?' Then Jesus said to them, 'The sons of the bridegroom are not able to fast as long as the bridegroom is with them' '' (Matt 9:14-15; Mk 2:18-20; Lk 5:33-34).

This is a responsive chreia. The situation prompting the speaker to respond is given; the speaker is identified; the quotation is given; and the entire unit is succinct. In Mark the unit is expanded slightly, the word order is altered, but the very words are held intact. Luke's version has almost ceased to be a chreia. It is expanded to fit into the wider context, and even the quotation is changed slightly, without changing the meaning. The clearest chreia here, as in the previous example, is in Matthew. This unit was not analyzed as a form either by Dibelius or Bultmann.

Since this is a chreia, the wider context of the gospel provides no clue about the situation that prompted the comment. Contrary to Lohmeyer,[4] it is very unlikely that it took place at the same meal as the previous chreia just because the Matthaean editor put the two chreias in the same chapter.

---

[4]Lohmeyer, *Matthäus*, p. 174.

Nor can the comment in poetry that follows the chreia be used to understand the initial meaning of the statement. Matt 9:15b was evidently added after the death of Jesus by the later church. Both M'Neile and Meyer[5] are correct in saying that the "sons of the bridegroom" are the friends of the groom or the guests at the wedding. Jewish and early Christian weddings lasted seven days, during which time there was much celebration before the entire party escorted the bride with the bridegroom to the home of the bridegroom. This was no time to fast. John's disciples, like the Pharisees, had fasted on certain occasions, long before John was killed. Therefore, the question was one of customary liturgical practices. The answer given, however, was in response to the fact that John had been killed by the time this was said. Jesus and his disciples were too busily engaged in their movement to take time out to fast. In the undercover business in which they were engaged, with Herod trying to stop them, the career of Jesus, like that of John, might be interrupted at any time, but Jesus was determined to continue each day until he would be stopped.

Commandment versus Tradition. "Then there came to Jesus *from Jerusalem Pharisees and scribes,* saying, '*Why do your disciples* transgress *the tradition of the elders,* because they do not wash their *hands* when *they eat bread?*' Jesus, in reply, *said to them,* 'Why do you also transgress *the commandment of God* for the sake of *your tradition?*' " (Matt 15:1-3).

This, again, is a responsive chreia. Neither Bultmann nor Dibelius discussed the literary structure of this unit. Dausch, Lohmeyer, M'Neile, and Meyer[6] all discussed these three verses as if they were an integral part of the entire discussion, Matt 15:1-20, not noticing this chreia on which the rest of the discussion is based. The chreia is the text for the commentary, Matt 15:4-20, and the text was composed before the commentary. It also had its own meaning apart from the commentary that was added later. There was probably an extensive discussion between the Pharisees and Jesus on the

---

[5]M'Neile, *Matthew*, pp. 120-21; Meyer, *Matthew*, p. 199; J. A. Zeisler, "The Removal of the Bridegroom: A Note on Mark 2:18-22 and Parallels," *NTS* 19 (1973):190-94, argued that the unit ends with Mk 2:19//Matt 9:15. He thought it referred to a condition at only one time, probably in Matthew's church when Pharisees and John's disciples fasted and Matthew's church did not, and they did not later either. This was an attack primarily against the Pharisees.

[6]P. Dausch, *Die Drei Älteren Evangelien* (Bonn, 1952), pp. 228-31; Lohmeyer, *Matthäus*, pp. 243-51; M'Neile, *Matthew*, pp. 221-29; Meyer, *Matthew*, p. 279.

topic of transgressing traditions. Jesus evidently did not justify his actions according to any law or custom. He simply replied *ad hominem,* "You transgress even the sacred scriptures!" This has all been capsuled into a chreia, so that it is no longer possible to know accurately what it was that they did to transgress the scriptures. This chreia seemed to the people who composed it clear enough to remember the details of the incident. Whatever the answer Jesus gave, it seems reasonable that there would have been another conflict with the Pharisees on the question of tradition since there were others of the same nature. If the later church had composed the chreia, it would have clarified the answer, so that the punch line would have given a message that gave meaning to Jesus' retort. Respect for quotations is shown in the fact that the Matthaean editor did not change the chreia but instead interpreted it by making an addition. This is what rhetoricians would have done.

Since Jesus left unanswered which commandment the Pharisees broke, Matthew supplied this lacuna with two quotations: (1) *Honor your father and your mother* (Exod 20:12; Deut 5:16) and (2) *He who curses his father or mother shall be put to death* (Exod 21:17). These are both texts dealing with the responsibilities of children to parents. Matthew frequently provided two proof texts when any were needed.[7] This was probably because in court two or three witnesses were required to prove a case. The tradition Matthew thought the Pharisees broke was in taking an oath not to provide for their parents. This is the way they did it: Pharisees say, "Whoever says to his father and mother, '[by the] gift! [on the altar], [may all these unmentioned curses come upon me], if you benefit from me' " (Matt 15:5-6).[8] When this happened, the Pharisees upheld the oath and the parents were neglected. This is the kind of vow men would take before joining a monastery where they were obligated to give all of their wealth to the community upon admission and take oaths not to hold on to any family ties of

---

[7]For example: Parading Virtue (6:2-5); Praying and Fasting (6:16-18); Birds and Flowers (6:26-29); Dogs and Hogs (7:6); Bread and Fish (7:9-11); volunteers (2 chreias: 8:19-22); Mingling and Fasting (9:10-15); Patches and Wineskins (9:16-17); Jesus and John (10:16-18). There are double proof texts in the following verses: 15:4; 19:5; 19:18-19; 21:13; 21:42; 22:37-39; 27:9-10. The following verses are "second endings" to chreias: 9:13; 12:50; 18:4.

[8]See GWB, "Some Oath and Vow Formulas in the New Testament," *HTR* 58 (1965):319-26.

any kind. Matthew thought those who became monks were breaking the two commandments he listed. This seems very unlikely to have been the original meaning Jesus intended in the commandment the Pharisees broke because Jesus also required his followers to take monastic vows that let the dead bury their own dead. Matthew represents the later church; he used the text in the way that was most useful to his day and supportive of his own legalism. Even though Matthew was the legalist, which Jesus was not, and even though he interpreted a chreia to suit his own needs, he also preserved unchanged chreias that were exactly contradictory to the message he defended. This is consistent with normal scribal integrity.

Matthew further followed his condemnation of Pharisees by using: (1) another proof text (LXX Isa 29:13); (2) a couplet on inner and outer defilement (Matt 15:11); (3) another chreia against the Pharisees (Matt 15:12-14); and (4) a final harangue about defilement and eating with unwashed hands. The whole discussion concludes with the final half of an inclusion, showing that the author considered these twenty verses the complete unit on this discussion. On Matthew's discussion, only the texts of the two chreias represent Jesus' sayings. The rest of the argument is of Matthaean composition.[9] This passage shows clearly the ways the later church used these chreias to compose its literature. In so doing, church scribes followed rules that were later used by Greek rhetoricians. The "later church" was probably not as late as Theon or Hermogenes. There were evidently accepted rules of exegesis employed by both Greek and Jewish homileticians before the time either of the gospel writers or of the later Greek rhetoricians. Mark also followed the same rules, but he developed this same text differently. His developed argument will be quoted here with words underlined which agree either generally or precisely with the chreia in Matt 15:1-3.

"Then there gathered together to him Pharisees and some of *their scribes, having come from Jerusalem,* and when they saw some of his *disciples* that with common hands, that is unwashed, they ate bread—for the Pharisees and all the Jews, if they do not wash their hands, they do not eat, holding fast to the traditions of the elders, and from the market places, if they do not cleanse themselves by sprinkling, they do not eat. Also many other things there are to which they hold fast by tradition, washing pots, kettles, and pans—then the Pharisees and the scribes asked him, *'Why do*

---

[9] Compare this with the homily developed by Epiphanes in chapter 2.

your disciples not walk according to *the traditions of the elders,* but with common *hands they eat bread?' Then he said to them,* 'Well has Isaiah prophesied concerning you hypocrites! as it is written:

This people honors me with their hands,
but their heart is far removed from me.
In vain they worship me,
teaching the commandments of men

(LXX Isa 29:13),

—leaving the commandment of God, you hold fast to the traditions of men.' *Then he said to them, 'You abandon the commandment of God* so that you may cling *to your traditions' "* (Mk 7:1-9).

Mark took the chreia from Matthew, expanded it internally, clarifying parts that his church would not understand, respecting throughout the verbal content because his dependence on Matthew's chapter 15 is shown in further interpretation of the chreia. Like Matthew, he quoted the two Torah passages, explained their meaning in terms of the oath that monks take, included the couplet on inner and outer defilement, followed by the same kind of harangue as Matthew had on this subject. He took the quotation from Isaiah that Matthew had later in the chapter and put it inside the expanded chreia. He omitted only the second chreia that Matthew used. It seems difficult to imagine how the relationship could have been the other way around, but this point is not important for the use of the chreia here. This simply shows how Matthew and Mark interpreted the chreia which they believed was a reliable text, preserving the true sayings of Jesus.

The interpretation that the later church gave to this chreia, however, is evidently not an accurate one because it is incoherent with the other chreias and parables. Since this is the only chreia that might be considered incoherent, it is very unlikely that the church composed it originally. It seems, rather, that it reflects a genuine conflict with the Pharisees on the subject of the tradition, even though it is impossible now to understand what it initially meant.

Inner and Outer Defilement. "While he was speaking, a Pharisee asked him if he would dine with him. After he had entered, he reclined. The Pharisee, when he saw it, was surprised that he did not first wash before the meal. The Lord said to him, 'Now, you Pharisees cleanse the outside of the cup and platter, but that which is from within you is filled with ravening and wickedness' " (Lk 11:37-39; see Kelim 4:4; 25:7-8).

"Woe to you, scribes and Pharisees, play actors! Because you cleanse the outside of the cup and saucer, but from within they are full of ravening and licentiousness. Blind Pharisee! Cleanse first the inside of the cup in order that its outside might become clean" (Matt 23:25-26).

The Lukan passage seems to be a chreia, even though it has an elaborate introduction which prompts the speaker to speak. It could have been reduced still more, saying something like, "When the Lord was a guest at the home of a Pharisee, the Pharisee was surprised to observe that Jesus had not washed before the meal." The Matthaean unit is clearly not a chreia. It is one of the seven woes to the Pharisees in a lengthy harangue against them. The teaching is basically the same in both gospels, although it is not clear how they got that way. One might have been dependent upon the other, or they may both have used the same source, or they may have used different chreias about the same incident.

Although Jesus was frequently shown in conflict with the Pharisees, he seems to have been sufficiently trusted by them for them to be willing to have him as a guest, at least at some point in his career. Even here he was under attack for not washing before the meal. Had he been an 'am ha' aretz, the Pharisee would have required him to bathe and change into the Pharisee's own garments before admitting him into his home.[10] When confronted with the question of uncleanness, Jesus brought up a well-known rabbinic law: Since hands only touch the outside of the dish, only the outside could be defiled.[11] There was a difference between what is ritually unclean and what is soiled or unsanitary. It was considered much worse to eat something that was unclean ritually than to eat something that was moldy, spoiled, putrid, or filled with disease germs. Jesus seems to have been arguing on the difference between what is ritually clean (טהור) and sanitarily clean (נקיא). The outside of the cup could become defiled, whereas the inside could become unsanitary.

The chreia comes to an end with this question of outside and inside of the dishes. The Matthaean and Lukan explanation of what this means is all the addition of the later church, but the chreia itself referred to the defilement which was within the Pharisee.

---

[10]SeeGWB,*Consequences*, pp. 194-210.

[11]See Kelim 4:4; 25:7-8; and G. Vermes, *Jesus the Jew* (London, 1973), p. 29.

The Last Word. "When the Pharisees, who were lovers of money, heard all these things, they began to mock him. He said to them, 'You are those who justify yourselves before men, but God knows your hearts' " (Lk 16:14-15).

This is a chreia which the Lukan editor understood to mean that God would bring down these self-exalted Pharisees. To the chreia, he added the couplet: "That which is exalted among men is an abomination before God." This interpretation seems a little stronger than the chreia shows. The point of the chreia is that God has the last word. He judges and it is impossible to fool him. This is a recurring ancient biblical theme. For instance, the story of David and Bathsheba is a story of a perfect crime. David got Uriah's wife pregnant; then he arranged for Uriah to be killed; everything turned out just as he had planned, but at the end of the story, the narrator reported, "But the thing David did displeased the Lord" (2 Sam 11:27). The brothers of Joseph plotted to get him out of the way, but the Lord arranged for Joseph to become second in command in the land of Egypt, where his brothers came seeking food (Gen 37:50). The rich man, who built bigger granaries to store all of his goods so that he could live in comfort, had all things arranged well until God demanded his life and the man died (Lk 12:16-21). The theme of the Magnificat (Lk 1:68-79) is that God upsets the best laid plans of men. He exalts the humble and humbles the exalted. When Jesus told the Pharisees that God was the final judge, he was only reminding them of something they already knew. The Pharisees may have been called those who love money because they gave only their tithes, refusing to give up all that they owned to follow Jesus. This chreia is another demonstration that Jesus was in verbal debate with the Pharisees.

Summary on Chreias. The chreias examined under the heading "Liberty and Law" pictured Jesus as one who broke the segregationistic laws of the Pharisees in his association with tax collectors and sinners. This caused him to be in conflict with the Pharisees on questions of the law. He sometimes justified his actions and at other times he simply accused the Pharisees in return. Some of these chreias provided texts for still more extensive arguments against the Pharisees, but these were the work of the evangelists and do not reflect the work done when the chreias were composed. It is not completely clear in all instances just what Jesus meant in his answers, but the chreias were consistent with one another in relationship with the Pharisees and in relationship to Jesus and the law. There are several parables of the same nature that spell out some of these points in more detail.

Parables

The Pharisee and the Tax Collector. "He told certain of those who believed that they, themselves, were righteous and despised the rest this parable: 'Two men went up to the temple to pray, the one a Pharisee and the other a tax collector. The Pharisee stood up and prayed thus to himself: "O God, I thank you that I am not just as the rest of men,[12] robbers, unjust, adulterers, or even as this tax collector. I fast twice a week; I give tithes of all I acquire." But the tax collector, standing at a distance, did not even want to raise his eyes to Heaven, but struck his chest, saying, "O God, be merciful to me, a sinner." I tell you this man went down to his home justified more than the other, because he who exalts himself will be humbled, and he who humbles himself will be exalted' '' (Lk 18:9-14).

The introduction and conclusion, telling why Jesus told this parable and what the parable meant may have been added by the Lukan editor. This commentary is consistent with the interpretive addition to the chreia on "The Last Word." The parable, itself, implies that Jesus thought the tax collector was in a better relationship with God than the Pharisee. The word "justified," however, may be the word of the editor. The picture given of two people facing judgment before God in the temple may be understood to have taken place on the Day of Atonement when Jews make a ritual of repenting of their sins, asking forgiveness from one another, and bringing their gifts to the altar in the hope of being forgiven. If this were the case, the Pharisee evidently had kept accurate count of all his sins and arranged for them to be forgiven the day they occurred. Therefore, he knew he had no secret sins; he had only an excess of merits, so this day of repentance was only a day of rejoicing for him.

The tax collector, on the other hand, had spent the entire year defrauding other Jews of their money, earning money under the employment of the foreign country that deprived the Jews of their liberty, mingling with Gentiles and keeping himself in a state of ritual defilement most of the time. Who could count his sins? How could he ever obtain forgiveness from his

---

[12]Compare with part of the Jewish morning service of worship: "Blessed are you, Lord our God, King of the age, who has not made me a Gentile (נכרי). Blessed are you, Lord God, King of the age, who has not made me a slave (עבד). Blessed are you, Lord our God, King of the age, who has not made me a woman (אישה)." From the *Authorized Daily Prayer Book,* ed. J. N. Hertz (London, 1960), pp. 5-6.

fellow Jews whom he had injured, so that God would consider his case and try him fairly? He approached the temple, knowing that God had kept record of all his sins and the books were open before him. He had no defense; he depended completely on the mercy of the court.

The editorial conclusion that the tax collector came away "justified" may be more accurately rendered "vindicated," because the implication was that he had won a court case. The teaching of the parable itself, however, is not that strong. It allows the reader or hearer to suppose that the tax collector, although guilty and therefore not vindicated, was forgiven. Dodd[13] correctly related this parable to the chreia on "The Sick Need the Physician" (Matt 9:10-13). The teaching is basically the same. It is a defense of the tax collectors against the Pharisees. Dodd's example of judging authenticity of parables on the basis of their ring is not sound, but this parable would make little sense told after the temple had been destroyed in A.D. 70. The center of activity in the parable was to have taken place in the temple at Jerusalem, taking this existence for granted. In the chreia on the sick and the physician, Jesus did not argue with the Pharisees in defense of the tax collectors on the basis that they were not sinners or sick. He conceded that, but tried to offer them healing. The same message is given here. The tax collector is an admitted and condemned sinner, but he is presented in comparison with the non-sinning Pharisee in such a way as to draw sympathy for the tax collector and not the Pharisee.

Wheat and Weeds. "The Kingdom of Heaven is like a man sowing good seed in his field. While men slept, his enemy came and sowed weeds in the midst of the wheat and went away. When, however, the stalk grew and produced fruit, then also the weeds became evident. The servants of the manager said to him, 'Sir, did you not sow good seed in your field? From where, then, does it have weeds?' He said to them, 'An enemy has done this.' The servants said to him, 'Do you want us, then, to go out and uproot them?' He replied, 'No! lest while you are gathering the weeds you uproot also the wheat. Let them both grow together until the harvest. Then, in the time of the harvest, I will say to the harvesters, "Gather first the weeds, and tie them into bundles to burn, but the wheat gather into my granary" (Matt 13:24-30).

---

[13]Dodd, *Parables*, pp. 117-18.

Like many other parables, without knowing the question it was intended to answer, the event is not completely rational. When a farmer finds weeds in his wheat, he does not normally assume that some enemy of his has deliberately planted them there while the farmer was not watching.[14] Weeds normally appear in seeded fields even without the interference of an enemy. Their presence is nothing that causes alarm and throws suspicion on anyone.[15] This probably means that the parable was intended to illustrate a situation in which the damage *was* caused by an enemy. Since the parable is no longer in its original context, we can only conjecture the *dramatis personae* involved and the situation that prompted the parable.

Since there were other chreias and parables that picture Jesus in conflict with the Pharisees in defense of the tax collector, this seems like the place to begin. In the case of the treasure hidden in the field, the field was the land of Palestine which was compared to the Kingdom of Heaven. This parable also is one in which the whole situation is compared to something related to the Kingdom of Heaven. In the promised land, there were weeds popping up everywhere, and, from the point of view of the Pharisees, these were the tax collectors. They did not come up voluntarily, however, the way weeds spring up in a field of wheat. These had been appointed by the enemy, Rome. Initially, these tax collectors seemed to be neighboring Jews, until suddenly they began to collect taxes for Rome. There were Zealots and Sicarii among the Jews who took every chance they could find to kill these tax collectors. Their answer, in the language of the parable, was to pull them up wherever they were found so that the good wheat could grow unimpeded. The counsel of the parable was that there might be some damage done that way to the wheat itself. Until the wheat had completely headed and was ready for harvest, some of these plants that seem to be weeds might turn out to be wheat. The weeds would surely get their just treatment. At the final time, they would be burned.

---

[14]W. G. Doty, "An Interpretation: Parable of The Weeds and Wheat." *Int.* 25 (1971):189, who thought of a parable as a miniature comedy or tragedy, missed the whole point of the enemy in pre-A.D. 70 Palestine. He commented, "They do not react to the enemy, but ask what they should do with the *weeds*. The enemy has no further function or role than sowing weed seeds among the good seed (wheat). He is then dismissed from the story."

[15]J. D. Crossan, "The Seed Parables of Jesus," *JBL* 92 (1973):260, said, " . . . the owner recognizes that inemical activity alone can explain the presence of (so many?) tares." But there is no indication in the text that this was an unusually large number of weeds.

When dealing with real weeds and real wheat, there is no way that waiting will change the outcome. Weeds keep on being weeds and wheat keeps on being wheat. They just have different destinies. With tax collectors, however, there was a possibility for change. The tax collectors were Jews by birth. They had been appointed tax collectors by an enemy. It is possible for them to repent and become loyal parts of the Kingdom of Heaven. Since Jesus was addressing himself to a serious recruitment program directed to these very tax collectors that the Pharisees wanted weeded out, it seems proper and necessary for him to compose parables such as this one to defend his actions. He had probably had enough success among these wealthy Jews employed by the enemy Rome to realize that there was some real talent there. There was also some latent loyalty to the Kingdom of Heaven when the need was properly presented to them. One of these tax collectors had repented and become one of Jesus' apostles. Another, Zacchaeus, was not only a tax collector, but a chief tax collector. When he received Jesus' message, he volunteered to take half of his possessions to repay former injustices so that he would have a clear conscience and no debits in the treasury of merits. The rest he would give to the poor, which probably means he would join Jesus' monastic movement, contributing all of the possessions left to the community called the poor (Lk 19:19). Success stories like this convinced Jesus of the wisdom of calling these ''sinners,'' ''harlots,'' and ''weeds'' to repentance before the ''harvest.''

The Fish Net. ''Again the Kingdom of Heaven is like a fish net, thrown into the sea. It gathers from every kind [of sea creatures]. When it has been filled, they draw it up onto the shore. Then they sit down and gather the good ones into a container, and they throw out the worthless ones'' (Matt 13:47-48).

This parable seems to have the same point as the previous one, except that the element of the enemy is not included so the parable follows more clearly. The parable seems to teach patience in judgment. Fishermen could not be selective about the fish they wanted to catch into their nets. Jews, of course, were forbidden to eat fish that did not have scales and fins; therefore, these were considered ''worthless.'' Just because Jews did not like eels, catfish, shell fish, frogs, and turtles did not mean these would never live in Palestinian waters. The person who refused to touch ''worthless'' fish would never become a fisherman because these lived side-by-side with the fish that had scales and fins. There was a time when these would have to be segregated, but that could not happen before the worthless ones had been touched. All the fish were drawn into the boat, and then they were divided. Only the good fish were kept. The "worthless" were thrown out. That is the way it would be in the Kingdom of Heaven. There existed, in Jesus' time, both faithful Jews and also those who had compromised with the Romans. These wealthy, liberal Jews were the ones the Pharisees wanted destroyed at once.

Jesus told parables like this one and the "Weeds and Wheat" to convince the Pharisees of the wisdom of waiting until it was certain which fish had scales and fins and which did not. Like weeds, fish without scales and fins would not change their character in a matter of days or weeks, but their counterparts in these parables, the tax collectors, could repent and become loyal supporters of the kingdom. If they did, they should be admitted before the judgment. On this point the Pharisees disagreed. A similar parable is the one that follows, "The Nonproductive Fig Tree."

The Nonproductive Fig Tree. "A certain man had a fig tree planted in his vineyard, and he came seeking fruit on it, but he did not find [any]. He said to the vinedresser, 'Look, for three years I have come seeking fruit from this fig tree, and I do not find [any]. Dig it up! Why does it keep the land nonproductive?' Then, by reply, he says to him, 'Sir, let it go also this year until I have cultivated around it and fertilized [it]. Then, if it produces fruit the following year, [well, and good], but if not you may dig it out' '' (Lk 13:6-9).

This is a difficult parable because it is removed from its original context, and it is not enough like other clear parables to conjecture with confidence that it has the same situation in mind as the others. This parable may have been told in conflict with the Pharisees, asking for a little more time for the tax collectors to repent. It could also have been told to leaders within the movement who were impatient for the revolution to begin. They were like Saul's soldiers at Gilgal; they had waited long enough and were about ready to give up the whole movement and go home (1 Sam 13:2-9). This may have been addressed to those who were not yet committed, reminding them of the small amount of time left to join or be rejected. In any of these cases, it seems likely that the "three years" may have been the actual time the recruitment program had been under way. The significance of the additional year is that by that time the magic three-and-one-half-year period between the defilement and the rededication of the temple reported in Daniel would be over. By that time either there would be positive results or the assurance that the signs had not been read correctly.

Another possibility for the three years is, as Plummer suggested, that a fig tree is expected to bear in three years. If it does not bear in four years, it probably will not bear at all.[16] Plummer's further suggestion that God is the owner and the people of Israel constitute the fig tree does not seem likely.

The Lost Sheep. "How does it seem to you? If a man has a hundred sheep, and one of them goes astray, will he not leave the ninety-nine on the mountains, and after he has gone, look for the one that has wandered? If he finds it, I tell you under oath that he will rejoice more over it than over the ninety-nine that did not go astray. Therefore, it is not the will of your Father in heaven that one of these little ones perish" (Matt 18:12-13).[17]

The following Matthaean chreia is used in Luke to enclose the same parable of the lost sheep. The words in the Matthaean chreia that are either identical or similar in Greek will be underscored to show the extent to which these chreias are similar.

"Now it happened, when he was reclining in the house, and look! many tax collectors and sinners had come and were reclining with Jesus and his disciples. When the Pharisees saw, they began to say to his disciples, 'Why does your teacher eat with tax collectors and sinners?' When he heard, he said, 'The healthy have no need of a physician, but those who are ill' " (Matt 9:10-13).

"Now all the tax collectors and the sinners were coming near to him, and the Pharisees and the scribes were saying, 'This man accepts sinners and eats with them.' He said to them this parable, saying,

'Which man among you, having a hundred sheep and has lost one of them, will he not leave the ninety-nine in the wilderness and go after the lost one until he finds it? After he has found [it] he will place [it] on his shoulders, rejoicing. And when he has arrived at his house, he will invite his friends and neighbors, saying to them, "Rejoice with me! Because I have found my sheep that was lost!" I tell you that thus will be the joy in heaven over one sinner who repents more than ninety-nine who have no need of repentance' " (Lk 15:1-7).

---

[16]Plummer, *ICC Luke*, p. 340.

[17]According to the Gospel of Thomas 98:22-26, the lost sheep was the largest of the sheep, one Jesus loved more than the other ninety-nine. The image of the *large* sheep seems to be an apt metaphor for the rich tax collector.

These parables differ in actual wording, but the message is the same in both. In both cases, the concluding sentence is not a part of the parable but was added to interpret it. This sentence was used in the Lukan parable to illustrate a chreia in exactly the way Greek rhetoricians taught their pupils. By doing this, Luke has shown that he thought the people who had no need of repentance were the same as the ones who had no need of a physician (Lk 15:1; Matt 9:13). In both cases these were the Pharisees and the tax collectors were the ones who were lost and needed repentance. Matthew's context is just as specific. He thought the lost sheep represented the "least of these," which were also called the tax collectors and harlots. The contrast between the safe majority and the lost minority seems to fit the parables well if the parable is interpreted as referring to the very religious and the ones who have been negligent. Dodd and Jeremias[18] both hold that this parable belongs to some context similar to the one Luke gives, illustrating again the relationship between Jesus and the Pharisees as well as the tax collectors. It is very similar to other chreias and parables that also teach acceptance of the tax collectors and show Jesus in conflict with the Pharisees on this point.

Many scholars[19] have been very inventive in their defense of the shepherd who left the ninety-nine sheep unattended on the mountains. He could not really have left them in danger, could he? But this is to miss the point of the parable. Jesus was not trying to give instruction on sheep care. He was speaking about lost tax collectors who got involved in business with the Roman government rather than a sheep that got lost on the hillside. The ninety-nine who are safely in the fold, needing no care, deliverance, or repentance represent the Pharisees, who are otherwise pictured in parables and chreias as "righteous," "healthy," "wheat," etc. If the wilderness where the sheep have been left is the same as the field with both weeds and wheat and the field where there is buried treasure, then we are talking about

---

[18]Dodd, *Parables*, pp. 118-20; Jeremias, *Parables*, p. 40.

[19]For example, see Jeremias, *Parables*, p. 133; M. J. Lagrange, *Evangile selon Saint Luc*, p. 417; F. Bussby, "Did a Shepherd Leave Sheep upon the Mountains or in a Desert? A Note on Matthew 18:12 and Luke 15:4," *ATR* 45 (1963): 93-94; and K. E. Bailey, *The Poet and the Peasant*, (Grand Rapids, c1976), pp. 149-50.

the promised land, the place where the Kingdom of Heaven[20] was expected to function as soon as the Romans were driven out. There seems to have been little danger of the Pharisees going astray there. They were the ones who thanked God that they were not like other men. Jesus conceded their righteousness many times, maybe satirically, but nonetheless, he started the argument with the same presuppositions as the Pharisees. Since that was the case, then, how should this Jewish sinner be treated in the promised land? The Pharisees would exclude him, whereas Jesus argued that he should be brought back into the fold which was part of Jesus' recruitment program.

The Lost Coin. "What woman, having ten drachmas, if she loses one drachma, will not light a lamp and search the house and seek carefully until she finds [it]? when she has found the lost coin, she will invite her friends and neighbors, saying, 'Rejoice with me, because I have found the drachma which I had lost.' Thus I tell you there will be joy in heaven before the angels of God over one sinner, repenting" (Lk 15:8-10).

Like the parable of the lost sheep, this one concludes with the finder rejoicing and inviting in all the neighbors to celebrate. This does not make good sense. The shepherd who has to kill two sheep or a fatted calf to feed his neighbors and friends as they celebrate the recovery of one sheep does not come out ahead, financially. The same is true of the woman who finds one small coin. This is not enough for a very elaborate celebration whether it be used to buy food or to decorate a dress as Jeremias and Bailey suggested.[21] In both cases, that which was really lost was the tax collector, whom Jesus had modestly, perhaps in intentional understatement, called "one of the least," "a sinner." Here he was represented by this small coin, but in reality, the tax collector was a very rich man, who could more justly be classified as an especially large sheep, as is suggested in the Gospel of Thomas version of the lost sheep (107). His repentance was an occasion for

---

[20]J. Klausner, *The Messianic Idea in Israel*, tr. W. F. Stinespring (New York, 1955), p. 235, said, "The Hasmoneans were influenced by a strong faith that the hour had come for the 'kingdom of heaven,' that is the kingdom of the God of heaven, to be revealed to the world and the kingdom of Greece to fall." Klausner seemed to think the Hasmoneans did not achieve their goal, because they did not destroy all Gentile nations and rule the entire world. Had they succeeded in doing that they would have acquired the Kingdom of Heaven.

[21]Jeremias, *Parables*, pp. 134-35, and Bailey, *Poet*, pp. 157-58.

feasting and rejoicing and Jesus may have been rejoicing in some of these feasts when the Pharisees criticized him for eating with sinners and harlots. If the tax collector really fit the classification the Pharisees gave him, then these celebrations would not make sense. Jesus' understatements may have been made deliberately to make the analysis of the Pharisees look ridiculous, just as the parable of the Pharisee and the tax collector in the temple did.

Luke obviously identified the lost coin with the lost tax collector, just as he did the lost sheep. This is evident from the fact that he also used this parable to illustrate the chreia about the sick who had need of a physician.

The Laborers and the Hours. ''For the Kingdom of Heaven is like a man who is a householder, who went out every morning to hire workers for his vineyard. He agreed with the workers on a denarius a day, and he sent them out to his vineyard. When he went out about the third hour, he saw others standing in the market place, idle. He said to them, 'Go work in my vineyard, also, and whatever is just I will give you.' So they went out. He went out again at the sixth and ninth hour and did the same. About the eleventh hour, when he went out, he found others standing, and he said to them, 'Why do you stand here all day idle?' They said to him, 'Because no one has hired us.' He said to them, 'Also you go to my vineyard.' When it was evening, the Lord of the vineyard said to the manager, 'Call the workers and pay their wages, beginning with the last [and continuing] until the first.' Those who went out at the eleventh hour received a denarius each, and those who went out first considered that they would receive more, but they also received one denarius each. As they received it, they grumbled against the householder, saying, 'These last worked one hour, and they received the same as we who worked and bore the burden and the heat of the day.' But he answered and said to them, 'Friend, I have not been unjust to you. Did you not agree with me on a denarius? Take what is yours and leave, but I want to give this last one also the same as you. Am I not permitted to do what I want with what is mine' '' (Matt 20:1-16).

This parable seems not to have been directed to the apostles as Allen thought.[22] Instead, it is more likely to have been aimed at the Pharisees.[23] Although the parable includes those who began work at 9:00 A.M. (the third

---

[22]Allen, *ICC Matthew,* P. 214.

[23]So also Jeremias, *Parables,* p. 38.

hour), noon, 3:00 P.M., and 5:00 P.M., the people in the parable who are most directly discussed are only those who came to work promptly at 6:00 A.M. and worked all day, in comparison with those who came at 5:00 P.M. and worked only one hour. Those who worked all day long for an agreed-upon wage were the Pharisees who had always kept the law and were expecting that God would fulfill his covenant with them and give them back the land. Those who began working just before the payment time were the tax collectors who had only recently accepted Jesus' call and invitation to work for the Kingdom of Heaven. In the eyes of the Pharisees, these were not just like people who loitered all day; they were working against the kingdom. They should not even be allowed to work this late in the day. They had been identifying themselves with the Gentiles. When the judgment day came, let them perish with the Gentiles! It would not be fair for them to be admitted into the Kingdom of Heaven without having worked for it all along.

It was not God, but Jesus, who was the hero in the parable. As the Messiah, he had the right to decide who would be admitted into his kingdom when the kingdom came. The Pharisees agreed that it was near the end of the age; the Kingdom would soon come. They had no suspicion that God would reverse Jesus' decision. The Messiah was a monarch. If he allowed these tax collectors into the kingdom, they would be admitted. Therefore, Pharisees were trying to persuade him to change his mind beforehand. This was not just idle speculation or nit-picking philosophy.

This had evidently been a continuing conflict that Jesus had with the Pharisees in justifying his efforts to include the tax collectors in the coming Kingdom of Heaven. Other Jewish writings later expressed the view that all Israel would have a place in the age to come (San 10:1) and that all would be equally treated at that time (4 Ezra 5:42). That is not precisely the teaching of Jesus, but this parable teaches that the tax collectors would have equal advantages in the Kingdom of Heaven. Other teachings indicate that they would have even preferred positions which is indicated by the fact that they were already associating with Jesus and receiving positions of leadership. Matt 20:16 is an editorial addition which implies that the late comers would actually receive more than those who worked all day. The parable teaches only that all will receive the same wages, but that the last will receive theirs first so that the first could see what happened and comment on it. The parable was structured specially to provide a setting to bring up this argument.

The idea that an employer is free to overpay if he or she wishes, so long as commitments have been fulfilled, would be challenged by labor unions today, but, in the ancient Near Eastern monarchies, kings could do as they pleased. In the parable, the employer was to be compared to a king or the Messiah in the new Kingdom of Heaven. The next two parables show the tax collectors, not only in equal position with the Pharisees in the judgment of God, but, like the parable of the Pharisee and the tax collector, they are judged more virtuous.

Two Sons and a Vineyard. "How does it seem to you? A man had two sons. He came to the first and said, 'Son, go out today and work in the vineyard.' He, by way of reply, said, 'I will, Sir,' but he did not go out. After he had come to the second, he said the same. But, by way of reply, he said, 'I do not want to.' Later, after he had repented, he went away [and worked in the vineyard]. Which of the two did the will of the father?" (Matt 21:28-31).

This parable is now preserved only in Matthew, worked into a whole dialogue which makes it difficult to separate clearly. The question, "Which of the two did the will of the father?" may not be a part of the original context. The same is true of the following repartee: "They said, 'The second.' Jesus said to them, 'I swear to you that the tax collectors and harlots will precede you into the Kingdom of God' " (Matt 21:31).

Perrin[24] followed Jeremias,[25] erroneously, in using one of the weakest texts, one that represents the first son as declining the invitation but later repenting and working in the vineyard. The argument is that if the first brother had accepted, the father would have had no reason to approach the second brother at all. There are two basic weaknesses with this argument apart from the textual support: (1) This assumes that the father needed only as much work done in the vineyard as one son could do. Therefore, if the

---

[24]N. Perrin, *Rediscovering the Teaching of Jesus*, pp. 118-19.

[25]Jeremias, *Parables*, p. 125. So also Meyer, *Matthew*, pp. 360, 368-69 and J. Weiss, *Die Schriften des Neuen Testaments*, 1 (Göttingen, 1907), pp. 363-64. J. R. Michaels, "The Parable of the Regretful Son," *HTR* 61 (1968):15-26, noted that there was still a third variant: The first son refused and then worked; the second consented but then did not work. Nevertheless, the second was considered the obedient one. Michaels rendered the passage "repented and went," "regretfully went away." Michaels conjectured that this was the original version, overlooking the two sons theme in the OT. This text, he said, if not simply the result of a careless scribe, reflects pro-Pharisaism in the early Matthaean church.

first son had consented, the father would not have asked the second. (2) This also presumes that the parable was expected to make sense in and of itself. But this is not always the case. The parable was intended to communicate a message even if it was sometimes strained or distorted a bit to make it fit the narrator's needs. Matthew has placed this parable in a context in which Jesus was defending the second brother, who was identified with the tax collector and the harlot (Matt 21:31) against the attacks of the chief priests and elders (Matt 21:23). Although this is the work of the editor, even if separated from its present context the content of the parable itself suggests an intended context that poses some such situation. Historically, the Pharisees did come first and they did agree to keep the law which was doing God's work. Historically, the tax collectors (also called harlots) did break the law.[26] It was only after Jesus had begun his recruitment program that some of them began to repent, give up all they had, and follow Jesus. Therefore the parable was designed to show their relationship. Since Jesus asked the tax collectors to give up their possessions, while the Pharisees were giving only their tithes, Jesus was in a position to compare the Pharisees unfavorably. They were not working in the vineyard the way the tax collectors were doing. They said they would, but they did not; the tax collectors said they would not, but they repented and did. That was the situation and Jesus made the parable fit his needs.

Although Jeremias acknowledged that the parable is not now in its original context,[27] he agreed with Dodd[28] in identifying the first brother with the religious leaders of the day and the second brother with the sinners and tax collectors. Most scholars agree with this identification.[29] The same is true of the following parable of a father who had two sons:

Two Sons and a Heritage. "A certain man had two sons. The younger son said to his father, 'Father, give me the portion of [family] property that

---

[26]For the metaphorical use of "harlot" to mean "liberal Jew," see GWB, *Consequences,* pp. 184-89. R. Augstein, *Jesus the Son of Man,* tr. H. Young (New York, c1977), p. 134, was not acquainted with such Jewish customs, so he referred to Jesus' "apparent companionship with gluttons, boozers, and whores."

[27]Jeremias, *Parables,* pp. 80, 125.

[28]Dodd, *Parables,* p. 120.

[29]Dausch,*Drei,* p. 284; Meyer, *Matthew,* p. 368; A. Plummer, *An Exegetical Commentary on the Gospel according to Matthew,* (London, 1909), p. 295; Weiss, *Schriften.* 1, p. 364.

falls to me.' So [the father] divided for them [the sons] his possessions. After not many days, the younger son gathered together all [his possessions] and went away into a distant land. There he scattered his possessions, living wastefully. After he had spent everything, there was a great famine in that country, and he began to be in need. He went and attached himself to one of the citizens of that land. [The citizen] sent him into his fields to herd hogs, and he was eager for his stomach to be filled with the husks which the hogs ate, but no one gave him [permission to do so]. After he came to himself, he said, 'How many hired servants of my father have more bread than they can eat, and I am here perishing in famine. After I have arisen, I will go to my father, and I will say to him, ''Father, I have sinned against Heaven and before you. I am no longer worthy to be called your son. Make me as one of your hired servants.'' Then he arose and went to his father. While he was still a long distance away, his father saw him and was moved with compassion. He ran and embraced and kissed him. The son said to him, 'Father, I have sinned against Heaven and before you. I am no longer worthy to be called your son.' His father, however, said to his servants, 'Quickly bring out the first robe and put it on him, and put a ring on his hand and sandals on his feet. Then bring the fatted calf, slaughter [it], and let us eat and be merry, because this son of mine was dead, and he came to life. He was lost and has been found'; and they began to celebrate.

''Now his older son was in the field, and as he came he drew near to the house, he heard music and dancing, so he called one of the servants to him and inquired what these things might be. He said to him, 'Your brother has come, and your father slaughtered the fatted calf, because he received him well.' He was angry and did not want to enter, but his father came out and begged him. He answered and said to his father, 'Look, all these years I have been serving you, and I never deviated from your commandment, but you never gave me even a kid that I might celebrate with my friends, but when this son of yours, who consumed your wealth with harlots, came, you sacrificed for him the fatted calf.' He replied to him, 'Son, I always have you with me, and all my possessions are yours, but it is necessary to rejoice and be glad because this your brother was dead and came to life; he was lost and has been found' '' (Lk 15:11-32).

This parable uses many idioms that are not normally known by non-Jewish groups and familiarity with these idioms is necessary to understand the parable. The term, ''hog,'' is frequently used, insultingly, to refer to a

Gentile.[30] The situation here was probably one in which the son had to seek employment among the Gentiles and would gladly have eaten food that was sold at the open market which would not have been *kasher*.[31] Religiously, "life" can take place only within the covenant, and according to some Jews, it can only occur on the land of Palestine when it is free from Roman rule. The term is sometimes used less restrictively to mean those who are faithful to their Jewish heritage. The term, "dead," is also used metaphorically to mean those who are not circumcised or who have become apostate.[32] Certain sects believed that all Jews of other sects were dead. When the younger son left his secure orthodox surroundings to live among the Gentiles, he was considered "dead" by the rigorous, law abiding Jews. He was also "lost." His return meant a restoration to the covenant where life was possible. He could feast on food that was acceptable to orthodox Jews. He was back home, so he was no longer "lost."

Bailey[33] has shown how impossible the proposed situation would be, both in antiquity and today. A son who asked for his heritage was saying he wanted his father to die. This type of insult would be unbearable in Near Eastern societies. Younger sons did leave home in search of better working and living conditions, but they did not take their heritage with them. Most of them had to go into business of some kind and mingle with Gentiles in commerce. This was considered "death" and living with "hogs." Those who did this were considered lost to the Jewish cause. The proud older son, who could stay home and retain possession of the family property and observe all of the orthodox practices, looked condescendingly at other Jews who did not, but younger brothers were sometimes forced by economic necessity into their role away from the family land.

The parable did not go into detail explaining whether or not the younger son was justified in his actions because Near Easterners would all under-

---

[30]GWB, *Consequences*, pp. 184-89.

[31]For a list of the explanations scholars have given for the situation, see Bailey, *Poet*, pp. 171-73. Scholars have tried to imagine how a person would literally want to eat food for hogs and not be able to obtain any. This misses the symbolism intended.

[32]GWB,*Consequences*, pp. 110-20.

[33]Bailey, *Poet*, pp. 161-67, has shown, both in antiquity and today, how impossible the situation proposed would be, but he overlooked one exception—Jacob, who left with Isaac's blessing and the heritage.

stand that he was not justified. It means to illustrate the situation in which
the tax collector had "left home" and was eating with the Gentiles (hogs).
Should he be allowed to leave his office of tax collecting and be welcomed
back into loyal Judaism? The position of the older son was that this was altogether unfair—especially the celebration of his return. If he were to be
accepted at all, he might be accepted as a servant.

There are enough references to the feasting and celebrating at the discovery of the "lost" to suspect that Jesus actually held feasts and celebrations when these tax collectors repented and joined his movement.
According to the Markan account, Jesus was accused by the Pharisees of
eating with tax collectors and sinners just after the tax collector, Levi, had
left his office of collecting taxes to follow Jesus (Mk 2:14-17). In relationship to the repentance and commitment to follow Jesus, Jesus offered to stay
with Zacchaeus in his home (Lk 19:1-10). This may have involved another
celebration feast. One of the reasons the Pharisees received reports of Jesus
eating with tax collectors and sinners was that not all of this was done in
just ordinary meals. There may have been special recruitment dinners
where tax collectors and other businessmen discussed with Jesus his program to regain possession of the promised land. There may also have been
celebration banquets held after each one of these wealthy businessmen gave
up his government office and his wealth to assist Jesus in his program.[34]
These conjectured events may not really have happened. An effort has been
made here to deduce the possible events that took place that evoked the
amount of attention they received from the Pharisees and were answered by
the kind of parables Jesus is reported to have told. Three of the parables related to Pharisees and tax collectors conclude with a celebration being held
because the "lost" had been found.

In NT times, Jews were called Jacob, and Romans, as well as Roman
collaborators like Herod, were called Esau or Edom. Probably every Jew
knew the story of Jacob and Esau. Esau was the *older* brother, but he was
not as clever or unprincipled as Jacob, so his younger brother tricked him
out of his just inheritance. The clever way in which Jesus prepared the story
of the prodigal son and the younger brother was to reverse the story. Jacob

---

[34]It would have been much more offensive to the Pharisees if Jesus had actually been
host to these banquets and invited tax collectors into his own home rather than accepting
hospitality in theirs. See Bailey, *Poet*, p. 143.

had managed to manipulate his father in such a way as to obtain Isaac's blessing as well as the heritage of Esau and then leave to go into a far country. Like the prodigal son, however, he returned and took over the heritage. His children became heirs to the entire promised land (Gen 25:19-34; 27:1-28:22; 32:1-33:20; 35:1-15). There are many points where the prodigal son story intentionally parallels the Jacob story.

It was the Pharisees who considered themselves, typologically, to be the true sons of Jacob. It was they who called the tax collectors Esau and Edom. Jesus told a parable that put the tax collector in the role of Jacob who had tricked his older brother out of his inheritance. The Pharisee was shown as the older brother, in this case, who had been left out of the celebration. More than that, this was of the older brother's own doing. Esau just was not as smart as Jacob, or as unprincipled, but the Pharisee still had a chance to belong to the celebration, too. If he did not enter, of course, it seemed that the tax collector, whom the Pharisee referred to as Esau, was really Jacob and he displaced the Pharisaic Esau. Like Jacob of old the tax collector would receive all the blessings. The same implication is involved in the story of the two sons and a vineyard. It was the second son who actually worked in the vineyard who was identified by the Matthaean editor as the tax collectors and harlots who would precede the first son into the kingdom.[35]

In the parables, themselves, no mention is made of tax collectors and sinners in relationship to these two sons. The stories obviously have the same point and each parable is found in only one of the single traditions. That is, the parable of the two sons and the vineyard is found only in Matthew, and the story of the two sons and the heritage is found only in Luke. Neither of these parables is dependent upon the other. Both Matthew and Luke have independently interpreted these parables to represent Jesus' reaction to the chief priests and elders or Pharisees and their scribes. Matthew considered the younger brother to be the "least of these," the tax collectors and harlots, whereas Luke thought the younger represented the tax collectors and sinners. Their separate sources and their separate interpretations by different editors to refer to the same groups of people make it seem more

---

[35]J. D. M. Derrett, *Law in the New Testament,* (London, c1970), pp. 116-18, noticed the importance of the two brothers theme in the OT and discussed the relationship of the older brother to the younger brother in law and in practice, but he failed to see the clever way in which Jesus turned the tables with this theme.

likely that these stories were not composed by the later church, but instead, were preserved by different branches of the church. The fact that their message is the same, and the stories are as clever and pointed as they are, points to the likelihood that one person told both parables to meet the same kind of situation. This kind of independent, coherent creativity accidentally occurring in two branches of the church and independently attributed to Jesus with the same interpretations seems unlikely.

The most reasonable explanation for the existence of these two parables is that Jesus told them, and they were remembered and written down by different people, separately, who understood the same meanings to the parables. The fact that these parables also are coherent with a number of chreias and parables in which two *dramatis personae* were involved: weeds and wheat, good and worthless fish, younger and older brothers, lost sheep and sheep not lost, etc., supports the hypothesis that all these chreias and parables represent basic teachings of Jesus. This does not mean that these are direct quotations from Jesus, but that Jesus seems to have taught something like this, and he trained his disciples to use arguments like these in defense of the tax collectors and in opposition to the Pharisees.

Not all scholars have concluded in agreement with these deductions. Jack Sanders, for instance,[36] argued that the parable is not a unit. Originally it ended with the younger brother returning home. The response of the older brother, said Sanders, is a Lukan addition. The hostility to the Pharisees is Luke's and it was he who revised this parable to show not only the *one* point that Jesus accepted the tax collectors, but he added that Jesus refuted the Pharisees when he told his parable. This accounts for the other Lukan parables, such as the Pharisee and the tax collector, the rich man and Lazarus, and the Good Samaritan. Sanders failed to note that this hostility is also present in Matthew against the Pharisees, as in Matt 23. He also overlooked (1) the important typological theme of two brothers that goes back to the OT, (2) the number of other parables and chreias, both in Matthew and Luke, that have two contrasting elements, and (3) the close relationship between the message of the two sons and the heritage and the two sons and a vineyard, one of which is preserved only in Matthew.

---

[36]J. Sanders, "Tradition and Redaction in Luke 15:11-32," *NTS* 15 (1969):433-38.

L. Schottroff[37] opposed those, like Sanders, who argued against its unity. She thought, however, that Luke himself wrote the whole parable. In opposition, both to her and to Sanders, Carlston[38] analyzed the vocabulary of Lk 15:11-32 in comparison with other Lukan vocabulary and concluded that it is all of one piece, and it is not Lukan, but comes from Luke's sources. He also supported this conclusion by comparing the theological points of view. This does not show that it comes from Jesus, but it opposes the position that it was created by Luke himself. This is also the opinion of Farmer,[39] who has shown that Luke 15 belongs to a source that was Semitic and closely related to Luke 13, which Luke used without making serious changes, and Bailey,[40] on the basis of poetic structure.

The Wedding Feast. "Again, Jesus answered and told them a parable, saying: 'The Kingdom of Heaven is like a man who is a king, who prepared a wedding for his son. He sent his servants to call those who had been invited to the wedding feast, but they did not want to come. Again he sent other servants, saying, ''Tell those who have been invited, 'Look, my meal is ready; my bulls and fatted animals have been slaughtered; and all things are prepared. Come to the wedding feast!' '' But they rudely went away, one to his own field, another to his place of business, [and the rest seized the servants, treated them dishonorably, and killed (them). Then the king became angry, and after he had sent his troops, he destroyed those murderers and burned their city]. Then he said to his servants, ''The wedding feast is ready, and the invited ones were not worthy. Go, then, to the secondary roads and whomever you find invite to the wedding feast.'' When those servants had gone out into the ways, they brought together all whom they found, evil and good, and the bridal chamber was filled with those reclining' '' (Matt 22:1-10; Lk 14:16-24; Gospel of Thomas 64).

The bracketed verses seem to be a later addition to the parable. Both the content and the style are different from that which precedes and follows. The later message which has been intruded seems to reflect either the his-

---

[37]L. Schottroff, "Das Gleichnis vom verlornen Sohn," *ZTK* 68 (1971):27-52.

[38]C. E. Carlston, "Reminiscence and Redaction in Luke 15:11-12," *JBL* 94 (1975):368-90.

[39]W. R. Farmer, "Notes on a Literary and Form Critical Analysis of Some of the Synoptic Material Peculiar to Luke," *NTS* 8 (1963):301-16.

[40]Bailey, *Poet,* pp. 159-61, 191.

torical situation in Judaea after Herod's death and before Archelaus had clearly been established ethnarch of Judaea and Samaria (*BJ* 2.1-105) or the period just before the fall of Jerusalem in A.D. 70. At the end of the Matthaean parable is another parable which is sometimes confused as being a part of the same parable. It is this:

"After the king had entered he looked over those reclining and saw there a man who was not dressed in a wedding garment, and he said to him, 'Friend, how is it that you have entered here without a wedding garment?' Then he was silent. Then the king said to the servant, 'After you have bound him hand and foot, throw him out into outer darkness' " (Matt 22:11-13).

Jeremias[41] correctly held that this was a later addition, partially because there is no known custom that required a wedding garment at a wedding in NT times. Jeremias and Via[42] thought Matthew added it to the other parable to correct the impression the other parable left that almost anyone was welcome to our Christian celebration. That is probably not necessary. Both in NT literature and in Rabbinic literature, editors tended to put under one heading all the material related to that subject, even if it was very remotely related. Here are two parables about weddings and wedding guests, so they were put together. That is all. There is no psychologizing needed to explain the fact.

It is difficult to deduce what this parable might have meant to Jesus, but in the later church the wedding garment was related to baptism. St. John Chrysostom invited those coming to be baptized to come as those being invited to a wedding and to a royal banquet, where, without cost, the one receiving baptism would receive a wedding garment.[43] Members of the Essene sect also attended meals dressed in special white garments they put on after they had bathed (*BJ* 2.127-31). Since they were communally organized, the "free" garment belonged to the whole group. Early Christians may also have provided the initiate a white garment when he was baptized which was called the wedding garment. Only after baptism was the initiate

---

[41]Jeremias, *Parables*, p. 65. R. Augstein, *Jesus*, p. 242, did not know how parables were classified, so he ridiculed the ethics of someone calling in people off the street and then demanding proper garments for the occasion.

[42]D. O. Via, Jr., "The Relationship of Form to Content in the Parables: The Wedding Feast," *Int*. 25 (1971):178.

[43]See *Hom* 8:23; T. Levi 11:9-20; 15:8; 21:2; Hermas, *Sim* 8:2, 3-4.

allowed to share in the holy meals or the eucharist with the rest of the community. Should anyone attempt to attend the eucharist or one of the holy meals without having first been baptized and having a "wedding garment" he or she would be expelled. This may have been the meaning of this "riddle." It was intended to warn against trying to receive communion without first being baptized. But this has to do with the parable which Jesus probably did not tell. The remainder of this discussion will deal with the "Wedding Feast," as it might have been interpreted in Jesus' time

With the exclusion of the additions of the later church (Matt 22:6-7, 11-13), this parable tells of only one event, a wedding feast for a prince. The king first sent his servants to tell the people they would be invited when everything was ready, so this invitation would not come as a surprise. Then, after everything was prepared, the servants went again to these same people to tell them to come, assuming that they would be ready, but they all made the same kind of excuses that Gideon accepted (Jdgs 7:2-7 and Deut 20:5-9) offered by soldiers to exempt themselves from military service, so that only the committed would be involved in war. These may have been included in the parable intentionally to give the listeners, who had ears, the clue that he was not really talking about a wedding but of a war and the people invited offered excuses allowed in the rules of holy warfare.[44] The result was that Jesus, like Gideon, was left with a relatively small number of shock troops with which to begin "the birth pangs of the Messiah."[45] But Jesus did not stop the story there. He needed more troops, so he invited those still less qualified, and these came![46]

Again, here is a parable in which two groups of people were involved. The first group, like the first son in the vineyard, was invited but did not

---

[44]L. Schottroff and W. Stegemann, *Jesus von Nazareth—Hoffnung der Armen,* (Stuttgart, c1978), p. 131, failed to notice the Deuteronomic origin of these excuses, so they held that the excuses " . . . can be understood as nothing else than foolish . . . *there are no reasonable excuses for the refusal* [italics theirs]. These may also have seemed foolish to the Romans. That was their intent.

[45]For the use and meaning of this expression, see GWB, *Revelation,* pp. 20, 23, 282, 310, 319, 533, 577, 583, 585.

[46]E. Linnemann, *Jesus,* pp. 25, 89-91, did not see this, so she did not think the host solved his problem of embarrassment by letting down his standards. Therefore she conjectured that the first one planned to come, but *not on time.* The main problem was not the host's embarrassment. It was the need to fill the ranks, and the real topic was not a wedding but a war, not guests, but recruits.

come. The second group, composed of those who had been invited only as a last resort, were like laborers who came at 5:00 P.M. to work in the vineyard, or like the second son who did not want to work in the vineyard but finally repented and worked. The second group was like the younger son who returned home and attended a feast held in his honor. This parable, then, seems to be another one of those attacking the Pharisees and justifying the admission of those tax collectors and other businessmen who were invited after the Pharisees had made legitimate excuses. In this parable, it was the Pharisees who were chosen first but the tax collectors who actually attended the feast. The image of a feast may also have been used to give a different slant to the criticism of Jesus' eating with tax collectors and harlots. The parable includes Jesus in the role of a king, a fitting place for one who aspired to be the messianic king of Israel. Jeremias correctly observed that in the Lukan narrative, the servant was sent out a third time, probably to the Gentiles after the tax collectors proved inadequate. This, Jeremias correctly thought, was an addition of the later church to include conditions that were not part of the situation when Jesus was recruiting followers.[47] There is still another parable dealing with a banquet.

Humility and Hospitality. "He began to tell a parable to the guests [of the Pharisee], observing how they chose the first seats, saying to them, 'When you are invited by someone to a wedding feast do not let yourself be reclined at the first place, lest someone more highly respected than you be invited by him. Then, after he has come to you and called you, he will say, "Make room for this one," and then you will begin, shamefully, to go down to the last place. But when you are invited, go and fall down at the last place, so that when the host comes, he will say to you, "Friend, come up higher." Then you will be honored before all those who are reclining with you, for everyone who exalts himself will be humbled, and everyone who humbles himself will be exalted' " (Lk 14:7-11).

Jeremias[48] did not find any problem with the form of this parable, but it clearly is not now in parable form. Parts of a parable have been incorporated into an exhortation. Originally this parable ended with a sentence or two that is not here, telling what happened after the person had been invited to "come up higher." It also would have begun with an introduction that is

---

[47]Jeremias, *Parables,* p. 64.

[48]*Ibid.,* pp. 191-93.

no longer here. That introduction would have told of a situation in which, probably, one person came to a feast and took the highest seat and another came and took the lowest seat, resulting in one being asked to have a lower place and the other being invited to come up higher. The *dramatis personae* given in that introduction would have provided whatever clues were necessary to indicate how the parable was used and what it was intended to mean.

In its context in Luke this is part of a whole collection of parables and sayings that are related to behavior at meals or stories about meals. After all the conflicts between Jesus and the Pharisees about dietary rules, it is surprising to find Jesus as a guest in a Pharisee's home. If he had been there, it would have been poor etiquette for Jesus to have attacked the host or his sect as the parable pictures him doing. Like the parable of the Pharisee and the tax collector, this parable may originally have shown a Pharisee taking the highest seat and the tax collector taking the lowest. The great reversal would come when the men were asked to exchange seats. Such a parable would be completely coherent with the other chreias and parables related to tax collectors and Pharisees, but to become a parable with these *dramatis personae* the very material necessary to identify the meaning of the parable would have been conjectured. Because there is little basis for this kind of circular conjecture, this narrative, which contains some parts of a parable, does not deserve much weight in determining the teachings of Jesus. The only value in its inclusion here is to show that its teachings are not incoherent with other chreias and parables. The same situation is partially true of the next parable, with some important differences: it now is a complete parable, although there are good reasons for doubting that it is now in its original form.

The Problem of Purity. "A certain man went down from Jerusalem to Jericho, and he fell among brigands who disrobed him, whipped him, and went away, leaving him half dead. By chance, a certain priest, going down that way, seeing him, went by on the other side. Likewise a Levite, coming to that place, when he saw him, went by on the other side. But a Samaritan, while traveling, came to the place where he was, and when he saw him, had compassion. He came to him, bound up his wounds, pouring on oil and wine. Then he put him on his own donkey and brought him to the inn and took care of him. The next day, he gave the inn keeper two denarii and said, 'Take care of him, and whatever you charge, when I return I will repay you' '' (Lk 10:20-35).

There are some problems with this parable—since Jews and Samaritans had nothing to do with one another, what business did a Samaritan have in Judaea, going from Jerusalem to Jericho? How did a Samaritan gain such prestige that he had credit with a Jewish inn keeper? The story is told as if the one who dealt mercifully with the wounded man was a person who was well-known, who traveled frequently in those parts, was trusted, and had credit. The parable also puts the Samaritan in a confused light—on the one hand he is praised as the one who helped the person in need, therefore being the hero of the story. But, on the other hand, he was presented with the questionable distinction of being, by definition, a person who had no religious principles and one who could be expected to have no concern for the commandments of the Torah.[49] This reflects an anti-Samaritan bias from a Jewish point of view. Samaritans were probably at least as careful in their ritualistic observances as Jews were. Both Jews and Samaritans insulted one another by calling the other defiled.[50] If this had been composed at one time by one person, the reader might expect a pro-Samaritan to have presented the Samaritan from a pro-Samaritan bias as the hero who was also pious. This would have required another situation altogether.

Initially this must have been neither a pro-Samaritan nor an anti-Samaritan parable. The benefactor would have been someone who contrasted in an important way with the priest and Levite, the "bad guys" in the story. The reason the priest and the Levite could not help the wounded man was that he was "half dead." Suppose he should die and become a corpse while they were trying to help him? The priest was going the wrong way to be under requirement to keep himself pure so that he could administer at the temple that day or shortly thereafter. If he had been assigned to assist in the temple service he would not have been permitted to touch a corpse for eight

---

[49]Not noticing this problem, J. D. Crossan, "Parable and Example in the Teaching of Jesus," *Semeia*, 1 (1974), p. 76, took the story at face value and said its goal was to put together two impossible and contradictory terms—good and Samaritan. He said whenever a person could say both together "then the kingdom of God has come upon him in this experience" (p. 77)—but not any kind of kingdom that would have satisfied Jesus or his followers.

[50]GWB, "The Samaritan Origin of the Gospel of John," *Religions of Antiquity* (Leiden, 1970), pp. 149-75. Jews considered Samaritan females defiled as menstruants from their cradles (Nid 4:1). Samaritans also classified Jewish women as defiled, but they did not think of *themselves* as being defiled, as this parable presumes. Samaritans, on the contrary, said it was Judah who brought adultery into the world (*Memar Marqah* 4.9, 168).

days before then. Of course, it was customary for Jews to have a reserve priest to meet such emergencies as these (Yoma 1:1), but priests and Levites coveted these prominent roles and did not want to be deprived of their privileges. Even though the priest was going away from Jerusalem and could have been purified before there was any service requirement for him, he still preferred to be undefiled at all times. The same was true for the Levite. The "good guy" could have been an ordinary Israelite or Jew who was not careful about purity rules. This would not have been a Pharisee or an Essene,[51] but someone like an *'am ha'aretz*, who was unlearned in legal practices, or more likely, a well-educated, informed Jew who did not observe all the Jewish rules that he knew. The character should have been one who would not have been insulted by the suggestion that he was non-observant. Since the benefactor seemed to have had credit and enough money to pay for things like this, he seems to have been at least moderately wealthy. This qualifies him as a candidate for the role of tax collector or some other wealthy businessman with whom Jesus associated, whom the Pharisees despised. Since this parable, like many others, has two classes of people being compared or contrasted, it fits perfectly the pattern of the Pharisee and the tax collector. Such a parable would also resemble the two sons and a vineyard, two sons and a heritage, the lost and safe sheep, the good and worthless fish, or the wheat and the weeds. The characters must have been switched by some Christian in the diaspora, like the author of Acts, who was interested in removing all signs of Christian disunity. He did not know any more about Samaritans than he had been told by Jewish Christians, so he presumed that they were almost synonymous with tax collectors—since both were always defiled according to Jewish Christians. So he tried to promote Christian unity among hostile Christians by replacing the term "tax collector" with its "synonym," "Samaritan," without realizing what an impossible situation he had created. Samaritans would not have been pleased by the anti-Samaritan insult attributed to Samaritans by the final edition of the parable.

From the Pharisaic point of view, the wealthy Jew who mingled with the Romans and became defiled was worse than useless. He was unpardonably damaged. Jesus frequently used understatements to plead the case of the tax collector who repented. In this situation, for example, the tax col-

---

[51]Contra C. Daniel, "Les Essenians et l'arriere-fond historique de la Parabole du Bon Samaritain," *Nov* 11 (1969):71-104.

lector could do that which priests, Levites, Pharisees, and other observant people could not do. He could be compassionate and save a man's life. The Pharisee, by way of contrast, would let a person die rather than become defiled, the way Jesus had done to be in communication with the sinners just so that he could call them to repentance. This parable may not only have defended the tax collector but even Jesus, himself, who, like the benefactor, willingly became defiled to save those, like the tax collectors, who had been left to die. The Pharisee was made to look as bad in this parable as he had in the parables of the two brothers, in which the Pharisee always came out as the older brother, Esau!

Like Matthew Luke had access to an adequate collection of parables that showed Jesus pleading for the tax collector in conflict with the Pharisees. He used many of them in his gospel but he may have had more which told the same basic message. Since he was omitting some, anyway, it may not have seemed wrong to him to alter just one to uphold his own views which he presumed were pro-Samaritan. If he really did that, he did not succeed very well because his changes were both positive and negative in relationship to Samaritans. If Jesus actually told this parable as it now is, it would show that Jesus not only wanted to show a Samaritan in a favorable light, but that he also had some unconscious, anti-Samaritan feelings that caused him to show the Samaritan as one who was unconcerned for the law. There is no other parable in the gospels to support this possibility.

Many scholars, such as Jeremias,[52] Lagrange,[53] Plummer,[54] and Schlatter[55] have raised no question about the authenticity of the Samaritan in the parable. Although it seems more reasonable that this parable should have been directed against the religious authorities in defense of the "sinners," the argument does not depend upon it. After all, there are the fol-

---

[52]Jeremias, *Parables*, pp. 87, 202-05.

[53]Lagrange, *Evangile*, pp. 312-15.

[54]Plummer, *ICC Luke*, pp. 286-88.

[55]A. Schlatter, *Das Evangelium des Lukas*, pp. 286-88. The same is true of such scholars as Crossan, "Parable," pp. 63-104, and G. Crespy, "La Parabole Dite: 'Le Bon Samaritain,' Recherches Structurales," *Etudes Theologiques et Religieuses* 48 (1973):61-79. G. Sellin, "Lukas als Geheimniserzähler: Die Erzählung vom Barmherzigung Samaritaner, (Lk 10:25-37)," *ZNTW* 60 (1975):19-60, however, considered the possibility that the Samaritan has replaced an Israelite.

lowing chreias and parables that bear the same basic message. If one, two, or more of them seem not to fulfill all of the criteria of form and coherence, the rest of the materials provide strong enough evidence to conclude that Jesus must have been in conflict with the religious authorities, chief of which were the Pharisees, on the subject of careful observance of Pharisaic rules. The primary offense was Jesus' willingness to eat with tax collectors and sinners. Jesus not only defended this action but told parables that pictured the Pharisees themselves as being less pious and ethical than the very tax collectors they attacked.

Chreias on Liberty and Law

The Sick Need the Physician......(Matt 9:10-13; Mk 2:15-17; Lk 5:29-31)
No Fasting at a Wedding......... (Matt 9:14-15; Mk 2:18-20; Lk 5:33-34)
Commandment vs. Tradition ....(Matt 15:1-3; Mk 7:109)
Inner and Outer Defilement............................... (Lk 11:37-39)
The Last Word...(Lk 16:14-15)

Parables on Liberty and Law

The Pharisee and the Tax Collector ....(Lk 18:9-14)
The Wheat and the Weeds............................... (Matt 13:24-30)
The Fish Net... (Matt 18:47-48)
The Non-productive Fig Tree ....(Lk 13:6-9)
The Lost Sheep................................(Matt 18:12-13; Lk 15:1-7)
The Lost Coin ....(Lk 15:8-10)
The Laborers and the Hours............................... (Matt 20:1-16)
Two Sons and a Vineyard................................ (Matt 21:18-31)
Two Sons and a Heritage ....(Lk 15:11-32)
The Wedding Feast ....(Matt 22:1-10; Lk 14:16-24; Gospel of Thomas 64)
Humility and Hospitality......................................(Lk 14:7-11)
The Problem of Purity .... (Lk 10:30-35)

Summary of Chreias and Parables

This chapter began with a chreia that showed Jesus defending his behavior of eating with tax collectors and sinners against the accusing Pharisees. This has proved to have been a popular theme among the chreias and parables. They all make sense together. The characters in the parables seem to play the same roles: Jesus offended the Pharisees by breaking their traditions and accepting tax collectors and sinners. The Pharisees are always presented as stringent legalists who objected to Jesus' behavior.[56]

The criticisms sometimes came to Jesus through his disciples which is not surprising. Like other regal pretenders of NT times Jesus was also a teacher. Some of his disciples—apostles or "fishers of men"—were commissioned to do part of the recruiting. Therefore, they also came in conflict with the Pharisees and disciples of John the Baptist. They had apparently been trained in stock answers and parables to use on certain occasions. When they were left without answers, they came back to Jesus, reported the incident, and Jesus then gave them the responses in case something like that happened again. By putting direct answers in chreia form for easy memory, the way the disciples of Diogenes did, and memorizing parables, these disciples became skilled in their debates. They also collected a large number of chreias and parables, like the ones given in this chapter, which have been preserved ever since. The method of teaching and administering his program that Jesus employed may account for the preservation of many of these teachings.

This is not the usual analysis given for the origin of the parables. Jeremias,[57] for example, said, " . . . each of them was uttered in an actual situation of the life of Jesus, at a particular and often unforeseen point. Moreover, as we shall see, they were preponderantly concerned with a situation of conflict." The care and skill which these parables reflect do not point to spontaneity and impromptu composition. Furthermore, the conflicts which Jeremias mentioned seemed to be of the same variety. In this chapter were many that would have been choice for any conflict with Pharisees while defending the acceptance of repentant tax collectors. Both Jesus and his apostles had a ready repertoire to meet this anticipated conflict. Knowing the kinds of conflicts that would confront the apostles, he seems to have prepared some apt parables in advance.

There are still other conflicts with Pharisees reported in forms other than chreias and parables. The following are some of them.

---

[56]S. Umen, *Pharisaism and Jesus,* (New York, c1963), p. 127, has tried to subdue Jesus' conflict with the Pharisees. He held that Jesus cannot have been against Pharisees as a whole, "but only certain ones whom he found to be unfaithful to Pharisaism either deliberately or through ignorance."

[57]Jeremias, *Parables,* p. 21.

Other Teachings

"At that time Jesus went through the wheat fields on the Sabbath, and his disciples were hungry and they began to pluck heads of wheat and eat. When the Pharisees saw, they said to him, 'Look! your disciples are doing that which is not lawful to do on the Sabbath!' Then he said to them, ['Do you not know what David did when he was hungry and those with him? How he entered the house of God and ate the loaves of the presence, which was not lawful for him to eat nor those with him, but for the priests only (1 Sam 21:1-6)? Or, have you not read in the law that on the Sabbath the priests abandon the Sabbath in the temple and are innocent? I tell you that something greater than the temple is here. If you had known what [the text,] "I want mercy and not sacrifice" (Hos 6:6) [means,] you would not have persecuted the innocent]. For the Lord of the Sabbath is the Son of man' " (Matt 12:1-8).

If this had once been a chreia, then the bracketed portion of this unit is a commentary added later to explain the punch line which claims that Jesus, like other political and ecclesiastical monarchs, was legally infallible. He made laws as he saw fit, so his position placed him, not only above the Sabbath, but above the law. Because he defined it, he could not be justly accused of breaking it. This means he was like David, so the interpreter quoted scripture to show the analogy. That justified his legal authority, but the second scriptural authority proved that he was no worse than priests when he broke the Sabbath. Although the accusation, attributed to the Pharisees, is consistent with other accusations made about breaking Jewish law, this is the first tine Jesus was attacked for breaking the Sabbath. By extension, this is coherent with the chreias and parables shown above, but it is more precise. Since none of the attacks against Jesus' breaking the Sabbath is now found in chreia form, there is more reason to think Jesus offended the Pharisees by breaking laws in general than that he broke just this particular one.

Doing Good on the Sabbath

Which man among you, who has one sheep,
and if it falls into a ditch on the Sabbath,
will he not seize it and pull it out?
How much more valuable, then, is a nan than a sheep?

(Matt 12:11-12; Mk 3:4; Lk 6:9)

This is an *a fortiori* argument: if this situation is true of the less valuable object, a sheep, how much more for a more valuable object, a person. Jewish legalists in NT times were not in agreement about whether or not a sheep should be pulled out of a well or a ditch or should be left there.[58] Luke has reported a similar argument:

Animals vs. Children of Abraham. "The Lord answered and said, 'Hypocrites! Each of you on the Sabbath day, will he not loose his cow or his donkey from his manger and lead them out to water? This is a daughter of Abraham whom Satan has bound—look! eighteen years! Was it not necessary that she be released from this bondage on the Sabbath day?' " (Lk 13:15-16; 14:5).

Tax Collectors and John. "I tell you under oath that the tax collectors and the harlots will precede you into the Kingdom of God, for John came to you in the way of righteousness, and you did not believe him, but the tax collectors and the harlots believed him. When you saw, you did not even repent and later believe in him" (Matt 21:31-32).

This seems to be a Matthaean addition to the parable of the two sons and a vineyard. It is addressed to the religious leaders and suggests that not only Jesus, but also John had inspired tax collectors and "harlots" to repent. The Pharisees are accused, not only of failing to respond to John, but also to Jesus. This is consistent with the Lukan report that the soldiers and tax collectors came to John (Lk 3:10-14). This accusation to the religious leaders (probably the Pharisees) is also in keeping with other teachings preserved in chreias and parables.

There are still other teachings and accusations of Jesus against the Pharisees (Matt 23:1-36).[59] They are the harshest sayings recorded of Jesus. They are well organized and consistent among themselves, but there are some reasons for thinking some of them, at least, are later than Jesus' time and are not completely coherent with the teachings in the chreias and parables. The woe against Pharisees on the technical matter of taking oaths presumes the existence of the temple, and therefore, was probably composed before A.D. 70 (Matt 23:16-22). On the other hand, it pictures Jesus

---

[58]Rigorous sectarians commanded, "Let no beast be helped to give birth on the Sabbath day; and if it fall into a cistern or into a pit, let it not be lifted out on the Sabbath" (CD 11:13-14; see also Yoma 85a; Shab 128b; Beza 3:4).

[59]See further H. Merkel, "Jesus und die Pharisaer," *NTW* 14 (1967/1968):194-208.

involved in precisely the kind of legalistic detail which he blamed the Pharisees for entertaining. The accusations against the Pharisees for all the bloodshed from the blood of innocent Abel to the blood of Zechariah (23:35) may be a reference to the mock trial of a righteous wealthy man, named Zechariah, whom the zealots killed after he was pronounced innocent. This happened near the end of the war of A.D. 66-70.

Conclusions

The sayings of Jesus reported in these chreias and parables, showing Jesus in conflict with the Pharisees, are some of the most coherent teachings in the gospels.[60] Furthermore, they are coherent with the chreias and parables related to recruiting followers under pressure. There are several kinds of checks and balances to support their authenticity. It seems very unlikely that any person or persons in any later church or churches could have attributed all of these teachings to Jesus, falsely, and kept them as consistent with each other and with the social and political conditions in Palestine in Jesus' day as these texts reveal. The parable of the tax collector and the Pharisee presumed the existence of the temple, which was destroyed in A.D. 70. In addition, the relationships shown between Jesus and his disciples as they brought in reports and were given instructions and answers are precisely those known to have existed between Greek philosophers and their students. They normally provided a situation whereby a teacher's messages could be used, recorded, and preserved.

Throughout this chapter Jesus appeared in support of a group of wealthy businessmen and tax collectors, with whom he associated, and from whom he obtained a following of very dedicated men. This is not the picture frequently given of Jesus in popular books about him. Was Jesus really closely associated with wealthy people rather than the poor, as he has often been shown? How could a poor carpenter gain access into the homes of wealthy leaders in Palestine? In this, as in the previous chapters, there have been many clues to associate Jesus, not only with wealthy people, but also with a monastic movement. In the next chapter attention will be given to these two items as possible factors in the career of the historical Jesus.

---

[60]Contra Umen, *Pharisaism*. Another defensive work is S. Zeitlin, "The Pharisees," *JQR* 52 (1961/1962):97-129.

CHAPTER FIVE

Monasticism and Economic Classes*

Jesus and the Upper Class

Paul's Collection. During his campaign to raise funds for the poor in Jerusalem, Paul promoted his cause to the Corinthians in the following ways: (1) He told of the sacrificial giving of the Macedonians toward this project. (2) He sent Titus to Corinth to assist the Christians there in their fund raising campaign and encouraged them also to contribute generously and willingly (2 Cor 8:6-8). (3) Paul reminded them of "the grace of our Lord Jesus, that on account of you, became poor when he was rich" (2 Cor 8:9). (4) He further encouraged the Corinthians to complete their fund raising project (2 Cor 8:10-12). Paul said this program of sharing was not intended to inflict undue hardship but to establish an economic equality

---

*The section of this paper dealing with Jesus and the Upper Class was first published in *Novum Testamentum* 8 (1964):195-209. That dealing with monasticism was published in *Religion in Life* 48 (1979):136-42. These have been reused with permission. Small changes have been made in topic headings, footnotes, and conclusions.

(ἰσότατος) among the saints (2 Cor 8:13-15). (5) Paul also recommended Titus and "the brother who is famous for preaching the gospel through all the churches" (2 Cor 8:18). Both of these men were to assist in the campaign at Corinth (2 Cor 8:16-23). (6) He asked the Corinthians to live up to the claims Paul had made for them and not to humiliate Paul before the Macedonians (2 Cor 8:24-9:5). (7) Paul assured the Corinthians of God's blessings for generous givers (2 Cor 9:6-14).

It is evident that his message was intended to persuade the Corinthians to give generously in terms of money. Of the two examples Paul offered them to follow, the first clearly referred to the Macedonians' financial contribution. In this context, it would seem that Jesus' example was of the same nature. Jesus, who had been a rich man (πλούσιος), made himself poor (by giving up his wealth) in accordance with the community related to him (2 Cor 8:9). Although this seems the most likely interpretation of the passage, there are four objections that require evaluation: (1) Some hold that Paul was interested only in the death and resurrection of Jesus and therefore shows no knowledge of Jesus prior to his death[1] (2) Second Corinthians 8:9

---

[1] A. Drews, *The Christ Myth,* tr. D. Burns (Chicago, n.d.), pp. 19, 169, 174-77, 181, 190, 192, 204, 207, 208, 224, 229-30, not only believed Paul did not know of the historical Jesus but that he invented the whole Christian faith by Judaizing the Adonis cult. More recently R. Bultmann, *Das Verhältnis der urchristlichen Christusbotschaft zum historischen Jesus* (Heidelberg, 1962), p. 9, said, "Paul proclaimed the incarnation, crucifixion, and resurrection; i.e. of the life of Jesus, the proclamation may only be the 'that' and the fact of the crucifixion of Jesus. . . . The eschatological and ethical preaching of the historical Jesus played no role with Paul." W. Schmithals, "Paulus und der historischen Jesus," *ZNW* 53 (1962):145-60, said the reason Paul recorded so little of the historical Jesus was that the primitive church rejected the consciousness of the historical Jesus κατὰ σάρκα and replaced it with a gnostic Christ of the Spirit. Hence Paul had no access to extensive historical information.

P. O. Moe, *Paulus und die evangelische Geschichte* (Leipzig, 1912), however, disagreed with the view that Paul knew practically nothing of the historical Jesus. He compared Paul's teachings with those in the gospels and held that their meaning was too close to be accidental. W. Morgan, *The Religion and Theology of Paul* (Edinburgh, c1923), pp. 31, 33, 35, 40, insisted that the risen Christ of Paul represented a generalized picture of the historical Jesus. A. Deissmann, *Paul, a Study in Social and Religious History,* tr. W. E. Wilson (New York, c1957), pp 195-96, also called attention to Paul's knowledge of Jesus. A. M. Hunter, *Paul and his Predecessors* (Philadelphia, c1961), pointed out passages in Paul's letters which he believed represented tradition about Jesus that Paul received from the primitive church.

Most views, like W. Wrede, *Paul,* tr. Lummis (Boston, 1908); G. B. Stevens, *The Pauline Theology* (New York, 1918), p. 207; W. Weinel, *St. Paul the Man and his Work,* tr. G. A. Beinemann (New York, 1906), pp. 314-18; and J. Klausner, *From Jesus to Paul,* tr. W. F.

seems to be paralleled in Philippians 2:6-8 which should be understood Christologically;[2] (3) The concluding clause in Second Corinthians 8:9, "in order that you, by means of his poverty, might become rich," seems not to refer to material riches. Therefore it would seem that his poverty also refers to spiritual poverty; and (4) Jesus has been understood to have come from humble origins and to have ministered to the lower classes of people.[3] These objections will be considered in order.

Stinespring (New York, 1943), pp. 436-37, do not exclude the possibility that Paul knew some historical tradition about Jesus, but they insist that he was primarily interested in the crucifixion and resurrection.

[2]So C. A. A. Scott, *St. Paul the Man and the Teacher* (Cambridge, 1936), p. 89; Stevens, *Pauline Theology*, p. 208; F. V. Filson, "The Second Epistle to the Corinthians," *The Interpreter's Bible*, 10 (New York, 1953):367-68; A. Plummer, *A Critical and Exegetical Commentary on the Second Epistle of St. Paul to the Corinthians* (New York, 1915), pp. 240-41; F. W. Beare, *A Commentary on the Epistle to the Philippians* (New York, c1959), p. 78; Deissmann, *Paul a Study*, pp. 194-95; Bultmann, *Verhältnis*, p. 9; Theology of the New Testament, tr. K. Grobel (New York, 1951) 1:175.

Moe, *Paulus*, interpreted 2 Cor 8:9 and Philip 2:6-8 together, but denied that 2 Cor 8:9 could be understood to refer to the incarnation. He understood ἐπτώχευσεν, however, to mean that Jesus was born in poverty (p. 25) and to have carried out his ministry while belonging to a low income group (pp. 97-98). He did not consider the possibility of Jesus' first having been rich before becoming poor. W. K. Grobel, "The Human Jesus Outside the Gospel and Acts," *New Testament Sidelights*, ed. H. D. McArthur (Hartford, 1960), said, "Without the controls at the gospels one might very easily draw sociological deductions from 2 Cor 8:9 and judge that Jesus on earth had once been wealthy and then had voluntarily descended to a much lower economic status" (p. 86). Although he considered this a "fallacious deduction," Grobel recognized the possible meaning of this text if not read from a specific theological viewpoint.

[3]For imaginative descriptions of the extent of Jesus' poverty, see W. Barclay, *The Mind of Jesus* (New York, c1960, 1961), pp. 9-10, and H. Branscomb, *The Teachings of Jesus* (Nashville, c1931), pp. 12, 92, 213-14. See also J. W. Bowman, *Jesus' Teaching in its Environment* (Richmond, c1963), p. 27; Deissmann, *Paul a Study*, pp. 27-28; and Klausner, *From Jesus to Paul*, pp. 440-41. Hunter, *Predecessors*, p. 11, commenting on 2 Cor 8:9, said, ". . . but his choice of the verb ἐπτώχευσεν would have been inept if he had not known that the earthly lot of Jesus was not one of affluence." J. G. Machen, *The Origins of Paul's Religion* (New York, 1923), p. 150, said of 2 Cor 8:9, ". . . although the reference may be primarily to the poverty of any human life as compared with the glories of the preexistent Christ, yet the peculiar choice of words is probably due to the details of Jesus' life of hardship." Drews, *The Christ Myth*, p. 115, said the suggestion that Jesus was the son of a carpenter reflects the influence of the Adonis cult. Kinyras, the father of Adonis, was also a carpenter or smith. Drews said further that if Paul had known of Jesus' sympathy for the poor this could have been especially adapted for effective proselytising (pp. 178-79).

Paul's Knowledge of Jesus. Although Paul's central concern for Jesus was his crucifixion and resurrection, he also indicated that he knew of Jesus as one "who was from the seed of David according to the flesh" (Rom 1:3). He also described the last supper to the Corinthians as a meal held in memory of Jesus on the night that he was betrayed (1 Cor 11:23-26). Romans were admonished to please their neighbors "for Christ did not please himself" (Rom 15:3). The clear distinction Paul made between his own judgment (1 Cor 7:12) and the counsel given by "the Lord" (1 Cor 7:10) evidently refers to Jesus' teachings on marriage and divorce (see also Matt 5:32; Mk 10:2-12). Paul's affirmation, "I know and am convinced by the Lord Jesus (ἐν κυρίῳ Ἰησοῦ) that nothing is ritually unclean in itself" (Rom 14:14), apparently indicates Paul's acquaintance with the teachings of Jesus.[4] This suggests that Paul knew something about the life and teachings of Jesus and that his conversion from Pharisaism to Christianity meant rejecting one faith and accepting another already known and related to Jesus and his ministry as well as his crucifixion and resurrection. Although the crucifixion and resurrection received primary attention in the letters of Paul, Paul did not hesitate to refer to an example or teaching of Jesus when the occasion required it. One such occasion seems to have been the appeal for funds to the Corinthians when the examples of Jesus and the Macedonians were used to prompt the Corinthians to share their financial possessions.

Second Corinthians 8:9 and Philippians 2:6-8. Lohmeyer[5] has called attention to the fact that Philippians 2:6-11, with the omission of "death on a cross," forms a unified poem of six three-line stanzas. Lohmeyer held that this was a primitive Christian hymn and was not Pauline.[6] Indeed, ever

---

[4]Paul's affirmation here is consistent with the anti-legalistic teachings of Jesus found in the synoptic gospels.

[5]E. Lohmeyer, *Die Briefe an die Philipper an die Kolosser und an Philemon* (Göttingen, 1956), pp. 90-91.

[6]Lohmeyer's view was supported by Bultmann, *Theology of the New Testament* 1:125, 131, 298; O. Cullmann, *The Christology of the New Testament,* tr. S. C. Guthrie and C. A. M. Hall (Philadelphia, c1959), pp. 174-81; Jean Hering, *Le Royaume de Dieu et sa Venue* (Neuchatel, c1959), pp. 159-70; Hunter, *Predecessors,* p. 122; and J. Jeremias, "Zur Gedankenfuhrung in den Paulinischen Briefen," *Studia Paulina* (Haarlem, 1953), pp. 152-54; Beare, *Philippians,* pp. 77-78, says Paul did not write the hymn but that it was probably written by "a gifted writer of his own circle" (p. 78). W. D. Davies, *St. Paul and Rabbinic Judaism* (London, 1958), p. 42, also suggested that the hymn was written either by Paul or

since Bauer,[7] some scholars have doubted the Pauline authorship of the whole letter to the Philippians. It has not held the same assured position among the authentic letters of Paul as has Galatians, Romans, and the Corinthian correspondence. This poem in Philippians was evidently written by some other Christian and quoted either by Paul or some later writer belonging to the Pauline school, or it may have been written later than the rest of the letter and added to it. In any event, it is judicious to hesitate before utilizing a non-Pauline letter in Philippians 2:6-11 to interpret a passage in one of Paul's letters in a way that apparently conflicts with its own context. Philippians 2:2-6 says that although Jesus was in the form of God, he chose the rank and status of a slave, accepting the humility of crucifixion. Second Corinthians 8:9, on the other hand, without mentioning Jesus' God-like status, his accepted role as a slave, or his crucifixion, in an appeal for funds, said that Jesus, though he had been rich, for the sake of his followers became a poor man. It seems likely that Second Corinthians 8:9 and Philippians 2:6-8 were written by two different authors and may have different meanings.

In Philippians 2:3, the Philippians were encouraged to make themselves humble in relationship to one another. The basis for this conduct was the example Christ showed when he took the form of a slave (Philip 2:6-8). Even though the Pauline authorship of Philippians 2:6-8 is not probable, a strong argument could be made to interpret Second Corinthians 8:9 Christologically if Paul regularly urged specific Christian behavior on the basis of the divine status of Christ which he voluntarily forfeited either at birth or at the crucifixion. A careful examination of Paul's bases for ethics, however, shows that this is not the case: Christians were to imitate Paul (1 Cor 4:15-16; Gal 4:12; Philip 3:17; 2 Thes 3:6-7) who, in turn, imitated Christ (1 Cor 10:32-11:1; 2 Cor 10:1; Philip 3:10-12) or they were to imitate

---

one of his disciples. L. Cerfaux, *Christ in the Theology of St. Paul,* tr. G. Webb and A. Walker (New York, c1959), pp. 374-77; C. B. Caird, *The Apostolic Age* (London, c1955), p. 114; E. F. Scott, "The Epistles to Philippians," *Interpreter's Theology,* tr. J. Marsh (New York, 1955), pp. 117-18, fn. p. 369, pp. 283-84, still hold that these verses are Pauline.

[7]F. C. Baur, *Paulus der Apostel Jesu Christi* (Stuttgart, 1845), pp. 458-75. For appraisals of the views of others who question the Pauline authorship of Philippians, see M. R. Vincent, *A Critical and Exegetical Commentary on the Epistle to the Philippians and to Philemon* (New York, 1911), pp. xxvi-xxx and H. A. W. Meyer, *Critical and Exegetical Hand-Book to the Epistles to the Philippians and Colossians,* tr. J. C. Moore (New York, 1885), pp. 4-6.

Christ's example directly (Rom 15:2-3). They could imitate Christ by pleasing their neighbors as Jesus did, or Paul could suffer as Jesus did (Philip 3:10; Col 1:24). But these are examples of the historical Jesus—not an interpretation of his origin, nature, or status. Some ethics were based on the character, purpose, or will of God (1 Cor 14:33; Philip 2:12-13; Col 3:13; 1 Thes 5:9-11, 12-22) or because of God's promises (2 Cor 7:1) or justice (Gal 6:6-10; Philip 2:14-15; Col 3:23-24; 2 Thes 1:5-12; 2:14-15). Paul further referred to teachings or commands of the Lord Jesus (Rom 14:14; 1 Cor 7:10, 12; Gal 6:2) or character that pleased the Lord or was fitting in the Lord (Col 3:18, 20). He also expected certain behavior because the Lord was at hand (Philip 14:5), and he exhorted Christians in the name of Jesus (1 Cor 5:3-4) or in the Lord Jesus (2 Thes 3:12). Paul further reminded the Christians of the implications of their new faith and freedom (Gal 5:1-16, 25; Col 2:6; 3:1, 5, 8, 12; 4:1). The relationship of Christ to the new community was such that Christians belonged to Christ (1 Cor 6:19-20); their bodies were members of Christ (1 Cor 6:15); and Christ, the paschal Lamb, had been sacrificed for the community (1 Cor 5:7). Therefore, sin against the brethren was sin against Christ (1 Cor 8:11-12; 10:14-16; 2 Cor 13:5), and certain ethics were required for the sake of the church (1 Cor 8:11-12; 12:12, 27; 2 Cor 2:10; Col 1:24), the sake of Christ (Philip 1:27), love (Phil 8), or friendship to Paul (Phil 14).

Other teachings and commandments of Paul were based on Paul's opinion (1 Cor 7:25), historic precedent (1 Cor 10:1-13), common sense (1 Cor 15:33), human merit or justice (1 Cor 16:10; 2 Cor 7:2), and appeal to help for a common cause (2 Cor 1:11) while some admonitions were not accompanied by any justification at all (2 Cor 13:11-12; Philip 1:27; Col 4:16). In none of these instances was the incarnation mentioned as a motivation for specific Christian behavior. The ethics motivated by the crucifixion were: (1) Christ's sufferings prompted Paul to share in his sufferings for the sake of the church (Philip 3:10-11; Col 1:24); and (2) Christ's sacrifice, considered the Christians' paschal Lamb, should have prompted Christians to cleanse their community of all ''leavened bread'' so that the Passover might be celebrated properly (1 Cor 5:6-8). The first is an example in the life of the historical Jesus that inspired similar action in the historical Paul. The second is an analogy which interpreted an act of Christ in a way that was intended to motivate an appropriate response, not an example to follow as in Second Corinthians 8:9.

The Relationship of Second Corinthians 8:9a to 9b. "The grace of our Lord Jesus Christ" (1 Cor 8:9a) was shown by Christ's becoming poor when he had been rich (2 Cor 8:9a). When understood in relationship to the Macedonians who had given money and the Corinthians who were asked to give money, it would seem likely that Paul also cited Jesus as an example of one who had given money. But the verse continues "in order that you, by means of this poverty might be rich" (2 Cor 8:9).

A Priori, the following three interpretations are possible for Second Corinthians 8:1-9: (1)The Macedonians had given generously of their money; the Corinthians were asked to give money; Jesus became spiritually poor so that the Corinthians might become spiritually rich. (2) The Macedonians gave money; the Corinthians were asked to give money; Jesus gave up his money so that the Corinthians might become financially rich. (3) The Macedonians gave money; the Corinthians were asked to give money; Jesus gave up his wealth so that the Corinthians might gain spiritual riches because of the merit he added to the treasury of merits.

Number one is the usual interpretation which needs no further support. Number two might be strengthened from the same context in Second Corinthians 9:10-11, in which Paul assured the Corinthians that their own giving would cause God to bless them more abundantly so that they would become rich (πλουτιζόμενοι) for all their generosity. Since money seemed to be Paul's concern at the moment, in Second Corinthians 8:9 he might have meant that Jesus voluntarily became economically poor so that the Corinthians might receive more abundant material blessings, but in another context, Paul thanked God that the Corinthians had "been made rich in everything in him" (1 Cor 1:5). "Everything" was pointed out more specifically as "every word and every knowledge" (1 Cor 1:5). Hence their newly acquired wealth referred to their gain in spiritual and intellectual insights. This evidence would favor either the first or the third possibilities. Arguments in favor of the third instead of the first are twofold: (1) Paul did not customarily refer to Christ's divine nature when urging Christians to follow a certain pattern of behavior; and (2) more than once, Paul referred to sharing material goods in exchange for spiritual benefits.

On his way to Spain, Paul hoped to stop at Rome that he might share with the Roman Christians some spiritual gift so that the Romans might be strengthened, or rather that both Paul and the Roman Christians might be "mutually comforted" while Paul was there (Rom 1:11). The comforting Paul expected to receive might have been partly spiritual, but it probably involved a financial contribution from the Romans so that Paul might be "sent on" to Spain by the Roman Christians (Rom 15:24). This is in harmony with Paul's admonition that he who is "taught the word" should "share all good things with him who teaches" (Gal 4:6; see also 1 Cor 9:11). The same kind of relationship between material and spiritual responsibilities was basic to Paul's reason for taking up the collection: "For if by means of their [the saints at Jerusalem] spiritual things, they shared with the Gentiles, [the Gentiles] are obliged also by means of fleshly things to minister to them [the saints of Jerusalem]" (Rom 15:27). Therefore it is within the realm of Paul's logic to have considered Jesus' financial contribution both to have brought spiritual riches to the Corinthians and to have motivated them to follow Jesus' example by making a financial contribution to the Jerusalem Christians. Since this is not the only possible interpretation, however, it will be necessary to examine the relationship Jesus had with the various social classes and some relevant Jewish customs in Jesus' time to learn whether or not there is any possibility that Paul in Second Corinthians 8:9 was actually reporting a historical event.

Jesus and the Social Classes

One of the reasons for thinking that Jesus was reared in the home of a laborer and belonged to the lower economic class is the question: "Is not this the son of a carpenter (ὁ τοῦ τέκτονος υἱός)?" (Matt 13:55).[8] Before concluding that a carpenter was inevitably a member of the lower classes, however, it will be necessary to examine the use of the word "carpenter" to learn the limits or extent of this profession in ancient times.

The Greek word that is translated "carpenter" is τέκτων. This has the basic meaning of one who scrapes, planes, hews, or builds. Words closely related to τέκτων are τεκνάζω, which means to employ, contrive, use cunning or practice; and τεχνή which means a way, means, or manner whereby a thing is gained. It is an art, system, set of rules of making or doing: τέχνημα is a work of art or treatise; and a τεχνιτής is a skilled workman in some special area, such as war, religious practices, theatrical art, or

---

[8]Matt 13:55-56 is an apparent expansion of a chreia. The chreia probably did not include the reference about the carpenter's son, which seems to have been added later. It is difficult, however, to imagine why the later church would add Matt 13:55-56 to a chreia if the statement were not true.

trickery. This is the term used to describe God who is the builder of the city which had foundations (Heb 11:10).

The breadth of meaning that has become attached to words related to τέχτων suggests that the word, τέχτων, may have expanded in meaning from the simple craftsman to one who supervises craftsmen. The Iliad provides two illustrations to indicate the extended meaning of the term, "carpenter." One is a reference to Harmon the τέχτων, whose hands were cunning to make all kinds of curious work. He built for Alexandros the trim ships, source of ills that were the bane of all the Trojans (*Il.* 5:59-64). It is not likely that Harmon made all the ships of the Trojans with his own hands. Credit for the work was given to him just as credit for a military victory is often attributed to the general in charge of a battle. In another context, Hector was seen entering the palace of Alexandros which Alexandros himself built with those who were the best carpenters (οἱ τότ ἄριστοι . . . τέχτονες ἄνδρες) then in deep-soiled Troyland. These made him his chamber, reception hall, and courtyard (*Il.* 6:313-16). This does not mean that Alexandros was a carpenter who built his own palace, but that he employed carpenters to build it. The most excellent carpenters were the ones in charge of the building, but unless they were very numerous, they did not do all of this work with their own hands. These so-called carpenters were probably contractors who designed and directed the building of the entire palace for Alexandros.[9]

If Jesus had been a carpenter who worked with his hands, then his home background was nowhere reflected in his teachings. There are only three references to building in the synoptic gospels: One is a quotation from Ps 118:22: " 'The very stone which the builders (οἰκοδομοῦντες) rejected has become the head of the corner' " (Matt 21:42; Lk 20:17). The second example compares the house whose foundation is built on rock with the one whose foundation is built on sand (Lk 6:46-49). This, however, is the type of insight one might expect from a contractor rather than a small craftsman.

---

[9]The argument would be stronger if some examples of an extended use of τέχτων could be found in NT times and if there were not a known-term, ἀρχιτέχτων, which sometimes described a chief engineer or person in charge of a building project (W. Dittenberger [ed.], *Orientis Graeci Inscriptions Selectae* 2:39; W. Dittenberger [ed.], *Sylloge Inscriptionum Graecarum*, 540, 160. So J. H. Moulton and Milligan, *The Vocabulary of the Greek Testament* [London, 1914] 1:82). Moulton and Milligan, ibid., p. 82, said further, "It is worthwhile to remember that τέχτων in its turn is wider than 'carpenter.' "

This is also true of the observation that one who wants to build a tower, first sits down and counts the cost to see whether or not he has enough money to complete the project (Lk 15:18-30). If these references give us any clue to the earlier occupation of Jesus, it suggests that his building activity was done on a larger scale than is normally thought and would be more closely related to business administration than to manual labor.[10]

The gospel teachings related to carpentry, however, are very few, hardly enough to establish Jesus' earlier career as that of a carpenter, much less to prove that his talents were employed in one particular class rather than the other. Furthermore, Jesus' teachings would not necessarily show the class from which he originated. It is probable that the teachings were prepared for the audience to which he spoke which might have been different from the social class in which he was reared. It is an impressive fact, however, that there are very few teachings of Jesus that reflect lower class associations, such as "The New Patch on the Old Garment" (Matt 19:16; Mk 2:21; Lk 5:36). In contrast are the teachings about "The Wheat and the Weeds" (Matt 13:24-30) and the "Unproductive Fig Tree" (Lk 13:6-9) in which the central figure was a gentleman farmer. "The Treasure Hidden in a Field" and "The Precious Pearl" (Matt 13:45) were discovered by men who were financially able to acquire their findings. The shepherd who found "The Lost Sheep" owned ninety-nine more (Lk 15:3-6). "The Unforgiving Servant" had borrowed ten thousand talents (Matt 18:23-25). The master

---

[10]G. H. Dalman, *Sacred Sites and Ways,* tr. P. Levertoff (London, c1955), said, "In the small market of the town, which serves a large district, there is today no special lane of *Carpenters* or *Joiners*. Only the forging of sickles and winnowing knives can be considered a trade characteristic of Nazareth" (p. 68). Dalman referred to Ludwig Schneller, *Kennst du das Land?* (1920), p. 58, who said Jesus "could only have been a bricklayer, since house-building in Palestine did not require any other kind of workmanship" (p. 69), but Dalman, eager to establish tradition, responded: "There must have been one or more workers in wood, who put up the roof-beams of the house and also supplied the modest requirements of a villager, as, for instance, ploughs and yokes, and spare parts of these; also doors, trunks, and bedsteads in particular" (p. 70). In the same context Dalman continued to comment on the economy of Nazareth: "Together with agriculture, the cultivation of fruit—especially olives, figs, and vines—must have been the chief occupation of the inhabitants of Nazareth. An old proverb says: 'It is easier to raise a legion of olives in Galilee than one child in the land of Judah' " [GenR 20.42b] (p. 70).

Dalman believed that Jesus was a carpenter because the NT and later Christian literature said so, but he had to imply the need for the trade in the town of Nazareth. It evidently never occurred to Dalman to consider the meaning of the word, "carpenter," in early times.

who entrusted his servants with talents (Matt 25:14-30; Lk 19:1-28), the manager who set one servant over his household (Matt 24:45-51), the landlord who leased his property to tenants (Matt 21:33-41; Mk 12:1-9; Lk 20:9-16), the man who hired laborers to work in his vineyard (Matt 20:1-16), the dishonest business manager's employer (Lk 16:1-9), and the householder in danger of robbery (Matt 24:43-44) were all property owners. Activities of kings were prominent illustrations in Jesus' teaching (Matt 22:1-14; see also Lk 14:16-24; Matt 25:31-46; Mk 3:24-25; Lk 11:17; 14:31-32). "The Good Samaritan" had credit at Jericho (Lk 10:30-37). "The Pharisee and the Tax Collector" were probably both wealthy men with different attitudes (Lk 18:10-14). The point of the parable about Dives and Lazarus (Lk 16:19-31) was pertinent only to those of Dives' income bracket. "The Wise and Foolish Virgins" were selected to participate in an elaborate, and therefore costly, wedding ceremony (Matt 25:1-13). Zacchaeus was a chief tax collector and very rich. In response to Jesus he volunteered to give half his goods to "the poor," the other half he needed to pay off his iniquities at the rate of four to one (Lk 19:1-10).[11] The man who wanted to inherit eternal life was described by Mark as rich (Mk 10:17-22) and by Luke as a ruler (Lk 18:18-23; see also Matt 19:16-22). "The Fool" was properly described as rich (Lk 12:16-20). The father of the "Prodigal Son" had enough wealth to give the younger son his share of the inheritance without breaking up the homestead (Lk 15:11-32). The accepted subordinate role of the servant who received no thanks (Lk 19:7-10) was directed to gentlemen farmers rather than servants.[12]

In some of the teachings the reference to wealth was needed to illustrate a point and therefore does not indicate the social class either of the teacher or his audience. Others however, would be pointless if told to people who had not enough wealth to entertain guests, hire servants, be generous in their contributions, etc. The audiences, at least, were predominately wealthy, and in the Near East where social position is recognized and re-

---

[11]L. Schottroff and W. Stegemann, *Jesus von Nazareth—Hoffnung der Armen* (Stuttgart, c1978), p. 138, tried to explain the "half" on the basis that John the Baptist asked those who had two coats to share with those who had none (Lk 3:11).

[12]S. Umen, *Pharisaism and Jesus* (New York, c1963), p. 116, evidently overlooked some of these factors when he concluded that Jesus "sought out therefore, the poor, the ignorant, the hated publicans (tax collectors for Rome), and those that for one reason or another had been expelled from their Jewish community."

spected, a teacher from the lower classes would have been less likely to have found his most attentive listeners among upper classes than a teacher who, himself, had been reared in upper class conditions.[13]

That Jesus did, in fact, direct his teachings to the upper class becomes more evident when his associations are considered: The Roman centurion (Matt 8:5-13; Lk 7:1-10), the ruler (Matt 9:18-25), Jairus, the ruler of a synagogue (Lk 8:40-56), and the Syrophoenecian woman (Mk 7:26-30) had some point of contact that moved them to seek the healing powers of Jesus. Jesus was also reported to have dined with a ruler who was a Pharisee (Lk 19:1-6). Jews involved in commerce would have been much more likely to have had dealings with the royalty and Gentiles than would craftsmen in small villages. For this reason one engaged in big business might have been more likely to have eaten with tax collectors and sinners (Matt 9:10-13; Mk 12:15-17; Lk 4:29-32; 15:1-2) than one who had been securely protected in an orthodox community. Jesus not only ate with these people, but he called Matthew (Matt 9:9) or Levi (Mk 2:13-14; Lk 5:27) a tax collector, and therefore a person of means, to become a disciple. Zacchaeus, described as a chief tax collector and very rich (Lk 19:1-10), was honored to have had Jesus as his guest. When James and John, sons of Zebedee, left their nets to follow Jesus, their work was left in the hands of Zebedee's servants, indicating that Zebedee also had a business large enough to merit the maintenance of a hired staff (Mk 1:19-20). Jesus did not object, as did his disciples, when a woman at Bethany poured expensive ointment on his head (Matt 26:6-13; Mk 14:3-9). Joseph of Arimathea, a disciple of Jesus, who provided the tomb, was reported to have been rich (Matt 27:57-60).

---

[13]For a good description of the relationship between a Near Easterner's wealth and social status and the receptiveness of the community to his counsel, see J. Pederson, *Israel its Life and Culture*, tr. Mrs. A. Miller (London, c1959) 1:213-26. Schottroff and Stegemann, *Jesus,* pp. 16-24, argued that Zacchaeus, the chief tax collecter who was very rich, was very different from the poor, subordinate tax collectors with whom Jesus mingled. Levi was also an exception (p. 114). Schottroff and Stegemann argued that Jesus' movement was like that of the Cynics, and his followers were beggars, slaves, cripples, the despised, and the oppressed (pp. 112, 117).

It is clear that Jesus mingled with at least one very rich tax collector, Zacchaeus. In the carefully stratified economic society of the ancient Near East, how could Jesus claim as associates both those of the upper class and at the same time those of the poverty class? Schottroff and Stegemann also misunderstood the titles "harlots" and "sinners" as belonging to the poverty class (pp. 24-26). Overlooking the homiletical character of Luke 6:20-26 in relationship to Matt 5:3-10, they called Luke 6:20-26 "the oldest Jesus tradition".

It was not unusual for a wealthy person in Jesus' time to give his wealth to a community that called itself "the poor" (1QHab 12:3, 6, 10; 1QM 11:1, 13, 14; 4QpPs 37:1, 9, 10) and to which he would at that time have been accepted as a full member. This was a requirement for admission into the Essene sect (Philo, *Apologia pro Judaeis* 9.4-5) or the order governed by the Rule of the Community (1QS 1:11-12; 3:2; 5:2-3, 13, 18-23; 9:8-10; see further "The Role of Purity in the Structure of the Essene Sect," *Revue de Qumran* 4 [1963]:37-46). Others outside of Palestine, like the Therapeutae (Philo, *De Vita Contempliva* 9:23) and Apollonius of Tyana (Philostratus, *The Life of Apollonius of Tyana* 1.xiii) gave their wealth to their relatives and chose the life of poverty. There is no way of knowing how many sects there were at the time of Christ that made requirements similar to those of the Essenes, [14] but Jesus would not have been out of character with Judaism of his time if he had given his wealth to some sect that had either existed previously or one that he founded and accepted the voluntary role of poverty. Furthermore, the conjecture that Jesus had once been a businessman but later joined a sect and became a scholar fits together well enough in the jig-saw puzzle of the historical Jesus to deserve a thorough examination of monasticism in NT times in relationship to gospel testimony about Jesus.

The Purpose of Celibate Orders

Levitical Purity. When the temple was not standing or was considered defiled by an improper priesthood or erroneous practices, groups of Jews isolated themselves from all defiling contacts and cared for their residences with the same levitical meticulousness as they thought the true priests should care for the temple area. They ate all meals in perfect levitical purity and according to all dietary laws. Since women during childbearing age were defiled half the time and stimulated defiling seminal discharges from men even when they were not defiled, these purity conscious men took vows of celibacy to prevent all this defilement.

---

[14]P. Parker, *The Gospel before Mark* (Chicago, c1953), pp. 94-99, strongly suggested that Jesus and John the Baptist belonged to a sect of Nazoreans. Later developments from this sect may be the Nasaraioi and Nazaraioi (Epiphanius, *Panarion* 18, 1:1-3:5; 29, 1:1-9:5). See also A. Schmidtke, *Neue Fragmente und Untersuchungen zu den Juden-christlichen Evangelien* (Leipsig, 1911), pp. 41-126, 248-49, and J. Thomas, *Le Mouvement Baptiste en Palestine et Syrie* (Gembloux, 1935), pp. 37-40, 156-62.

Social Security. Since celibate males could not procreate children, groups had to establish an economic insurance policy to provide for old men the way children would normally care for parents. This policy was a communal structure whereby all members of this group, upon final admission, were required to break all family ties and give all their goods to the community. Under this type of administration the organization owned even the clothes the members wore and assumed financial responsibility for all the members' needs. Probably because all members took vows of poverty, the community was called "the poor."[15] The Essene community allowed members no important decisions, except that they could voluntarily help others and give charity without consent of the administration, but even these privileges were limited to people other than relatives (*BJ* 2.134). Members on admission were required to give all their possessions to the community and take "terrible oaths" (*BJ* 2.139-42), some of which probably involved breaking completely with their families and promising not to provide for them again. If they were allowed to continue making charitable contributions to parents, the members would be tempted to provide for all the needs of their parents as the commandments dictated. If this were done, however, the community would soon be undermined financially and loyalty would be divided between the community and the family. To avoid any such confusion, a sharp distinction was made between the group members and all others. There are some indications that Jesus belonged to some such monastic group and invited others to accept its discipline and demands.

Celibacy

The Parents of Jesus. One of the indications that Jesus was a member of a monastic group is the rejection he showed his mother. He never displayed any affection to her or called her his mother. In fact, he denied that she was. At the wedding in Cana, when she addressed him, he replied, "Woman, what do we have to do with each other?" (Jn 2:4). When those around him told him his mother and brothers had come to see him, he replied, "Who is my mother? and who are my brothers?" Then, pointing to his immediate followers he said, "Look! My mother and brothers" (Matt 12:46-50). This implies that Jesus had rejected the mother who had given

---

[15] "At first the [poor] tithe was divided into three parts—(1) one to friends who were priests and Levites; (2) one to the treasury; and (3) one to the poor and the *haverim* who were in Jerusalem" (JM.Sh. 5:9, 56d).

him birth and transferred his family loyalty to another group which included those around him just as other monks did. On another occasion a woman from the crowd shouted, ''Blessed is the womb that bore you and the breasts that nursed you!'' This is a figurative way of offering a blessing for Jesus' mother, but he rejected it just as he rejected his mother and brothers when they came to see him. He responded, ''Rather, blessed are those who hear the word of God and keep it'' (Lk 11:27-28). In both cases, Jesus reminded the people around him that he had no longer any allegiance to the family into which he had been born. At the cross he said to his mother, ''Woman, look! your son,'' and indicated someone else (Jn 19:26).

There is no report of Jesus mentioning his own father and that is not surprising. We told his disciples to call no man father on earth (Matt 23:9). Since the disciples had rejected their families, they must live as if their original family never existed. Their only father was God; their only brothers were members of the order; and their family loyalty was transferred to another group. The Lord's prayer, taught to Jesus' apostles, addressed God as ''Father'' (Matt 6:9). The celibate community governed by the Rule of the Community (6:10) referred to its members both as ''neighbors'' and ''brothers.'' When Jesus gave directions for the terms by which people could join his group, he said, ''If anyone will come to him and does not hate his father, mother, children, brothers, sisters, and even his own soul, he cannot be my disciple'' (Lk 14:25-26). This seems to mean that the followers of Jesus were required to break all ties with their families.

This measure seems severe to many Protestants but not to rigorous monastic orders. The same requirements were made of those who joined the community governed by the Community Rule. These rules governed whom the members of the sect should hate and whom they should love. They were to love all the sons of light—the members—and hate all the sons of darkness—all the rest, including former family members (1QS 9). Jesus insisted that he did not come to bring peace but division. He would separate father from son, mother from daughter, mother-in-law from daughter-in-law (Lk 12:51-53). Prospective followers of Jesus were not allowed to postpone their commitment until they had fulfilled the commandment to honor their parents by caring for them while they lived and burying them respectfully after they had died. Those outside the group, called ''dead,'' were given the responsibility of burying corpses of others who were considered dead while they still breathed (Matt 8:21-22). Followers were to break with their families and join a community that displaced the family. This was evidently a celibate, communal, masculine group.

Angels of God. Jesus told the Sadducees that in the resurrection there would be neither marrying nor giving in marriage, but all would be like the angels of God in heaven, who were celibate (Matt 22:23-30). Only those who fell, and sinned, had intercourse with women. Their indulgence was the cause of the flood (Gen 6-8). Jesus concluded his discussion on divorce, concurring that it was profitable not to marry, although some were not able to accept celibate demands. Others, however, like Origen, made themselves eunuchs for the Kingdom of Heaven (Matt 19:10-12). This was an even greater demand than celibacy, but it was for the same purpose—to keep an undefiled camp, so that the Lord could be present. The 144,000 elect ones on Mount Zion were celibate, not having defiled themselves with women (Rev 14:1-4). If Jesus really belonged to a celibate community, as the evidence indicates, and believed that the age to come would be only for celibate males, it seems likely that he would also have belonged to a community that was communal like the Essene community or the community governed by the Community Rule. This seems likely from the rules attributed to Jesus and teachings reported from him.

Celibate Orders

Communal Economy. The Essene economy was communal with a special officer assigned to manage finances. Individual members were relieved of the anxieties of the world. They could come to the monastery at mealtime and expect food. They could change clothing as they needed from the community wardrobe. If they traveled to other communities they could visit other Essene homes or monasteries and receive hospitality.

Christian disciples were also sent out without extra clothing, money, or food, with the understanding that "worthy" houses in other towns would provide for them, free of charge (Matt 10:8-13). One of their members was in charge of the treasury (Jn 12:6). They were encouraged to be unconcerned about food, clothing, and material needs (Matt 6:19-34). Like other monks, they were not supposed to acknowledge any earthly father. Like other monastic brotherhoods, members were not to compete for offices but for opportunities to serve one another. Like other brotherhoods, they were all brothers with some kind of equality, whereby the greatest and strongest served the smallest and weakest (Matt 23:7-9, 11-12; see also 1QS 6:2). Although men in general avoided any type of work normally done by women in the Near East, all work in monasteries was done by men. Because of this peculiarity, it would not seem odd for the apostles to wait at the edge of the city until a man appeared, carrying water. If they followed him, as they did, they would likely come to the only monastery in the area where other monks would be welcome to celebrate their Passover (Mk 14:12-16).

When a man came to Jesus asking what he might do to inherit, "life," Jesus told him to keep the commandments as all good Jews should. When the man said he had always done this, Jesus thought he might be prepared to go further, so he said, "If you want to be perfect, go, sell all you have and give to the poor, and you will have treasures in heaven. Then, come and follow me" (Matt 19:16-21). The commandment to be perfect evidently involved giving all he had to the "poor." Therefore it seems likely that Jesus was inviting that man to fulfill the qualifications for belonging to a perfect, celibate community for which giving all of one's possessions was only part of the requirement. The immediate disciples had left everything to follow Jesus. This meant leaving houses, parents, brothers, sisters, wives, children, and lands for the sake of Jesus (Matt 19:27-30). The commandment to be perfect may have been a commandment to become a monk (Matt 5:48).

Monastic Ethics. The righteousness of the group governed by the Sermon on the Mount was expected to exceed that of the Pharisees (Matt 5:20) who only gave tithes (Matt 23:23). Those who accepted Jesus' call, however, gave all they had to the community that called itself "the poor." The severe, celibate discipline of the Rule of the Community is similar to that of the Sermon on the Mount which prohibited anger and insult to the brothers (Matt 5:21-22). They were not only forbidden to commit adultery, but even to look at a woman to lust after her. For a community that was kept levitically pure, lust had to be prevented because it causes defiling nocturnal emissions and severe methods had to be applied to prevent this. If the eye that wandered caused defilement, it was to be plucked out and the hand that caused defilement was to be cut off (Matt 5:27-30). Rabbis similarly observed that frequent examination for a woman was meritorious (it let her know at once that her menstrual period had begun so that she could isolate herself and avoid defiling others), but for a man, they said, "Chop off his hand" (Nid 2:1). Frequent examination for a man was considered to be masturbation which increased defilement and had to be prevented. This was the same punishment demanded by the Sermon on the Mount, evidently for the same offense, associated with adultery. A monk, Abba Antonio, said,

"The one who sits in the wilderness and is silent is released from three wars: (1) hearing, (2) speaking, and (3) seeing. He has one [battle] alone [to fight]—adultery" (MPG 65.77.11). The only adultery a monk could commit while alone in the wilderness was masturbation. The primary reason for celibacy was to avoid defilement and even monks had a problem keeping an undefiled area or community. Paul described the conflict between his mind and his members that afflicted him when "the commandment came" with his Bar Mitzwah obligations (Rom 7:7-25).[16]

Members of the rigorously disciplined community governed by the Sermon on the Mount were forbidden to take oaths which were accompanied by curses (Matt 5:33-37) and were required to walk a second mile and turn the second cheek to the attacker (Matt 5:38-42; cf. 1QS 6:25-27), doing good to enemies (Matt 5:43-47). Receiving undeserved punishment and doing good that could not be repaid canceled debts in the heavenly account and helped provide a sinless community. If anyone in the sinless community sinned and refused to repent, he was expelled like a Gentile and a tax collector so the rest of the community could be sinless or perfect (Matt 18:15-17). The community governed by the Rule of the Community also required celibate members to be perfect or walk in a perfect manner (1QS 8:1, 20, 21; 9:2, 5, 6, 8-9, 19; 11:11). The monastic group of holy men was intended to be a sanctuary for Aaron and a house of perfection and truth in Israel (1QS 8:8-9) who would not mingle their wealth with the men of deceit. Such rigorous communities were necessarily small (Matt 7:13-14) with "narrow gates" for entrance. Only celibate communities, following the kind of discipline demanded by the Sermon on the Mount, 1QS, or the rules governing the Essenes, could hope to be perfect, but those who did were compared to the angels of heaven and the heavenly Father himself (Matt 5:48; 22:29-30).

Conclusions

Since the discovery of the Dead Sea Scrolls, scholars have had to revise their former conclusions that monasticism originated in Egypt in the fourth century A.D. It was obviously an established institution among the Essenes before the time of Christ and Jesus seems to have been very much involved

---

[16]GWB, *Consequences*, pp. 181-84.

in it. There are a few, like Phipps,[17] who have conjectured that Jesus was married, the chief reason being that marrying is normal for the emotionally mature in twentieth century America. Therefore, Jesus must have met these demands. There is absolutely no scriptural evidence for this conclusion, however, and there are many good reasons for thinking that Jesus was a celibate monk who observed all the demands he made of others. He did not insist that people marry. On the contrary, he made severe family demands of his followers that could be fulfilled only by celibacy. He probably gained part of his authority by the sincerity with which he, himself, accepted these stringent limitations. He also made equally severe demands on people's wealth, sometimes successfully. This would not seem possible to the stratified Near East if Jesus, himself, had not come from the upper classes. How else could he get a hearing with these upper class tax collectors? People evidently took Jesus seriously, as indeed would be expected from a person who had grown up in wealthy surroundings, received privileged opportunities in education, training, and leadership, but then gave all his money to a community that called itself "the poor," accepted vows of poverty, celibacy, and obedience, and devoted the rest of his life to inviting others to share his goals.

Although there is no evidence that Jesus was married, Luke described Jesus' birth in humble surroundings, and two of Jesus' apostles were accused of being uncultured and provincial. Not only Luke, but also the author of The Infancy Story of Thomas (13:1) presumed a lowly birth. Justin (*Dialogue* 88) described Joseph's occupation as a carpenter who made plows and yokes. Origen, (*Celsus* 1:28-29), accepted the accusation that Jesus had been born of laboring parents in conditions of poverty. According to the Apocryphal Book of James (1:1-52), however, Mary's father was described as very rich. The large, stone tomb in the Kidron Valley is attributed to Jesus' brother James. What poor family could have afforded this? The Acts of Pilate show Jesus to have been a person to whom Pilate felt obligated to defer (1:2ff.),even though Jews said he was a carpenter's son (1:1). The accusation that he was born of fornication was refuted (2:3-6), and prominent people, like Joseph of Arimathea, Nicodemus, Jairus, and various rabbis, elders, priests, and Levites defended him or bore witness to him (12:1 ff.). The Apostle of Edessa also described Jesus in royal correspondence

---

[17]W. E. Phipps, *Was Jesus Married?* (New York, 1970).

before his crucifixion and one of his apostles accepted the invitation to heal King Abgar. Most of these reports seem legendary.

Being born in a manger did not imply poverty in antiquity. Mandaeans regularly arranged for babies to be born in mangers to avoid defiling their houses. Why would anyone concerned for purity defile a whole inn full of people?[18] The implication of the offering (Lk 2:24) is that it is the gift of a poor family, "a couple of pigeons or two turtle doves." The early church evidently pictured Jesus the way they wanted him to be, and fabricated legends accordingly, so this is not the place to look for historical evidence. There is much more likelihood that the historical Jesus is reflected in chreias and parables (as shown in chapters three and four) than in later church legend. Several of these make good sense against a background of monasticism. They also show Jesus addressing his teachings to people who had enough wealth to act on the basis of his teachings. In chapter 3 Jesus was shown making rigid demands of followers that would involve giving up their wealth and joining a celibate community. Chapter 4 pictured Jesus associating with wealthy tax collectors and in conflict with the tithing Pharisees whom he considered hypocrites. The next chapter will examine Jesus, managing his campaign under the nose of the Roman authorities.

---

[18]See E. S. Drower, *The Mandaeans of Iraq and Iran* (Leiden, 1962), p. 41.

The Mystery
of the Kingdom
# of God

Introduction

The first chapter defined the Kingdom of Heaven as a religious monarchy which was designed to exist on the same land as the Davidic kingdom with its capital city at Jerusalem. There were hopes of territorial expansion, even to the extent of the entire Roman empire, but this is the place where things would begin. Chapter six will deal with both aspects of that religious kingdom. On the one hand, it will examine the basic providential teachings of Jesus—without this conviction any attempt to overthrow the Roman empire would seem ridiculous. On the other hand, this chapter will show why such a term as Kingdom of Heaven was used to describe this anticipation and program. Neither of these emphases could be distinguished from Judaism or early Christianity on the basis of dissimilarity. Hypothetically, these teachings might all have been added by the later church or derived from earlier Judaism because the convictions and the methodology were basic to both. Belief in providence was so fundamental to Judaism and Christianity that Jesus would have been strange indeed if he had evolved from this environment without this firm conviction. When he said, ''Do not be afraid . . . it is your Father's good pleasure to give you the kingdom'' (Lk 12:32), he expressed a cardinal Jewish belief both in God's care for his chosen people and the confidence that the kingdom was attainable. His entire program was undertaken on these two bases which have been reflected in teachings organized under other chapters. The subversive method of attaining this kingdom had been developed in Egypt, Babylon, and Palestine under the Seleucids. The teachings in this chapter will simply show how these Jewish beliefs and practices were implemented by Jesus.

The God Who Cares

God as a Gardener. ''Then, after the disciples had arrived, they said to him, 'You know that the Pharisees, after they heard the report, were offended.' He said in reply, 'Every plant which my heavenly Father has not planted will be uprooted' '' (Matt 15:12-13).

This is a responsive chreia from the literary point of view. The situation is given to which Jesus responded. His response is quoted and the unit is very brief. It is also one of the teachings that grew out of a council meeting held after the apostles had returned from one of their missions. They were giving Jesus an account of the events that occurred while they were ''fishing for men.'' It was in sessions like these that much of the information was communicated that was recorded in chreia form. This chreia is also coherent with other teachings in parables and chreias. Here, Jesus is shown in conflict with the Pharisees, as has been evident in previous chapters. He also used metaphors related to farming or gardening which are similar to those used in the parable of the weeds and the wheat. The final scene of that parable pictured the weeds being thrown into the fire with the wheat safely stored in the granary. When the ''harvest'' comes, only the grain that has been planted will be reaped.[1] When the disciples were concerned about the Pharisees being offended and not following Jesus' movement, Jesus responded that this indicated their position in God's original plan.

---

[1] Meyer, *Matthew*, p. 282, argued mistakenly that the plants to be burned were not the Pharisees but their teachings. Just as ''weeds'' represented sinners in the parable of ''wheat and Weeds,'' so the ''plant'' here represents rejected members of the community (Matt 3:10; Isa 5:7; Sira 3:28). So also T. Zahn, *Das Evangelium des Matthäus* (Leipzig, 1910), p. 525, and M'Neile, *Matthew*, p. 227.

In other parables, Jesus was shown in direct conflict with the Pharisees, some more than others. This conflict evidently became worse as time went on. There may have been a time when Jesus and the Pharisees worked together because the disciples seemed alarmed that Jesus had fallen out of their favor. It is only a conjecture that the reason for their fall-out was Jesus' association with the tax collectors. That is the issue about which he seemed to be in greatest disagreement with them, but no record is given of Jesus before he began to associate with tax collectors and sinners.

Mustard Seeds and Mountains. "The apostles said to the Lord, 'Add to our faith.' The Lord said, 'If you had faith like a mustard seed, you would have said to this sycamine tree, "Be uprooted and planted in the sea," and it would have obeyed you' " (Lk 17:5-6; see also Matt 21:21; Mk 11:22).

"Then, approaching, the disciples said to Jesus, alone, 'Why were we not able to cast it out?' He said to them, 'Because of your little faith. I tell you under oath, if you had faith as a mustard seed, you would say to this mountain, "Be moved from here, there," and it would be moved, and nothing would be impossible for you' " (Matt 17:19-20).

The Lukan version is a chreia; the Matthaean version is not. In the Lukan version, there is a question, and answer, and it is all succinct. In the Matthaean version, the chreia has been interrupted to adapt it to the preceding story in Matthaean context. The contexts, however, do not help with the meaning. These units once existed independently. This is clear, not only by the chreia form in Luke, but also because the preceding context (Lk 17:1) referred to Jesus' followers as "disciples," whereas the chreia discussed "apostles." The chreia called the respondent, "Lord," whereas Luke 17:19, called him "Jesus." Both deal with the effectiveness of faith, but have possibilities of different interpretations.

The Lukan version showed the apostles asking for help in faith. His response may have been a rebuke like the one in Matthew. "If you had," implying that they did not, unless he had meant, "If you had *only,* implying that, of course, they had more. The point of the mustard seed seems to be its small size rather than its growth potential. Whether intended as a rebuke or an encouragement, this message showed that Jesus was confident that God would do a great deal for his people if they had only a little faith. The suggestion that the mountain or the sycamine tree would be moved for them seems to be hyperbolic, but there is another possibility with the mountain. Zechariah promised that in the day of the Lord the Mount of Olives (this mountain) would be split in half. Half would move southward; half would move northward (Zech 14:1-5). He may have meant that the day of the Lord would come by faith. It was this day for which all zealous Jews aspired, when God would intercede and defeat the foreign nations for Israel. It was a standard tenet of holy war theology that God would act against Israel's enemies, utilizing all of the forces of nature. He made the stars in their courses fight against Sisera (Jdgs 5). Splitting a mountain was no more miraculous than dividing the Reed Sea or the Jordan River. This is consistent with the belief that God would pull out all that he himself had not planted. God was in charge.

None Good but God. "Now a certain ruler asked him, saying, 'Good teacher, What good must I do so that I will inherit life of the age?'[2] Jesus said to him, 'Why do you call me good? None is good except One, God' " (Lk 18:18-20; Matt 19:16-17).

There is nothing exceptional about this. Most Jews believed that God was One and that he alone was good—that which is impossible with men is possible with God (Matt 19:26; Mk 10:27; Lk 18:27). Jesus simply reminded the questioner of a creed he already accepted and recited every morning. This was basic to the belief expressed in the following parables.

The Sower. "Look! A sower went out to sow. While he was sowing, some fell along the path, and after the birds came, they ate it. Others fell on rocky ground where there was not much soil. It sprouted quickly, because there was no depth of soil, but when the sun shone, it was scorched, and because it had no roots, it withered. But others fell among the thorns and the thorns came up and choked them. But others fell on good ground, and it produced grain, some a hundred, some sixty, and some thirtyfold" (Matt 13:3-8; Mk 4:4-9; Lk 8:5-8).

White[3] has corrected Jeremias' explanation of Palestinian farming methods. Near Eastern farmers, White held, never sowed on hard ground and they knew their fields well enough to avoid sowing on paths and rocky ground. This parable probably does not provide an ideal picture of the way frugal farmers farm, but that was not its intention. Instead, it pictured the scattered way in which Jesus and the apostles had to communicate through

---

[2]The expression "Life in the age," often translated "eternal life," refers to life in the age to come or life in the age of Jewish rule over the promised land. See further GWB, *Consequences,* pp. 136-49.

[3]K. D. White, "The Parable of the Sower," *JTS* 15 (1964):300-307.

the parables in hit-or-miss fashion. It was told to convince the hearers that even hit-or-miss farming was profitable as would be their methods of reaching the multitudes by telling parables to large groups. Even careless farmers could count on the good soil and adequate rain to produce a profit, even though there were losses. When preaching to Jews, apostles could also count on God to produce a response even though they did not know in advance which Jews would respond.

Jeremias has also noted the eschatological emphasis on this parable.[4] By the time the parable concluded, it is harvest time, and harvest in scripture frequently refers to the booty taken after war, at the time of the Messiah's arrival, the last judgment, and the beginning of a new age. Gerhardsson's argument against Jeremias is not convincing.[5] Gerhardsson said the point of the parable is not the harvest but the manner of hearing, based on the Shema' (Deut 6:4-9), but this requires the acceptance of the later interpretation (Matt 15:18-23) as being the meaning intended by the chreia itself. Some of the important harvest texts are as follows:

As men rejoice in harvest time
as they rejoice when they divide the spoil (Isa 9:2).
Though a man may go forth in tears,
when he sows the seed,
he will come again, rejoicing,
carrying with him his bundles of grain.

(Ps 126:6)

John the Baptist compared the Messiah to a harvester, coming with a winnowing fan in his hand (Matt 3:12; Lk 3:17). Joel described an anticipated bloody battle in the Kidron Valley at the edge of Jerusalem in terms of harvesting both grain and grapes (Joel 3:9-17). In Samaria, Jesus found the fields white with harvest (Jn 4:35).

Part of the reason for this analogy is that Jews believed that ages, like days, weeks, and years, grew old and came to an end. This was all part of God's plan.[6] Therefore Jews could be sure that this evil age would reach its

---

[4]Jeremias, *Parables*, pp. 149-51, contra J. D. Kingsbury, *The Parables of Jesus in Matthew 13* (St. Louis, c1977), p. 36.

[5]B. Gerhardsson, "The Parable of the Sower and the Interpretation," *NTS* 14 (1968):165-93.

[6]GWB, *Consequences*, pp. 15-18.

end and Jews would have the harvest that was predestined to come. It was their belief in God's providence that gave them hope that the Kingdom of God would soon come because they had already endured the earlier seasons with their labor and pain. This teaching of Jesus is consistent not only with other parabolic teachings and those reported in chreias, but with basic Jewish belief.

The Father's Hospitality.

> Ask, and it will be given to you
> seek, and you will find
> knock, and it will be opened to you,
> for everyone who asks, receives;
> and he who seeks, finds;
> and to one who knocks (see P.R. 176a),
> it will be opened.

Which man among you, if his son asks him for bread,
will instead give him a stone?
Or, if he asks for fish,
will instead give him a serpent?
If, then, you who are evil know how to give good gifts
to your children,
how much more your Father in heaven
will give good things to those who ask him!

(Matt 7:7-11; Lk 11:11-13)

This is neither a chreia nor a parable. It is somewhat parabolic and it is consistent with other teachings of Jesus about God. It cannot be proved to be a true teaching of Jesus on the principle of dissimilarity because it is at once Jewish and Christian, but if someone else composed it and attributed it to Jesus, he or she did it fairly. Jesus has been shown in parables and chreias to have taught that God can be trusted to provide for the needs of his children, the chosen people.

These poetic teachings are based on Near Eastern hospitality customs.[7] Although orthodox Jews were very careful not to accept into their homes people who did not keep the hospitality rules the same way they did, they were required by the rules of their faith to provide for the needs of the members of their sect. They were required to open their doors for orthodox guests and give them changes of clothing and ample food and shelter. Since

---

[7]Ibid., pp. 199-201, 243, 274-75, 279.

Essenes provided in this way for other Essenes, Pharisees also provided for other Pharisees, and sectarians related to the Gospel of Matthew and the Johannine epistles were obligated to provide this kind of hospitality for their fellow sectarians, why should God's chosen people think that God would not provide for them in the same way if they appeared at his doorstep? This is typical *a fortiori* logic that occurs many times in Greek rhetoric and rabbinic literature.[8] It means if something is true of something light, weak, or small, it is all the more true of something heavy, strong, or great. The same logic is applied to the examples of the Father who provided hospitality for his son.

It was a Jewish father's responsibility to see that his son was properly trained in Jewish laws. This included dietary laws. The father should have taught his son never to eat anything that comes from the water that does not have scales and fins, like catfish, bull heads, shell fish, and eels (Lev 11:12). All of these were referred to as creeping things or serpents. When a son came to his father's house, hungry, and wanted bread, his father would not deceive him and give him a rock that looked like bread, would he? Neither would he cook him some catfish and serve it to him, telling him it was carp. It was not the father's intention that his own son break the law, unconsciously. He wanted his son to keep the law as he had taught him. Therefore, the son could be confident that in his father's house the food served would be approved by all the dietary laws. If this was true of a human father, how much more should the chosen people trust their heavenly Father to meet their real needs!

It is not possible to distinguish the teachings of Jesus from those of other early Jews and Christians on the matter of God's providence, the way Jesus' teachings can be distinguished from those of the Pharisees on the question of accepting tax collectors and sinners. These are teachings that would be suitable to most Jews and early Christians.

Midnight Hospitality. "Which one of you will have a friend, and he comes to him in the middle of the night and says to him, 'Friend, provide me three loaves, since my friend has arrived from a journey, and I do not have anything to set before him.' That one, from within, by reply would say, 'Do not trouble me. Already the door is closed, and my children and I are

---

[8]Aristotle, *Rhetoric* 1.iii.9; ix.29; 2.xxiii.4-6; Mekilta, *Pisha* 11:70-75, 97-103, passim.

in bed. I am not able to get up and give you anything.' I tell you, even if he will not get up to give him anything because he is his friend, because of his desperate situation, he will rise and give him whatever he needs'' (Lk 11:5-8).

The friend in this parable may have been just any next door neighbor, but he may also have been a shopkeeper who normally sold bread during working hours. Therefore, the needy neighbor knew he had bread on hand. The problem was that this was after hours, the shop was closed, and the family was all in bed. This was not the time to come expecting to conduct business, but there was the question of hospitality obligations. Everyone in the Near East knew about these.[9] When a guest came, his host was under extreme social pressure to meet all of his needs. Consider, for example, Rahab's willingness to betray her family and town to protect the Israelites whom she had accepted as guests into her home (Josh 2); Lot's willingness to forfeit his virgin daughters in order to protect his guests (Gen 19:1-8); or the Danite's willingness to provide equally for his Levitical guest (Jdgs 19:1-26). This was the implication of the parable. This kind of demand a person would not make on a friend just to meet ordinary needs, but when faced with hospitality demands, the host was obligated to leave no stone unturned. Furthermore, the reputation of the whole village would be injured if a guest could not find hospitality there. It was considered an honor for the entire village for a guest to lodge there overnight. Therefore the host would make unusual requests of others and be willing to pay unusual prices for needs rather than treat his guest improperly. The friend who has awakened also realized that this was an unusual situation for which he too had some responsibility. He could not leave this man and the entire village to be embarrassed in this rude way. This was a community crisis so the man awakened could be expected to help meet the extenuating circumstances.

Since the parable itself does not reveal the intended teaching, it is not certain what Jesus wanted to teach by this parable. Luke used it to introduce the exhortation that Jews should not hesitate to ask God for their needs which makes better sense than any other possibility that comes to mind. When Jews had circumstances as extenuating as those of a host without food, they need not hesitate to disturb their heavenly Father about their

---

[9]GWB, ''The Spiritual Commandment,'' *JAAR* 26 (1968):126-27.

problems. His reputation was also at stake. They could count on him to respond. A similar *a fortiori* parable was reported about the unjust judge.

The Unjust Judge. "There was a certain judge in a certain city who neither feared God nor deferred to human beings. Now there was a widow in that city, and she came to him, saying, 'Vindicate me from my adversary!' He did not want to at that time, but afterward he said to himself, 'Even if I do not fear God nor honor human beings, because of the trouble this widow causes me, I will vindicate her, so that she will not finally wear me out by her coming' " (Lk 18:2-5).

Both Jews and Christians were warned not to take their problems to a Gentile court (1 Cor 6:1-11). Paul referred to Gentile courts as the courts of the unjust (1 Cor 6:1). Just as rabbis often meant a Gentile king when they told parables of a "king of flesh and blood," so Jesus probably meant a Gentile judge when he told a parable of a judge who did not fear God. This makes the *a fortiori* argument all the more extreme. This was not just a crooked Jewish judge who could be bribed by those who had money. He was a Gentile judge who would not show special favor to God's chosen people. This widow did not have the money to bribe him even if he had been susceptible to bribery. There was nothing she could do but make a nuisance of herself until the judge vindicated her.[10] Luke put this parable in a context comparing the widow's incessant pleading to the prayers of the chosen people to a just God who would show favoritism to his chosen people.

The comparison of prayer to God with a plea before a judge is very apt because a case brought before a judge is a prayer, and this is a metaphor, taken from a law court, that best describes a request made to God. In both cases a law court scene is presumed. One of the rabbis explained prayer as follows: "*If they cry aloud to me I will surely hear their cry* (Exod 22:23). Whenever he cries I will hear, but if they do not cry, I will not hear. The scripture says, *I will surely hear their cry,* in any event. Then why does the scripture say, *If they cry aloud to me I will surely hear?* except that I will hurry more to punish when someone *cries* than when he does not *cry.* Now look! These words constitute an *a fortiori* argument: If when an individual

---

[10]For a more recent example of the same sort, a woman appearing before a Moslem judge, see N. B. Tristram, *Eastern Customs in Bible Lands* (London, 1894), p. 228.

cries the Lord *hears his cry,* how much the more so when the congregation *cries''* (Mekilta, *Nezikin* 18:74-81).

In addition to these teachings in chreias and parables, there are other instructions attributed to Jesus that are consistent with these. For example, in an *a fortiori* argument, Jesus reminded his listeners that two sparrows were sold for a farthing, yet neither of them would fall to the ground unnoticed by the heavenly Father. But God's chosen people are to be treasured much more than sparrows! (Matt 10:29-30). God has counted even the hair on Jewish heads (Matt 10:30). God clothes the lilies of the field and he feeds the birds of the heavens, therefore God's chosen people need have no anxiety about whether or not he will provide for them adequately (Matt 6:25-34). These are not all the teachings attributed to Jesus that encourage trust in God. God's providential care is implicitly understood in many of the chreias and parables that are principally directed to recruitment of followers or conflicts with the Pharisees in relationship to tax collectors and sinners. It is also implicit in some of the teachings that follow related to secrecy and sabotage in relationship to the movement planned to bring about the Kingdom of Heaven.[11]

Mystery and Sabotage

Introduction. Even though Jesus was convinced that God was prepared to give the Kingdom of Heaven to the Jews of his time with him as the new Messiah to sit on David's throne at Jerusalem, it was very important that the Romans not realize that he was at that very time recruiting followers and raising funds to undertake a movement that would evict the Romans from power. Therefore this movement had to be undertaken as quietly as possible without attracting undue attention from the Roman leaders until he was prepared to handle all the resistance they would provide. How could this be done? Somehow he had to be able to talk to mixed groups in such a way as to appear innocent to the Romans and their collaborators while at the same time communicating something more to those Jews whom he wanted to arouse to follow him. This was not difficult to do in relationship to the well-trained sectarians who were acquainted with the secret codes. This secret knowledge and these code terms were evidently taught as part of a catechism. To some groups it was called ''the mysteries of the Kingdom of

---

[11]Linnemann, *Jesus,* p. 121, argued that this is certainly not a parable of the historical Jesus, but an addition of the later church.

God'' (Matt 13:11; Lk 8:10; Gospel of Thomas 62). Others called it "Gnosis'' (γνῶσις or דעת). Rabbis called this the "oral Torah'' (שבעל פה תורה) or the "memorized Torah.''[12] This is the Torah which legalists kept on the tips of their tongues. Rabbis said God forbade Jews from writing down the Mishnah because it was the mystery only for the just (Tanh. Gen—Buber, p. 98). Jewish Christians insisted on three months' training before baptism. During this time, the person being prepared for membership was taught "the mysteries of the Kingdom of Heaven'' (Clementine Recognitions 3:67). The word "parable'' was both an analogy and also a "riddle.'' Jesus reportedly spoke in "riddles'' to those who were not trained in the mysteries of the Kingdom of Heaven (Matt 13:10-13). In riddles, those who were good Jews, and therefore familiar with tradition and scripture, could still understand the intended meaning whereas the Romans would not get the point.[13]

---

[12]R. E. Brown, *The Semitic Background of the Term 'Mystery' in the New Testament* (Philadelphia, c1968), held that the NT term "mystery'' belongs to a Semitic thought-form and needs no interpretation in relationship to the Greek mysteries. Initially it meant council, referring to the secret councils of the gods. Then it came to mean divinely communicated secrets. See Sira 39:2-3; Enoch 63:3; 2 Bar 48:8-9; 4 Ezra 10:38; 12:36-37; 1QHab 7:8. The Habakkuk Commentary called the mystery the hidden meaning of prophecy. See also 1QS 4:6 and B. Reicke, "Traces of Gnosticism in the Dead Sea Scrolls?,'' *NTS* 1 (1954/55):138. Early Christians were warned to be cautious not to reveal mysteries to those not worthy (Gospel of Bartholomew 4:66-67). Those worthy of the Lord's mysteries were also worthy to become heirs of the heavenly kingdom and temple of God (Acts of Thomas 88, 94; see also 2 Esdras 14:46-47). The rabbis said the Lord would not prevent Gentiles from translating the Torah and claiming that they were Israel, but he said, "I know, but the ones who have the mysteries are my sons. What is this? This is the Mishnah, which is given orally'' (Tanh. *Ki Tisa'* 34; see also *Wayara'* 5, Buber ed. 6, 44b). Although "mysteries'' in the gospels and some other writings refer to a secret teaching, in others it had a sacramental meaning, similar to those of the Greek mystery cults. It is necessary to examine the context case by case to learn its meaning.

[13]D. O. Via, Jr., *The Parables* (Philadelphia, 1967), p. 8, and "Matthew on the Understanding of the Parables,'' *JBL* 84 (1965):430-32, said that so far as Mark was concerned the parables were useless, since neither the disciples nor the outsiders could understand them. It is true that Mark sometimes failed to comprehend the significance of the message, but Matthew understood. Nonetheless, Via presumed Markan priority. Does this mean Matthew understood the parables Mark wrote but did not understand? W. Manson, "The Purpose of the Parables; A Re-examination of St. Mark 4:10-12,'' *ET* 68 (1957):240-44, also missed the underground nature of parables when he held that Jesus directed parables to the patient mystics rather than to the zealotish apocalyptists who heard and left. It was neither the pacifists nor the zealots, but the Romans, from whom Jesus was keeping his message.

Martin Buber,[14] explaining the relationship of saga or myth to history said, '' . . . it is wrong to talk of a 'historization of the myth'; it might be preferable to describe them as a mythization of history, while remembering that here, unlike the concept familiar in the science of religion, myth means nothing other than the report by ardent enthusiasts of that which has befallen them. And it may very well be doubted whether, in the last resort, the report of an unenthusiastic chronicler could have come closer to the truth.''

An example of this kind of saga is Daniel in relationship to the Maccabean Revolt.[15] This was told in relationship to Jewish history from the Fall of Jerusalem in 587 B.C. to the Hasmonean period. During this period, Palestine was ruled by four Gentile powers, the kings of Babylon, Media, Persia, and Greece. The Seleucid dynasty ruled in Syria when the Maccabean rebellion broke out. After the ruling king, Antiochus Epiphanes, was blocked by the Roman troops and prevented from taking Egypt, he sacked the temple at Jerusalem. This was the straw that broke the camel's back and the Hasmoneans led a revolt that continued until Israel was free from foreign rule and foreign taxation ceased. An important turning point in the war was Judas's victory over the Syrians at Beth-horon, after which the temple was cleansed. Then worship was renewed.

When this story was told mythologically, the narrator pictured the various dynasties of pagan countries that had ruled Palestine as monstrous beasts that came up out of the sea, each one more vicious than its predecessor. The last monster had ten horns; from the tenth grew a little horn that was speaking great things. This was Antiochus Epiphanes, described mythically. Then appeared in the vision a judgment scene, with God acting as judge, mythically called the "Ancient of Days." This Judge opened the books, studied the briefs, and passed judgment against the beasts. The fourth beast was sentenced to death by burning and the others had their ruling authority removed. Then came the enthronement scene, with the accompanying clouds to indicate divine presence. After this, one "like a Son of man" came up before the Judge and was respectfully received.[16] He had

---

[14]M. Buber, *Moses* (New York, 1958), p. 17.

[15]For a fuller explanation of the relationship of Daniel to Judas, see GWB, *Hebrews*, pp. 38-51.

[16]In the judgment scene in Daniel, the Son of man was not the heavenly judge but the plaintiff—a point overlooked by such scholars as N. Perrin, "The Son of Man in the Synoptics," *Biblical Research* 13 (1968):3-15.

evidently been the plaintiff in the case and had received a positive verdict. Then the Judge decreed that he would give political authority to the "one like a Son of man" to rule over a kingdom, together with all the accompanying glory.

What did this saga mean? It meant that Judas had won a military victory over the Seleucid Greeks and was accepted as leader of the Jews around Jerusalem. It also meant that God approved this action. It was God who had decreed that the Seleucids should be destroyed and the Hasmoneans enthroned. The "time, two times, and half a time" that took place between the defilement and the rededication of the temple was the crucial struggle between Israel and a great military power that marked the "end of this age" and the beginning of the "age to come." The age that ended saw the last foreign power ruling, and the age to come was one in which Israel was ruled by her own leader.

In a situation of domination by a foreign power, those who planned to lead a revolution would not have been speaking openly about messiahs, military victories, and the like similar to those led by Judas the Maccabee. The Romans would have recognized the importance and meaning of messianic movements, but Jews could speak of the books being opened, the beast being destroyed, the Son of man coming with the clouds, the end of the age, the "time, two times, and half a time," or any other mythical expression that alluded to this saga, and it would communicate the unmentioned military planning involved. Since the analysis of history from the Babylonian captivity was spelled out mythologically in terms of seventy weeks of years, the final half week of which occurred just before the temple was rededicated, future anticipations could be discussed in the same mythological terms: the fourth beast, the end of the days, the judgment day, and the "Son of man" were code terms which could be used in "riddles" told in public without the Romans ever learning what was being communicated.

After the Hasmonean age, Herod the Great ruled for thirty-four years with the military backing of the Roman empire. Since he was an Idumean, he and the Roman power that was behind him were referred to mythologically as "Edom." When Jews said "Edom" it not only helped them to feel and express mythologically all of the hostility that Jacob felt against Esau, but also all the vengeful hostility expressed in Ps 137 and Obadiah who cried out against the Edomites after they had helped the Babylonians capture Jerusalem in 587 B.C. From "captivity" they longed for the day of revenge: Happy would be the one who took Edomite children and dashed their heads against the rocks! (Ps 137:9). At a time when Jews had to acquiesce to Roman domination, they could call Rome "Edom" and communicate mythologically to one another the hostility they had against this power. All the while they were communicating these feelings, mythologically, they were also planning underground movements by which they hoped to over-throw Rome just as the Maccabees had earlier overthrown the Seleucids.

After Herod's death, during the short time that it took for Archelaus to go to Rome and gain authority to lead the country, three leaders arose very suddenly and led extensive military movements. The bulk of the royal troops, that ostensibly had been loyal to Herod and Rome, deserted to the rebellious movements (*BJ* 2.52). One of these guerrilla leaders was Judas, a Galilean rebel. He broke open the royal arsenals and obtained weapons to arm his troops and then he began his resistance movement. It seems obvious that he had been working quietly, preparing followers for any opportunity that should present itself (*BJ* 2.56; *Ant* 17.271-72). Another leader was Si-mon, one of the royal officers of Herod's kingdom. While pretending to support Herod's government, he had also been organizing a guerilla move-ment behind the scenes, probably among Herod's own forces. He was very quickly able to organize troops, burn down the royal palace at Jericho, and destroy many other stately mansions. He was finally killed in a conflict with Roman soldiers (*BJ* 2.57-59; *Ant* 17.273-77).

A third leader was named Athronges. He was a man whose only qual-ifications, said Josephus, were a strong body, a courageous soul, and four brothers very much like himself. That which he lacked that made Josephus speak of him disparagingly, was a great family name, like one of the Has-moneans or sons of David. The fact that Josephus singled him out for this pejorative description probably means that these other guerrilla leaders had royal family histories and support. Athronges suddenly appeared, well or-ganized with troops lined up under different brothers depending on the mil-itary engagement. He himself acted like a king, wearing a crown, and making all major decisions. He evidently had a well-organized administra-tion, prepared to break out into the open whenever it seemed wise. The goals of Athronges and his brothers as well as his followers had been estab-lished long before the death of Herod. He wanted to be king of the nation, to overthrow Herod and his Roman supporters. All of these brothers were finally silenced by the Romans, but before that happened, Josephus said they had made all Judaea a scene of guerrilla warfare (*BJ* 2.60-65; *Ant* 17.276-84).

In the short seven weeks between Passover and Pentecost, these three military movements arose and tried to overthrow the government of Archelaus before he could get control of it himself. Archelaus's departure for Rome seemed to them like a sign from Heaven. Although it happened suddenly, like lightning, or a thief in the night, it is more than likely that all three of these men had met many times with small groups of trained followers, who, in turn, had organized still other subordinate groups of Jews who were unhappy with their current regime and were willing to risk their lives and fortunes to change the leadership. These men were probably impatient people who had urged open action many years before action was actually initiated. During that time, followers may have asked, ''When will these things take place? and what is the sign of your *parousia*?'' This is conjecture, but there was another leader, a few years later, who also led a movement that never broke out into military rebellion, so far as we know, but there are clues of the secret nature of the movement.

Jesus told his disciples that the beautiful temple at Jerusalem would be destroyed, so that not one stone would be left intact. The disciples asked, ''When will these things be, and what is the sign of your *parousia* and the end of the age'' (Matt 24:1-3)? ''The end of the age'' was a mythical expression related to Daniel, which meant the end of the foreign rule. After some unknown period of secrecy, earlier guerrilla leaders, like Mattathias the Hasmonean, Athronges, Simon, and Judas, finally made their public appearances. These were their *parousiai*. A twentieth century example of this took place in Iran. After thirteen years as an exile in France, Khomeini finally flew back to Iran to lead the country, after his secret followers had expelled the Shah. At the time of Jesus' discussion with his disciples, Jesus had not made his plans public. There had been no *parousia*; the disciples of Jesus were impatient, as were others who tried to take Jesus by force and make him king (Jn 6:15). When speaking to his disciples, he could employ ''the mysteries of the Kingdom of Heaven,'' but to outsiders, he spoke in riddles. Some of the riddles he told are just as puzzling to Americans and Europeans today as they were to Romans two thousand years ago.

Contemporary Confusion. Jesus often spoke in a language that did not make complete sense to the average listener who had no special knowledge to suspect that he was really saying something other than the obvious.[17] He spoke of foxes having holes and birds of the heaven, tents (κατασκηνώσεις)—but birds do not have tents; they have nests (νεοσσία) and there are separate words both in Hebrew and Greek for these terms.[18] Jesus told a story of a mustard seed that grew up and became a tree, when every farmer in Palestine would have known that mustard seeds grow up to become plants—not trees that reach heaven. The farmer who learned there were weeds in his wheat field knew at once that an enemy had sown them, whereas Palestinian, European, and American farmers all know that weeds grow even without enemy interference. The woman who lost a small coin, amounting to one day's wages for an unskilled laborer, upon recovery, invited guests and neighbors in to celebrate her good fortune. The celebration might have cost more than the lost coin. The same is true of the shepherd who held a celebration after he found his lost sheep—and what shepherd would leave ninety-nine sheep untended in the mountains while he looked for one that was lost? The woman who was making bread "hid" some leaven in the dough, whereas most people making bread just add the leaven with the other ingredients, since there is nothing secretive about it. Jesus told a story about a king who held a wedding feast and invited the most qualified guests. When they made excuses for not coming, they used exactly the excuses Deuteronomy prescribed as admissible for exemption from military service (Deut 20:5-9; Judges 7:2-7). Why? When the disciples of John asked if Jesus was the one who was to come, he told them to remember what they had heard and seen: (1) blind people could see, (2) lame could walk; (3) lepers were cleansed; (4) deaf could hear; (5) dead were raised; (6) the poor received the good news, and (7) the one who took no offense in Jesus would be blessed (Matt 11:2-6). So, what did he tell John? Was he, or was he not? There were evidently ways by which messages could be commu-

---

[17]Contra Linnemann, *Jesus*, p. 3, following Bultmann, *History*, p. 174, " 'The image in the *similitude* is taken from real life as everyone knows it, and refers to the things that happen every day, to circumstances that even the most ill-willed must admit exist.' This is how it *always* [emphasis added] happens when leaven is added to meal (Matt 13:35), when someone sows mustard seed (Matt 13:31 f.), when grain ripens to harvest (Mark 4:26-29).''

[18]C. F, D. Moule, "The Individualism of the Fourth Gospel," *Nov* 5 (1962):177, held that Jesus is reported in Acts 1:4 to be bivouacking with the disciples.

nicated to those who had ears to hear. Some of these were parables or "riddles."[19]

Solutions to Riddles. Fiebig[20] discovered long ago that the NT parable is not the same as the Greek analogy or fable. It more closely resembles the Hebrew *mashal* or the Aramaic *mathla'*, which can mean either an analogy or a riddle. An OT example of a *mashal* is a story which Nathan told David of a rich man who killed a poor man's only little ewe lamb. This is easily understood because we have the setting and the outcome reported. But what could we know about this parable without the response, "You are the man!" (2 Sam 12:7)?

The parables told by rabbis were not especially apt. If you did not know the question the rabbi was trying to answer, the parable would not make much sense. For example, "Rabbi Shimon ben Yohai was once asked by his disciples, 'Why did the manna not come down to Israel once a year?' He replied, 'I will give you a parable: This may be compared to a king of flesh and blood who had one son, whose maintenance he provided once a year. [This meant that the son] would visit the father only once a year [to receive his allowance]. Thereupon, [the king] provided for [the son's] maintenance day-by-day, so that [the son] would call upon [the king] every day. The same is true with Israel. One who had four or five children would worry, saying, "Maybe no manna will come down, tomorrow, and all will die of hunger." Thus they were found to turn their attention [day-by-day] to their Father in heaven'" (Yoma 76a). The rabbi knew how often the manna fell and attempted to explain it in this parable. He did not really know how kings managed their economic or family affairs. It is not likely that a prince would see the king only when he needed money or that the king would dole out money only upon personal request, but the rabbi had to tell a parable that would explain the real situation that dealt with the manna, so he made up a story with that goal in mind. Therefore, the parable makes sense only in context.

---

[19]This is much different from the existential interpretations that are currently popular. Trying to communicate in a revolutionary environment is not the same as dramatizing an ontological possibility (as D. O. Via, Jr., *The Parable* [Philadelphia, 1967], p. 49, would have it) or philosophizing about the situational or contextual character of human existence (Ibid., p. 131), or "the autonomy of the aesthetic object" (Ibid., p. 120).

[20]P. Fiebig, *Alt Jüdische Gleichnisse und die Gleichnisse Jesu* (Tübingen, 1904). See also H. P. Müller, "Der Begriff 'Rätsel' im Alten Testament," *VT* 20 (1970) 465-89.

In dealing with the parables of Jesus, we no longer have the context. We have some parables of Jesus which do not make sense as simple stories. We have to deduce the question Jesus was really trying to answer. There are two places where we may look for clues to the question: (1) OT scripture, and (2) known Jewish tradition. Jesus spoke so that those who were trained in the mysteries of the Kingdom of Heaven (Matt 13:10-13) could understand the special code, but he also wished to communicate with other Jews who were not so trained. To those he spoke in parables based on scripture and tradition because he expected them to know these.[21] This did not require special code but still the Romans could not understand it. This technique enabled him to recruit openly and publicly without arousing the suspicion of the Romans. Since scripture is quoted in some of Jesus' parables, we can begin studying his message with those. The first of these is a seemingly innocent story of seed that grows mysteriously.

Mysterious Growth. "The Kingdom of God is like a man who throws seed on the ground and sleeps and rises night and day, but the stalk shoots up and grows in a way he does not know. Mysteriously, the land produces grain, first the blade, then the stalk, then the full grain in the stalk. When it yields the grain, *he puts in the sickle, because the harvest is ready*" (Joel 4:13; Mk 4:26-29).[22]

To the Roman listener, this would seem like an innocent story of farming. The "Kingdom of Heaven," however, is a code word the Romans would not have understood. This riddle was told so that even those Jews who did not understand "the mysteries of the Kingdom of Heaven" but knew their scriptures and the general Jewish tradition would be able to understand a message that was not innocent. What was the tradition and scripture they

---

[21]This is not the same as C. H. Cave, "The Parables and the Scriptures," *NTS* 11 (1964/ 65):374-87. Cave has tried to conjecture scripture texts *not quoted in the parables* that may have been the synagogue readings which the parables illustrated. There are few, if any, controls for Cave's kind of conjecturing. Bornkamm, *Jesus,* p. 70, was mistaken in saying that the parables required no knowledge, education, theoretical judgment, or goodness. They required a knowledge of Jewish scriptures and tradition.

[22]J. D. Crossan, "The Seed Parables of Jesus," *JBL* 92 (1973) 253, did not like the vengeance motif of the Joel passage, so he concluded that it was a later gloss, not present in the original parable. Crossan held that since the verse is not explicitly quoted in the Gospel of Thomas 85:15-18, the "sickle" mentioned there could be dismissed. There was more pacifism and less vengeance in the early church than among the apostles in Jesus' time.

needed to know, and what was the secret message they would have received?

According to the old Pentacontad calendar that was still observed by some Jews in NT times,[23] unleavened bread was eaten after the end of the old year, right up until New Year's Day, the very day that later became Christian Easter.[24] On the first of the New Year there was a ceremony of cutting the first of the new year's grain. This ceremony was so important to tradition that it was preserved even after the lunar calendar was accepted and New Year's Day was changed to Autumn. According to the old calendar, New Year's Day always fell on the first day after the Sabbath, but that was not so of the lunar calendar. According to the lunar calendar, this might even fall on the Sabbath, but if it did Pharisees still conducted the ceremony. People from neighboring towns gathered and when it was dark, one of the messengers of the court said, "Is the sun set?" The crowd then answered in unison, "Yes!" Three times the question was asked and answered in unison. Then he asked, "Is this a sickle?" and they answered, "Yes!" This was done responsively three times. The same procedure followed with the basket. Finally, he asked, "Shall I reap?" and the crowd answered in unison, "Yes!" This also happened three times before the messenger of the court put the sickle into the new grain (Menahoth 10:3). Then they cut the grain and brought it into the Temple court in baskets. There it was parched and ground into flour. It could be consumed after it had been properly tithed and the priests had received their portions (Menahoth 10:4).

Also on the New Year's Day the Lord was believed to open the books and judge the people. If they were judged meritorious, they would be given back the land and the enemy nations would be subdued. If they were believed to be still in their sin, they would continue in captivity to pagan nations. Judgment was to take place in the land of Israel when enemy nations would be gathered and utterly defeated by God's judgment (Ezek 38:19-

---

[23]See further J. and H. Lewy, "The Origin of the Week and the Oldest West Asiatic Calendar," *HUCA* 17 (1942):1-152a

[24]See J. and H. Lewy, "Origin"; J. Morgenstern, "The Calendar of the Book of Jubilees," *VT* 5 (1955):34-76; Morgenstern, *Some Significant Antecedents of Christianity* (Leiden, 1966), pp. 20-22.

29).[25] The author of Joel probably had the judgment day associated with New Year's Day in mind when he wrote the following poem describing a war in terms of a harvest scene.[26] This is the very scripture quoted in this cleverly constructed parable of Jesus:

> Sanctify war, stir up the mighty men
> beat your plowshares into swords,
> and your pruning hooks into spears . . .
> Let the nations arouse themselves,
> and come up to the Valley of Jehoshaphat . . .
> for there I will sit to judge
> all the nations round about.
> *Put in the sickle, because the harvest is ready.*
> Come, tread the grapes, for the press is full.
> and the vats overflow . . .
> Mobs, mobs, in the Valley of Verdict—
> The Day of the Lord is near
> in the Valley of Verdict . . .
> The Lord roars from Zion,
> and utters his voice from Jerusalem.
> The Lord is a refuge to his people,
> a stronghold to the people of Israel.
> So you shall know that I am the Lord your God,
> who dwells in Zion, my holy mountain.
> Jerusalem shall be holy, and foreigners
> shall never again pass through it.
>
> (Joel 4:9-17)

---

[25]See L. Landman, *Messianism in the Talmudic Era* (New York, 1979), p. xii, and H. J. Kraus, *Die Königherrschaft Gottes im Alten Testament* (Tübingen, 1951), pp. 50-57, 69-70, 106. Also see *RH* 4:5; *TRH* 1:11-13; *LevR* 19:1.

[26]Although this seems to be an obvious allusion to a New Year's Day judgment scene, the following commentaries on Joel overlooked it: L. C. Allen, *The Books of Joel, Obadiah, Jonah, and Micah* (Grand Rapids, c1976); A. Cohen, *The Twelve Prophets* (Chesham, c1948); F. W. Farrar, *The Minor Prophets* (New York, n.d.); Mag. H. Frey, *Das Buch der Kirche in der Weltwende: Die Kleinen Nachexilischen Propheten* (Stuttgart, n.d.); H. Henderson, *The Book of the Twelve Minor Prophets* (London, 1845); K. Marti, *Das Dodekaphropheton* (Tübingen, 1904); C. Von Orelli, *The Twelve Minor Prophets,* tr. J. S. Banks (Edinburg, 1897); E. B. Pusey, *The Minor Prophets* (New York, 1886); G. L. Robinson *The Twelve Minor Prophets* (New York, c1926); Th. H. Robinson, *Die Zwölf Kleinen Propheten: Nahum bis Maleachi* (Tübingen, 1954).

Those who had ears to hear knew that Jesus was referring to a very special New Year's Day celebration when he mentioned putting in the sickle. This parabolic language was understood, not only by those who knew "the mysteries of the Kingdom of Heaven," but many others who understood Jewish scripture and traditions. One of these was the author of Rev 14:14-20.

> *I was watching, and look! (Dan 7:13), a white cloud, and upon the cloud* (Dan 7:13) was seated one *like a Son of man* (Dan 7:13), having upon his head a gold crown and in his hand a sharp *sickle* (Joel 4:13). Then another angel went out from the temple, shouting loudly to the one seated upon *the cloud* (Dan 7:13), *"Put in* your *sickle* and harvest, *because the time to harvest has come* (Joel 4:13), because the harvest of the land is ripe."* Then one seated upon *the cloud* (Dan 7:13) put his *sickle* (Joel 4:13) to the land, and he harvested the land. Then another angel went out from the temple which was in heaven, having also himself, a sharp *sickle* (Joel 4:13). Another angel went out from the altar, who had authority over fire, and he called out in a loud voice to the one who had the sharp *sickle* (Joel 4:13), saying, *"Put in* your sharp *sickle* (Joel 4:13) and gather in the grapes of the vine of the land, because its grapes are ripe." Then the angel *put* its *sickle* (Joel 4:13) to the land, gathered the vines of the land, put them into the wine press of the great wrath of God, and *trampled the wine press* (Isa 63:3; Joel 4:13) outside the city. The blood from the wine press reached the bridles of the horses for two hundred miles around.

The Valley of Verdict is identical to the Valley of Jehoshaphat which is the Kidron Valley just outside of Jerusalem near the temple area. Therefore the city, outside of which the wine press was to be trampled, is Jerusalem. The author of the Apocalypse understood the code words necessary to use such terms as "sickle" when referring to Joel and the judgment at the Valley of Jehoshaphat and the "wine press" which also involved the final battle between the Gentiles and the Jews when the "harvest" was gathered. The angels who went out from the temple and the altar were near at hand to the valley where all of this was expected to take place. When they put in their sickles to "gather" grapes, they put them into the Gentile troops that were to be gathered in the valley to attack Jerusalem (See Ezek 38:1-39:29).

All of this is involved in that seemingly harmless and innocent expression in Jesus' parable, "When it yields its grain, *he puts in the sickle, because the harvest is ready*" (Joel 4:13; Mk 14:29). As people were wondering when the Romans were going to be driven out and the messianic kingdom be installed, Jesus, through this parable, told how the Kingdom of God would come. He said that the new government was already in process. Inauspiciously, quietly, almost without notice, things were happening. At the appointed time, before anyone really realized it, there would be a judgment day. At that celebration, when the Gentiles all gathered against Jerusalem, the Lord would cut them all down like grain. This was a parabolic way of saying, "The Kingdom of Heaven has come near" (Matt 3:2; 4:17; 10:7—but, of course, the Romans would have missed the message. Similar to this parable is the following, which is designed as a riddle to be understood only by those who had ears to hear.

The Mustard Seed. "The Kingdom of Heaven is like a grain of mustard seed, which a man took and sowed in his field. On the one hand, it is the smallest of all seeds, but on the other hand, when it is grown, it becomes greater than the vegetables, and becomes a tree, so that the *birds of the heaven come and dwell in its branches*" (Dan 4:12, 21; Matt 13:31-32; Mk 4:30-32; Lk 13:18-19).[27]

McArthur[28] was convinced that the best reading of the texts shows that the tree is original, but he objected, " . . . *contrast* is a legitimate part for a parable but not *incongruity*. The contrast between the small mustard seed and the large plant makes a point in the contrast of Jesus' ministry, but a mustard seed that turned into a tree would be a monstrosity not characteristic of the parables correctly attributed to Jesus." McArthur and Crossan[29]

---

[27]Mark 4:31-32, not realizing the significance of that Daniel quotation, modified the parable so that the mustard seed grew up—not to become a tree—but, "the greatest of all garden herbs." This made it rationally acceptable for those, like Mark, who did not understand the code to these riddles. Scholars like G. E. Post, "Mustard," *Hastings Dictionary of the Bible* 3, p. 463; Meyer, *Matthew,* p. 258; and Plummer, *ICC Matt,* p. 194, have also tried to justify the parable by holding that mustard plants sometimes grow large in the Near East—ten to twelve feet tall, and Arabs sometimes call herbs, "trees." This still is not a tree that "reaches heaven." Those who understand "the mystery of the Kingdom of Heaven" or parabolic code would not have this problem.

[28]H. K. McArthur, "The Parable of the Mustard Seed," *C* 33 (1971):198-210, quote from p. 210. R. W. Funk, "The Looking-glass Tree is for the Birds," *Int.* 27 (1973):3-9, argued that Jesus deliberately picked a small mustard bush in contrast to the cedar of Lebanon because of the humble size. Even though he studied this passage in relationship to Ezekiel and Daniel, he did not see the reason for these references.

[29]Crossan, "Seed Parables," p. 255, asked, "Why use a mustard plant if one intends to have birds *nesting in* its branches?" Even though references to birds in branches occur in all synoptic accounts, as well as the Gospel of Thomas 84:32, Crossan concluded that the original parable did not have any reference to a tree or birds' nests (pp. 253-59), so he dismissed the quotation from Daniel.

missed the point at which this resembles other parables. Like many other parables of Jesus, this riddle was not intended to provide a lesson on agronomy. Most Near Eastern farmers would have known that mustard seeds do not grow up to become trees. They grow up and become mustard plants, but it is precisely this distortion which would have given the one who had ears to hear the clue to the intended message of the parable.

There were probably three messages for those who had ears to hear (1) All they had to do was remember the content of Daniel 4 or go back and look it up to learn that the tree was part of a dream that represented a kingdom that reached heaven and its dominion extended to the end of the earth (Dan 4:22). The Kingdom of Heaven was to be like that. (2) The second message was that the Most High rules the kingdom of men and gives to whomever he chooses (Dan 4:17, 25, 32) and he would force even Gentile kings to acknowledge him (Dan 4:37). (3) This kingdom, represented by a tree, was ruled at one time by Nebuchadnezzar, but after it had passed through the hands of three other beasts, it was finally given to the Jews under the leadership of the Son of man (Dan 7:13) at exactly the time when Judas overpowered the Syrians sufficiently to cleanse the temple. This knowledge enabled Jews to understand the third message which was that the Kingdom of God was like the Hasmonean kingdom that had been ruled by the foreign nations until the Son of man was vindicated in the heavenly court. The Romans in the group probably missed all of that.[30]

Leaven and the Land. ''The Kingdom of Heaven is like leaven which a woman took and hid in three measures of flour until the whole [dough] was leavened'' (Matt 13:33; Lk 13:20-21).

The importance of the leaven metaphor is that leaven is very infectious. It is not necessary to add yeast to flour to make it leavened. It has only to be moistened to be considered leavened. For Passover, it is important to have flour that has not been leavened. Therefore care must be taken that no moisture reaches the wheat from the time it heads out until the flour is moistened just before the bread is put into the oven. There must elapse only eighteen minutes between the time the flour is moistened until the unleavened bread is taken out of the oven. Most Jewish bakers can manage this operation within eleven minutes. If any flour is accidentally moistened or becomes

---

[30]The secretive way in which messiahs communicated is evident when Sabbatai Zevi carried a fish around in a baby basket to let Jews know that under the zodiacal sign of Pisces Israel would be redeemed from pagan rule. See J. Kastein, *The Messiah of Ismir,* tr. H. Peterson (New York, 1931), p. 73.

moldy, it must be discarded. Vessels that can hold moisture must be broken. If a small bit of leavened flour falls into a pot of dough, sixty times as large as the leavened flour, the whole is considered leavened. The dough must be discarded and the pot must be broken.[31] Because leaven is considered infectious, it was used metaphorically to describe a political or religious movement. That is what Jesus meant when he warned his disciples to watch out for the leaven of the Pharisees, Sadducees, and Herod (Matt 16:6; Mk 8:14-15; Lk 12:1). He meant that these groups were busy propagating their doctrines everywhere. Like leaven, they were corrupting the nation. Rabbis complained to the Lord: "Master of the ages, it is revealed and known to you that we want to do your will. Who is hindering? The leaven that is in the dough and subjection to the Gentiles. May it be your will that we may escape from their hands" (Ber 17a). This was also true of leaven that must permeate into loaves.

When leavened bread is desired, there is no need to hide the leaven that is used.[32] It can just be added since there is no secrecy involved, but Jesus was using coded language. At the time he was speaking, the Kingdom of Heaven was in hiding. The Romans did not know that it existed. This was an underground movement that was quietly, infectiously, working its way through the land. With the rapidity of leaven in a loaf, this undercover movement would take control of the whole situation, and everyone would find out what had been happening.[33] This parable is consistent with the parable of the seed growing secretly or the mustard seed that grew up and became a tree. At the right time, the grain would be ready for harvest and the leavened loaf would be ready for the oven. These were different metaphors for the same event. It meant that the Kingdom of Heaven was about to come into existence in the land of Palestine.

---

[31]L. I. Rabinowitz, "Mazzah." *Encyclopaedia Judaica* 11, pp. 1155-58.

[32]There is also no reason to think the number three refers to the deity, as Funk thinks (R. W. Funk, "Beyond Criticism in the Quest of Literacy: The Parable of Leaven," *Int* 25 [1971] 149-70, esp. p. 167). Funk said "leaven" is the loss of the received world; "hide" means mystery; and "three measures of meal" equals the presence of God (p. 167). Three measures would make a fantastically large number of loaves, but that was intended to alert the Jewish listener that Jesus was not really talking about bread at all.

[33]With Constantine's conquest, Eusebius said all those Christian disciples, who had been consecrated to the Word and yet were secretly concealed, appeared openly (*HE* 10.iv.60).

The Bell on the Cat. "How can anyone enter the house of a strong man and seize his goods if he does not first bind the strong man? Then he can plunder his house" (Matt 12:29; see also Isa 49:24-26; Ps Sol 5:4).

In one of the nursery stories told to almost every American child, the mice held a council meeting to decide how to deal with the new cat that had arrived on the scene and reduced the rodent population. After much meditation, some mouse suggested that they would have to pin a bell on the cat so that every mouse could hear him coming. They all thought it was an excellent suggestion, but the next procedural question was, "Who will pin the bell on the cat?" That was the end of the project. At the beginning of this parable, the situation sounded very much like that, but the conclusion was different. The conclusion was that they *would* go through with the project and get the strong man bound so that they could plunder his house. What were they really talking about that would make sense in the same context as these other parables?

The strong man who controlled the "house" that the Jews wanted to plunder in NT times was probably Rome.[34] Most Palestinian Jews would have liked to plunder Rome's possessions in Palestine and drive Rome out, but that was easier said than done. Rome first had to be bound and made helpless, mostly without Rome realizing what was happening. This was a big job, but no greater than that undertaken by the Hebrews in Egypt and the Hasmoneans with Syria. It would require various kinds of sabotage— Jews could get themselves appointed to important Roman posts where they could control things. From these positions they could either weaken Rome by steady sabotage or apparently be good Roman officers until the whole web was woven and Jews controlled enough important posts that they could make Rome functionally helpless. This meant "binding the strong man." Afterwards they could take over the entire country, and that was the plan.

That this sort of thing was going on is evident from the activity that took place when Aristobulus left the country to get authority to rule the country when Herod the Great died. When Jews were in Babylon, they negotiated with Cyrus of Persia for Cyrus to grant them many concessions, one of which was permission to return to Palestine. They undoubtedly did some

---

[34]B. Weiss, *A Commentary on the New Testament* (New York, 1906) 1:104; Meyer, *Matthew*, p. 241; Plummer, *Matthew*, p. 178, rightly thought the strong man was Satan, but Jews also identified Satan with Rome.

things to help the Persians take over Babylon to make it worth Cyrus's concessions. The same was true with Constantine and the Christians. If Jews had been better organized and had been able to offer Constantine more assistance than Christians did at that time, Constantine would probably have negotiated with them, instead, and the Christians would have continued as a strong upper class minority.[35] In order to get the concessions they did, Christians were expected to participate in many active ways that enabled Constantine to take over the Roman government. This probably involved skilled sabotage on the part of the Christians.

We have no record of Jewish sabotage within Syria at the time of the Hasmonean Revolt, but there were many Jews there at that time. They had been given citizenship privileges more than a century before (*Ant* 12.119-120) and probably held positions of influence by Hasmonean times. There were Jewish soldiers in the Syrian army brought to fight against Alexander Jannaeus. When they actually got near the battle lines, six thousand Jews defected to Alexander (*Ant* 13.377-80; *BJ* 1.95-99). At the time of the revolt of the Jews against Rome in A.D. 66-70, Josephus and Tacitus both report the great amount of civil strife and internal conflict within the Roman government that made it easier for Jews to rebel. There is no report that Jews were involved in the Roman government, getting and keeping this unrest and insecurity going, but it may have happened. This is all part of what is involved in ''binding the strong man'' and both Jews and Christians have a long history of sabotage and fifth column activity from the time of Moses on.

After as much success as Jews had had prior to NT times, it is not surprising that they would have dared to try to undertake a sabotage program against the great Roman empire, at least enough to obtain freedom for the promised land. It is also reasonable to suppose that they would not venture open conflict with Rome until their sabotage program was well under control. When Jews finally did risk open conflict in A.D. 66, they had things under such control on all sides that they became a serious threat to the Roman empire. This could not have happened accidentally. Behind the scenes there must have been a lot of careful planning and an extensive intelligence operation, employing Jews in every country who were already in strategic places as part of their normal occupations. Jesus seems to have been aware

---

[35]See further, GWB, *Revelation*, pp. 10-12.

of such possibilities, surely inside of Palestine, and maybe throughout the Roman empire.

The Undercover Government. "When he had been asked by the Pharisees when the Kingdom of God would come, he answered them and said, 'The Kingdom of God will not come by observation, and they will not say, "Look here! or there!" Look, the Kingdom of God is in your midst' " (Lk 17:20-21).

This responsive chreia is frequently used as proof that the Kingdom of God is not a political entity at all, but means only the ruling authority of God in the hearts of people. After all, it does say the Kingdom of God is *within* you, does it not? Of course, most scholars hold that this means the Kingdom of God is in the midst of the community involved and not just in the hearts of individuals.[36] Although it is difficult to understand how a ruling power or territorial kingdom can exist psychologically or sociologically in a non-political way, most scholars have not examined this passage in relationship to sabotage and fifth column activity. Nonetheless, when dealing with a revolution, this is a normal part of the program. Long before the revolt, there must be behind-the-scenes plans functioning like seeds growing secretly or like leaven working through a loaf, until the strong man is finally bound and it is time to "put in the sickle." When the harvest is ready for the sickle, and the mustard plant becomes a tree that reaches heaven, and the strong man is bound (Matt 12:29), the Son of man[37] will come with the clouds, and that which was once told in secret would be shouted from the housetops (Matt 10:26-27). These are all parabolic terms which would have the political effect of a messiah ruling as king from Jerusalem with his twelve cabinet members ruling over the twelve tribes of Israel (Matt 19:28). This is what had been going on in Iran before the Shah was removed from the country and Khomeini was brought in to make his *parousia*.

There are enough references in this chapter to the teachings of Jesus that are coherent with one another, that also are consistent with the beliefs taught

---

[36]RSV, for instance, renders this passage, "in the midst of you." C. H. Dodd, *Historical Tradition in the Fourth Gospel* (Cambridge, 1963), p. 401, fn. 1, preferred the translation, "within your reach" or "within your grasp." H. A. W. Meyer, *Critical and Exegetical Hand-Book on the Gospels of Mark and Luke* (New York, 1884), p. 491, preferred *"in your circle."*

[37]Bornkamm, *Jesus*, p. 176, without knowing the mythological nature of the title, "Son of man," said some references to the title "undoubtedly" can be traced back to Jesus.

in God's providence and willingness to give Jews the Kingdom, to suspect that Jesus really believed and taught something like this. They are also coherent with the chreias and parables related to a recruitment program under pressure that involved tax collectors and stirred up the hostility of the Pharisees. The evidence has been growing that depicts Jesus as one who was intimately related to plans for an open revolt against Rome whenever the time was ripe. There is still one more passage that reflects open communication through code in parabolic or mythical language. This is the coded message to the disciples of John the Baptist.

Fulfilled Prophecy. Some of the rules by which Jewish and Christian historians and theologians of NT times functioned are these: (1) Whatever is in the world is in the scripture. Therefore the only place to search for hidden knowledge is in the scripture. (2) All prophecy will be fulfilled in the days of the Messiah. Since Jews believed that the days when Jesus and John the Baptist lived were days of the Messiah, prophecy was expected to be fulfilled. One needed only to study carefully to determine what was prophesied that is somehow related to current events. To those who knew scripture, this also became a coded means of communication for those who had ears to hear. The rest missed the point.

The Message to John. At the time when John was in prison for insurrection (*Ant* 18.116-19) and "had heard the works of the Messiah, he sent through his disciples, and said to him, 'Are you the coming one, or should we anticipate someone else?' Jesus, in reply, said to them, 'Go, report to John the things you hear and see: *The blind receive their sight*; the lame walk; the lepers are cleansed; *the deaf hear*; the dead are raised; *and the poor receive the good news,* and blessed is the one who is not made to stumble because of me' " (Matt 11:1-6).

Now just what did Jesus tell the messengers to tell John? Was he the coming one (i.e. the Messiah) or not? Was there ever going to be anything done to release John from prison? The answer seems to be a clear, "Yes!" but it was said in mythical language that only those familiar with the OT would understand. It would not have been clear to the Romans. John the Baptist should have been one of those who had eyes to see and ears to hear (Matt 13:16-17; Lk 10:23-24) and Jesus' message was aimed at him. The scripture John needed to know was Isa 29:18-20:

"In that day, *the deaf will hear* the words of the book; from the gloom and darkness, the eyes of *the blind will see*; *The poor will increase in the joy* of the Lord. and *the humble of men will rejoice* in the Holy One of Israel;

for the terrible one will come to nothing, and the scoffer will be finished; and all those who watch to do evil will be cut off."

To those who recognized this scripture, Jesus seemed to be saying, "These are the days of the Messiah. Prophecies are being fulfilled. Just notice, Isaiah said that in the days of the Messiah, (1) the blind would see, (2) the deaf would hear, (3) the poor would become happy, and (4) the terrible one would be finished off. Now of these prophecies, the following have been fulfilled: (in addition to those added to confuse the issue for those who were not intended to hear the message) (1) the blind receive their sight; (2) the deaf hear; (3) the poor are receiving the good news and are therefore happy. Now what do you suppose will happen next?" The messengers were to assure John that he would be blessed if he did not lose hope but realized that his release was next on the agenda. This involved getting rid of Herod—the terrible one.[38]

Jesus seems to have planned to find release for John, somehow, probably in a way that would remove Herod, but before that could happen, Herod put John to death, and this frustrated the plans Jesus and John had for their messianic movement. When the news came to Jesus, he reportedly responded again in code so that those who had ears to hear could hear. Since he was closely related to John[39] and John had been executed as an insurrectionist, it was important for him to be very cautious. He just said, "This is the one about whom it is written, *Look, I am sending my messenger before your face, who will prepare your way for you*" (Mal 3:1; Matt 11:10). Those who remembered Passover liturgy knew that Elijah was expected to come just before the Messiah, to prepare the way for the Messiah who would follow. This had been prophesied in Malachi. When Jesus quoted this passage and identified it with John, he also was saying that he was the Messiah who was to come right after John. Had he announced openly at that time, before Romans, that he was beginning to lead a revolutionary movement, he would have been put in prison or killed at once to prevent further insurrection, so he said the same thing by quoting scripture. This was the way an insurrectionist could communicate in public without being suspected. To those of

---

[38]Overlooking the important purpose of the Isaiah passage, W. G. Kümmel, *Jesu Antwort an Johannes den Täufer* (Wiesbaden, 1974), pp. 129-59, argued for the genuineness of this encounter.

[39]Contra M. S. Enslin, "John and Jesus," *ZNW* 66 (1975):1-18.

the same group, he could speak through ''the mysteries of the Kingdom of Heaven.'' To the rest he spoke in riddles, so that well-trained Jews could understand, but the Romans would miss the point.

The Messianic Secret

Secrecy was closely associated with messiahs. Trypho said, ''But even if the Messiah has already been born and lives somewhere, he is not known, and he does not even recognize himself [as the Messiah]. Nor does he have any kind of power until Elijah has come, anointed him, and revealed him to everyone'' (Justin, *Dial.* 8). There are also rabbinic legends of the Messiah being in hiding in the Great Sea or Rome.[40] In his letter to the Jews at Yemen, Maimonides told them prophecy would return to Israel at A.D. 1210, after which the Messiah would come. He warned them, however,to keep this information from becoming public[41]—three guesses why!

By using mythological language, Jews were able to tell ''the truth'' upon interrogation without disclosing facts. For instance, some sons of David were brought before Domitian with the suspicion that they were potential insurrectionists. They were asked about the Messiah and his kingdom and they replied by saying that the messianic kingdom was ''heavenly'' and would be instituted only at the end of the age (Eusebius, *HE* 3.xxx.1.4. This seemed harmless to Domitian, so they were released. Had he known that the expression ''Kingdom of Heaven'' was a code word for the promised land under Jewish control, and that the ''end of the age'' would take place whenever Jews were liberated from Rome, Domitian might not have been as lenient as he was. It was only a few years later (A.D. 132-35) that another messianic pretender engaged in a bloody war with Rome, trying to bring about the same ''heavenly kingdom'' at a time he hoped would prove to be the ''end of the age.''

At the beginning of the twentieth century the ''messianic secret'' was a popular topic in NT circles. William Wrede and Albert Schweitzer offered scholars different solutions the same year. Wrede said the secret of Jesus' messiahship was not historical. This was a motif which the author of Mark deduced from the early church after the resurrection and transferred

---

[40]Midrash *Bereshit Rabbati*, daf. 84-85; *Lamentations Zuta* 1:2; *Lamentations Rabbati* 2:1-2. See GWB, *Revelation*, pp. 452-62.

[41]GWB, *Revelation*, p. 90.

back into the life of Jesus. Schweitzer's solution was that Jesus kept his messiahship a secret because he was not yet the Messiah. He received the secret at his baptism and kept it a secret until his crucifixion. He let only a few know beforehand that he *would be* the Messiah and the Son of man when that time came. With his death came the end of the Kingdom of God and eschatology, and the church was liberated from a narrow nationalistic messianism to be a world-wide religion.[42]

Both scholars looked for solutions that would not identify them with Reimarus.[43] The most obvious reason for a pretending messiah to keep his plans secret was to avoid the certain death that would follow if his revolutionary plans should become known to Romans or Roman sympathizers.

The literary forms used in this chapter are as follows:

Chreias

God as a Gardener .... (Matt 15:12-13)
Mustard Seed and Mountains..(Lk 17:5-6; Matt 21:21; Mk 11:22)
None Good but God.................(Lk 18:18-20; Matt 19:16-17)
The Undercover Government .... (Lk 17:20-21)

Parables

The Sower .... (Matt 13:3-8; Mk 4:4-9; Lk 8:5-8)
The Midnight Hospitality .... (Lk 11:5-8)
The Unjust Judge....................................... (Lk 18:2-5)
Mysterious Growth...................................(Mk 4:26-29)
The Mustard Seed..... (Matt 13:31-32; Mk 4:30-32; Lk 13:18-19)
Leaven and the Land...................(Matt 13:33; Lk 13:20-21)
The Bell and the Cat ....(Matt 12:29)

Others

The Father's Hospitality.............. (Matt 7:7-11; Lk 11:11-13)
The Message to John ....(Matt 11:1-6)

---

[42]A. Schweitzer, *The Mystery of the Kingdom of God*, tr. W. Lowrie (New York, 1950), p. 159.

[43]H. S. Reimarus, *The Goal of Jesus and his Disciples*, intro. and tr. GWB (Leiden: E. J. Brill, 1970), has long been considered a heretic because he believed Jesus and his disciples were trying to recover the promised land.

The messianic secret was kept by using various kinds of code expressions in the form of parable and known religious myth, like some of those discussed in this chapter. Among other things, the next chapter will consider the function of forgiveness in this whole military-religious enterprise of acquiring the Kingdom of Heaven.

CHAPTER SEVEN

The
Royal
Treasury

Introduction

Treasury Terms. Initially, the religion of Israel from which modern Judaism and Christianity sprang was a state religion. The synagogue and the church evolved from the diaspora as unplanned spin-offs, but the religion that developed on the promised land was a state religion. The king was both a political and religious leader. The tithes that were required met both the costs of maintaining the temple and the priesthood as well as the entire national economy. Because this was true, theological language developed in terms of national leadership and function. Among these terms are those related to a royal treasury such as "reconcile," "forgive," and "redeem" are treasury terms used in dealing with finance. When these became transferred into theological concepts dealing with sin and righteousness, there was also presumed a heavenly treasury and a bookkeeping system whereby sins and merits could be recorded just as deposits and withdrawals are recorded in a banking system.

Mythical Terms. When the banking/borrowing concept is transferred mythically to the realm of sins and virtues, a treasury or bank of some kind is necessary to make sense out of the whole metaphor. Jeremiah spoke to the people of Judah, telling them that they had committed so many sins that they had overdrawn their account. They were at that time bankrupt, according to his diagnosis, so the Lord would foreclose on them, driving them out of the land until they had paid, in terms of virtue, double for all their sins (Deut 15:18; Jer 16:18). Second Isaiah told Jews of Babylon some fifty years later, that they had at that time paid double for all their sins, so they would soon be released from their imprisonment and be allowed to return to the promised land (Isa 40:2).

Later Jews presumed that this was so. Whenever they were in exile again they would have to act in the same way before they could be restored. Since Jews did not go into exile or return one by one, it was evident that they all contributed to and withdrew from the same treasury. When they were overdrawn, the treasury had to be reimbursed. This is what the first generation or two of Jews of Babylon did. They suffered for the sins of earlier generations.[1]

On the basis of past Jewish experience, Jews in NT times were obligated to keep a careful watch on their deposits and withdrawals in this heavenly treasury. If they were to become free from the Romans, they would first have to pay off the indebtedness which had been established by earlier generations. Therefore there are many teachings in the NT about forgiveness and reconciliation. In the business world, books could be cleared every seven years for personal debts and every forty-nine years when land was held in security (Lev 25:8-10). In the mythical banking system, there was an opportunity given for reconciling differences once a year on the Day of Atonement. On that day, God would forgive Jews their sins if they first met certain conditions: (1) they had to become reconciled to one another, leaving no grudges, no sins unreconciled, no wrongs not corrected with one another; (2) they were required to repent of their sins, and (3) they had to bring to the altar the specified offerings for their sins against the Lord.[2] If all of

---

[1]Christians inherited this mythology from Jews. Eusebius, for example, explained the success of Constantine by saying that the church had paid the just penalty for her sins, so she was once again restored (*HE* 10.iv.60). See further GWB, *Consequences*, 128-31.

[2]Ibid., pp. 222-37.

these were done, and if every Jew met all the requirements, then all sins would be forgiven. Since the only reason they were not in control of the promised land, according to this doctrine, was that they were in debt to God, it followed logically that when all their sins were forgiven they would receive back the promised land. God was in control of the books and there was no way Jews could check his records. The only way they could judge the status of their account was the results: was the promised land in their control, or was it not? In NT times Rome was in control of the promised land, and the longer this condition continued, the harder Jews tried to pay off their debts. Small groups were formed that tried to be "perfect," believing that even a small remnant could redeem Israel and provide the Lord a perfect place in which to dwell. Some of these admonitions to repent and forgive sins are preserved in chreias attributed to Jesus.

Chreias on Repentance and Forgiveness

Become like Children. "At that time the disciples came to Jesus, saying, 'Who is great in the Kingdom of Heaven?' After he called a child, he stood it in their midst and said, 'I tell you under oath, if you do not turn and become as the children, you will not enter the Kingdom of Heaven' " (Matt 18:1-3; Lk 9:46-48a; expanded in Mk 9:33-37).

In Judaism of NT times, girls were taught very few laws, had very little legal authority, and therefore were not held responsible for very many offenses. Responsibility was delegated to males in that chauvinistic society. Until their circumcision at eight days, boys were not considered part of the Jewish community. From eight days until their Bar Mitzwah, boys were not legally responsible for their sins. Their fathers were. For this period of twelve or so years children were absolutely innocent, no matter how bad their behavior. Jesus was evidently telling the disciples that they, too, must become sinless, and that could happen once a year for those who "turned" or repented and met the other demands of the Day of Atonement. Commenting on Ps 102:18, rabbis said, "*A people will praise the Lord*: These generations, which were like corpses in their deeds, come and pray before you on *Rosh Hashanah* and you create them a new creation." The Lord promised Jews that if they would do penance even for a ten day period between New Year's Day and the Day of Atonement, then on the Day of Atonement he would judge them innocent and create them a new creature (*PR* 40, 169a). Rabbis also promised that if they accepted the yoke of the Torah, the Lord would say to them, "Just as you enter into judgment before me on New

Year's Day and leave in peace [that is, with all sins forgiven], I will redeem you as if you had been made a new creature . . . as if you had never sinned" (JRHS 4.i.59c, 60).[3] The only way Jews could know if they had repented adequately was by the results—did they get the land restored? If they did not, then they had some sins that had not been reconciled.

The Sign of Jonah.

Then certain of the scribes	Then the Pharisees and Sadducees, tempting,
and Pharisees answered him saying, "We want to see a sign from you." He answered and said to them, "An evil and adulterous generation seeks a sign; a sign will not be given it, except the sign of Jonah, the prophet" (Matt 12:38:39).	asked him to show them a sign from heaven. He answered and said to them,* "An evil and adulterous generation seeks a sign; a sign will not be given it, except the sign of Jonah" (Matt 16:1-2a,4).
Now the Pharisees came out and began to interrogate him, seeking from him a sign from Heaven, tempting him. After he had groaned in his spirit, he said,	While the crowds were gathering, he began to say,
"Why does this generation seek a sign? [May all these unmentioned curses come upon me] if a sign will be given to this generation" (Mk 8:11-12).	"This is an evil generation; it seeks a sign, but a sign will not be given it, except the sign of Jonah" (Lk 11:29).

Three of these are responsive chreias. Luke's chreia is an assertive chreia in which the statement was prompted by a situation rather than a person. Matthew has not even strained to keep the exact wording in his two examples, but there is no question about the message given. There *is* a question about its meaning. This is true of all forms of this message. Mark's version differs more than the others since it is given in the form of an oath, but all chreias make it clear that Jesus was not going to provide the kind of

---

[3]The guiltlessness of the child—not necessarily a feeling of helplessness, patience, and thankfulness, as P. Dausch, *Drei,* p. 254, held, or "the beauty of the childlike temper," as Plummer, *Matthew,* p. 249, thought. Childlikeness is not necessarily a virtue for adults, but repentance and sinlessness were necessary for entrance into the kingdom.

*Some texts add here: "When it is evening you say, 'It will be a good day, tomorrow, because the heaven is red,' and at dawn, 'Today will be cold, because the heaven is red and stormy.' " This is an interpretative addition that destroys the chreia.

sign they wanted. He would only give them the sign of Jonah—whatever that meant![4] They evidently knew what it was, but we do not. Our closest guess is that it is a call to repentance such as Jonah gave to the people of Ninevah, but that is not certain. They wanted a sign that would show them that the same things were about to happen as happened with Moses and Aaron, Joshua, or one of the Hasmoneans. If Jesus had just struck a rock and made water appear, cleansed someone of leprosy, as Moses did with Miriam, brought down manna from heaven, or divided the Reed Sea, that would have satisfied them. These were miracles they expected to see again in the days of the Messiah. Jesus refused to give any such sign. The next chapter will discuss at length the logic by which they looked for signs.

Tragedies around Jerusalem. "Some were going along at the same time they were telling him about the Galileans whose blood Pilate mixed with their sacrifices. He answered and said to them, 'Do you think that these Galileans were worse sinners than all [other] Galileans because they suffered these things? No! I tell you if you do not repent, all of you will perish in the same way—Or, those eighteen upon whom the Tower of Siloam fell and killed [them]—do you think they were worse sinners than all the [other] men who lived in Jerusalem? No! I tell you, if you do not repent, all of you will perish in the same way' " (Lk 13:1-5).

This seems to be a unit comprised of two parallel chreias put together and abbreviated by omitting one of the situations that prompted the speaker to speak. The assumption given is that both responses arose at the same occasion. This is one of those literary units that allows us to test it for geographical and chronological validity. The place where sacrifices were made and the place which zealots often tried to conquer the Romans was the temple at Jerusalem. The Tower of Siloam was evidently a part of the wall built around Jerusalem in the area of Siloam in the Kidron Valley. Therefore both of these incidents are reported to have occurred within the borders of Jerusalem. This evidence comes from the chreia itself and not the Lukan context. Jesus' activity was in Palestine and Jerusalem was its capital city where many Jews went three times a year for festivals. This was the city where Jesus was crucified. Had this geographical location been Spain,

---

[4]Hiers, Kingdom, p. 58, said this was perhaps a mistake for the sign of John, meaning John the Baptist, but all four editions of this chreia say, "Jonah." Meyer, Matthew, p. 245, and Allen, ICC Matt, p. 139, took it to mean Jesus' resurrection.

Rome, Corinth, or some location where Jesus had never been, it would be necessary to rule out this account as something possibly related to Jesus himself. But that is not the case.

There is also a personality included in the account—Pilate—the procurator of Judah from A.D. 26 to 36. This event is also reported to have taken place under the same Roman procurator who crucified Jesus. Therefore this concurs both chronologically and geographically as an event that could have happened in the life of Jesus just as it is reported. That does not prove that it did, but that it is possible. It is also consistent with the behavior expected of Roman procurators, especially Pilate (*Ant* 17.213-23; 18.55-59; 20.105-12; *BJ* 2.3,3; 9.4; 5.1,5).

Of course, any Christian writing historic fiction might have known enough facts to have taken this into account and made up the whole event so that it would sound reasonable. How can we test that? Consider those Galileans whose blood Pilate mixed with their sacrifices: Which Galileans were they? Would the average Christian in Rome have known fifty years later? There were many attempts at festivals to overthrow Rome. At those occasions, Rome regularly got out her troops and stilled the rebellion. How could this event be distinguished from all the rest, from the pericope given? Or, those eighteen killed when the Tower of Siloam fell: What eighteen? Now did it happen? Was it a construction accident or a military battle? No historian has reported either of these events. When Mark wrote his gospel and came across things his readers did not know, he stopped and explained that which was not known; for instance, what the customs of the Pharisees were (Mk 7:1-9). The stories in Luke 13:1-5 are given without explanations, implying that the people addressed knew the details and did not have to be told. Had the authors written down these events in chreia form many years later, they would have given explanatory details. At a time when there were no newspapers, no radios, no televisions, and no other expedient means of communication, how many years after the events could this be done? Five, ten, fifteen years? Would the number be greater in Jerusalem than in Capernaum, Antioch, Alexandria, or Rome?

There was a time in the United States when everyone could say, "Wrong way Corrigan," or later, "payola on TV," and almost everyone would understand what was meant without explanation. Now, anyone speaking publicly to the average audience, using these expressions without explanation, will fail to communicate the desired message to the majority of his or her listeners. This is true even though we have modern means of communication so that almost everyone who is alive at the time the events take place can now know the expressions associated with them. They are also written down in the archives of American history so that later generations can look them up and learn what they mean. Most people do not, however, so popular speakers have to explain situations before using earlier expressions. Only in certain, special groups, like a group of senior citizens, all of whom were alive when Corrigan made his famous flight, can a person use the expression, ''Wrong way Corrigan,'' and be understood. The same logic can be applied to ''payola on TV'' or ''Watergate.''

All of these facts rebel against the suggestion that the later church composed this literary unit, making up the events told in it, and attributing sayings to Jesus which Jesus never said. A later author, writing for the general church, could not presume a knowledge of events that were assumed by the person who put this down in writing. Once something was written down, and a well-known leader was quoted, however, there was a strong scribal tradition to maintain it just as it was, even though it was not understood. Had the apostles put these in chreia form for their own use in recruiting and preaching, they would have needed no more details than the unit gives.

The situation reported makes good sense in the history of the period to which it is ascribed. During the time of Pilate there were many military conflicts between zealous Jews and Roman military personnel. There were probably more than Josephus has reported, one of which was this clash described in Luke 13. On the other hand, after A.D. 70 the church tried to modify the amount of insurrectionist activity with which Jesus had been associated, leaving the impression that Jesus and his followers were always peaceful people who were never sympathetic with any kind of insurrectionist activity. No one knows how much important Christian historical material was destroyed at that time. One of the reasons parables were admitted was that they could be understood in nonrebellious ways. In that situation, this account of the clash between Pilate and the Galileans does not seem to be the kind of report the church would have wanted to propagate if it were not necessary, whether the church liked it or not.

The message of location and time is coherent with the situation shown by the teachings in chreias and parables considered earlier. Jesus was shown organizing a movement, quietly, while making great demands on volunteers, using coded speech and avoiding conflicts with Herod. The content of the message in these two parts of the unit is also coherent with other teachings in this chapter that picture Jesus urging people to repent and forgive one another.

There are so many objections to any consideration that the later church might have composed this unit the way it is and still have it coherent in message, time, and location with the activity of Jesus, that it would take a great deal of credulity to accept such an assumption as that. The most likely explanation is that it is historically accurate. It really happened and it reports faithfully the response of Jesus to the questions posed.

Extensive Forgiveness. ''Then approaching, Peter said to him, 'Lord, how many times will my brother sin against me and I forgive him? seven times?' Jesus said to him, 'I do not say to you, ''Until seven times,'' but ''until seventy-seven times'' ' '' (Matt 18:21-22).[5]

If your brother sins, warn him;
if he repents, forgive him.
If he sins against you seven times a day,
and seven times he turns to you, saying,
'I repent,' you must forgive him (Lk 17:3-4).

This teaching in Matthew's account is clearly a responsive chreia. The message in the Lukan account is basically the same, but clearly not a chreia. Instead, the first sentence is a command and the second sentence is an explanatory elaboration. Dibelius[6] identified Matthew 18:21-22 as a chreia.

Since pious Jews believed the arrival of the Kingdom of Heaven was contingent upon the forgiveness of sins and the reconciliation of believers, every effort had to be made to get sins cancelled. This required an effort on the part of the sinner to correct his offense and also on the part of the person offended to forgive the sin. Jesus was teaching the necessity of forgiveness. The question was not whether the person wanted to forgive or not; he was obligated to do so for the sake of the kingdom. If a Jew came to the altar, bringing his atonement offering but had not been completely reconciled with all of his fellow Jews, he would not be forgiven for his sins against God.[7] Therefore, if he came bringing a gift to the altar and there remem-

---

[5]So also Meyer, *Matthew,* p. 332, in agreement with Origen and Augustine, but against Jerome (see also Yoma 86b; Sira 28:2; Enoch 50:4).

[6]Dibelius, *Tradition,* pp. 159-60.

[7]GWB, *Consequences,* pp. 222-37.

bered some sin that had not been reconciled, he should leave his gift there and go back and become reconciled before offering his gift (Matt 5:23-24). In order to avoid forgetting sins, members were obligated to help one another, reminding other members of their sins every day. If any member refused to repent, he was told of his sins before two or three witnesses. If he still refused to repent, he was brought before the whole church; if he refused to repent before that body, he was to be excommunicated so that the rest of the community might be free from sin (Matt 18:15-17). This is the theology behind the teachings of the chreia. It is coherent with other teachings of Jesus with reference to tax collectors and sinners, such as the parable that follows.

A Parable on Repentance and Forgiveness

Two Debtors.

The Kingdom of Heaven is like a human king who wanted to settle accounts with his servants. When he was beginning to settle, one was led to him who owed him ten thousand talents. Since he was unable to repay, the lord commanded that he, his wife, his children, and all that he owned be sold and [the proceeds from the sale] be paid to him. The servant, then, prostrated himself before him, saying, "Be patient with me, and I will pay it all back to you." Since the lord of that servant had compassion, he released him, and forgave him the loan. Then, after he had left, that servant found one of his fellow servants who owed him a hundred denarii. He seized him and choked him, saying, "Pay back what you owe!" His fellow servant fell down then and begged him, saying, "Be patient with me, and I will repay you." But he did not want to. Instead, he went out and threw him into prison until he paid the debt. Then when his fellow servants saw the things that had happened, they were very much disturbed, so they reported to their lord all the things that took place. Then his lord called him in and said to him, "Wicked servant! All that debt I forgave you, since you pleaded with me. Is it not necessary that you be merciful to your fellow servant, just as I had been with you?" Then his lord was angry and gave him over to the torturers until he should pay back all that he owed him. Thus also my Father who is in heaven will do to you, if you do not forgive each one his brother from your hearts (Matt 18:23-25).

A certain creditor had two debtors: one owed him five hundred denarii and the other, fifty. Since they were not able to pay, he forgave them both. Which of them will love him more (Lk 7:41-42)?

Derrett[8] argued that the Matthaean parable is not exaggerated but makes sense, just as it is, in Near Eastern business of two thousand years ago. People were sold into slavery to pay debts and servants who were tax collectors dealt in huge sums of money. They collected a lot and had large overhead expenses. Therefore, ten thousand talents was not an exorbitant figure. Josephus, however, said the taxes from Coele Syria, Phoenicia, Judaea, and Samaria totaled only eight thousand talents (*Ant.* 12.175), so it is not likely that one of the tax collectors in Judaea or Samaria alone would have been working with so much capital that he could have expected to earn enough in one year to pay this back. Derrett was probably right in saying that the servant was asking his employer only for an extension on the loan, but, like other parables, it is not necessary that every detail of the parable cohere statistically with business practice. That was not the primary point. The point was that the employer who was also the creditor forgave the servant an extensive loan[9] and the amount was probably made in hyperbolic proportions to dramatize the huge indebtedness in contrast to the small loan of the other servant.

The term "human king" probably has the same connotation in Greek as the rabbinic expression "a king of flesh and blood," which means a human king, sometimes specifically a Gentile king. This was a favorite parabolic designation for God in rabbinic parables and it probably has the same significance here. In NT times the word "debt" often referred to a debt in the treasury of merits. It was a sin that had not been corrected and justified. Jews and Christians were conscious of the great debt they had run up because of their sins and they often spoke of them in hyperbolic terms. How could all of this be repaid? Micah asked, "With what shall I come before the Lord? Will the Lord be pleased with thousands of rams, with ten thousands of rivers of oil?" (Micah 6:6, 7). The understanding of the Day of Atonement theology, however, was that once each Jew was reconciled to his fellow Jew, Jews had a chance that God would forgive the debt of their sin against him. In Pharisee-tax collector terms, it was the Pharisee who would not forgive. Jesus compared him to the debtor who owed ten thousand talents to God and would not forgive his fellow Jew a hundred denarii or even

---

[8] J. D. M. Derrett, *Law and the New Testament* (London, c1970), pp. 38-39.

[9] About 600,000 times as large as the loan he refused to forgive. So M'Neile, *Matthew,* p. 169.

wait for him to pay it back. According to Atonement Day theology, the tax collector could not be forgiven on that day unless the Pharisee forgave him his sin and chose to be reconciled to him. The Pharisee realized this, but Jesus suggested that a just God would not hold the Pharisee innocent either on the judgment day if he refused to be reconciled.

In the Lukan version, the parable is almost lost in a narrative. The assumption is that the one who had been forgiven more would be most grateful. This seems to have been Jesus' experience. These sinful tax collectors, once forgiven and accepted back into the fold, became grateful and very loyal followers. These chreias and this parable on forgiveness were not only coherent with one another but consistent with the teachings of Jesus in relationship with the Pharisees and tax collectors. There are still other teachings in the gospels on forgiveness, not in chreia or parable form, which have been attributed to Jesus.

Unpardonable Sins

Although Jesus called Jews to repent (Matt 4:17), there were some for whom it was too late—they had already committed the unpardonable sin:

Every sin and blasphemy will be forgiven men;
blasphemy against the Spirit will not be forgiven.
Whoever says a word against the Son of man
will be forgiven,
but whoever speaks against the Holy Spirit
will not be forgiven,
neither in this age nor in the age to come

(Matt 12:31-32).

Because modern Christians think that this is extreme and pictures God as petulant and peevish, theologians have psychologized it in various ways, but the meaning is clear. Blasphemy means speaking disrespectfully about the Holy Spirit. Although the punishment for this offense seems unreasonable today,[10] it did not seem unreasonable in Judaism and Christianity of NT times. The following quotations will show that this is no distinctive teaching of Jesus.

Whoever swears by the Name which is honored over
every name . . . either for fear of persecution or
for any reason whatever, shall be separated [from

---

[10]Therefore scholars have been creative in inventing ways to minimize its force. See Meyer, *Matthew*, p. 242 for example.

the community] and not allowed to return again

(1QS 6:27-7:1).

[He shall not] swear either by *Aleph* and *Lamed* (El, Elohim) or by *Aleph* and *Daleth* (Adonai), except for oaths of enrollment [which are taken] with the curses of the covenant. . . . If he swears by the curses of the covenant before judges and then transgresses, he is guilty; and [even] if he confesses and repents, they will not forgive him (CDC 15:1-4).

Profaning God's name was the same whether it was done publicly or privately, intentionally or unintentionally (Pirke Aboth 4:4). Some Jewish groups listed other sins as well for which there was no forgiveness, such as sinning excessively, sinning in a righteous generation, sinning with the intention of repenting (ARN 39), profaning holy things, despising the set feasts, showing off before one of the brothers in the congregation, nullifying the covenant with Abraham, and revealing secret meanings of the Torah which were not according to the *halakah* (Pirke Aboth 3:11; see 1 Macc 1:15). In the Christian communities, there was a "sin unto death," meaning one which demanded excommunication (1 Jn 5:16-17). Both Hebrews (6:4-6) and the Shepherd of Hermas (Vis. 2.ii; Mandate 4.iii; Sim. 6.ii) agreed that those who were once enlightened and then sinned could not be forgiven.

According to this quotation which is attributed to Jesus, Jews might be forgiven if they spoke insultingly of human beings or the Messiah, but the Day of Atonement would not be effective for the one who depreciated the Holy Spirit.[11] This quotation might be expected of almost any rabbi or Christian leader of NT times. Therefore it would not be strange for Jesus to have said something like this.

The expression "binding and loosing," is an idiom that means having the authority to throw into prison and punish or to release from prison. In a sectarian context, this refers to forgiving sins or refusing to forgive. Any sect that refused to forgive a member his sins excommunicated him. Those excommunicated or not admitted to the community were "bound" in their sins. Those "loosed" were forgiven and accepted into the community. It was presumed that the community acted with God's authority and that God

---

[11]It was not as difficult as Plummer, *Matthew*, p.179, and Allen, *ICC Matt*, p. 137, imagined to distinguish between the Messiah and God's Spirit. The Messiah was the agent, and God was the principal. The Spirit was understood to mean God.

would reject those whom the community rejected. Therefore "outside the church there is no salvation" (see Matt 16:19; 18:18).

These references to unpardonable sins and excommunication practices are neither in chreia nor parable form, but the quotations from the gospels are coherent with other forgiveness teachings attributed to Jesus in parables and chreias. There is nothing specially distinctive about Jesus' teaching about repentance and forgiveness. Jesus' claim that repentance and forgiveness of sins were necessary for the acquisition of the Kingdom of Heaven only reminded Jews of that which they already knew.

More about the Kingdom

The primary purpose of Jesus' organization and program was the acquisition of the Kingdom of Heaven. Apostles were commissioned to go to all of the villages and cities in Israel, announcing that the Kingdom of Heaven was near (Matt 10:7; cf. Matt 4:17; Mk 1:15; Lk 9:2). To Peter were given the keys to the Kingdom of Heaven, according to Matthew 16:19. Jesus told the scribe who knew the law and kept it from his youth that he was not far from the Kingdom of God (Mk 12:34). Jesus' ability to cast out demons by the spirit of God was a sign the Kingdom of God had broken upon them (Matt 12:28). This was what Moses and Aaron had done before in Egypt.

One of the puzzling passages about the kingdom, which has been attributed to Jesus, is the following:

From the days of John the Baptist until now
the Kingdom of Heaven is forced,
and forceful men seize it (Matt 11:12-13).

The idiom "from . . . until" is a *merismus,* pointing to both ends of a period to include all the time in between. Normally, this is used to express a considerable length of time,[12] but Jesus was a contemporary of John the Baptist. For this reason it is probable that the later church added this to show the time from John's early ministry (ca. A.D. 5-25) until the war broke out with Rome (A.D. 66). There was a stormy period beginning with the rebellion of Judas the Galilean and Zadok the Pharisee (A.D. 6/7) and continuing until the all-out war broke out against Rome (A.D. 66). In between there were many bloody guerrilla battles. The editor may have included this state-

---

[12]Contra Meyer, *Matthew,* p. 225.

ment because it was associated with John the Baptist, as are other items in Matthew 11. It has been attributed to Jesus, but it seems unreasonable to assume that Jesus really said it.[13] Because of passages like this some scholars have said that we cannot know anything about the historical Jesus. If even one quotation was added by the later church, the church may have added it all. Although this may be falsely attributed to Jesus, the expression, Kingdom of Heaven, here is coherent with other teachings that referred to the promised land which zealots were trying to recover from Rome.

The Remnants

The procedure of this study has been to provide the reader with as many of the materials as possible that are being considered for judgment. This is to enable the reader to pass judgment on the data before accepting the given conclusions or forming her or his own conclusions. Furthermore, an effort has been made to see that all test cases are fair. This has been done by including, not just representative examples, but *all* of the material belonging to most categories. The exception to this is the impossibility of including all of the chreias contained in Mullach's collection of sayings of Diogenes. Judgments were made on the bases of *all* of these, although they are not easily available to the reader. In comparing the chreias of Theon with those of Doxapatres, *all* chreias included in the writings of both rhetoricians were given. In tracing the chreia related to John and Cerinthus, every example that could be found was given. When dealing with the chreias and parables of the NT, *all* genuine chreias were included and distinguished from those conjectured chreias which had been expanded by later commentators. Also *all* of the parables attributed to Jesus have been considered. Chreias and parables were classified in the way that seemed most natural to each, independently, only to discover that nearly all of them naturally belonged to the same categories: (1) those showing Jesus recruiting and maintaining a very committed staff of apostles, (2) those picturing Jesus in conflict with the Pharisees on the question of accepting tax collectors and sinners into his group, (3) those that indicated Jesus' methods of communicating with Jews in a coded way without being discovered by the Romans, and (4) Jesus' teachings about repentance and forgiveness of sins.

---

[13]Some who think Jesus did not say this are: Allen, *ICC Matt*, pp. 116-17; M'Neile, *Matthew,* p. 155; Plummer, *Matthew,* p. 162.

There are a few, however, that do not fit into these divisions. They are at least partly coherent with them, and they are in expanded chreia or parable form and so are part of the data to be considered. Since there are not enough of these to form a chapter for each topic, they will be grouped here together, regardless of their content.

Marriage and Divorce.

Then Pharisees arrived, tempting him, and saying, "Is it lawful to divorce a woman for any reason?" He said in reply, "[Do you not know that he who created from the beginning, *male and female he made them* (Gen 1:27), and he said, *For this reason a man should leave his father and mother and be united to his wife, and the two shall be one flesh* (Gen 2:24), so that they are no longer two but one]. That which God has joined, let no man separate" (Matt 19:3-6).

The bracketed portion appears to be a Matthaean commentary, including two proof texts to strengthen the case, as is typical of this editor. If the bracketed portion were omitted, this would be a responsive chreia, but since it required editing to make this claim it cannot be done confidently.

The Messiah was a pretending king. Kings made laws in those days for their entire nation. Therefore it was fair to ask a messiah any legal question and expect him to have an opinion on the subject. The answer given here was a reasonable one, considering the social situation. Women had almost no rights. If a woman were divorced, she would have to go back to live with her father, if he were alive, or her brother, if she had one. Without these, she had no way of obtaining a livelihood except by prostitution. The responsibility belonged to the man; he could either marry or divorce, according to the law. She could not choose to divorce him (*Ant* 15.259). Since this was so, it was important for the husband to continue to be responsible for her. If this is really a chreia, as has been conjectured, then the added commentary with modifications does not belong to the original statement. Judging from other chreias and parables, this was not a topic that Jesus would have initiated. His own interests were first of all in acquiring the kingdom. For that, he urged men to leave their families, but this was not the same as divorcing a wife.

Rock and Sand.

Everyone who hears my words and keeps them, will be compared to a wise man who built his house on the rock. The rains came down, the rivers came, and the winds blew and struck against that house, but it did not fall, for it was founded upon the rock. Everyone who hears my words and does not keep them is like a fool, who built his house upon the sand. The rain came down, the rivers came, and the wind blew and struck that house, and it fell, and its destruction was great'' (Matt 7:24-27).

This parable is now placed, fittingly, at the end of the Sermon on the Mount. The words mentioned in the parable refer to the laws included in the Sermon on the Mount. If Jesus told this parable at all, it probably was not in this context. This is rather a general parable that could be applied to many situations. It is very aptly used as a summary parable for the Sermon on the Mount. Jesus may not have told such a parable. This may have been a parable possessed by the editor of the Sermon on the Mount who placed it fittingly where it now appears. It is coherent with the teachings of Jesus, but it does not directly advance the program that seemed most vital to him.

Old and New.

Every scribe, after he has been
instructed in the Kingdom of Heaven,
is like a man, a householder,
who brings out from his treasure chest
both new and old (Matt 13:52).

Like the parable on Rock and Sand, this is a summarizing parable—the kind useful to an editor. It was properly placed at the end of the parables on the Kingdom of Heaven in Matthew 13. The one instructed in the Kingdom of Heaven would have had a large repertoire of parables and chreias—some recent and modern and others that were classical and ancient. Jesus' apostles were probably well-trained in these materials, so he may have given it a different context.

Chreias

Becoming Like Children .... (Matt 18:1-3; Lk 9:46-48a; expanded
in Mk 9:23-37)
The Sign of Jonah ... (Matt 12:38-39; 16:1-2a, 4; Mk 8:11-12; Lk
11:29)
Tragedies Around Jerusalem .... (Lk 13:1-5)
Extensive Forgiveness .... (Matt 18:21-22; Lk 17:3-4)
Marriage and Divorce .... (Matt 19:3-6)

Parables

Two Debtors .... (Matt 18:23-25; Lk 7:41-42)

Rock and Sand .... (Matt 17:24-27)
Old and New ....(Matt 13:52)

Summary

Bultmann said there were so many parables circulating in Judaism in NT times that any Christian who wished could appropriate some of them and attribute them to Jesus. Therefore, these were unreliable units for examining the historical Jesus. This study has not confirmed his judgment. Surprisingly, when organized according to topic headings under which they naturally fall, all but the last two summarizing parables in this chapter have fit under the same major categories as the chreias that were independently classified in the same way. There are only three parables that seem to have been composed by the later church or added by it to those belonging to Jesus. Two are these summary parables and the third is the parable about the wedding garment in chapter four. Even these parables are not in conflict with the message of other supportive parables. There are no unexpanded chreias that do not fit under these four major headings. This speaks strongly for the validity of both. Some of the sayings attributed to Jesus that were considered under the same headings as chreias and parables were neither. Some of these also seemed convincing, but others did not. There seemed more possibility for the later church to make additions in the form of commentary or narrative statements than to interfere with a literary unit that was already complete, like a parable or a chreia.

Of the parables and conjectured chreias considered, those classified as "remnants" seemed to be the least reliable of all. Although they are possibly valid sayings of Jesus, there are also other possibilities. Although Bultmann's skepticism is hypothetically justified, the analysis given here shows that the church was not very careless in attributing parables to Jesus. The only three parables that arouse suspicion in the entire collection are these two, which are summary parables and not the kind that would affect Jesus' fundamental teachings, and the parable about the wedding garment which may have been added because of the subject matter. In the next two chapters the church's points of view and historical methodology will be considered to learn how the church reasoned when it filled in the areas that were missing in the account of the historical Jesus. First, however, some general conclusions will be reached on the basis of this entire study up to this point. What can we now know about the historical Jesus?

The Historical Jesus

Mythology and History. When mythological terms are understood mythologically, parabolic terms parabolically, and historical terms are considered historically, the written reports provided in the gospels seem adequate for understanding a great deal about the historical Jesus. This knowledge, however, reflects only one period in his life—that period when he was leading a movement to recover the promised land from the hands of the Romans. The chreias and parables considered here grew out of the movement he was leading as an adult. These were teachings he provided for his apostles to use in their offices during the campaign. The leaders needed only stock parables and answers to questions that were expected to arise as they recruited followers into the program. Since these were the ones they learned, these are the ones that were preserved. They tell nothing about when or where Jesus was born, where he went to school, his family background, the sequence of events in his life, the sect to which he belonged, his height, weight, color of his eyes or hair, his language or his ability to perform miracles. Many lines of evidence converge to indicate that he came from a wealthy family, gave up all of his wealth, and joined a movement that required vows of poverty, celibacy, and obedience. He committed himself completely to the task of recovering the Kingdom of Heaven which seems to have been a mythological term or a code term for the promised land.

The expression "Kingdom of Heaven" was used by Jesus, and probably his apostles, while communicating with other Jews to deceive whatever Romans were present. Although he did not openly refer to himself as messiah or king, that is the leadership role which he undertook. He used the term "Son of man" for his title.[14] This was the mythological name which most Jews understood from Daniel 7 to apply to the Messiah. There is almost no probability that the church first came to think of Jesus as the Mes-

---

[14]G. Vermes, *Jesus the Jew,* (London, 1973), p. 172, had not thought of the possibility. of "Son of man" as a code term when he said that it could not be a title. S. Matthews, *Jesus on Social Institutions,* ed. K. Cauthen (Philadelphia, c1971), p. 112, was not aware of the political situation in Palestine or he would not have concluded that Jesus was not a socialist, a monarchist, or a democrat.

siah after his death.[15] If he had not been understood as a messiah before his crucifixion, his crucifixion would not have convinced many Jews that he was one. Some other code words Jesus used were: (1)Esau, Edom, the enemy, the evil one, Satan, or the devil = Rome; (2) hog or dog = Gentile; (3) "end of the age" = end of the Roman rule and beginning of Jewish rule; (4) Heaven = God.

Faith and Freedom. Jesus was leading a religious movement. He believed that God would give Israel back the Kingdom of Heaven if Jews met the terms. This was part of the normal Jewish belief in covenant theology.

The severe demands Jesus made and the time limitations of his promises imply that he thought the calendars and signs were right to mean that God was about to restore the kingdom to Israel, but he was dependent upon unknown anticipated signs to tell him exactly when and how to act. There was more than one calendar circulating in those days and various sects disagreed on which days the festivals fell, but people did count sabbath years and jubilees, and Jesus seems to have had some understanding about these that convinced him that Jews must act quickly.[16] He probably had also studied similarities between events in his day and those related to Hebrews in Egypt and Jews in Babylon just before the release. When he said, "The time is up," he probably meant the time of the Gentile rule was over. This was the time for Jews to act so as to be ready to receive the Kingdom of Heaven which God was willing to return.

Jesus was sufficiently confident in his time schedule to promise Jews that the Kingdom would come in their generation or even before the next Passover. Since these prophecies were not fulfilled it seems unlikely that the church would have invented them after the fall of Jerusalem (A.D. 70) just to show that Jesus had made false predictions.

Jesus and his Apostles. Jesus called Jews to repent and commit themselves completely to the cause he was leading. His sincerity and skill were sufficiently impressive for him to have been able to convince wealthy tax

---

[15]So also J. C. G. Greig, "Messianic Interpretation in Jesus' Ministry," *Studia Evangelica* 6 (1973); 197-220, but the following scholars thought Jesus became a messiah at his crucifixion and resurrection: W. Wrede, *The Messianic Secret* tr. J. C. G. Greig (London, c1971), pp. 48-49, and A. Schweitzer, *The Quest of the Historical Jesus* tr. W. Montgomery (London, 1956), p. 343, and R. Bultmann, "Study," p. 71.

[16]But there is not enough data to be as precise as A. Trocme, *Jesus and the Nonviolent Revolution* tr. M. H. Shank and N. E. Miller (Scottdale, 1973), pp. 38-40.

collectors and businessmen to join him in this enterprise as ''fishers of men.'' In preparing them to inform the nation of his plans and needs, he taught them the parables and chreias as stock answers to questions that arose in the campaign. It may be because of this that we have preserved these parables and important sayings in chreia form. The messages disclosed in these literary units do not picture the apostles as a group of unlettered, ignorant men who were common day laborers. They seem to have been intelligent businessmen with good leadership and administrative skills, necessary educational backgrounds, and other qualities that enabled them to extend the goals Jesus promoted. It was in part due to their ability and organization that enabled the church to continue after Jesus had been crucified.

Chreias and Confidence. The literary bases of the so-called form critics were inadequate to examine the teachings of Jesus. Dibelius misunderstood the chreia and Bultmann's apophthegms were nondefinitive. Dibelius's conjectured paradigms had no literary justification in antiquity. The chreia, however, proved to be a viable literary unit for examination. It was carefully defined and used by rhetoricians of NT times. Philosophers, historians, and other authors collected chreias and published them in books as early as the fourth century B.C. These were not considered biographies or histories, but shorthand recollections upon which biographies and homilies could be constructed. When students of philosophers, like Lucian and Xenophon, wrote about their teachers, they expanded these chreias into more detailed reminiscences. When the chreias of Diogenes were studied, they presented a reasonable, coherent picture of a real human being.

Rhetoricians apparently did not create chreias, but they copied the ones that had been preserved. They practiced using these chreias in debate and oratory, but they were not primarily inventive leaders from the standpoint of data. They were skilled copyists. The definitions and examples given by Theon and Aphthonius were carefully copied and preserved by Doxapatres nine hundred years later than Theon. The one chreia reported by Polycarp was faithfully reported nine hundred years later by Paulus. This does not mean that the chreias were preserved exactly, word-for-word, but their messages were faithfully reported. Because this is true there seems to be little basis for the anxiety that has been shown by NT scholars to accept a chreia that was not included in ''the earliest gospel.'' Although Markan priority is rapidly losing support among NT scholars, it would not make much difference in the validity of a chreia if it were preserved in a document that was earlier or later than the other by twenty or thirty years. Therefore it is legitimate to use chreias from the gospels wherever they are found, without considering the possible date of the document in which they are now preserved.

Some chreias include such geographical locations as the temple area in Jerusalem or the Tower of Siloam, both of which belong to the geographical territory with which Jesus was familiar. They also record the names of such political leaders as Herod and Pilate, both of whom governed when Jesus lived in Palestine. These chreias alluded to local knowledge without explanation that might be necessary for their comprehension which presupposes that the data were written down soon enough after the event to need no elaboration. No chreia contains a geographical reference to an area where Jesus had never been or a chronological date either before or after the lifetime of Jesus. All of this speaks in favor of the reliable reporting by chreias of things Jesus said and taught. This does not claim that these all contain the very words of Jesus, but it allows the historian to use these forms confidently as he or she tries to reconstruct the period in Jesus' life which these reflect.

Parables of the Kingdom. The messages of the parables were the same as the messages of the chreias used as riddles for communicating to the Jewish masses without the Romans understanding the content. Parables could be readily decoded and understood by those who had ears to hear. They were not primarily stories about gardening, herding sheep, recovering lost coins, and administering business, but were stories about the Kingdom of Heaven, which was understood as a code word for the promised land under the control of Jews with their own messiah ruling in Jerusalem. Some of the stories had intentional distortions to give listeners a clue to the hidden message, if they had ears to hear. Sometimes the real point was disclosed through a passage of scripture and sometimes there was a well-known Jewish tradition or event in earlier history subtly revealed. These parables taught the importance of giving up everything for the sake of the Kingdom of Heaven, the importance of accepting such wealthy ''Reform Jews'' as tax collectors and sinners when they repented, trust in God's faithfulness and care for his chosen people, and the importance of repentance and forgiveness of sins. These illustrate the messages taught in the chreias. Different historians may assess this data differently, but few will deny that these main themes are topics that Jesus taught.

The Death of Jesus. Although the chreias and parables say nothing about Jesus' death (as they probably would if they had been the creation of the later church), later Christian testimony is so consistent that there is little doubt that Jesus was crucified at the hands of the Romans near the time of the Passover feast. The apostle Paul, who became a follower of Jesus at least three years before the death of Aretas (A.D. 40), referred to Jesus as one who had been sacrificed as the Christian's paschal lamb (1 Cor 5:7). He also reported to the Corinthians that "the Lord Jesus, on the night that he was betrayed" broke bread with his apostles (1 Cor 11:23-24). Paul did not say further who it was who betrayed Jesus or under what conditions it was done. Matthew reported that Jesus was crucified on the charge that he was "king of the Jews." He was also crucified with two others, both of whom were insurrectionists (Matt 27:37-38). In the eyes of the Romans, there were three insurrectionists crucified together, one of whom was pretending to become king of the Jews. N. A. Dahl has said that any attempt at reconstructing the life of the historical Jesus would have to take into account the way he died.[17]

The program reflected in the chreias and parables points out very clearly the activity of a leader intent on taking control of the promised land away from the Romans. This kind of subversive activity is that which Romans wanted to stop as early as possible to prevent thousands of deaths and preserve their own control of the country. Dahl correctly reasoned that Christians would be offended by the facts they would discover if they set about to learn what the real historical Jesus was like.[18] This is not because this historical activity was so much out of harmony with the conditions or ethics of the time or the ideals of the Jewish or Christian religion of the period. It is offensive because two thousand years have elapsed since then and standards of ethics have changed accordingly. That which seems heroic at one period in history seems offensive at another period. Christians have labored so long under the delusion that Jesus exhibited exactly the kind of ideals and ethics that have pleased us in every age that many have thought we could never tolerate a knowledge of the real historical Jesus in relationship to Palestinian social and political conditions of that day.

---

[17]N. A. Dahl, "The Problem of the Historical Jesus," *Kerygma and History* tr. ed. C. H. Braaten and R. A. Harrisville (New York, c1962), pp. 138-71.

[18]Ibid.

After the Bar Kokhba rebellion (A.D. 132-35), Christians and Jews were forced to accept a more tolerant attitude toward Rome. Marcion led an anti-holy war theology movement, holding that Christians had no part of this rebellious religion of the Jews. He established the first Christian canon composed only of the Gospel of Luke as it was then (about half as big as it is now) and ten letters of Paul. The fact that he did not represent all of Christianity is evident from his excommunication from the church at Rome and the extension of the canon to include much of the Jewish literature he omitted. Included in that literature were parables and apocalyptic literature, both of which were composed in coded language that could be understood only by those who had ears to hear. Like other Jews, Christians did not give up their political aspirations with the defeats of A.D. 70 and 135 but continued their subversion right up until the time of Constantine. The coded nature of parables and apocalyptic literature allowed this literature to be preserved while being misunderstood by the opponents. It also made it possible for it to be misunderstood by Christians themselves, as it has been for many years.

Pharisees and Monasticism. The literary units examined showed on the one hand that Jesus lived as a celibate monk and demanded the same rigorous ethics of his followers. On the other hand he seemed willing to eat with tax collectors and sinners in a way that was ritually offensive to the Pharisees. How does it happen that these two characteristics occur in the same person? There are at least two possibilities: (1) Vermes argued that Galileans had quite different standards from those of the Judaean Pharisees. In Vermes' opinion the laxness toward Levitical code that Pharisees observed in Jesus' following was typically Galilean.[19] The conflict between Jesus and the Pharisees was part of an on-going dispute between Galileans and Judaeans. (2) Another possibility is a very practical, administrative explanation. Jesus restructured his program and reconsidered some of his practices after the death of John the Baptist. This possibility will be considered in detail.

Jesus was evidently baptized by John the Baptist, considered him to have been the greatest of all the prophets, and based his authority on the authority of John. John neither ate nor drank (Matt 11:18). This did not mean he starved, but it meant he was very careful about his dietary rules.

---

[19]Vermes, *Jesus*, p. 57.

He did not eat with tax collectors and sinners but ate only locusts and wild honey—both of which could be served on the same table with either meat or milk and never be in danger of "boiling the kid in its mother's milk" (Exod 23:19; 34:26; Deut 14:21). If, however, Jesus had been lax in his legal observances from the beginning he probably would not have worked well with John.

Parker has made a good case for believing that Jesus and John at one time belonged to the same Nazorean sect, one which still exists in the Fertile Crescent today and traces its roots back to John the Baptist.[20] While John was alive Jesus probably observed the same sectarian rules as John. At that time John and Jesus may have thought of themselves as the Aaronic and Davidic messiahs through whom God would recover the promised land.[21] With the death of John, however, the plan would have been frustrated and forced Jesus to rethink his role and his program. It is from this period on that we have a record of his activities in chreias and parables. Prior to that time he may have got along very well with the Pharisees, but when he changed his program, they objected. This monk who had been very rigorous in his observance and had unselfishly given all that he had to this community of poor Nazoreans suddenly began to engage in discussion with the wealthy Reform Jews who later became his followers. This was the same kind of Torah expediency that the Hasmoneans employed in their war with the Syrians. They decided it was better to break the Sabbath law and preserve the nation so that all of the Torah could be kept than to observe the Sabbath rigorously and be held in subjection to the Syrian Greeks.

To develop a fiscally sound, efficient organization, Jesus needed the money and leadership skills of these wealthy businessmen who had mingled with the Romans. He reasoned that the goal was worth the legal offense that was required to bring this about as the chreias and parables show. This, however, brought him into conflict with the Pharisees. He did not stop being very demanding of himself and his followers; he broke only the laws nec-

---

[20]P. Parker, *The Gospel before Mark*, (Chicago, c1935), pp. 94-99, and B. Gärtner, *Die Rätselhaften Termini Nazoräer und Iskarot* (Lund, 1957).

[21]K. G. Kuhn, "Die Beiden Messias Aarons und Israels," *NTS* 1 (1955):168-79. Contra R. E. Brown, *The Birth of the Messiah* (Garden City, 1977), p. 267.

essary to form an effective organization. It was at that point that Jesus was called

an eater and a drinker of wine,
a friend of tax collectors and sinners (Matt 11:19).

This did not mean, as modern translations suggest, that he was a glutton and a drunkard. The offense was not how much he ate and drank but the people with whom he feasted—tax collectors and sinners—those people who had mingled with the Romans and broken traditional Jewish laws of hospitality.

Unanswered Questions

Although there is a good basis for trusting the teachings in chreias and parables, there are still some puzzling questions: Was the entry into Jerusalem on a donkey Jesus' *parousia*? Was the action in the temple really a military attempt to take over the temple? Did Jesus actually lead a war? If this is so, how did Paul and other early Christians become converted to a pacifistic Christianity shortly after Jesus' death? The answers to these questions cannot be made with certainty because the data are not all one-sided. Therefore the most important issues will be presented here, and different readers will be persuaded differently on the basis of the same data.

Jesus, the Warrior. It is not possible for an objective historian to dismiss all the military inferences related to the teachings of and about Jesus. He began his ministry in association with John the Baptist who was later killed for insurrection. Jews at that time were anticipating two messiahs, one a son of Aaron to be the high priest, and the other a son of David to lead the war and become the new king. Since John was a priest and Jesus is reported to have been a son of David, they may have planned to fulfill these messianic roles together. Jesus claimed his authority on the authority of John the Baptist (Lk 20:1-8). Jesus had among his apostles such unpeaceful people as James and John whom he called "sons of thunder," one Simon, called "the zealot," and another Simon, called "the terrorist" (*barjona*). Judas was called the "dagger bearer" (*sicarius*). If he had been leading a nonviolent revolution he apparently selected a noncooperative group.

At one point in his program he told the apostles to sell their garments and buy weapons. When he was told that they had two swords there, he said that was enough (Lk 22:35-38). This would not have been enough weapons for any open warfare, but suitable for small guerrilla attacks, like the ones undertaken by the sicarii. There were many isolated guerrilla actions during the lifetime of Jesus. None of these has been associated with Jesus, but there is no certainty that he and his apostles were not involved. The Pharisees warned that Herod was trying to capture him and Herod is reported to have associated Jesus' movement with the insurrectionist activity of John the Baptist. The apostles who were assigned guard duty on the evening of the Last Supper were armed and one is reported to have drawn his sword against the oncoming forces (Matt 26:51; Lk 22:50). These loosely related items indicate that Jesus was associated with a group who expected him to lead a war and he is not reported to have done much to correct them.

The Pacifistic Church. With all of these indications of a military movement, there are some conflicting facts to consider. The same apostles whom Jesus called and trained while he was alive led a movement after his death that converted militaristic Paul from zealous Pharisaism to a devoted pacifism sometime before A.D. 37. How did that happen? Not only Paul but other leaders of the church, such as the authors of the Sermon on the Mount, 1 Peter, and early church martyrs were convinced pacifists. Both the militaristic and the pacifistic movements in early Christianity were emphatic parts of conquest theology, basic to pre-Christian Judaism.

Militarists traced their ethics to the typology of Joshua, David, and the Hasmoneans who took up the sword in the name of the Lord and trusted the God of armies to give them the victory, no matter how great the odds. Gideon slew the members of the Midianite camp with only three hundred committed soldiers; Jonathan and his armor bearer alone conquered a fortress; with only clubs and stones the armies of Deborah and Barak conquered the troops and chariots of Sisera (Jdgs 5). Many times the Hasmoneans defeated armies of the Syrians that were much greater and better armed. This was possible, Jews believed, because God and his angels were among their troops, destroying the enemy. Even the stars in their courses fought against the enemies of Israel. These militarists had as their forefather, Phineas, the priest, who took the law in his own hands and killed Zimri and his new pagan bride with a spear. As a result of this, God reckoned his act as righteousness; he was granted an eternal priesthood; and the disease the Israelites were suffering went away. Phineas and his followers despised the passive acceptance of mingling with foreigners. The Hasmoneans led the war against the Syrians in the name of their forefather Phineas, who was zealous for the law. Before his conversion to Christianity Paul was a zealous Pharisee, advanced in the tradition of his fathers, and he persecuted Christians. The zealots who fought against Rome in the first century A.D. probably got their name from their allegiance to Phineas and his zeal for the law.

There is only one other place in the OT where anything was reckoned to anyone as righteousness. This was Abraham, who did not act at all; he only believed and that was reckoned to him as righteousness. After Paul became a Christian his basic proof text for his ethics was Gen 15:6: "And Abraham believed God, and it was reckoned to him as righteousness" (Rom 4:3). This is best understood as not only emphasizing the pacifistic ethic of conquest theology, but as arguing against those who were following Phineas for his zeal. Paul said these people were zealous but mistaken (Gal 4:17-18). Just as the militarists could claim the acquisition of the land by Joshua and the Hasmoneans through holy warfare, so the pacifists could point to the suffering service of the first generations of Jews in Babylon who did not resist but only suffered patiently to pay for the debt of sin against Israel. When this was done, God gave Jews back the land. In pre-Christian times a faithful Jew took his son out to a cave so as not to break the Sabbath, knowing they would be killed there. The purpose of this was that they wanted God to punish the enemy for their innocent blood and reward Israel by restoring the kingdom (*regnum*) (Assump. Mos. 9:1-10:10).

The Community Rule prescribes that sectarians should give to their oppressors the work of their hands and whatever goods they required, but they should also hate them with an everlasting hate and wait for the day of vengeance (1QS 9:21-23). The covenanter pledged; "I will not repay anyone evil [for evil]. I will pursue a man with goodness, for judgment belongs to God, and he will repay to everyone his deserts. I will not enter into conflict with the man of perdition until the Day of Vengeance, but anger I will not turn away from the man of deceit, and I will not be content until he establishes justice" (1QS 10:17-20). They counted on God to punish their enemies worse than they could. Paul was of the same opinion. He urged the Romans to live as peacefully as possible with all, taking care not to avenge themselves. Instead they should let God do the avenging. They should provide their enemies with food and drink when they had such needs, for by so doing they heaped coals of fire upon the heads of their enemies (Rom 12:18-20)! They were paying off Jewish debt in the treasury of merits and helping their enemies to overdraw theirs at the same time, resulting in God's foreclosing on the enemy and punishing him severely. This is also the basis for the counsel not to resist the evil doer but to turn the other cheek, walk the second mile, and love the enemies (Matt 5:39-48). This would be more effective than the militarism of the zealots.[22]

Jewish and Christian pacifism was no more humane or kind than militarism. Both were designed to destroy Rome and establish the Kingdom of Heaven on the promised land. The difference was purely tactical, but Jews of Jesus' time disagreed on which was the best tactic for obtaining the desired result. Since Jesus was a very religious man who believed that God wanted Jews to have the Kingdom, it is evident that he was seriously trying to do exactly what God wanted him to do. Jesus was not willing to *give* signs, as the people demanded; he was *waiting* for signs from Heaven so that he could act in accordance with God's will, saying that no one knew the exact hour or day—not even the Son, but the Father only. Jews had to be prepared to wait. Had Jesus been given a sign such as those given to Moses or Gideon that directed him to attack the Romans at a feast, he probably would have done that. Had he been given a sign like the one the Babylonian Jews received, namely, Cyrus arising and being willing to negotiate with Jews in Babylon for their assistance in overthrowing Babylon, then he probably would have negotiated with the Parthians, Gauls, or any country that was prepared to attack Rome.

Jesus and John may at one time have been confident that God wanted them to lead an open conflict against Rome as the two anticipated messiahs. That plan was partially frustrated, however, by the death of John the Baptist. This may have given Jesus an opportunity to rethink his role. It was at that time that he began to reorganize his program to include wealthy, Jewish businessmen and tax collectors. He expanded his program in size and financial support to be prepared for a war with Rome, if that seemed to be the will of God. He may also have reconsidered, at the same time, whether or not God willed an open war at that time. The death of John may have been understood as a sign to the contrary. There are some indications that Jesus struggled with this issue seriously. Without presuming that the temptations narrative or the prayer at Gethsemane are actual, historical accounts, it is reasonable to think that they may have been designed to give mythical expression to an experience that the apostles recognized during their train-

---

[22]See K. Stendahl, "Hate, Non-retaliation, and Love," HTR 55 (1962):343-55; GWB, *Consequences,* pp. 18-21, 31-37; and J. Licht, "Taxo, or the Apocalyptic Doctrine of Vengeance," *JJS* 12 (1961):95-103.

ing. This vacillation on Jesus' part may have caused the apostles to become impatient and finally caused some of them to reject him. It was not until the supper at Jerusalem during the Passover Feast that Jesus was betrayed and Peter denied him. The apostles evidently expected his *parousia* to take place at that time, but Jesus still postponed it. He said it would happen before the *next* Passover. To some of them this may have seemed to be sabotaging the program, but he continued to wait for a sign from Heaven. If God did not approve their efforts they would fail. Jesus was a religious leader not just a secular militarist. He was apparently ready to fight or die to bring in the Kingdom of Heaven. When the Romans came to capture him, he did not try to force God's hand, utilizing the forces at his command, and expect God to defeat the enemy. This may have been understood as a sign from God that he was expected to respond passively, assuming that God would use Jesus' suffering as payment against the indebtedness of sin still held against Israel.

The apostles were evidently impatient with Jesus at some points, but very quickly after his death they were able to interpret his death in terms of passive suffering and Day of Atonement theology. One explanation for this is that they had this as a part of their training before the crucifixion.

This does not provide an absolute explanation of the data. It is only one conjectured possibility. It is also possible that Jesus actually entered Jerusalem, publicly announcing himself as the Messiah. There may have been a much more serious conflict in the temple area than the accounts admit. Since the temple was also the national treasury and the strongest national fortress, it is unlikely that it could have been taken by someone who only upset a few tables. Brandon, Carmichael, and others may have been right when they suggested that the war had already broken out by the time Jesus was captured by the Roman soldiers.[23] If this had been the case, however, and the apostles had only trained to prepare for a military involvement, it is surprising that the crucifixion did not put an end to the movement, the way it did for Judas, Simon, and Athronges. The survival of the church after the crucifixion as a passively oriented organization, committed to martyrdom more than militarism, suggests that some preparation for alternatives had been made by Jesus before his death. Readers should not expect historians and theologians to solve all of these problems for them, dogmatically. The

---

[23]S. G. F. Brandon, *Jesus and the Zealots* (Manchester, 1963), pp. 322-58, and J. Carmichael, *The Death of Jesus* (New York, c1962), pp. 133-62.

data is here and readers are free to analyze it themselves and arrive at their own conclusions. That may not happen all at once. These are serious issues that require a great deal of thought and discussion. In the meantime, still more data will be introduced.

Summary. This study has indicated only what the historical Jesus was doing during those years, probably after the death of John the Baptist, when, as an adult leader, he was organizing and directing a campaign to recover the promised land. It is customary for historians to concentrate on any leader's active leadership period more than any other time of his or her life. In Jesus' case it was only after he had begun to call, organize, and commission apostles to extend his program that parables and chreias were needed, so these literary units are confined to that time. There is still a lot of unknown data about the historical Jesus. What was his relationship to John the Baptist? What did Jesus teach and observe before John's death? What kind of training did he receive? Was John his principal teacher? Chreias and parables tell nothing about this. The later church, however, tried to recover parts of this unknown history. The next two chapters will show some of the historiographical methods the church employed to discover still more about the historical Jesus.

• CHAPTER EIGHT •

Cycles
of Time
and Their Signs

Introduction

Cultural background. Not only the Greeks, but Egyptians, Mayas, and
Aztecs thought time moved in cycles.[1] Cyclical views of Plato and Aristotle

---

[1]L. Cottrell, *Lost Civilizations* (New York, c1974), said the following about the Mayas
in Central America: "The Maya believed that only by understanding and accurately meas-
uring these recurrent cycles of time could one explain the present or predict the future. Their
calendrical system was superior to that of the ancient Egyptians or our own. They could
measure time not merely in years and centuries but millions of years. And they did this without the least understanding of the universe. They believed the earth to be flat and that the
sun-god, like the Egyptian God Re, reached the eastern horizon by travelling through the
underground passage . . . the solar year of 365 days was called the *tun*. It had eighteen divisions (equivalent to our months but of twenty days each) and one evil period of five days.
So far, so good, but now the system becomes complicated. In addition to the *tun*, and run-
ning concurrently with it, was a ceremonial year of 260 days. This consisted of thirteen day
numbers and twenty named days. The two systems interlocked to form a unit of fifty-two
years, the calendar round—equivalent to our century but in Maya terms (pp. 103-104).

" . . . They discovered that this solar year is approximately 365.2422 days long (p.
105). . . . Moreover, in later times the sacred period of time was the *katun*-"twenty solar
years, each *katun* being the province of a particular deity. After thirteen *katuns*—260
years—the cycle began all over again, history repeating itself and the god or goddess governing the first *katun* reasserted himself or herself" (pp. 105-106).

were developed and modified by later Stoics and Neoplatonists.[2] Iamblicus said some of the older Greek philosophers thought time was like a folk dance where people held hands and circled around the now.[3] Proclus claimed that real time was the ideal number of all the number of cycles (περιόδων).[4] Damascius thought time was everlastingly present and apparent in things that are born to pass away, cyclically.[5]

Trompf began his important study on cycles with Polybius whose philosophy held that governments rotated in a certain predictable order.[6] Polybius called this phenomenon "recycling of governments" (πολιτειῶν (ἀνακύλωσις) (*Hist.* 6.ix,10). According to Polybius governments began with a monarchy that rose, degenerated, and fell. This sequence of events was followed by an oligarchy that also rose, degenerated, and fell. The third step was the rise, degeneracy, and fall of a democracy. By this time the cycle was complete and prepared for the ascendancy of a new monarchy.[7] Trompf supposed Polybius found the basis for his philosophy from such predecessors as Empedocles, Plato, and the Pythagoreans, although Polybius, himself, invented the very theory he proposed.[8] Plato had asked rhetorically, " 'Have not thousands upon thousands of city-states come into existence, and on a similar computation, have not just as many perished? And have they not in each case exhibited all kinds of constitutions many times every-

---

[2]J. L. Russell, "Time in Christian Thought," J. T. Fraser (ed.), *The Voices of Time* (New York, c1966), pp. 68-69.

[3]S. Sambursky and S. Pines (trs.), *The Concept of time in Late Neoplatonism* (Jerusalem, 1971), p. 34.

[4]Ibid., p. 60.

[5]Ibid., p. 76.

[6]G. W. Trompf, *The Idea of Historical Recurrence in Western Thought* (Berkeley: University of California Press, c1979), pp. 4-115. Trompf analyzed historians from Polybius to the Reformation in this volume and promised a second volume that would continue this analysis through Toynbee in the twentieth century. See also his "Notions of Historical Recurrence in Classical Hebrew Historiography," *Vetus Testamentum-Supplements* vol. 30, pp. 213-29.

[7]Ibid., pp. 5-6.

[8]Ibid., pp. 8-9, 37-45.

where?' '' (*Leg.* 2.676B-C).[9] Trompf called this cyclical rise and fall of governments "the anacyclic zigzag" or "recurrence."[10] He designed a chart (Chart 1) to illustrate Polybius's historical philosophy.[11]

CHART 1

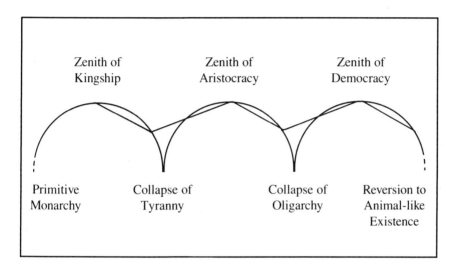

Zenith of Kingship   Zenith of Aristocracy   Zenith of Democracy

Primitive Monarchy   Collapse of Tyranny   Collapse of Oligarchy   Reversion to Animal-like Existence

---

[9]Ibid., p. 11.

[10]Ibid., p. 25.

[11]Some details of Trompf's chart are omitted here.

One advantage of this chart is that it shows the cycles of history as they continue across a period of time. This is not the same as the cyclical view that all history would be precisely repeated, as Vergil assumed: "And the great Achilles sent to Troy once more" (*Ecologues* 4,34-36; cf. 46-47). According to Polybius, one government rose and fell to be followed by a different government of that same nation that also rose and fell. Nonetheless, the same data which Trompf shows in half circles could also be shown in a complete circle with radii forming "slices" within that circle.[12] This would not point out so clearly the passage of time, as Trompf's chart does, but it would indicate more picturesquely the fact that the rotation had turned completely around to the same position of generation or degeneration as it had been long before.

It is easy to understand how agricultural peoples could come to such conclusions as these. Seasons followed one another with a dependable degree of regularity, always returning to the same seasons again and again. Summer and winter, sowing time and harvest, rainy and dry seasons were expected in a certain order. In relation to this, certain feasts were structured to happen every year in a consistent sequential relationship to one another. Days of the week followed one another in a certain order before starting all over again. The same was true with months, pentacontads, sabbath years and jubilees. There seemed to be a predestined structure about all of this which was apparently accepted by many ancient peoples. Polybius called it "Fortune."[13] Against this background, different peoples and individuals evidently developed their peculiar local variations and theological interpretations.

The purpose of this study is to try to understand from the available literature the ways in which Jews and Christians appropriated these philosophical concepts and applied them to their theology and way of life. This will require an analysis of various and sundry bits of Jewish and Christian literature, extending from OT times to medieval Jewish and Christian history, that express certain implications, related to their understanding of time. These will be studied, one after the other, to show their relationship

---

[12]Trompf, *Recurrence*, p. 25, acknowledged this: "In review, then, the *Anacyclosis* appears to be reducible to a single cycle, one with similar conditions at both the beginning and the renewal point, and one characterizable in terms of organic growth and decay."

[13]Trompf, Ibid., p. 64.

CHART 2

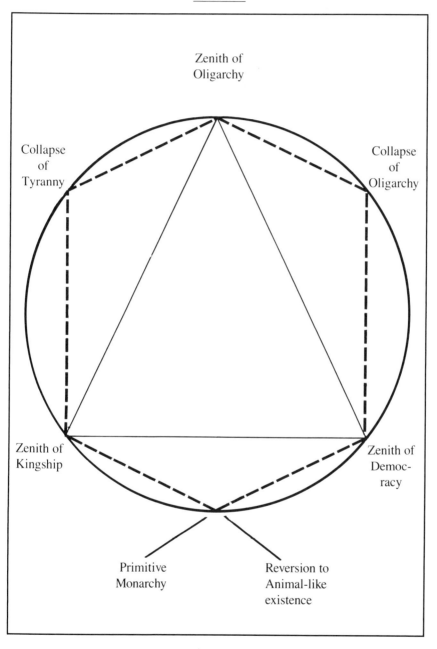

to one another and the importance these convictions had for their future expectations.

Development of the Data. (1) The first step will be to show early Jewish testimony to cyclical time. (2) The second step will examine the Jewish concept of ages. (3) The third division will show Second Isaiah's typological deductions from cyclical time. (4) Next will be an analysis of Daniel's cycle in comparison with earlier history. (5) The cycle before the fall of Jerusalem in A.D. 70 will then be compared to specific points in Daniel's cycle. After these have all been considered, their importance will be shown in relationship to typological and cyclical signs during the time of Jesus and in later Jewish and Christian eschatology.

Cyclical Testimony

Josephus, the Koheleth, the Sibyl, and the Scrolls. After Josephus had described the destruction of Jerusalem in A.D. 70, he marvelled at the exactness of the cycle [of destiny] (περιόδου) which predestined the temple to burn at the hands of the Romans on the very month and day on which it was burned by the Babylonians, years before the second fall (*BJ* 6.268-269). Josephus' easy allusion to cycles was no isolated example, completely removed from normal Hebrew and Jewish thought. In the OT itself, the Koheleth held that events in time circled like the wind, so that the events that happened currently had already happened before and would happen again (Eccles 1:6, 9). "The Psalm of the Seasons" in the Community Rule (1QS 10:1-9) took both cycles and seasons for granted and considered them all occasions for praise to God. The poet praised God at the beginning of the administration of light which continues through its course, after which it is withdrawn, and darkness rules for an appointed time. Then, at the end of the darkness, at a predestined time, darkness rotates into light again (1QS 10:1-2). The word used for changing from light to darkness and back to light is תקופה, meaning turn, roll, or rotate. Just as days rotate and are renewed; so also are weeks and jubilees—all of which become seasons for praise (1QS 10:1-9).

The Sibyl narrated history in terms of cycles of times, cycles of seasons, and cycles of years.[14] Whenever any of these units of time was com-

---

[14]Χρόνοις περιτελλομένοισιν; = *circumvertentibus*—Sib. Or. 3:289; also 3:158; περιπλομέναισιν ἐν ὥραις = *redentibus horis*—Sib. Or. 3:627; and περιτελλομένων ἐνιαυτῶν = *redentibus* [or *ferentibus*] *annis*—Sib. Or. 3:563.

pleted, it was thought to be fulfilled. For example, a Jewish author concluded that Moses' years had been fulfilled when he was ready to die (Assump Mos 1:15). After Jacob had fulfilled seven years, Laban gave him Rachel (Gen 29:28). Jeremiah said seventy years were required to fulfill the sentence for the destruction of Jerusalem (Dan 9:2). The initiate into the community governed by the Community Rule took steps one year at a time. The rules dictate what should happen to him "until there is fulfilled for him (עד מלאת לו שנה תמימה) a full year," meaning until his first year was up. "When there is fulfilled for him the second year" (לו השנה השנית ובמילאת) (1QS 6:17-21), additional action would be taken. This meant it would happen at the end of his second year. Fulfilled time was not necessarily filled with some mysterious content, as many theologians have supposed. It was simply used up and finished. It would never recur until the cycle reached that point again in its rotation.

Predestination and Time. Because of the repetitious nature of cyclical time, it was assumed that certain things should fall on certain days routine to fit the destined cycle. For example, rests were scheduled sabbaths, and fasts and feasts were routinely set for specific days of the week, specific states of the moon, or specific days of the year. The predestined cycle would be upset if the wrong day were observed, and many sectarian conflicts were based on just this point. There were so many natural things of life which happened at only certain points in the year that it was not difficult to suppose that all the events in the cycle were predestined.

One Jewish author reasoned: "God created all the Gentiles which are on the circle of the earth as well as us. He foresaw them and us from the beginning of creation of the circle of the earth until the departure of the age, and nothing has been neglected by him even to minute details, but everything he foresaw, and he moved everything forward as a whole" (Assump Mos 12:4). The Jewish prophet seemed to think that God predestined Jews and Gentiles to relate to one another across the ages of time according to a certain plan. Second Baruch spelled this out more clearly. He said the time between Adam and the Messiah was divided into twelve periods of alternative good and bad fortune for Israel. These periods were probably considered twenty-four ages or twelve complete cycles of time (2 Bar 53:12; 56:1-69; 4 Ezra 14:11-12). According to the NT seer, the four messengers were released from the river Euphrates where they had been bound and prepared "for the hour and day and month and year" (Rev 9:15). Just as a woman could not postpone birth after a nine month pregency, so the scheduled order of times could not be retarded or hastened (4 Ezra 4:40-43). The predestined nature of events was presumed by the author of the Fourth Gospel who reported that Jesus acted or did not act in a certain way because his hour had or had not yet come (Jn 2:4; 7:30; 8:20; 12:27; 13:1; 16:21; 17:1).

Cycles and Ages

Cullmann's position. Cullmann agreed with most scholars that the words for age, עוֹלָם and αἰών, were both names that referred to units of time.[15] He also agreed with others that the expression, which literally means "into the age" (לְעוֹלָם = εἰς τὸν αἰῶνα), meant "eternity." Cullmann, however, argued that "eternity" was a term that described endless time and could not be confused with the trans-temporal Greek ideal of eternity.[16] Cullmann was on the right track, but he should not have called this expression "eternity" or "endless time" at all. עוֹלָם very, very rarely has a spatial meaning, and the temporal meaning is never trans-temporal, trans-spatial, or endless, in Jewish or Christian testimony. Temporal עוֹלָמִים or αἰῶνες refer only to units of this-worldly time.[17] The second step of this study will be to analyze the usage of the term "age" in Jewish and Christian literature.

Ages in the literature. The smaller units of time, such as weeks, years, and weeks of years, were all parts of larger cycles, called ages. According to Hebrews, God made the ages and set them in order (Heb 1:2; 11:3). Ages were of an indefinite length. Changes of fortune for Israel indicated to Jews that ages had changed. For example, Noah saw three ages: the time before the flood, the flood, and the restoration. Moses saw three ages: the time when Israel was forced into slavery in Egypt, the term of slavery, and the redemption. Mordecai saw the time before the enslavement of Haman, the time of the decree, and Israel's redemption. Job saw the initial period of perfection, his torture, and his healing. All of these ages fell in the same sequence in the cycle. Rabbis referred to divisions of time with changing fortunes as "ages" (Tanhuma, *Wayashev* 90b). R. Joshua interpreted

---

[15]O. Cullmann, *Christ and Time*, tr. F. V. Filson (Philadelphia, 1950), pp. 52, 61-63. Cullmann was only one of the many biblical scholars who thought Jewish time was linear. For a long list of others, see Trompf, *Recurrence*, pp. 117-118.

[16]Cullmann, *Christ*, pp. 45-48. See also E. Jenni, "Das Wort 'Olam im Alten Testament," *ZAW* 64 (1952):195-248, esp. 221.

[17]GWB, *Consequences*, pp. 136-47, and *Revelation*, pp. 31-33.

"from generation to generation" (Ps 72:5) to mean from "life in this age" to "life in the age to come" (Mek., *Amalek* 2:186-188). The word *dor* in Hebrew is derived from the Akkadian *darum*, which refers to a period of fifty years. An age was therefore thought by some to be about the length of a generation, which is approximately the same length as a jubilee.

The arguments for claiming that an age was fifty years were mostly offered as exegesis of the term עבד עולם or "slave of an age" (*JKidd* 59d; *Ikkarim* 4.42, 10-11; Mek., *Nezikin* 2:83,86-90). The expression was also used in the flattering wish, "King, live for ages!" which wished him to reign more generations than one. There were, however, other possibilities.

An age changed whenever power changed from the rule of one people to the next. Thus the four beasts or kings mentioned in Daniel, from one point of view, represented four ages—Babylon, Media, Persia, and Greece (Dan 7:3-7; 11:23). From another point of view, they all constituted one age—the age of the Gentile rule or the evil age. Jews were most concerned about two ages, the age when other nations ruled (this age) and the age when Jews ruled (the age to come). The Gentile age was called "this age," because the literature was always written when Gentiles were in power. When Jews were in power, they hoped for still greater blessings, but no radical shift in ages. The Gentile age and the Jewish age were opposite sides of the same cycle (4 Ezra 7:50).

Ages and administrations. The concept of a complete cycle consisting of one age of Gentile rule and one age of Jewish rule in a zig-zag fashion makes sense also against other Jewish reports. "The Psalm of the Seasons" at the end of the Community Rule offers praise to God at the beginning of the administrations (ממשלת) of light, which continues through its course until it is withdrawn, and darkness rules for an appointed time. When the appointed time of darkness ends, the rule of light begins to dawn (1QS 10:1-2). According to the poet, time moves in predictable, predestined order and always in cycles or rotations. He followed the Genesis poem of creation (Gen 1:16) in using the term "rule," "administer," or "govern" (ממשל) to describe the relationship of light to day and darkness to night. Jews also thought of themselves as sons of light and the Gentiles as sons of darkness, perhaps following the analogy of day and night, as predestined parts of one cycle of time. Just as Gentiles ruled the age of darkness, so Jews would rule the age of light, and they believed the rule of the Jews was predestined to follow the Gentile rule just as certainly as day followed night.

At the Turn of the Ages. In Daniel the Gentile Age of Darkness ended the rule of the Syrian Greeks; the Jewish age or the age of light began with the Hasmonean rule. In between was a shadowy, three-and-one-half year period of war, followed by a divine judgment and the installation of one like a Son of man who brought an end to the rule of darkness and introduced the rule of light.

This war of judgment was dramatized by the one like a Son of man, presenting his case before the Ancient of Days. This three and a half year period was also later called "the birth pangs of the Messiah,"[18] referring to the painful military struggle before the "parousia" of one like a Son of man, or the judgment day marked the end of one age and the beginning of the next age (4 Ezra 7:112-113). When the judgment was in Israel's favor, the "age to come" was a period to which Jews looked with eager expectation. In none of the literature is the age to come identified with the Gentile age. The Sibyl considered the arrival of Cyrus on the horizon to have been the judgment day when God judged men with blood and flames of fire (Sib. Or. 3:86-87). He further spoke of the woes that accomplished the circling of years from the Seleucid rule until the Maccabean peace (Sib. Or. 3:562-572). Second Baruch spoke of twelve ages, with black waters representing Gentile rule and white waters representing a time of favor for Israel (2 Bar 56:1-69:5).

One important change of ages occurred with the end of the Seleucid rule over Israel and the establishment of Hasmonean rule. This new age or age to come began with the rededication of the temple by Judas the Maccabee. At the beginning of this age "those who make the many righteous" were expected to shine like the stars for "the age and until" (לעולם ועד) (Dan 12:3). RSV renders this verse, "forever and ever," but that reads a lot into the phrase that is not in the text. It may mean just "for the age of the Jewish rule and until . . .," meaning "until it comes to an end, and the predestined Gentile age rules in its place." Hai Gaon said of the Jewish age, "They [the Jews] will dwell in their kingdom until the end of the [Jewish] age. There are some who say until the completion of seven thousand years from the

---

[18]See *Revelation*, pp. 20, 23, 282, 310, 319, 323, 533, 577, 583, 585.

days of creation (i.e. A.D. 3240).[19] There are [others who say] many thousands [of years] with no known limit," but this second opinion was wishful thinking.

The very logic by which Jews concluded that the cycle would eventually turn around to Jewish rule implied that the Jewish rule would also come to an end, just as rhythmically as it began. It may have been the same reasoning which required the author of Rev 20 to predict that Satan would be bound in the bottomless pit for a thousand years, after which he would be released again (Rev 20:1-3). Jews often minced oaths and used euphemisms to avoid actually expressing a condition that they did not want to take place. This translation, "for the age and until," seems like a minced expression used to avoid mentioning the predestined bad fortune for Israel that the full expression would contain. Even though the expression was minced, there were some Jews in the time of Maimonides who believed that those who shone like the stars would only shine for their predestined millennium of rest before Gentiles inherited their turn at the cycle again.

Ages and Politics. The change in fortune in which Jews were most interested in NT times was the change whereby Israel would replace Rome as the ruling power. This involved the change from the age of Esau-Edom-Rome to the age of Jacob-Israel. Just as one end of a man is his extended hand and the other end his stretched-out foot, so Jacob's hand was at Esau's

---

[19]On the basis that a day in the sight of the Lord is as a thousand years, Jewish eschatology was based on the assumption that the world was created to form one great cycle of seven thousand years. The sixth millennium began at A.D. 1240. From A.D. 1240 to 2240 was to be the messianic age. During this millennium the Messiah was expected to appear, overthrow all of the Gentile nations, and establish Jewish rule over all the world. The age to come or the age of rest was the next millennium. This was the millennium of Jewish rule over all the world and would last until the end of the sabbath "day" of a thousand years, i.e., until A.D. 3240, as Hai Gaon suggested (*Revelation*, p. 129). Many Christians also believed in a week of millennia. St. Augustine, for instance, not only believed there would be seven millennia, but he also expected an eighth (*De Civitate Dei* 22.xxx), indicating that, like Hai Gaon, he expected another age to begin after the Sabbath age. For Augustine, however, this was not to be an age of regression, but one of increased felicity. The day after the Sabbath is the first day of the week, the day on which Christ arose. Therefore, there would be a corresponding resurrection millennium after the Sabbath millennium of rest.

heel, which meant Rome would have to come to an end before Israel could rule.

Mythologically, this was predestined from the births of Esau or Romulus and Remus, followed immediately by the birth of Jacob, or, historically, from the origins of Rome and Israel (4 Ezra 6:7-10), in Jewish judgment. Jacob would overtake Esau, or Israel would displace Rome when the times changed over Israel for good, and Jews would see the consolation of Zion (2 Bar 44:7). As the cycle of time moved around, contemporary ages grew ripe and old (2 Bar 70:3; 4 Ezra 5:55; 14:10-11, 16) before they passed away and came to an end (4 Ezra 6:20; 11:44; 12:25; 2 Bar 4:11; 2 Cor 5:17). As one age rolled past, another age rolled into its former place. It would then be a long predestined time before the wheel of time moved far enough around for that period in the cycle to repeat itself, but it was destined to do so, in Jewish judgment. The longings of Israel were described during the evil ages, when Jews were living under foreign rule. It was then that they counted, calculated, and studied the signs to learn how long this wicked age would last. The messianic age, the age to come, the comfort of Israel, and the promised rest were all names for the new age that was destined to follow the current age that was sure to come to an end.

Second Isaiah's Analysis of Cycles

The Babylonian Point in the Cycle. Once Jews found themselves in Babylonia, away from the promised land, they were reminded of a similar period in Egypt, so they assumed that they had made a complete cycle, from one captivity to the other. Therefore, they called their existence in Babylon, "slavery" even though they did not make bricks, either with or without straw either metaphorically or actually. Since they knew what had happened to their ancestors in Egypt, from that history they could deduce what events would happen in Babylon and in what order. By studying the sequence of events that happened from their entrance into Egypt until the United Kingdom was established under David and Solomon they could predict the events that would take place in Babylon from their entrance until the kingdom was reestablished in the promised land under a Jewish king, since all of this was predestined by cycles (see Isa 41:22-23; 42:9; 48:5-7). As the Koheleth said, "That which has been is that which will be" (Eccles 1:9). Before the age in which the land would be restored, there would be water flowing from the rock in the wilderness; miracles of healing would take place; there would be manna from heaven for the redeemed as they returned. The time in which this kind of prophecy would make sense would not be a horizontal line, but a series of circles, with smaller circles round the rims of the larger circles to represent the weeks, years, sabbatical years, and jubilee years—all of which were completed within still larger circles, each of which contained two ages—one, a Gentile age, and one, a Jewish age. The following chart shows only these two larger cycles which the author of Second Isaiah apparently compared in his deductions of the events that would still follow after his time.

The period of history covered from the time the sons of Israel went down into Egypt until the Babylonian captivity is here called the "Egypt-Canaan Cycle." This was the historical cycle of events with which the author of Second Isaiah was familiar and upon which he based his analysis of the Jewish position in the "Babylonian-Jerusalem Cycle." He reasoned that Jews of his day were half-way through the next cycle and were just about to enter the coming age of Jewish rule. This was the good news which he had to announce.

Signs of the times. After about a jubilee of years had taken place in Babylon, Second Isaiah predicted the events destined to happen before the return of Jews to Palestine, at just the right time (Isa 49:8). Under the leadership of the Lord's servant, Moses, Hebrews were led out of Egypt, but not directly to Palestine (Num 12:7-8; Deut 34:5; Josh 1:1, 7, 13, 15; 8:31; 9:24; 11:15; 12:6; 13:8; 14:7; 18:7; 24:4-5, 29). They had to pass through the wilderness, but the Lord was with them there. He provided them water in the wilderness (Isa 48:21), quails and manna to eat (Isa 49:10), miracles of healing, and protection from wild beasts and military enemies. At the destined time, God would again provide a servant to enable Jews to escape from Babylon (Deut 18:18). At that time the wilderness would blossom like a rose (Isa 35:1), the blind would receive their sight; deaf people would hear; lame would walk (Isa 35:6). There would be pools of water in the wilderness (Isa 35:7; 41:17-18; 43:19-20; 44:3-4), and guidance for all those who returned through the wilderness to the promised land (Isa 35:3-10; 40:10-11; 42:16-20; 50:3; see also Deut 26:8). Just as the Lord brought the Hebrews out on eagles' wings to establish them in their destined portion (Deut 32:8-11), so the Jews in Babylon would mount up on wings as eagles (Isa 40:31). As the Lord guided the Hebrews through the Reed Sea to escape from the Egyptians (Exod 14:15; Isa 63:12-14), so he would again lead them through the waters (Isa 43:2; 51:11). Just as the Lord had sent his angel before them as a pillar of fire by night and a pillar of cloud

CHART 3

Temple to be Rebuilt
Judgment Day
ca. 536 B.C.

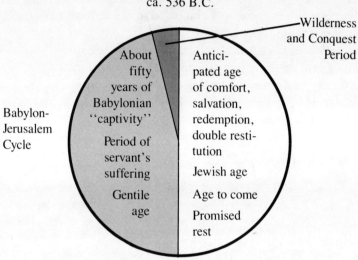

Temple Built
Judgment Day
ca. 1000 B.C.

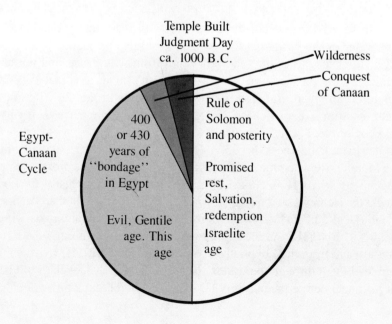

by day and followed them across the Reed Sea the same way (Exod 14:19-20), so Jews would return with the Lord before them and behind them (Isa 52:12; 58:8). Just as the Lord's servant, Moses, volunteered to bear the sins of the people when they sinned with the golden calf (Exod 32:35), so the Lord's servant again willingly accepted the sins of the Jews (Isa 53:4, 12). Just as the Lord drove away all of Israel's enemies, showing himself to be the "Man of war" (Exod 15:3), so the Lord, as a "Man of wars" (Isa 42:13) would prevail against the enemies of the Jews (Isa 41:12; 54:14-17); his arm was not shortened that he could not save (Isa 50:2; 59:1). All of this was destined to happen in order, just like clockwork, except, in this case, the Lord shortened one of the time periods in the cycle. Whereas the Hebrews had spent more than four hundred years in Egypt (Exod 12:40-41), Second Isaiah foresaw time passing in Babylon in about a jubilee. The second wilderness and conquest periods were probably also thought to have been shortened to pass as quickly as Jews could walk from Babylon to Jerusalem and take control. This may not be as precise as the early Stoic concept of the great cyclical year,[20] but it is more precise than Polybius was. Polybius ventured to make general predictions of Rome's future on the basis of the rise and fall of other nations,[21] but he did not offer a time schedule. Polybius presumed that good leadership and citizens with good character could retard the degeneration of a nation. It was not a blind, mechanical movement that could not be influenced at all by human beings.[22] The cyclical zig-zag which Polybius understood to be normal for the rise and fall of governments was understood by Israel as being times of Jewish and Gentile rule. The differences between Jewish and Greek thought about recurrence in history or cycles in time are not nearly as radically different as Jewish and Christian scholars have presumed.[23]

If Second Isaiah had not thought the second return to Palestine after the second captivity was predestined to follow the pattern of the first return from the Egyptian captivity, it would have been normal for him to have routed the Jews around the Fertile Crescent, over well-travelled roads to Je-

---

[20]Russell, "Time," p. 70; Trompf, *Recurrence*, pp. 11-12.

[21]Trompf, *Recurrence*, pp. 56, 66, 81, 101-102. See also p. 83.

[22]Ibid., pp. 64, 105-06.

[23]So also Trompf, "Notions," p. 229; *Recurrence*," pp. 117-119, 170, 176.

rusalem, rather than planning a journey that crossed both waters and a wilderness, as he did. Jeremiah had expected them to return from the north as they had apparently travelled when they left for Babylon (Jer 3:18 13:20 15:12; 16:14-15; 23:7-8; 31:8; 46:20). Second Isaiah followed the outline of events in the Pentateuch, rather than any map of topographical and geographical expediency to design the order of events in his prophecy. The parallels which Second Isaiah was able to deduce are impressive. He was not the first to prophesy the future on the basis of past events. Both Isaiah and Jeremiah had done so before the Babylonian Captivity, but they had not read the signs of the times as extensively as Second Isaiah had. Like his God, Second Isaiah was able to recount what had happened before and foretell what would happen again. This is what God had revealed to him through the Pentateuch (Isa 41:21-23; 42:9).

The author probably could not have been able to point out these signs as joyfully or confidently as he had if he had not also known one other sign—Jews had already negotiated with Cyrus of Persia and agreed to perform the sabotage in Babylon that was necessary for Cyrus's success in return for Cyrus's willingness to allow the Jews to return to Palestine (Isa 44:28; 45:1). These are the data that made him anticipate the return and start looking for signs to prove that this was God's destined plan. The "prophecy" of Daniel was composed in the same way.

After the Hasmonean victory, Daniel interpreted the events of his recent past as the fulfillment of previous prophecy, which he calculated in such a way that it pointed exactly to the end of the Greek age with the rededication of the temple after the defeat of the Greeks by Judas the Maccabee.[24]

The Hasmonean Cycle

Daniel's Update. Whereas Second Isaiah understood that the age of captivity in Babylon was much shorter than the bondage in Egypt had been, Daniel reasoned that it was even longer. Instead of fifty years, Daniel said 490 years were required under Gentile rule until Jews had paid for their sins and could be restored from captivity (Dan 9:24). These 490 years seem also to have begun with the Babylonian captivity, just as Second Isaiah's fifty were.

---

[24]For a defense of this position see GWB, *To The Hebrews* (Garden City, c1972), pp. 38-52.

CHART 4

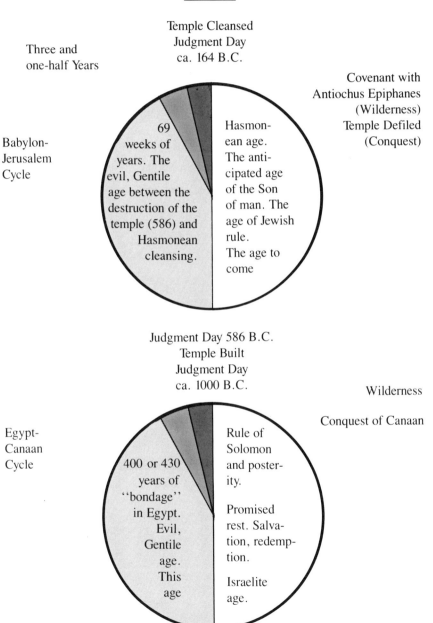

Temple Cleansed
Judgment Day
ca. 164 B.C.

Three and
one-half Years

Covenant with
Antiochus Epiphanes
(Wilderness)
Temple Defiled
(Conquest)

Babylon-
Jerusalem
Cycle

69 weeks of years. The evil, Gentile age between the destruction of the temple (586) and Hasmonean cleansing.

Hasmonean age. The anticipated age of the Son of man. The age of Jewish rule. The age to come

Judgment Day 586 B.C.
Temple Built
Judgment Day
ca. 1000 B.C.

Wilderness

Conquest of Canaan

Egypt-
Canaan
Cycle

400 or 430 years of "bondage" in Egypt. Evil, Gentile age. This age

Rule of Solomon and posterity.

Promised rest. Salvation, redemption.

Israelite age.

The seventy weeks of years he understood Jeremiah to have predicted were divided as follows: (1) Seven weeks of years were spent without a temple, evidently in Babylon. (2) Sixty-two weeks of years were spent in privation with a temple in a poor state of repair. (3) The last week of years was divided into two equal halves, the first, concluding with Antiochus's defilement of the temple and the second, ending with its cleansing. This last half week of years was probably the period he called the "end of days," meaning the end of the Gentile age (Dan 2:28; 10:14; 12:6-7, 13).

The Hasmonean Return. Just as it was covenant with Cyrus that prompted Second Isaiah to "recognize" the signs of the time and foretell a new exodus from Babylon, so the historical events associated with the Maccabean victory prompted the author of Daniel to interpret this return to the promised land as the fulfillment of Jeremiah's prophecy. The Maccabean rebellion was instigated by the oppressive action of Antiochus Epiphanes which involved defiling the temple. It required three and a half years, more or less, for the Hasmoneans to regain control over enough of Jerusalem to rededicate the temple. This was a sign to the Hasmoneans that God was on their side and that they would win, sooner or later. It took more than twenty more years to regain the complete Davidic kingdom and remove the foreign tax, but the die had been cast, in their judgment.

Deliverance in History. Part of the reason the Maccabean Revolt had been successful was the lack of governmental stability in Syria.[25] After one of Judas's early victories, when the Syrian commander, Seron, was killed (*Ant.* 12.292), Antiochus Epiphanes collected troops to take vengeance on Judas, but when he checked his resources, he discovered that he was not financially able to undertake a full scale attack until he collected tribute from colonies in Persia (*Ant.* 12.293-294). He attacked the Persian city of Elymais so as to strip its temple of riches, but he was defeated and forced to flee. He became ill and died there, never to return to take Jerusalem (*Ant.* 12.354-357). The mythological account of this is that the Ancient of Days condemned the fourth beast to death by burning (Dan 7:11). In the mean-

---

[25]It would not have been inconsistent with their faith for Jews to have had representatives in the Syrian government to help create the inner-governmental confusion. In Antioch, Jews were granted citizenship rights by the beginning of the third century B.C. By the time of the Maccabean rebellion there would have been numerous Jews in strategic positions there (*Ant* 12.119-120). They also had precedents in Egypt and in Babylon for this type of activity.

time, Judas had won important victories over the Syrians and rededicated the temple (*Ant* 12.309-326). A few years later (ca. 162 B. C.), after Antiochus Eupater captured Bethsur, he had held Jerusalem under seige for several months until Judas and the few who still remainded there were almost completely out of provisions and nearly forced either to starve or surrender, when a message came from Antioch that Phillip was coming from Persia to take over the Syrian government. Antiochus had to act quickly. He ordered Lysias, his commander at Jerusalem, to make a treaty with Judas so that they could return. This came just in the nick of time to save the Hasmonean cause (1 Macc 6:28-63; *Ant*. 12.375-383).

During Jonathan's leadership, Demetrius had threatened Jonathan with war unless the Jews paid all the kinds of tribute that had been required of them before the Maccabean Revolt began. Jonathan would not have been able to refuse this if Tryphon had not returned to Syria from Arabia and successfully taken the crown from Demetrius (*Ant*. 13.143-147).

These are a few of the most obvious occasions when the Hasmoneans were saved because of internal problems of Syria that demanded attention. Jews believed that God had acted in behalf of the Jews to stir up this internecine strife, just as he had earlier hardened the heart of Pharaoh, to deliver his chosen people from oppression. Syria had gone through many civil wars during this period, and there were three kings from 164-162 B.C. and five rulers from 128-124 B.C. Rebellion in other colonies distracted attention and military forces from Palestine. The high cost of civil and external wars also drained the national treasury, thus reducing the intensity with which Syrians could fight the Jews. Since Jews were fighting a religious war to recover their liberty to live according to the laws and customs of their fathers (*Ant*. 12.303), they believed God was using these distracting forces to enable the Jews to regain control of the promised land.

The Beth-horon Victory. The victory won shortly before Jews cleansed and rededicated the temple, according to Josephus (*Ant*. 12.312), "contributed not a little" to Jewish acquisition of freedom. When Seron heard Judas was regaining strength he began his march against Judas, camping at Bethhoron, northwest of Jerusalem on the road from Jaffa to Jerusalem through Lud. Judas prepared to meet Seron's army with a small troop of committed soldiers who fasted before the battle in which Seron was killed, and the Syrian army was forced to flee to the sea coast after eight hundred of them had been killed (*Ant*. 12.288-293). Shortly thereafter Antiochus sent three of his most competent leaders with 40,000 foot soldiers and 7,000 horsemen to overpower Judas and take Judea. Judas saw their camp at Emmaus, between Beth-horon and Jerusalem. Like Gideon of old, Judas dismissed all newly married men and those who had recently acquired property, so that all soldiers would be fully committed to battle. Gorgias took part of the Syrian army to attack the camp itself while the enemy was divided. He caught them off-guard and killed more than three thousand as they fled across the plain, scattering themselves toward the west, southwest, and northwest. When Gorgias learned what had happened, he also fled with the rest of the Syrian force, leaving the Jews completely victorious. Their thanksgiving and celebration continued with the rededication of the temple and the institution of the first Hanukkah (*Ant.* 12.298-312).

These victories were interpreted religiously and celebrated together with Hanukkah, in memory of God's acts in behalf of Israel at the end of the days of Greek dominance over Palestine. Twentieth century Jewish prayer books still include a prayer of gratitude for the miracles associated with the Hasmonean victory.[26] This was the period marked by Daniel as the end of days. Between the ages, judgment was held, the plaintiff won the verdict, and the kingdom, power, and glory were given both to the one like a Son of man (probably Judas)[27] and the saints of the Most High (Jews who were contemporary with Judas) (*Ant.* 12.316-326; Dan 7:13-28). This was the beginning of the new age of favor for the Jews.

After full control of Palestine was acquired (about 142 B.C.), this Hasmonean age lasted only a little more than 70 years before Romans began to gain control (63 B.C.), but later generations looked back to this age as one of the important ages for Judaism.

Dates and Theories. Although Second Isaiah had proclaimed a new exodus, and there had been a return to Palestine under Ezra and Nehemiah, not all of the Davidic kingdom was reestablished until the completion of the Maccabean rebellion. The pro-Hasmonean author of Daniel reasoned that this later period really represented the end of the evil age that began with the Babylonian captivity. He then traced the events that had happened between the end of the Jewish age in 586 B.C. and the end of the Gentile age at about 164 B.C. Second Isaiah had traced the historical events up to the end of the Jewish period (586 B.C.), and Daniel complemented this anaylsis of

---

[26]GWB, *Revelation*, p. 235.

[27]See fn.24.

cyclical time by listing the events that followed that period (586-164 B.C.). He did this in terms of Sabbath cycles. There were seventy weeks of years between the pre-Babylonian Jewish age and the Maccabean Jewish age of the saints of the Most High. Sixty-nine weeks of years elapsed from the Babylonian captivity until the time when some Messiah was cut off (Dan 9:24-26). A covenant was made at that time for one week[28] at the end of one half of that week of years, the temple was defiled; by the end of the second half of the same week of years, the temple was reestablished, and the age of the Greeks was beginning to collapse. This totalled seventy weeks.[29] In the judgment of the author of Daniel, this was the end of the Greek age of darkness and the beginning of the Jewish age of light. Rededication of the temple marked the end of "this age" and the beginning of the "age to come." This all had been predestined from the creation of the world and the ages (Heb 1:1). From the dogmatic point of view of a religious cyclicist, this all worked out perfectly, but the author of Daniel had to force history to fit his sabbatical time system.[30]

The time from 586 to 164 B.C. is 422 years and not 490 years, as Daniel calculated. The author was accurate about the last seven years. The rest was forced to fit into 69 weeks of years. It took more than twenty years for the Hasmoneans to gain complete control under the rule of Simon, when all foreign tax was discontinued. Jews referred to the removal of the tax in Simon's reign as the beginning of a new era (*BJ* 1.53; *Ant.* 13.213). The Hasmoneans ruled until 63 B.C. when Pompey entered Jerusalem and imposed a tax upon the country (*BJ* 1.118). Herod's rule began at 38 B.C.; the procurators began control of Palestine with the renewal of taxes collected by a foreign government, about A.D. 6-7. This was 170 years after the temple had been rededicated. From the beginning of Simon's reign (142 B.C. to Pompey's entrance was 79 years (*BJ* 1.53; *Ant.* 13.213; 1 Macc 12:41-42), but the rabbis (San 97b) also forced the period into a length of 70 years to coincide with ten sabbath years in a cycle of ages, according to Jeremiah.

---

[28]This apparently refers to the holy covenant Antiochus made with the Jews which he broke when he defiled the temple (Dan 11:30; *Ant* 11.249).

[29]Others followed Daniel's pattern. See the divisions of time in the Sibylline Oracles, the Apocalypse of Paul, etc. For a more extensive defense of this argument, see GWB, *Hebrews*, pp. 38-51.

[30]According to Trompf, Polybius also sometimes forced history to fit his philosophy (*Recurrence*, p. 94).

This was the good Jewish age which rolled past into an evil Gentile age again. Daniel had promised that the Jewish kingdom would last for "the age and until." By A.D. 6-7 the extent of that age was known. After the fact, this Babylonian-Jerusalem cycle was something like the following diagram.

The Post-Hasmonean Cycle

Resistance to Change. When the final judgment came, accompanied by the taxation under Quirinius in A.D. it was clear that the victories gained under the Hasmonean leadership had been completely lost, and Jews were back again under the control of some other foreign power. Although Jews at that time believed in cycles of time, they were not so completely convinced of the unchangeability of time for them to have been willing to sit around and wait for another seventy weeks of years until their turn came again. They began at once to see if they could reverse this change and regain the age that had just been fulfilled. Beginning with Judas of Galilee and Zadok the Pharisee, leaders appeared regularly at feasts, prepared to lead rebellious movements against Rome. After the Romans killed the necessary number of Jews to restore peace, Jews agreed that the time was not yet ripe. They would try again next year. This continued until they received enough positive assurance from their efforts to convince them that they had received a sign from Heaven. They had reached the time to rebel as the Hasmoneans had and they believed that by doing just as the Hasmoneans had done they could obtain the same results the Hasmoneans had. The signs they received to convince them occurred during the Battle of Beth-horon, after which they were "ready" to fight. The situation was desperate inside the city, and Jews may have remembered a similar situation when Judas almost had to surrender. Then, for reasons unknown to the Jews, Cestius gave up the siege and began to retreat. This encouraged the Jews to follow him in hot pursuit, killing many foot soldiers and cavalry. After some of his officers had been killed, Cestius abandoned baggage and fled through the same Beth-horon ravine by which he had come. Once in the ravine, the Jews had him cornered, just as Judas had done with the Greeks on two other occasions about two hundred years earlier. After one of those occasions, the turning point of the war, the temple was rededicated; the other victory brought death to Nicanor, the Syrian general, and was later celebrated by the Jews as Nicanor's day (*Ant.* 12.400-412). On the occasion of the later antitype, Jews boxed in the Romans from both ends of the ravine and slaughtered many before the Romans finally got through to the plain during the

CHART 5
Temple Cleansed
Judgment Day
ca. 164 B.C.

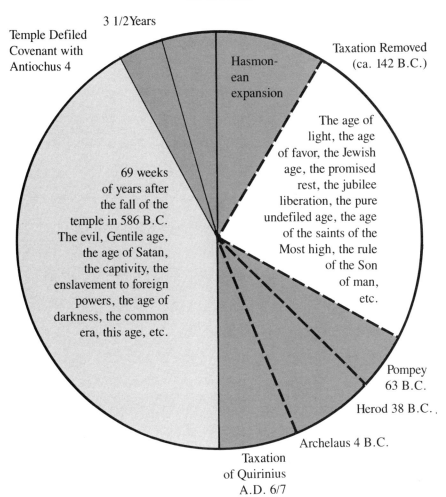

3 1/2 Years

Temple Defiled
Covenant with
Antiochus 4

Taxation Removed
(ca. 142 B.C.)

Hasmon-
ean
expansion

The age of
light, the age
of favor, the Jewish
age, the promised
rest, the jubilee
liberation, the pure
undefiled age, the age
of the saints of the
Most high, the rule
of the Son
of man,
etc.

69 weeks
of years after
the fall of the
temple in 586 B.C.
The evil, Gentile age,
the age of Satan,
the captivity, the
enslavement to foreign
powers, the age of
darkness, the common
era, this age, etc.

Pompey
63 B.C.

Herod 38 B.C.

Archelaus 4 B.C.

Taxation
of Quirinius
A.D. 6/7

A.D. 6/7
Judgment Day

night. The Jews, then, returned to Jerusalem and assembled in the temple to organize their troops and prepare for an all-out war with Rome (*BJ* 3.255-259).

Josephus wrote his history so as not to show any relationship between the Maccabean zealots and the zealots who fought against the Romans in the war of A.D. 66-70, but, as Farmer has demonstrated,[31] it is very unlikely that the holy war soldiers who drove Cestius and his troops to retreat through the Beth-horon ravine failed to see the typological relationship between this victory and Judas's critical victories over Seron, Gorgias, and Nicanor at the same place.[32] For Judas, these were crucial points of the war. For the Jews who fought against the Romans, this was the occasion for organizing troops and appointing officers for the extensive war with the Romans. At that point Jews were exuberant and confident. They were sure God was on their side. They more than likely considered themselves to be at the same point in the time cycle as the Maccabees had been at the cleansing of the temple. There were still other signs of the times which led Jews to think that their war with the Romans was an antitype of the earlier victorious war with the Syrian Greeks. It was this confidence that enabled them to fight against overwhelming odds to the very end, and they held out for a time, two times, and half a time.

Antitype for Syrian Instability. The conflict that broke out into open warfare with the Battle of Beth-horon in A.D. 66 began at a time when there was more internal and external conflict in Rome than there had been in Syria at the time of the Maccabean Revolt. Tacitus described the period beginning with A.D. 68 as one "rich in disaster, terrible in battles, torn asunder by civil conflict, horrible even in peace. Four emperors fell by the sword; there were three civil wars, even more foreign wars, and often both of these at once" (*Hist.* 3.1-2). Just as the Hasmoneans interpreted the Syrian instability as God's action on behalf of his chosen people, so the Jews, after the Battle of

---

[31]W. R. Farmer, *The Maccabees, Zealots, and Josephus* (New York, c1957).

[32]Greek historians also saw parallels between figures and periods in history. For example, Plutarch (*Vit.* [*Demetrius and Anthony Compared*] 3.1 ff.) compared Demetrius 1 to Anthony. Dio Cassius compared the times of Julius Caesar to those of Sulla (*Vita Cari* 3.1). Note also the crossing of the Reed Sea (Exod 15) and the Jordan (Josh 4:23), the Egyptian and Babylonian captivities, *et al.*

Beth-horon, thought God caused Rome all these problems so as to liberate his elect. After the war had been fought for more than three years (a time, two times, and half a time—Dan 9:27), during the civil war Vespasian led against Vitellius, Rome was burned. Rome had been sacked and burned before, but this was the first time the Capitol with its temples had been set afire by the Romans themselves so all Rome was in despair, fearing still more divine punishment (*Hist.* 3.71-72). At this time, when the merchants wept and the stock market crashed (Rev 18:9-19), the zealous holy war soldiers in Jerusalem understood Rome's fire as the punishment which God had sent upon Rome, just as he had earlier sent plagues against Egypt and civil wars against Syria (Rev 18:4-8). Rome's burning was no tragedy to those zealous Jews, and it was probably at this time that they shouted, "Rejoice over her, Heaven, saints, apostles, and prophets, because God has avenged her for you" (Rev 18:20). They exclaimed, "Halleluyah! . . . because the smoke of her burning goes up for ages of ages" (Rev 19:2-3).

During this crucial period there had been three emperors in Rome within one year. Vespasian had conquered most of Palestine and had cut off all access routes to Jerusalem, as Lysias had done years before. Then, just as miraculously as Lysias's withdrawal, the civil conflict became so intense in Rome that Vespasian withheld a direct attack on Jerusalem to organize a campaign against Vitellius (*BJ* 4.486-502). This was clear proof to holy war soldiers that history was repeating itself. Jews in A.D. 69-70 were at the very point in the cycle where Hasmoneans had been about two hundred years earlier—or so they thought. It seemed the perfect antitype or recurrence of Lysias's withdrawal, and also of a withdrawal of an earlier Assyrian king whose soldiers had surrounded Jerusalem. After Hezekiah prayed, a plague came upon the Assyrian soldiers, killing 85,000 of them in one night, after which the king was forced to return to Nineveh (2 Kgs 19:1-36). Jews probably thought these events related to the Assyrians, the Syrians, and the Romans all happened at the same point in the cycle of time. In the Roman cycle, first Vespasian withdrew to Egypt to plan his strategy. When the conflict opened up in Rome itself, the Capitol was set aflame. This occurred just half a week of years after the war with Rome had begun. Soon Jews would be a free people again. The signs seemed obvious. In the eagle vision, the eagle (Rome) heard a voice like a lion (lion of Judah) accusing the eagle of being the fourth beast to rule the world before the saints of the Most High received the kingdom (4 Ezra 11:37-46). The author of Revelation also identified Rome typologically with the fourth beast.[33] Sooner or later the Messiah of the seed of David was destined to destroy the fourth beast (4 Ezra 12:22-23). The only question after Vespasian withdrew was that of deciding which of the Jewish generals was the true Son of man— John, Simon, or Eleazar. These three messianic pretenders fought in armed conflict to find out and succeeded only in weakening the Jewish military power and burning all of the grain stores in Jerusalem while Vespasian was gone.

Erroneous Typology. When Titus returned to continue the war he found Jerusalem considerably weakened by famine and destruction. The earlier exuberance had been reduced to lamentation, but religious soldiers fought until the temple burned, expecting a miracle right up to the last minute. Josephus said there had been numerous false prophets who had deluded the people during this war. One of them assured Jews, even when the temple was in flames, that God was right at the point of showing the signs of deliverance (*BJ* 6.285-86). After the temple had been burned, Josephus observed that the cycle was exactly in agreement with the earlier type. The temple had been burned first in 586 B.C. and again in A.D. 70 on exactly the same month and day, according to Josephus (*BJ* 6.268-70). Whereas the false prophets had recognized the signs of the times to be exactly in correspondence with the period before the Maccabean victory, Josephus, following the same typological, cyclical understanding of predestined time, concluded, *after the event,* that the prophets had been false, and the type they had identified was the wrong one.

This was neither the beginning nor the end of Jewish reliance on signs and interpretations. During the forty or so years after the crucifixion of Jesus, Josephus reported four leaders who promised deliverance to contemporary Jews. They also offered signs to prove this would happen. Their signs were all modern equivalents of earlier prototypes that would show they were then in the very place in the cycle of time where these events occurred in the first place. Theudas promised that the river Jordan would open

---

[33]Rev 13 not only identified Rome with the fourth beast but attributed to Rome the qualities of all four monstrous beasts. For a discussion of typology in antiquity, see M. Eliade, *Cosmos and History*, tr. W. R. Trask (New York, 1959). A. Farrer, "Important Hypotheses Reconsidered, 8. Typology," *Exp. Tim.* 67 (1956):228-31, said, "There never has been, nor in a sane world ever could be anything called 'the typological hypothesis' " (p. 228). For a demonstration of his conclusion, see the rest of the article. Typology is not a hypothesis, but a fact, according to Farrer.

for him as it had for Joshua (*Ant.* 20.97-98). Another figure led the Jews to the wilderness to see signs of liberation (*Ant.* 20.167-68; *BJ* 2.259). A third promised that the walls of Jerusalem would fall before him as those of Jericho had before Joshua (*Ant.* 20.168-72; *BJ* 2.261-63). A fourth led Jews into the wilderness to receive salvation and rest (*Ant.* 20.188). These happened so often that Jews were also warned not to go out into the wilderness to meet these messiahs (Matt 24:25). The signs they promised to repeat first occurred prior to or during the first conquest of Canaan. Followers hoped to see proof that they were then at the same point in the cycle of time as when these first occurred.[34]

During the fifth century some Jews in Crete were told by a Jew who pretended to be Moses that he had been sent to Crete from heaven to open the Mediterranean Sea so that they could walk on dry land back to the promised land. On the day he gave the sign, they hurled themselves into the sea and most of them drowned or were shattered by the rocks.[35]

In A.D. 723. Jews who lived in Spain and France abandoned their possessions at the instruction of a certain messiah to go to Syria, where the Messiah was to be congregating the Jewish believers. Local authorities confiscated their property while they were gone.

At the beginning of the Crusades, Jews in Salonika and other nearby Greek towns were fasting, receiving flagellations, and repenting of their sins in expectation of the Messiah. They had heard that the Christians were gathering forces and going to the promised land. They thought that this was God's activity, sending the Christians to prepare the way for the Jews, just as Cyrus of Persia had done for them in their captivity at Babylon. They went out, joyously, to meet these deliverers and were slaughtered (A.D. 1096). Somehow they misread the signs; the typology did not reveal the outcome accurately.[36]

On bases of astrology, counting years and feasts on calendars, studying typology and cycles, Jews deduced years and days on which the Messiah was expected to arrive. Some of the exact dates offered were as follows: A

---

[34]There were non-Jews who expected the past to be reenacted just as precisely as this. Thucydides (*Hist.* 1.22[4]), for instance, said, " . . . events like this will occur again."

[35]Socrates, *HE*, 8.xxxviii.63-64; *MPG* 67:825-828; GWB, *Revelation*, p. 175-76.

[36]J. Mann, "Messianic Movements in the Days of the First Crusade," *Hatekuphah* 23 (1925):253-59; GWB, *Revelation*, pp. 106-112.

prophet in France said Elijah would gather Jews together in A.D. 1226, and
the Messiah would appear in A.D. 1233.[37] In 1235 Jews in Prague were
forced to disperse, because they were preparing to raişe an army and were
displaying letters, saying that the Messiah had come.[38] Judah Halevy said
the proper date was A.D. 1130, at which time the power of the Christians
and Moslems would be broken.[39] In some of the texts for *The Book of Ze-*
rubbabel, both the dates of A.D. 960 and A.D. 1060 are given as the time to
expect the Messiah.[40] None of these proved correct, but this did not cause
either Jews or Christians to give up their belief about the ages or the conviction that it was possible to deduce future events on the bases of cycles,
typology, and prophecy.

The events leading up to Constantine's victory were interpreted typologically as the new exodus and resurrection (*HE* 9.5-8; 10.11-12). Both
Christians and Jews fought the Crusades with the belief that this was the
right time for each to gain possession of the promised land.[41] A millennium
of years before, both John the Baptist and Jesus probably interpreted their
times on the bases of such factors as calendars, cycles, typology, and prophetic writings, the way other Jews did. They called Jews to repent, because
they believed the time of the Jewish captivity was up; the age of the Gentiles
had been fulfilled; and the Kingdom of Heaven was at hand. The land of
Israel was not restored to the followers of Jesus at that time, anymore than
it was won by later Jews in the bitter war against Rome, but a knowledge of
this way of thinking provides many clues for understanding how some of the
material in the gospels came to be written.

Conclusions

There is a lot of imperfect logic revealed in Jewish and Christian attempts to deduce from cyclical time an understanding of their own history
that would enable them to predict the future. Although Polybius predicted
the future downfall of Rome on the basis of the rise and fall of earlier na-

---

[37] A. Z. Aescoly, *Jewish Messianic Movements* (Jerusalem, 1956), p. 188; GWB, *Revelation,* pp. 202-203.

[38] Aescoly, *Jewish,* p. 190; GWB, *Revelation,* p. 203.

[39] GWB, *Revelation,* pp. 239-40.

[40] Ibid., p. 370.

[41] Ibid., pp. 18-23.

tions, he did not attempt to predict specific events that would occur within given time limitations. In some ways Jews and Christians had more confidence in the reliability of cycles than many Greeks had. Jewish and Christian understanding of cyclical time was more of a rationalization or a means for justifying their dogmatic hopes than a scientific instrument for objective research. On the one hand, their concept of cyclical time provided a basis for believing all the events in history were predestined and foreordained from the beginning of creation. Historical events followed one another in predestined sequence. When the cycle of predestined events had been completed the cycle would begin all over again, with the same events happening all over again in the same sequence. This was basic to the logic. If this were carried out explicitly, then the sons of Israel would have spent four hundred years in Egypt; Moses would have led them out; they would have spent forty years in the wilderness; Joshua would have been followed by Saul, David, and Solomon in acquiring the kingdom. About four hundred years after Solomon, the cycle would have been completed, and the sons of Israel would again have journeyed into Egypt, spent more than four hundred years there again, followed by another forty years in the wilderness under the leadership of Moses, etc. That is the kind of precision Vergil and some Pythagoreans evidently expected, but Polybius did not. Second Isaiah was different from both. On the one hand, he was less universalistic than Polybius; he related the cycles only to Jewish expectations. But on the other hand, he allowed a great deal of variation in time limitations and allowances. He considered the fifty years spent in Babylon to be the equivalent of the four hundred years spent in Egypt. He thought the forty year wilderness period and the extensive conquest of Canaan would pass in the length of time it would take Jews to travel from Babylon to Jerusalem. They would not enter exactly the same kind of Canaan Joshua found, but a kingdom twice as glorious as that of Solomon and David.

Daniel was more reasonable in his chronological judgment, because he equated the period in Egypt, the wilderness, and the conquest of Canaan with the four hundred, ninety years spent between the beginning of the Babylonian captivity and the rededication of the temple in 164 B.C. After the Romans had taken complete political control of the promised land in A.D. 6-7, Jews were not so completely convinced of the unerring cycle of predestined events that they were prepared to wait around for four hundred years until the Egyptian section of the cycle was over. They could ignore all the negative evidence held up for their observation and pick out two or three clues to convince them that they were again in the last half week of years of the old, evil, Gentile age, the age of the fourth beast. This was the end of the days, the wilderness period before the entrance into the promised land. Later Jews expected this wilderness period to last half a week of years or even as little as forty-five days.[42] Within this brief period the prison sentence would be fulfilled, and the Kingdom of Heaven would be restored to the promised land. Prophets calculated and calculated; they studied and studied the current events in relationship to their past history to find some justification for their undying hope that they would again regain political supremacy, when Gentiles would prune Jewish vineyards and tend Jewish flocks. When rabbis listed the order of events that would take place during the last week of the Gentile age, they said in the sixth year there would be voices and in the seventh year, wars. Rabbi Joseph observed that there had been many weeks like this, but the son of David did not come. Rabbi Abave retorted, ''Were there in the sixth [year] voices, and in the seventh [year], wars? And were they, further, in their [prescribed] sequence?'' (San. 97a).

Although the basis for their convictions was many times very slim, they risked their lives on the likelihood that it was correct. When predictions failed, neither Jews nor Christians gave up their belief in cyclical, predestined time. They just went back to their drawing boards and recalculated. Rabbis thought this calculation was so important that Jews were forbidden to associate with any Jew who was capable of calculating, but did not (San. 75a).

Although medieval Jews seemed obsessed with their calculations, based on some kind of cyclical concept of time, they were not unique. They only varied in details and degree with Jews of pre-Christian times and Christians of NT times. Trompf also found an amazing consistency in the philosophies of Greeks as early as Polybius and Christian and non-Christian historians up to the time of the Protestant Reformation. Whereas Trompf concentrated on the philosophies of historians, the emphasis here has been the way in which Jews and Christians applied their philosophy to their religious doctrines and expectations. Trompf presumed that Jews and Christians held an overall linear view of time which applied to eschatology and apocalyptic literature. Within that framework they also held normal Greek cyclical views of historic recurrence He showed over and over again

---

[42]Ibid., pp. 384, 402, 415, 424-25, 432.

cyclical themes within this so-called linear concept of history. This study, on the other hand, has shown that the basic view was *cyclical* and that the eschatology fit into *that* framework. The end expected was not the end of the world, but the end of an era, a segment of the cycle, or, to use Trompf's diagrams, a significant point in the recurrence or anacyclical zig-zag.

Cyclical time was not the only factor to be considered in their eschatological expectations; there was also the expectation that OT prophecies would be fulfilled in the days of the Messiah. There were convictions about jubilee and sabbath justice, and astrological signs in the heavens. But with all these refinements, Jews and Christians continued to watch for miracles like those performed in Egypt, the wilderness, or those promised by Second Isaiah. They looked for the recurrence of events like those that had happened between the defilement and rededication of the temple in the Hasmonean period. These identities would reassure them of their position in the cycle, and if the signs were those close to the end of the Gentile age, covenanters would abandon their current occupations and secular positions to invest all they had in the campaign to reestablish the new government in the age to come, when they would again be in positions of political and economic prominence. This is what eschatology was all about.

CHAPTER NINE

The Church
Writes
History

Introduction

After the death of Jesus the early church had at its disposal the chreias and parables that the apostles had learned and preserved. This told only of Jesus' activity during his campaign on behalf of the Kingdom of Heaven. It is not surprising that they knew no more. Most people know very little about their national leaders prior to the time when they begin to function as officers. For example, very few citizens of the United States know where or when Gerald Ford, Jimmy Carter, or Ronald Reagan were born, went to grade school, high school, and college. Their family trees, previous employment, hobbies, and interests are equally unknown.

In countries ruled by dynasties, where there have been no dynasty changes for hundreds of years, citizens become informed about the royal families beginning with infancy, but that is not the case with rulers like David, Saul, Herod, Alexander the Great, and Vespasian—all of whom gained their positions by military force. Neither would that be the case with any of the pretending messiahs in Palestine. Because of this, sycophantic authors attributed to great leaders who attained their positions by their own military proficiency birth stories that are obviously mythical, somewhat miraculous, and belonging to a peculiar type of narrative that has many distinctive characteristics. There were miraculous birth stories about leaders like Sargon of Akkad, Xerxes of Persia, and Moses, and philosophers like Pythagoras and Plato. The Matthaean birth story is very much like the birth story about Sargon, more than two thousand years earlier. The claim to virgin birth in those days was not based on scientific observation; it was a confession of faith expressed in mythological terms.

Not until Alexander the Great had conquered his empire did he declare that he was the son of Zeus. When his mother, Olympias, heard of it, she said, ''Will that young man not stop accusing me to Hera?!''[1] Philo of Alexandria, a Jewish philosopher and exegete who was a contemporary of Jesus, claimed that Isaac was virgin born.[2] All Jews who had read Genesis knew how Sarah complained that she could not bear a child, so when she finally bore Isaac, Philo called this virgin birth! On what basis? Not on scientific examination and documentation. Philo reasoned that when a virgin had intercourse with a man she became a woman. When a woman had intercourse with the Lord, however, she became a virgin again. Philo meant by this that he believed Isaac was at least as great as all the kings who were said to have been virgin born. Since their greatness could not be explained by their endowments received through natural ancestry, they were said to be born of the gods which meant they were virgin born.

Virgin birth was a mythological explanation for greatness that was readily understood in NT times. Since the early church did not know the details of Jesus' birth, it could assume that it was fair to structure the narrative in virgin birth terms, because, in the church's judgment, there had never been a greater leader in the world. This was the basis upon which historians of the early church began to write their narratives, but that was not the only ground upon which they based their conclusions. Luke and Matthew have different birth narratives. Their authors reached their conclusions

---

[1]Theon, ''Progymnasmata,'' *Spengel* 3.v, p. 460.26-29.

[2]Philo, *On the Cherubim* 50. Philo also claimed that God was Isaac's father (*Allegorical Interpretation* 3.219; *On Dreams* 1.173). R. E. Brown, *The Birth of the Messiah* (Garden City, 1977), pp. 522-23, has argued that (1) miraculous births among pagans would have had no influence on Christian concepts, (2) Christians probably would not have known about them, anyway, and (3) parallels are not exact. This kind of dismissal is based on wishful thinking.

on the basis of different historiographical emphases, but both authors conjectured their narratives on the basis of accepted Jewish methods of historiography and they probably utilized all of the factual data they could muster. The first to be considered here is Luke's infancy and childhood narrative.

Lukan Tradition

When the "historian," Luke, set out to reconstruct the early life of Jesus, he was familiar with certain Jewish customs that would apply to all Jewish males: birth, circumcision, purification of the mother, Bar Mitzwah and age requirement for holding an office of national leadership. Around these traditions, Luke used the factual data at his disposal to reconstruct the narrative.

The "historian" began with the known history about Jesus. He had been crucified under Pontius Pilate (A.D. 26-36). Luke evidently also knew that a national officer had to be at least thirty years of age and no more than fifty years of age (CDC 14:8-9; 1QSa 1:8-10).[3] On this basis, John said Jesus was not yet fifty years old (Jn 8:57) and Luke held that he was about thirty when he began his ministry (Lk 3:23). Working backwards from A.D. 36, he came to the important event of the Roman taxation by Quirinius (A.D. 6/7).[4] There was a mythological reason for thinking that Jesus would have been born at the same time as the Roman taxation. The taxation was a great tragedy in the eyes of Jews and they believed that the Messiah would be born at some time when the chosen people were suffering extensively. This is the way it was with Moses (Exod 1:1—2:10). There are two narratives in later Jewish literature that describe the birth of the Messiah on the very day on which the temple was destroyed in A.D. 70. The confession was that on this most depressing of all days, the Lord provided Israel with the source of restoration.[5] This provided Luke a mythical date for the birth of Jesus that was also reasonably close to the time when an adult who was at least thirty years of age during Pilate's term of office might have been born. This was a good place for a saga author to begin.

---

[3]GWB, "Dates, Discrepancies, and Dead Sea Scrolls," *The New Christian Advocate* 2 (1958):50-54.

[4]Against those who try to conjecture an earlier date see Ibid., pp. 51-52.

[5]GWB, *Revelation,* pp. 452-58. C. T. Ruddick, Jr., "Birth Narrative in Genesis and Luke," *Nov* 12 (1970):344-48, suggested that Luke 1-2 was patterned after Genesis.

The difference between a saga or myth and history is that the saga is more interested in telling how people *feel* about events than in the precise historical details. Josephus, for instance, wrote a history of the Maccabean revolt; the author of Daniel wrote a saga about the same event. Josephus told of the battles that took place and the events that succeeded one another; Daniel told of the beliefs and religious interpretations the people gave to these events. Luke was something of a historian. He tried to relate his beliefs to actual, datable events in history, but he was primarily dealing with saga or myth. Therefore Luke's historical reporting is mingled with his beliefs about the religious significance of Jesus to Jews.

When Luke wrote this narrative he evidently had the following traditions at his disposal: (1) Jesus lived in Nazareth; (2) as the son of David he was predestined to be born in Bethlehem; (3) from either Josephus (Slavonic text *BJ* 2.110-3) or another source Luke learned that John the Baptist was actively leading a movement during the reign of Archelaus (4 B.C.-A.D. 6/7); and (4) Jesus was closely related to John the Baptist.

To follow this kind of logic it is necessary to presume that Herod's son was also sometimes known as Herod and that he might have been considered a king when, in reality, he was only an ethnarch. Even with this transfer of Herods there are still some chronological inaccuracies in the narrative. Statistically, this implies that Jesus was crucified before he began his ministry, but these are the kinds of details that disturb historians more than authors of sagas. In saga it was more important to communicate the meaning of the event than to report historical details accurately. For example, the author of Daniel considered the period from 586 B.C. to 164 B.C. to be four hundred, ninety years, because that is the number he needed to make seventy weeks of years as a possible fulfillment of Jeremiah's prophecy of seventy years. Actually there were only four hundred, twenty-two years between these two dates, but that fact did not disturb sabbatical eschatologists, nor did the chronological inaccuracies in the Lukan birth narrative bother the author of that saga or the early Christians for whom it was intended.

With these facts before him, Luke composed his document which involved filling in only the details of the myth, whose outline was obvious in the judgment of the author. Before the birth of Jesus, there is the miraculous birth of John the Baptist taking into account John's priestly heritage. Elizabeth's condition was patterned after the typology of Sarah giving birth in her old age (Gen 21:1-7), and Hannah, whose son, Samuel, was born after

Hannah's vow to the priest, Eli, in the temple (1 Sam 1:9—2:10). Prophecies related to Elijah and Samson were applied to John (Jdgs 13:4-5; Mal 3:1, 23-24; Lk 1:15-17). This was accepted historiography for Jewish and Christian theologians since these were days of the Messiah and all prophecies were made to be fulfilled in those days (San 99a; Ber 34b). The Magnificat was composed following the typology of the Song of Hannah on the presumption that many OT prophecies were being fulfilled in the birth of the Messiah.[6] The Benedictus (Lk 1:68-79) was also composed on the basis of many prophecies that were thought to be fulfilled in the days of the Messiah in relationship to the Messiah and his leadership role for Israel.[7] The reason Jesus was reportedly born in a manger, rather than at the inn in Bethlehem, was that mothers were always considered defiled when birth took place. Therefore it was customary for mothers to give birth in stables or in corners of their houses that had been walled-off so that the rest of the family would not be defiled. This is still the practice of the Mandaeans today. Some later commentator, who did not know Jewish customs, explained, erroneously, "because there was no room at the inn" (Lk 2:7).[8] The messenger of the Lord (Lk 2:9-10) who announced good news to the shepherds was like the messenger of the Lord who brought good news of peace to Zion (Isa 40:9; 41:27; 52:7). Just as the prophecy of Isa 44:20 was for the Lord's chosen people, so the good news to the shepherds was:

> Glory to the Most High God,
> and on the land, peace,
> for his chosen people (Lk 2:14).[9]

Because of the numerous prophecies, typologies, and traditions associated with the Messiah, Luke was able to compose an extensive saga around the birth of Jesus. With the traditions about Nazareth and Bethlehem, Luke had only to deduce how Jesus could be born in Bethlehem and live in Nazareth. The taxation of Quirinius gave him a basis for explaining how the two locations were resolved. There was not much tradition or leg-

---

[6] For an analysis of these see Brown, *Birth*, pp. 355-60, and D. Strauss, *The Life of Jesus* (London, 1898), pp. 106-20.

[7] Ibid., pp. 378-92.

[8] E. S. Drower, *The Mandaeans of Iraq and Iran* (Leiden, 1962), p. 41.

[9] In a nationalistic context the Greek here means "the land of Palestine" rather than "the earth," and "men of [God's] good pleasure" are the chosen people.

end about the circumcision of the Messiah, so Luke took care of that detail in one verse, noting that Jesus was both circumcised and named on the eighth day as was normal for Jewish males. The next event in the normal life of a Jewish male was that he and his mother would be cleansed after the required forty days had been completed, just as the scripture directed (Lev 12:1-4). For Jesus, Luke supposed that this would take place in the temple at Jerusalem (Lk 2:22-23) and he reported that Mary gave the atonement offering required of someone who was not rich (Lev 12:8). Luke also took this occasion to insert a prophecy of Simon, based on Isaiah 40:5; 52:10; 42:6; 49:6; 25:7; and 46:13, and the prophecy of Hannah, relating Jesus to those who expected the redemption of Jerusalem (Lk 2:38), but he did not mention Jesus as being virgin born.[10]

Since there was no reported tradition about what a Jewish male should do between the ages of forty days and twelve years, Luke skipped over this period and reported what he conjectured to have happened to a Jewish boy destined to be the Messiah at the time of his Bar Mitzwah.[11] Luke was consistent in holding that Jesus lived in Nazareth, so he arranged a situation whereby he could get to Jerusalem so that this event could take place in the Holy City before the greatest of all rabbis. All Jewish boys were given chances to show their knowledge of the law before adult males of their congregations, but it would seem that the Messiah would have excelled all normal performances. Instead of the local synagogue, it was the temple; instead of the laymen, this was before the scholars. The situation was centered around a normal trip to Jerusalem for one of the feasts which Jews attend three times a year.

The next age that is important to Jewish males is twenty.[12] At that time, the youth becomes an adult; he is no longer a minor; he is responsible for bearing arms, paying taxes, offering sacrifices, and is allowed to marry. There is no special ceremony about this, and since Jesus was celibate, there

---

[10]So J. A. Fitzmyer, "The Virginal Conception of Jesus in the New Testament," *TS* 34 (1973):269-72. See also P. J. Thompson, "The Infancy Gospels of St. Matthew and St. Luke Compared," *Studia Evangelica* 1 (1959), p. 217.

[11]Brown, *Birth*, p. 473, says this was not a Bar Mitzwah, but for arguments and information Brown overlooked, see GWB, *Consequences*, pp. 181-82.

[12]See GWB, "The Old Testament Meaning of the Knowledge of Good and Evil," *JBL* 75 (1956):114-20; also GWB, *Consequences*, pp. 181-84.

was no occasion to relate the events that might have taken place at that time. Therefore, Luke skipped all of the history from twelve years until about thirty, when Jesus presumably began his public leadership role (Lk 3:23).

Matthaean Deductions

Fulfilled Prophecies. The author of the Matthaean narrative worked with many of the same assumptions as the Lukan narrator. There were some differences of emphasis. Whereas Luke began with the conception of John the Baptist and tried to tell what must have happened at the most important periods in a Jewish boy's life, Matthew began with the birth of Jesus and then told nothing of Jesus' life until he confronted John the Baptist for baptism as an adult. Furthermore, he emphasized the importance of prophecies fulfilled and typologies repeated more than Luke did. On the basis of five OT prophecies Matthew structured the saga under consideration. (1) Isaiah 4:14 prophesied: "Look! a virgin will become pregnant and will bear a son, and they will call his name Emmanuel." Since all prophecy is made only for the days of the Messiah and these were the days of the Messiah, this prophecy must apply to the birth of Jesus. The Semitisms in this narrative indicate that the author knew Hebrew very well and could have rendered his own translation of the Hebrew which means "young woman," instead of the Greek in the Septuagint, whose translation of the same word was rendered "virgin." Matthew chose the Septuagint text, however, probably because he wanted to apply to Jesus a proof text that would claim for him all the glory claimed by other great kings. This verse in Isaiah justified the virgin birth story. (2) From Micah 5:1, 3 Luke found the following prophecy: "And you, Bethlehem, are by no means the least among the chiefs of Judah, for from you will come a chief who will shepherd my people Israel." This text provided proof that the Messiah was predestined to be born in Bethlehem, so there would be no reason to interview witnesses to learn where Jesus had been born. Since he was the Messiah, there was no other possibility. The scripture was the only place to look for information, so the author of the saga prepared a narrative that took Bethlehem into account. Since Jesus was born there, the author also assumed that his parents had lived in Bethlehem at the time. (3) Hosea had said, "Out of Egypt I have called my son." Since the Messiah was the only Son of God, this text must apply to Jesus; the only question was how. Somehow the Messiah must have been in Egypt so that the Lord could call him out from there, as he had done with Moses. The task of the ''historian'' was to deduce how this could have come about. (4) Jeremiah prophesied,

The voice in Ramah was heard,
mourning and great lamentation
Rachel weeping for her children,
and she did not want to be comforted,
because they were not (Jer 31:15).

Rachel, of course, had lived more than a thousand years earlier and would not have known about the children around Bethlehem at the time of Herod the Great, but that was no deterring factor. According to the rabbis, there is no before and after in scripture (Hor. 8a; CantR. 1:2). Jeremiah was a prophet. Therefore, he would have been speaking only of the days of the Messiah. Why would there be weeping in Herod's day? Herod must have slaughtered Rachel's descendants the way Pharaoh had done with the Hebrew children in Egypt. (5) Knowing that Jesus had been called a Nazoraios, the author presumed that this also must have been prophesied. Upon studying the scripture, he learned from Judges 13:5 that, with reference to Samson, it was said, ''He shall be called a Nazarite.'' Here, then, was another prophecy that was fulfilled in the days of the Messiah. This prophecy accounted both for the fact that Jesus was called a Nazoraios and the likelihood that he lived in Nazareth. Parker[13] has shown that the word Nazoraios does not come either from Nazarite or Nazareth. It was the name of an early Jewish sect which has survived to this day in the Fertile Crescent. Nazaraions are members of the Mandaean sect whose members trace their religious ancestry to John the Baptist. When Paul became a Christian he was also considered a member of the Nazoraios sect (Acts 24:5) associated with Jesus, the Nazoraios (Acts 26:9).

Since the Matthaean author deduced the town Nazareth from the prophecy in Judges rather than learning it from local records, Jesus may never have lived in Nazareth at all. Luke's reference to Nazareth (Lk 4:16) may have been derived from Matthew's deduction, and John may have obtained the information the same way (Jn 1:45; 2:12), and on the basis of this, like Matthew 4:13, arranged for amove from Nazareth to Capernaum (Jn 1:12) where Jesus apparently lived (so also Mk 1:9, 21). When he was

---

[13]P. Parker, *The Gospel Before Mark* (Chicago, 1953), pp. 92-96. See also J. Thomas, *Le Mouvement Baptist in Palestine et Syrie* (Gembloux, 1935), pp. 157-6O, and N. J. Schoeps, *Theologie und Geschichte des Judenchristentums* (Tübingen, 1949), pp. 10, 285.

in his house (Matt 9:7), Jesus was at Capernaum, not Nazareth (Mk 2:1). John also had a report of Jesus teaching in the synagogue at Capernaum (Jn 6:59) and of a poor reception from his home community of Capernaum (Jn 11:22-24). Much of Jesus' activity was centered around Capernaum and the Sea of Galilee and John wrote as if it were common knowledge that Jesus was from Galilee, but the precise town of Nazareth may simply be the deduction Matthew made on the basis of the similarity of the words, Nazarite, Nazoriaos, and Nazareth. Since one of these words was included in a prophecy (Jdgs 13:5), this would have been considered adequate proof of historical reality in Judaism of those days, but it is not acceptable to modern historians.

These five prophecies provided Matthew all the scriptural authorization he needed for composition of the narrative, but these were only his proof texts. He constructed his saga primarily on the basis of typologies to determine what was predestined to take place about that time.

Typologies. Part of the reason gospel writers believed that Jesus was the Messiah was their analysis of the turn of the cycles of time. They had seen signs in their contemporary history that they could match with events related to the exodus from Egypt. Furthermore, they had probably calculated sabbaths, jubilees, and periods of time from strategic events that convinced them that the time of the Gentile rule had been fulfilled. They were then living in the last days of the Gentile era and were about to enter into the new era of Jewish rule, the age to come. In the predestined schedule of events, God must have been ready to deliver his chosen people from the new Egypt. Matthew structured his entire gospel after the Hexateuch to indicate the position of his generation in the new exodus.[14] The birth narrative was only part of this structure, but it was an important factor that the author worked

---

[14]See A. Farrer, "On Dispensing with Q," D. E. Nineham (ed.), *Studies in the Gospels* (Oxford, 1955), pp. 75-77; W. D. Davies, *The Setting of the Sermon on the Mount* (Cambridge, 1964), p. 78; and B. Gärtner, *Die Rätselhaften Termini Nazoraer und Iskariot* (Lund, 1957). For decrees like, "the future redeemer will be like the former redeemer," see RuthR 5:6; NumR 11:2. See also R. Bloch, "Quelques Aspects de la Future de Moise dan la Tradition Rabbinique," *Moise l'Homme de l'Alliance* (Tournai, c1955), pp. 93-167 in *Cahiers Sionens* 7-8 (1953/54):211-85; L. Landman, *Messianism in the Talmudic Era* (New York, 1979), pp. xxxi, 27 (15), 30 (18); and J. Klausner, *The Messianic Idea,* tr. W. F. Stinespring (New York, 1955), p. 17.

in with the fulfillment of prophecies. The very beginning of Matthew was designed to remind the reader of the Book of Genesis:

Gen 5:1: "This is the Book of the   Matt 1:1: "The Book of the Gene-
Genesis of men. . . ."   sis of Jesus the Messiah. . . ."

The quotation taken from the Septuagint was probably used as a representative quotation, defining the whole etiological section (Gen 1:1—11:32), on the one hand, and as an introduction to the Book of Genesis, on the other. The etiological stories provide a background for the history of the Hebrew people beginning with Abraham (Gen 12:1).

The next Genesis section includes the stories of the patriarchs, beginning with Abraham, giving lists of their posterity down to the activity of Joseph (Gen 12:1—36:43). The equivalent section of Matthew lists the patriarchs, beginning with Abraham, as the ancestors of Jesus. These ancestors reach as far as Joseph (Matt 1:2-17).

Following the patriarch section, Genesis 37:1—50:26 includes stories of Joseph of Egypt, including his dreams and chastity in relationship to Pharaoh's wife although to outsiders the whole situation looked suspicious. This section also tells of Joseph's migration to Egypt, a move which later seemed to have been predestined to save the sons of Israel. The corresponding section of Matthew tells of Joseph's dreams, chastity, and virtue in relationship to Mary. Out of concern for the Son, he fled with his family to Egypt (Matt 1:18—2:15). Here ends the "Genesis" section of the Gospel of Matthew, but the parallels continue into the "Exodus" section:

EXOD 1:2—2:25: Changes of kings; slaughter of male children by the king; Moses' flight from Egypt.

MATT 2:16-23: Slaughter of male children by the king; change of kings; journey of Jesus and family from Egypt to Nazareth.

EXOD 4:27-31: Aaron addressed the Israelites; the people believed and rejoiced that God had visited his people. They believed and worshipped.

John addressed the Israelites. All Jeruslaem, Judaea, and all the region around the Jordan, came to him, confessing their sins and being baptized.

EXOD 14:1—15:21: Children of Israel approached the Reed Sea and came through it.

MATT 3:13-17: Jesus approached the Jordan River and was baptized.

EXOD 15:22—17:16: Moses and the Israelites were taken up from the sea and went into the wilderness.

The Israelites were thirsty and hungry, and they tempted the Lord.

Moses provided miracles to meet the needs of the people.

MATT 4:1-11: Jesus was led up from the River Jordan into the wilderness by the Spirit.

There he was tempted by the devil. After forty days and nights of fasting, Jesus was hungry.

He refused to perform miracles, thereby also refusing to tempt the Lord his God.

This is not the end of the Matthaean parallels with the Torah, but it is enough to show Matthew's conscious attempt to reconstruct the early history of Jesus' movement in parallel with early Hebrew history. He prepared a genealogy that went from Abraham to Joseph, just as Genesis provided. Mary was betrothed to Joseph, who was the antitype of Joseph of Egypt, being exceptionally meritorious about sexual propriety and having dreams to meet his problems. This all fit together with the prophecy of Isaiah to provide a virgin birth narrative. Herod was the antitype for the pharaoh that did not know Joseph. Just as Pharaoh slaughtered the infant male children, the author presumed Herod must also have slaughtered infant male children, but just as Pharaoh missed Moses in the process, so also Herod missed Jesus. Since the ancient Joseph spent his fruitful years in Egypt, it was necessary for the Matthaean narrator to arrange the Joseph antitype to get to Egypt. Otherwise readers might not notice the intended correspondence between the two. In the judgment of the author, he was not fictitiously composing stories. He had discovered by studying the scriptures the proximity between the cycles of time at the exodus from Egypt and his own which was the function of a prophet. This was no tragic poet or fiction writer; he was one who knew earlier cycles of history so well that he understood just where his generation was in the corresponding cycle of time. He probably did not first see the prophecy of Jeremiah and then find a corresponding typology that supported it. It was probably the other way around. Knowing that there had been a slaughter of infants in Egypt, he reasoned that there must have been a corresponding slaughter of infants with the birth of Jesus. Once this had been "established," he supported this conviction with a proof text of Rachel weeping for her children. With two such strong witnesses, who could doubt that it had really happened? Many twentieth century Americans would, of course, but not many persons who lived in Jesus' time. Two witnesses were enough to condemn a man to death in court; therefore, Matthew was careful to provide two or three illustrations as biblical witnesses to most of his arguments. In the birth narrative, his two major witnesses were typology and prophecy.

It was only because the scripture said, "He shall be called a Nazarite," and because Jesus had also been called "the Nazoraios" that Matthew presumed Jesus' home must have been in Nazareth. This also supplemented the reputation he and his followers had of having come from Galilee. Since he had been born in Bethlehem, according to prophecy, it would be necessary to get Jesus to Nazareth, somehow. Again, prophecy came to the aid of the author. Hosea said, "Out of Egypt I have called my Son." This meant Jesus was to leave Egypt. This was also indicated by the death of Herod. Here were two witnesses to prove what must have happened. Joseph's dreams also came to the rescue. Through a dream Joseph was told to go to Nazareth rather than return to Bethlehem. This dream was confirmed by the proof text, "He shall be a Nazarite." In the judgment of the literary artist, he was only putting together obvious data to interpret the events that must have taken place.

Summary. Like the author of the Lukan narrative, Matthew really was composing a saga rather than a historical report, but that was the kind of history Jews were writing in those days. It was not enough to tell the bare facts of history; the author had a religious, prophetic obligation to tell what the facts meant. The virgin birth narrative was designed to attribute to Jesus that which was the heritage of the greatest kings. By using this medium, the author told how he felt about Jesus. He also confirmed this feeling by other testimonies that were suitable for kings. For Matthew, this was the arrival of the Magicians from the East; for Luke this was the Magnificat, the Benedictus, and the Nunc Dimittus, giving poetic content to OT prophecies confessing the conviction that this child was predestined to grow and become the one who would redeem Israel from the hand of the oppressor. Although the typological identities prove nothing actual about the events that happened in NT times, they show how the author felt and how he understood the times in which he lived in relationship to the general cyclical plan of God. He thought he had been reading the signs correctly, so he designed the narrative in such a way as to convince his readers that his analysis was correct. It was much more important to Jews of his day to know how long it would be before God would expel the Romans and restore the promised land than to know the exact age of John or Jesus when they began their public ministry.

Both Luke and Matthew were more like prophets than historians, but they were scholars believed to be astute in deducing unknown history on the bases of prophecy, typology, Jewish customs, and other convictions which were central to their messages. Other materials, such as the date of John's conception, the length of Mary's pregnancy, the date of the Roman taxation, and the number of miles between Nazareth and Judah were secondary details. According to Matthew, Jesus was called Joshua which means "Jehovah saves" because he was predestined to "save" his people from their sins (Matt 1:21). This passage makes sense in a Semitic language, not in Greek, indicating that it was written originally in Hebrew or Aramaic.

From the historian's point of view, these sagas do not provide much information about where and when Jesus was actually born. According to John, people said Jesus did not qualify as a messiah because the Messiah was expected to be of the seed of David and be born in Bethlehem, whereas Jesus came from Galilee and people seemed to think he had been born there (Jn 7:41-43). Matthew and Luke followed different logic: *Since* Jesus was the Messiah, he *must* have been born in Bethlehem, and he *must* have been a descendant of David's line, so they wrote their sagas to express that conviction. The fact that they believed the prophecies were accurately fulfilled, however, does not mean their sagas represent historical fact. The same is true of the prophetic basis for claiming Nazareth for Jesus' home town. This is conviction and not necessarily historical fact. From these attempts of religious leaders to write sagas, we learn their convictions but not history. If we did not have the reports of the Hasmonean revolt in 1 and 2 Maccabees and the histories of Josephus we probably would not be able to deduce all of this from Daniel alone. From the birth narratives, in the same way, historians have to be agnostic about such reports as the place and time of Jesus' birth, the place where the family lived, the appearance of a star, the visit of the wise men, the shepherds, the slaughter of the infants, the trip to Egypt, the virgin conception of Mary, the dreams of Joseph, and all other ideas of these sagas that are based on prophecy or typology rather than known historical facts. These narratives were attempts of the later church to reconstruct the earlier history of Jesus' life on the basis of their convictions and their understanding of typology and history. Luke had still another way of writing history. He took reports that he had received from other sources and expanded them midrashically.

Jesus' Homecoming Sermon

Matthew's Text.

The following text appears both in Matthew and Mark with so few variants that it is impossible to determine which source Luke used. In both cases this appears to be a chreia that has been expanded. The conjectured expansions are indicated by brackets. The words used in Luke's commentary are underscored, whether exactly or in some variation.

> And after he came to his home town, he taught them in their syn-
> agogue, so that they were astonished and said, "From where does this
> man get this wisdom and these miracles? [Is not this the son of the car-
> penter? Is not his mother called Mary, and are not his brothers James, Jo-
> seph, Simon, and Judas? Are not his sisters all with us? Then, from where
> does he get all these things?]" And they were offended by him. But Jesus
> said to them, "A prophet is not without honor except in his own home-
> town and in his house" (Matt 13:54-57).

If the bracketed portion were omitted, this would be a chreia. Luke, however, used either this entire text, the Markan parallel (6:1-6), or the source used by both, because commentary is made both to the chreia and to the expansion, as the underlining shows.

Luke's Homily.

> And he came to Nazareth, where he had been brought up, and, according to his custom on the Sabbath day, he entered into the synagogue, and stood up to read [scripture]. Now there was given to him the scroll of the prophet Isaiah, and, after he had opened the scroll, he found the place where it was written:
>
> "The Spirit of the Lord is upon me,
> because he has anointed me
> to announce good news to the poor.
> He has sent me to proclaim release to the captives,
> and the opening of the eyes for the blind,
> to provide release to the prisoners,
> to proclaim the year of the Lord's favor" (Isa 61:1-2).
>
> Then he closed the scroll, gave it back to the attendant, and sat down. The eyes of all those in the synagogue were directed to him, and he began to say to them, "Today, this scripture is fulfilled in your ears." Then all bore witness to him and were astonished at the gracious words which went out from his mouth, and they began to say, "Is not this the son of Jo-

seph?'' Then he said to them, ''You will surely tell me this parable, 'Physician, heal yourself! The things that we heard had happened in Capernaum, do also here in your home town.' '' Then he continued, ''I tell you under oath, 'A prophet is not accepted in his home town.' Truly, I tell you, there were many widows in Israel during the days of Elijah, when the heaven was closed for three years and six months, and there was a great famine upon all the land, but to none of them was Elijah sent except 'to Serepta of Sidon, a widow woman' (1 Kgs 17:9). There were also many lepers in Israel in the days of Elisha, the prophet, but none of them was healed except Naaman, the Syrian.'' Then, after they had heard these things, they all were filled with anger, and they arose and threw him out of the city, and they led him to the edge of the cliff upon which the city was built in order to throw him down, but he passed through their midst and left (Lk 4:16-29).

Observations. Luke developed the text from Matthew, Mark, or their source, filling in many of the uncertainties. Matthew's text did not say what Jesus' home town was; Luke identified this, perhaps inaccurately, as Nazareth. Luke distinguished this from the other possibility of Capernaum, where Jesus had apparently performed miracles. From his text, Luke learned that Jesus taught in the synagogue, meaning that he taught them many times. Luke altered this to concentrate on one special event when Jesus gave his opening sermon. Luke further understood the text's statement, ''He taught them,'' to mean that he first read a text and then sat down and interpreted it, so Luke added the appropriate text from Isaiah which itself was a commentary on the Leviticus text on Jubilee release (Lev 25:10). Then, returning to his text, Luke gave the response of the congregation with some expansion. Apparently acquainted with the methods the rhetoricians taught for developing a homily from a chreia, Luke supplied Jesus with a proverb (which he called a parable) and two illustrations from the OT to support his argument, after which he gave further response on the part of the congregation, accentuating the extent of Jesus' rejection.

This was another way in which the church wrote ''history.'' Luke had already traced events in Jesus' life from birth to the beginning of his campaign. Here he provided a specific occasion for that beginning, but he did not construct the narrative as fiction. He based his construction on a text that he had already received and believed to be reliable. Luke simply developed that text, homiletically, the way other gospel writers did (Matt 15; Mk 7). When he did this he employed some of the very homiletic devices the rhetoricians trained their students to use,[15] but he did not learn this from such rhetoricians as Theon, Nicolaus, or Aphthonius, all of whom came later. These methods of exegesis had evidently been developed before the time either of Luke or Theon. This method of exegesis became popular no matter who first introduced it and preachers have been elaborating texts in much the same way ever since. This method was accepted among the rabbis and church fathers as well as rhetoricians. This expansion of the expanded chreia, rather than historical fact, is somewhat of a distortion, and the modern historian would not accept this as historically valid. The text Luke used may once have been an unexpanded chreia, telling, rather generally, that Jesus received less than a hearty welcome with full support from his home town, whatever that was. Since Jesus, reportedly, had singled out Capernaum for condemnation because of its rejection (Jn 11:22-24) and since Jesus is also reported to have taught in the synagogue there (Jn 6:59), there is a little more evidence for thinking Jesus' home town was Capernaum than Nazareth, as Luke specified.

Even though Luke's attempt at filling in unknown parts of Jesus' history seems to be inaccurate, it would still be unfair to attribute to this author improper motives or accuse him of deliberately falsifying history. He applied accepted methods of homiletics when he composed this homily. He just did not write history as Thucydides, Herodotus, or Polybius would have done.

Thucydides also warned against reporting as fact any supernatural events said to have taken place. The historian, he said, could only report that people *said* this or that miracle had happened. The gospel writers, however, wrote "history" from a different point of view, with different rules. Those who made the rules in the first place were dogmaticians rather than objective historians. The next step here will be to consider whether the miracles were historical events or deductions of "historians."

The Historicity of the Miracles

Problems. The miracles attributed to Jesus provide a problem for the historian, because there is no real way by which miracles can be tested as teachings can. Did they happen, or did they not? The evidence is inconclu-

---

[15]Not noticing the relationship of Luke's homily to the text on which it was based, M. Burrows, "The Origin of the Term, 'Gospel,' " *JBL* 44 (1925):31, was followed by E. F. Scott in saying "[this Lukan homily] is one of the most historical incidents in the Gospel narrative."

sive, and different readers will assess it differently. An attempt will be made to show what factors should be taken into account in making a decision.

There is a great deal of similarity between ancient demonology, angelology, and emotional healing performed by ancient magicians and described in ancient mythology and that currently applied by psychoanalysts through guided imagery. Ancient mythologists and magicians probably understood that one of the important ways to emotional truth and health was through fantasy.[16] The ancient magician was as well respected in antiquity as the psychoanalyst is today and probably for the same reasons.

Jesus would not have been unique if he performed miracles. Pharisees of his day were held to have performed miracles (Matt 12:27). In those days miracles were attributed to many great leaders. Rabbis were said to have performed miracles; many people were claimed to have been healed in temples of Asclepius; Moses and Aaron had a wand through which they were said to perform miracles in Egypt and the Wilderness. Messiahs were expected to prove their office by performing miracles (Matt 24:24). In the seventh century A.D. a messianic pretender gathered a following because he had healed a leper.[17] Much later another pretender, Moses Dari, predicted that on a certain day it would rain blood and it did.[18] In France a certain Ben Arieh attracted followers because he was able to flutter through the air in the tree tops at night.[19] Some messiahs, however, were accepted without miracles. One of these was Bar Kokhba in the second century A.D. and another was David Alroy during the Crusades.[20]

Prophecies. Those who believed that all prophecy was fulfilled in the days of the Messiah and that Jesus was the Messiah looked to the OT to learn that which was predicted to take place in their days. Some of the passages they could have found were as follows:

> Then the deaf will hear the words of the book,
> and the eyes of the blind will see

---

[16]See further M. Watkins, *Waking Dreams* (New York, 1976) and G. Adler, *The Living Symbol* (New York, 1969).

[17]GWB, *Revelation*, p. 97.

[18]Ibid., p. 98.

[19]Ibid., p. 100.

[20]Ibid., p. 191.

out of deep darkness.
The humble will rejoice again in the Lord,
and the poor will exult in the holy One of Israel

(Isa 29:18-19).

Then the eyes of the blind will be opened,
and the ears of the deaf, unstopped
then the cripple will leap like a deer,
and the tongue of the dumb will sing for joy.
Waters will break out in the wilderness,
and streams, in the desert;
the burning sand will become a pool of water,
and thirsty ground, springs

(Isa 35:5-7).

"Those who despoil you shall become a spoil,
and all who prey on you I shall make a prey.
For I will restore health to you,
and your wounds I will heal,"
says the Lord

(Jer 30:17).

For thus says the Lord: "Look!
I will bring them from the north country,
and gather them from the ends of the earth.
Among them will be the blind, the lame,
the pregnant woman, and the one bearing
a child together"

(Jer 31:7-8).

Thus said the Lord God, "Look! I will open your graves and raise you
from your graves, O my people. I will bring you home into the land of
Israel, and you shall know that I am the Lord, when I open your graves"
(Ezek 37:12-13).

As in the days when you came out of the land of Egypt, I will show them
marvelous things

(Micah 7:15).

Typologies. In addition to prophecies, it was expected that the Messiah
would perform the miracles that had been performed by the great leaders
before him. Moses, for instance, controlled the waters of the Reed Sea so
the people could pass over it on dry land (Exod 14:16-29). He healed Miriam of her leprosy (Num 12:10-16), brought down manna from heaven for
food (Exod 16:4-30), and struck the rock and made water flow (Exod 17:5-

7). When Joshua wanted to cross the Jordan, the waters parted for their crossing (Josh 33:14-17). When the Hebrews marched around Jericho, the walls of the city fell flat (Josh 6:1-20). Elijah multiplied the meal for the widow of Zerephath (1 Kgs 17:8-16) and revived her son (1 Kgs 17:17-24). Elisha multiplied the loaves (2 Kgs 4:42-44), called down fire from heaven to consume approaching soldiers (2 Kgs 1:10-12), healed Naaman's leprosy at long distance (2 Kgs 5:1-14), revived the Shunamite's son who had died (2 Kgs 4:18-37), and filled the oil jars magically (2 Kgs 4:1-7). These were all miracles that had been performed by prophets and great leaders in the past. In the days of the Messiah, it was presumed that they would all happen again.[21] After all, in the predestined cycles of time, all of these things would be repeated. So certain were Jews that they were living in "the last days" of the Roman era, when the new exodus would begin, that many Jews followed a messianic pretender, Theudas, who said he would lead them to the Jordan River and the waters would separate for them so that they could cross over on dry land. Fadus sent his cavalry out to meet them. They killed many, took the rest prisoners, and beheaded Theudas (*Ant* 20.97-99). An Egyptian pretender led a Jewish following up to the Mount of Olives and promised to make the walls fall as they had for Joshua at Jericho. Roman troops again interfered (*Ant* 20.169-72). Another guerrilla leader met with a multitude in the wilderness, promising to renew the wilderness miracles, but Festus killed most of the group and took the rest as slaves (*Ant* 20.188).[22] The failure of these movements did not weaken Jewish resolve; Jews expected miracles to happen in their day as they had in periods of earlier deliverances.

Jesus and Miracles. The chreias show that when people asked Jesus for a sign, he said no sign would be given (Matt 12:38-39; 16:1-4; Mk 8:11-12; Lk 11:29). Nevertheless, Jesus is pictured in the gospels, performing many miracles. How did this come about? One possibility is that he really performed this come about? One possibility is that he really performed miracles, even though he said he would not. The other is that the church knew

---

[21]For miracles in the messianic age, see L. Landman, *Messianism*, p. xxiv.

[22]Sometime before A.D. 1492, a large Jewish army was gathered near Ancone, Italy, in a desert, prepared to attack Rome. Another group was to attack Arabia, and still a third would march against Edom to deliver the Jews from exile. They were organized according to Numbers 2 and had the Tetragrammaton and ten commandments as standards. So. J. Mann, "Glanures de la Gueniza," *REJ* 74 (1922):148. There were messianic movements through the sixteenth century. See GWB, *Revelation*. These were organized in various ways to fit typologies. See also J. Kastein, *The Messiah of Ismir*, tr. H. Peterson (New York, 1931), pp. 17-18, 33, 73.

he must have performed miracles because the Messiah was foretold to do this. On the basis of typology and prophecy, the church might have deduced that miracles had been performed even though they had no record of them. Therefore, the role of the mythologist was to learn from scripture the kind of miracles the Messiah was predestined to perform and fill in the details.

There are some indications that this was done, at least in some instances. For example, after Peter's mother-in-law's fever left, Matthew reports that at evening they brought many to him who were possessed with demons and he cast out the demons and healed the sick. "This was to fulfill that which was spoken by the prophet Isaiah, 'He took away our sicknesses and bore our diseases'" (Isa 53:4; Matt 8:16-17). After he healed a man with a withered hand, many followed them, and he healed them all so as to fulfill the prophecy of Isa 42:1-4.

In addition to these Matthaean miracles that are explained as fulfillment of scripture there are also others patterned after the miracles of Elijah and Elisha in the Fourth Gospel and synoptic parallels. The miracles of Elisha are also anti-types of the Elijah miracles, but there are fourteen, rather than seven, because Elisha was promised a double portion of Elijah's spirit (2 Kgs 2:9-12). Their miracles are as follows:[23]

ELISHA PARALLELS	ELIJAH MIRACLES	ELISHA MIRACLES
2	A. Stopped rain (1 Kgs 17:1-6)	1. Divide waters of Jordan (2 Kgs 2:2-14)
2, 8, 9	B. Provided widow's meal and oil (1 Kgs 17:8-16)	2. Purified water at Jericho (2 Kgs 2:19-23)
6, 7, 10, 14	C. Revived widow's son (1 Kgs 17:17-24)	3. Called bears to destroy 42 boys (2 Kgs 2:23-24)
4	D. Called down fire from heaven (1 Kgs 18:1-40)	4. Filled stream bed with water (2 Kgs 3:13-20)
3, 11, 13	E. Fire consumed soldiers (2 Kgs 1:9-10)	5. Filled son of prophet's wife's oil jars (2 Kgs 4:1-7)
	F. Fire consumed soldiers (2 Kgs 1:11-12)	6. Provided son for Shunamite woman (2 Kgs 4:8-17)
1, 12	G. Parted waters of Jordan (2 Kgs 2:8)	7. Revived Shunamite's son (2 Kgs 4:18-37)

[23]This discussion on Johannine miracles was previously published by GWB, "The Samaritan Origin of the Gospel of John," *Religions in Antiquity* (Leiden, 1970), pp. 149-75.

8. Purified stew (2 Kgs 4:38-41)

9. Multiplied loaves (2 Kgs 4:42-44)

10. Cured commander's leprosy (2 Kgs 5:1-14)

11. Afflicted Gahazi with leprosy (2 Kgs 5:19-27)

12. Made ax head float (2 Kgs 6:1-7)

13. Struck Syrians with blindness (2 Kgs 6:15-19)

14. Man revived who touched Elisha's bones (2 Kgs 13:21)

When the seven miracles of Jesus in the Fourth Gospel are compared with the miracles of Elijah and Elisha, the units fit in this chart as follows:

ELIJAH PARALLEL	ELISHA PARALLELS	SIGNS OF JESUS
B	2, 4, 5, 8	1. Changed water to wine (2:1-11)
	10	2. Healed centurion's son (4:46-54)
		3. Healed lame man at pool 5:2-9)
B	9	4. Multiplied loaves (6:4-14)
G	1, 12, 13	5. Walked on water (6:16-21)
		6. Healed blind beggar at Pool of Siloam (9:1-7)
C	7, 14	7. Raised Lazarus (11:1-44)

Some of the more obvious parallels are the following;

JESUS (JN 1:1-11)	ELIJAH (1 KGS 17:1-6)	ELISHA (2 KGS 4:1-7)
1. Woman recognized need; host unable to fulfill hospitality obligation	Woman in need; embarrassed by hospitality obligation	Woman in need; unable to meet obligation to creditor
2. Asked Jesus for help		Asked Elisha for help
3. Response seemed unreasonable: ''What have you to do with me?''	Request seemed unreasonable.	Response: ''What shall I do for you?''

4. Mary: "Do whatever he tells you."	Elijah: "Do as you have said."	
5. Jesus ordered jars filled with water and taken to the steward		Elisha ordered jars brought and filled
6. Order fulfilled	Order fulfilled	Order fulfilled
7. Abundance of wine	Abundance of meal and oil	Abundance of oil
8. Hospitality obligation paid	Hospitality obligation paid	Financial obligation paid

The miracles of Elisha are similar enough to each other in instances where he provided for people that the Johannine sign has parallels with all of them (2 Kgs 2:19-20; 3:13-20; 4:38-41). But the parallels involving women, both with Elijah and Elisha, are closer types from which the Johannine story was probably formed.

"The Centurion's Son"

JESUS (JN 4:46-54)	ELISHA (2 KGS 5:1-14)
1. Official's son ill.	Army officer had leprosy.
2. Came to Jesus for help.	Came to Elisha for help.
3. Jesus questioned his faith.	
4. Jesus told him to leave; his son was well (distance healing).	Elisha sent messenger to give directions (distance healing).
	(3) [John out of sequence] Officer questioned that this would work.
5. Officer believed and left.	Officer decided to follow instructions.
6. Son (a child) was well.	Officer's flesh restored like that of a child.

Two other healing miracles Jesus performed took place at pools. The first man healed (5:2-9) expected to have to be dipped in the pool as Naaman was directed by Elisha to go and wash, but Jesus told him to get up, take his cot, and walk. The blind man at the Pool of Siloam (9:1-7), however, was instructed to wash in the pool as Naaman had been told to bathe in the Jordan. Like Naaman, after he had done so, he was healed; he had received his sight.

"Multiplication of Loaves"

JESUS (JN 6:4-14)	ELISHA (2 KGS 4:42-44)
1. Great crowd arrived at Passover time.	Sons of prophets gathered.
2. Andrew brought boy with barley loaves and fishes.	Man from Beal-shalishah came with barley loaves and fresh grain.
3. Andrew, Jesus' disciple, said it was not enough.	Elisha's servant said there was not enough.
4. Jesus blessed the food and had it distributed.	Elisha commanded that the men be fed and promised some would be left.
5. All ate and were filled and twelve baskets full of food were left over.	All ate, and they had some left as Elisha promised.

There is some resemblance between miracles and the occasion when Elijah multiplied the meal and the oil for the widow (1 Kgs 17:1-6). In all instances hospitality was required of people who apparently had not enough to provide it. In all instances the prophet involved performed a miracle which made the small amount of food there was become more than enough.

"Nature Miracles"

The power Jesus had over the forces of nature was shown in his ability to walk on the water (6:16-21). The same power was shown by Elijah and Elisha when they divided the water of the Jordan and walked across on dry lang (2 Kgs 2:8, 14). Elisha showed that he had a double portion of his master's spirit by also making an ax head float (6:1-7). Details of these miracles are not very close.

"Raising the Dead"

JESUS (JN 11:1-44)	ELIJAH (1 KGS 17:17-24)	ELISHA (2 KGS 4:18-37)
1. Jesus had special relationship with family at Bethany.	Elijah received hospitality from widow of Zerephah.	Elisha had received special hospitality from Shunamite woman.

| 2. Lazarus became ill and died. | Widow's son became ill and died. | Shunamite's son became ill and died. |
| 3. Mary and Martha blamed Jesus: "If you had been here, my brother would not have died." | Widow blamed Elijah for her son's death. | Shunamite blamed Elisha for deceiving her by giving a son and taking him away again. |

Some other details suggest that these similarities are more than coincidental. The picture of the Shunamite woman weeping at Elisha's feet after the death of her son (2 Kgs 4:27) resembles Mary who fell at Jesus' feet after the death of her brother (Jn 11:32). The resurrection miracle was the seventh miracle that Elisha performed and also the seventh that Jesus performed. Since Elisha had a double portion of Elijah's spirit, he also performed a second resurrection miracle, even after his death, when a corpse that touched his bones revived (2 Kgs 13:21). This was Elisha's fourteenth miracle. The miracles of Elisha follow a type that is similar to the miracles of Elijah. This does not mean that every miracle Elijah performed had exactly two counterparts in the Elisha stories. One has no parallel and another has four, but some are closer than others, and the total is exactly twice as many as Elijah had performed. The miracles of Jesus in the Gospel of John follow the typologies of Elijah and Elisha to about the same degree, being closer to the miracles of Elisha and Elijah.

Observations. No attempt will be made here to examine every miracle, one-by-one, to see how many can be explained directly in terms of typology and/or prophecy being fulfilled. It is obvious that there were prophecies that could be understood to need fulfillment in this way. It was also clear that pretending messiahs tried to validate themselves by performing some of the signs that were characteristic of the exodus either from Egypt or Babylon. The gospel writers themselves explained miracles as the fulfillment of prophecy and the miracles of the Fourth Gospel seem intentionally patterned after the prototypes of Elijah and Elisha miracles. Furthermore, some of the miracles are accompanied by peculiar situations: Jesus healed someone before thousands of people and then told them not to tell anyone (Matt 12:15; Mk 3:12)! That is no way to keep secrets, but it may have been a way the gospel writers had of explaining how it happened that no one had seen any of Jesus' miracles if he had performed so many. That device at once argues that there had been many witnesses and they had all been told to keep the miracles secret. If Jesus had been so skillful in performing miracles it would have been to his advantage to have performed one before the Sanhedrin or Pilate, but no such miracle appeared. Furthermore his answer to those who asked him for a sign from Heaven was that one would not be given.

There is enough evidence to cast some serious doubt on some, if not all, of the miracles attributed to Jesus.[24] There is none of the confidence in dealing with miracles of the gospels that there is in dealing with the chreias and parables, but this is not the whole story. When the disciples of John asked Jesus if he was the one who was to come, he answered: "Go, tell John what you see and hear: The blind receive their sight; the lame walk; the lepers are cleansed; the deaf hear; the dead are raised; and the poor receive the good news; and blessed is he who is not offended in me" (Matt 11:4-5). Does this not say clearly that Jesus was performing all of these miracles? Probably not. The real message Jesus wanted John to hear was that the prophecy of Isa 29 was being fulfilled. The important prophecy was one he could not say out loud before the Romans: "The terrible one (Herod) will come to nothing, and the scoffer (Herod) will cease" (Isa 29:20). Since he could not tell John directly that he was working on getting rid of Herod, he told them a list of things, some of which were quotations from the verses just before the one he wanted to communicate. Those who knew scripture would have recognized this subversive allusion and returned encouraged. It is not likely that they actually *saw* all the things he mentioned. Who had been raised from the dead before their eyes? If that had really happened it probably would have received more "press coverage" than it did, but there is still one more objection: In a chreia, when the Pharisees told Jesus that Herod wanted to kill him, he responded, "Tell that fox, 'Look! I cast out demons and perform cures, today and tomorrow. . . .' " (Lk 13:31-32), seeming to claim that Jesus was actively involved in healing.

Different readers will appraise this evidence differently. It is not a closed case, but some of the methods the early church had of reconstructing unknown areas of Jesus' life have been shown to indicate how these authors reasoned. They were not malicious fiction writers. They presented what they believed were the normal conclusions of their beliefs on the basis of scripture, typology, and accepted methods of exegesis. They searched the

---

[24]Contra R. Bultmann, *Jesus and the Word*, tr. L. P. Smith and E. H. Lantero (New York, c1958), p. 173, who said, "But there can be no doubt that Jesus did the kind of deeds which were miracles to his mind and to the minds of his contemporaries . . ."

scriptures and when they found two supporting proof texts or typologies they believed that proved that the item involved was fact. They had only to record it. Another blind area, not included in parables and chreias, consists of the events around the cross. That will be considered next.

The Final Agony

The Problem. When Jesus was captured, the apostles soon vanished. How, then, could later generations know how Jesus reacted to this time of suffering? What happened at the cross? How did Jesus respond, and what were his thoughts and feelings? Without witnesses, Herodotus or Thucydides might have said they did not know. Authors like Matthew and Luke, however, who had been trained in rabbinic research and exegesis, would not have felt so severely limited as historians would have been. They could always look to the scripture to find what had been prophesied. What were the typological possibilities for a person facing death unjustly? There were two lengthy Psalms expressing the feelings of men in despair, crying out to the Lord. Jesus must have reacted as an anti-type to these. Therefore Matthew wove these two Psalms (22 and 69) together to recover this unknown part of Jesus' life.

The Prophecies. Psalm 22 begins with a cry of despair of one who thought God had forsaken him. In times past Israelites had cried to the Lord and he delivered them. The Psalmist, however, had become an object of ridicule. People mocked him for trusting the Lord. The Psalmist suffered hunger, thirst, and physical pain. People pierced his hands and feet, divided his garments among themselves, casting lots. Nevertheless, the author cried to the Lord in confidence, assured that God was not far off. He vowed that he would continue to praise the Lord, knowing that he alone ruled over nations and that all the proud people of the earth would have to bow down to the Lord.

Psalm 69 describes a man who had become hoarse from crying out; he was sunk into the mire, with no place to stand. Multitudes gathered around attacking him with lies, desiring his death. No one came to his rescue; all his friends had forsaken him; he was given poison for food and vinegar to drink. All of this suffering and embarrassment was because of the Psalmist's defense of the Lord. Therefore, he called on the Lord to come to his rescue, destroy his foes, rescue the Psalmist, and blot out his enemies from the Book of Life. Then the Psalmist would praise the Lord for his salvation.

The Projections. With these two Psalms as the required two witnesses to prove his case, the Matthaean mythologist reconstructed the experience of Jesus at the cross. There his attackers must have offered Jesus vinegar to drink (Matt 27:33-34) because this was prophesied in Psalm 69:22. They also must have divided his garments, casting lots for them, because this was prophesied in Psalm 22:19. They blasphemed Jesus, shaking their heads (Matt 27:38), because that is what Ps 22:9 foretold. They mocked him for trusting in God, thinking God would rescue him (Matt 27:43). This was obvious because Psalm 22:2 predicted it. While he was on the cross, Jesus must have cried out, "My God, my God! why have you abandoned me?" (Matt 27:46) because that would be the anti-type of the Psalmist (22:2). Again they offered him vinegar to drink because the Psalmist prophesied it (Ps 69:22; Matt 27:48-49).

Convinced that Jesus was the Messiah and armed with these two Psalms, the author of this narrative did not at all presume that he was composing fiction. As a good research student, he was simply applying the scripture that was available to him as the only source in the world. That which was prophesied there must have been fulfilled in the days of the Messiah, even if there had been no nonscriptural witnesses to see it happen. Like the wise man, Daniel, Matthew knew some mysteries that the pagans did not know. He employed these to reconstruct the past; these same tools could be employed to discern the future.

Historical Jesus and the Origin of the Churches

Introduction. The question that is often raised but left unanswered is, " How did the church originate from the life, actions, and teaching of Jesus?" Absolute answers cannot be given, but some of the possible ingredients that may have contributed to its formation will be offered here. These have all been discussed in earlier chapters. They are: (1) the Jewish doctrine of atonement, (2) the two sides of conquest theology, (3)fulfillment of prophecy, (4) the Pentacontad calendar, and (5) apostolic administration. These will be reviewed in order.

The Doctrine of Atonement. Redemption is a mythological term for Jewish liberation from foreign control of Palestine. This is based on the belief that God keeps records of virtues and sins. Every year on New Year's Day, the Lord holds judgment, weighing the merits and sins of Jews in comparison with Gentiles. If the merits are inadequate to compensate for the sins, Jews are destined to continue in captivity, serving out their term as debtor captives. Words like redemption, treasury of merits, forgiveness, and reconciliation are all finance oriented metaphors. When the account is overdrawn, the creditor in normal Jewish borrowing systems is free to demand payment in terms of work at half wages until the debt is paid. This makes the debtor a captive or prisoner, and Jews removed from the promised land speak of themselves in those terms. No matter how many good works are applied to the credit of Jews, they always think of being redeemed by God when liberation takes place. Some Jews believe that Jews can never pay back their debt of sin to the Lord. Therefore, relief can only come when the Lord chooses to redeem Israel by forgiving Israelites their sins.

The Two Sides of Conquest Theology. Conquest theology is the belief of a people that considers God's will to be involved in acquiring a certain portion of land for a given people. Since it is God's will, God approves and supports the people involved in all their battles to gain possesion of the land. One way of acquiring the land was through warfare, believing that God was the Lord of armies who would fight alongside the soldiers to overpower the much larger forces of the enemy. If Israel should ever acquire the land by military force the leader of the troops, as well as the Lord, would be considered a savior.

The other way of acquiring the land was to increase virtue on the part of Israel and disfavor for the enemies. By walking the second mile, turning the other cheek, and yielding to mistreatment without retaliation the covenanter was actively engaged in redeeming Israel by paying off her indebtedness of sin. On the Day of Atonement, if Israel were judged meritorious, God would wreak vengeance upon Israel's enemies and restore the promised land. Any leader who added enough merits to the treasury to obtain a positive verdict from the Lord on the Day of Atonement would also be a savior, because he or she would save Israel from her sins (Matt 1:21) and would therefore be as much responsible for the acquisition of the land as if he had led armies to overpower the enemy. If this happened, on the Day of Atonement God would wreak vengeance upon Israel's enemies and restore the promised land. Both types of conquest theology were possible choices in NT Times.

The strong emphasis Paul made against retaliation (Rom 12) shows how much this topic was argued. Some Jews may have believed both methods were effective, depending upon the time and the conditions. Since both have scriptural support, the question was which should be applied at this time. Should Jews suffer or fight? Jesus may have considered both possibilities, waiting for a sign from Heaven to show which way he should go. The fact that the apostles were prepared to become involved in a war and betrayed or denied Jesus only after he seemed to them to be stalling unnecessarily indicates that military action was a genuine consideration. He was obviously organizing as effective a following as possible, in case a military action seemed dictated. He apparently also discussed with the apostles the other option—suffering to pay off Israel's sins, because the apostles quickly interpreted Jesus' death as an atonement sacrifice given to redeem Israel from her sins.

This does not mean that every reference in the gospels that reports Jesus saying, "The Son of man must suffer," is a valid, historical quotation from Jesus. Neither does it mean that the temptations account or the report of the agony at Gethsemane are literal, historical quotations. Both are obviously mythical accounts of inner experiences, but these sayings may indicate a genuine spiritual struggle the apostles realized Jesus had been undergoing in his effort to understand what God wanted him to do at this time. When Jesus was actually captured without a struggle, apostles assumed that Jesus had voluntarily chosen suffering rather than fighting. With their theology of the Day of Atonement, they believed that a messiah's suffering unjustly would contribute much more to the treasury of merits than any ordinary Jew.[25] Perhaps this alone would be enough to turn the tide; this would be the required Atonement offering necessary for redemption and forgiveness of sins. If so this would mean Jesus' claim that the Kingdom of Heaven was near could still be proved to be accurate! There was also scriptural evidence for believing this was true.

Fulfillment of Prophecy. Since all prophecy was destined to be fulfilled in the days of the Messiah and since Jesus was the Messiah who had voluntarily accepted suffering rather than conflict, it was obvious that he had fulfilled the prophecy of Second Isaiah. After all, it was the suffering servant of Isaiah that provided the basis for nonretaliatory suffering and here it had been fulfilled! The proof text was Abraham's faith (Gen 15:6), but this kind of righteousness was vindicated through the suffering servant at the time of the Babylonian exodus. It was the first generation or two of Jews in Babylon who constituted the suffering servant at that time,[26] but in the days of the Messiah, it was the Messiah who had fulfilled this prophecy. As this suffering provided the means for return in the days of Ezra and Nehemiah, so Jesus' suffering would be the redeeming agent in the days of the Mes-

---

[25]GWB, *Revelation*, pp. 342-43.

[26]For a defense of this position see GWB, *Consequences*, pp. 123-31.

siah. On the Day of Atonement God would forgive Jews their sins and restore the promised land if Jews met the following conditions: the covenanter was required to (1) repent, (2) be reconciled to his fellow Jew, and (3) bring the required atonement offering to pay for the sin committed against God.

Jews quickly understood that Jesus fit into this picture by providing all of the atonement offering required. That which was left was repentance and reconciliation among covenanters, so Paul and others set about preaching reconciliation and repentance. As the Messiah, Jesus was considered God's apostle or agent (Heb 3:1). This means he could speak with the authority of God. Legally, he was identical with God within the limits of his authority. This was as high a rank as human beings could attain. From that lofty position, he voluntarily accepted the role of the suffering servant of Isa 53. The early church was quick to point out the great reduction in rank between messiahship and servanthood:

> Have this mind in you which was also in Christ Jesus,
> who, being in the status of God,
> did not consider [legal] equality with God
> something to be retained,
> but he reduced his own rank,
> accepting the status of a servant.
> While he was like human beings,
> in human physical form,
> he reduced his own rank,
> being obedient to the point of death,
> death on a cross (Phil 2:5-8).[27]

After encouraging Christians to avoid sin by submitting willingly to any oppressor so as to gain merit and favor with God, the author of 1 Peter (2:11-20) said, "For to this you have been called, because Christ also suffered in behalf of you, leaving an example so that you might follow in his tracks, who *committed no* sin, *neither was any deceit found in his mouth* (Isa 53:9), who, when he was reviled did not revile; while suffering, he did not threaten, but he gave himself over to the one who judges justly. *He himself bore our sins* (Isa 53:4) in his body on the tree, so that we might be rid of sin and live righteously. Of his *wounds you have been healed* (Isa 53:6), for you were *as straying sheep*" (Isa 53:6; 1 Peter 2:21-25).

---

[27]Contra J. G. Machen, *The Origins of Paul's Religion* (New York, 1923), p. 150. This does not refer to Jesus' economic class as a laborer but to his rank as a voluntary suffering servant of Isaiah. This happened at his death, not at his birth.

Those whose faith was based on the fulfillment of scripture, the doctrine of atonement, and conquest theology were not depressed by the death of the Messiah. To be sure, the messianic movement had failed. Historically that which happened was that the Messiah had been captured by the Romans and crucified; mythologically, however, the program was a success. God would still bring about the desired end, they believed. All that was left to obtain atonement for the nation was the forgiveness and reconciliation of the covenanters. The early church set about teaching the necessity of forgiveness and reconciliation, the unfulfilled demands for redemption. This was current agenda.

The messianic movement, which involved the historical Jesus, was not only not continued, but Christian leaders, like Paul, taught that the active militarism of Phineas and Paul's own former Pharisaism was a mistaken zeal. This new movement had the same goal as the old one, but its methodology was pacifistic in nature, rather than being activistically, militarily oriented. The basis for this mythology was that the sacrifice necessary for atonement had already been made. From the standpoint of the Day of Atonement theology, this was the important contribution Jesus made to the enterprise. It was not organizational skill of the Messiah and the commitment of his supporters to resistance against Rome that was important then. At that point the covenanters' ability to repent was the chief item on the agenda.

The event that made this possible was not military action but the voluntary sacrifice of the Messiah. The death of the Messiah was the only historical event important then. That was the basis for the new proclamation of good news, the new saga, the myth. The sacrifice of Jesus, involving his death, was considered the "work" of Christ, as distinct from the earlier deeds of the historical Jesus. This was not a militarily based resistance movement but a mythologically based political movement, structured according to the theological doctrine of forgiveness and Day of Atonement theology, but this new saga would not have been conceivable if Jesus had not been known as the Messiah before his death.[28] It was the *Messiah's* suffering that would provide enough merit to bring about redemption. No other Jew's merit would be adequate.[29] This emphasis on conquest theology cap-

---

[28]Contra A. Schweitzer, *Quest*, p. 345; *The Kingdom of God and Primitive Christianity*, ed. U. Neuenoschwander, tr. L. A. Gerrard (New York, c1968), p. 78; W. Wrede, *The Messianic Secret*, tr. J. C. G. Greig (London, c1971), pp. 48-49; E. Käsemann, "The Problem of the Historical Jesus," *Essays on New Testament Themes* (Naperville, c1964), p. 31; and Bultmann, "Study," p. 71.

[29]GWB, *Revelation*, pp. 73-74.

tured more interest from later Christians than has the historical Jesus, but both the historical Jesus and the saga of forgiveness are parts of the same Christian heritage. Neither Christianity nor Judaism, however, has ever given up the militaristic emphasis of conquest theology. Sometimes we have rejoiced in our sufferings, but at other times we have gone into battle, confident that God was on our side.

The Pentacontad Calendar. The oldest calendar in the Fertile Crescent was organized completely around sevens.[30] There were seven days in a week, seven weeks to a unit of forty-nine days, called a pentacontad or "fifty." There were seven of this units in a year, bringing the number to three hundred, fifty days. There was an additional period of fifteen or sixteen days between the old year and the new year, so that the new year would begin at the opening of harvest every year. This period was not counted as part of the year; neither were the fiftieth or "pentecost" days. At the end of every seven weeks there was a celebration before the first day of the new pentacontad began. The following diagram will show how the year was divided:

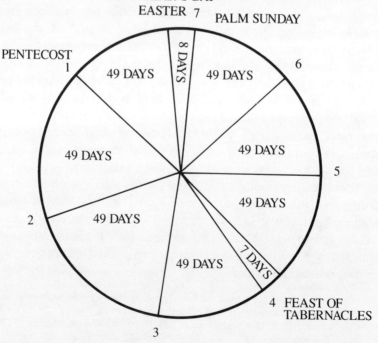

NEW YEAR'S DAY

EASTER 7   PALM SUNDAY

PENTECOST 1   49 DAYS   8 DAYS   49 DAYS   6

49 DAYS   49 DAYS

5

2   49 DAYS   49 DAYS   49 DAYS

49 DAYS   7 DAYS

4 FEAST OF
TABERNACLES

3

---

[30]J. and H. Lewy, "The Origin of the Week and the Oldest West Asiatic Calendar,"

Each pentacontad celebration fell on the day now called Sunday. Israel made some adjustments in this calendar by dividing the fifteen or sixteen days into two units, one, the Feast of Tabernacles, at the end of the fourth pentacontad, and the other at the end of the seventh pentacontad, just before the new year.[31]

There used to be a festival at the end of the seventh pentacontad in which large numbers of townspeople would walk in procession to a temple outside of town where they remained until New Year's Day.[32] That happened at the end of the old year. Before that festival began, the people destroyed all of the produce from the old year, believing that it was bad luck to carry any over into the new year. During the week in between the old and new years, they ate unleavened bread. On New Year's Day they put the first sickle into the grain and began to eat from the new grain.[33] Like the Christian Pentecost, the feast of the first pentacontad occurred fifty days after New Year's Day. On that day ancient Hebrews celebrated the presence of the Lord.

During the winter Jews would not move camp, knowing that the real presence of the Lord was in the smoke that huddled around camp, not forming a straight pillar to heaven.[34] The first pentacontad celebration was far enough along in the Spring that there was no danger of further rain. Campfire smoke went up like a pillar, so they celebrated the Lord's presence at that time.

This old calendar was gradually replaced by a lunar calendar, but not all at once. Jews continued to celebrate the harvest and New Year's Day by the preceding fast of unleavened bread and the liturgy of cutting the first grain. They also expected God to judge the world on that day. After they moved New Year's Day to Autumn, Jews really celebrated two New Year's Days. This old calendar is still reflected in some of the Dead Sea Scrolls,

---

HUCA 17 (1942/43):1-152. See also R. North, "The Derivation of the Sabbath," *Biblica* 36 (1955):182-201 and R. North, *Sociology of the Biblical Jubilee* (Rome, 1959).

[31] J. Morgenstern, *Some Significant Antecedents of Christianity* (Leiden, 1966), p. 20-21.

[32] J. Morgenstern, "The Calendar of the Book of Jubilees, its Origin and its Character," *VT* 5 (1955):34-76; Lewys, ibid., pp. 105, 111. Unaware of this calendar and the customs associated with it, R. Augstein, *Jesus the Son of Man,* tr. H. Young (New York, c1977), p. 144, said Jesus probably entered Jerusalem on Sukkoth.

[33] Morgenstern, "The Calendar," p. 40-42; Lewys, ibid., p. 81.

[34] Morgenstern, ibid., pp. 53-54.

the Book of Jubilees, and some parts of the Pentateuch, and it is still observed by some Oriental Jews and Christians. Belief in the resurrection was also associated with New Year's Day.[35]

The procession on Palm Sunday may have been a celebration that carried on the old tradition of the Babylonians and Assyrians of walking in procession to the temple on that day. Jesus' observance of the Passover meal a full day before popular Judaism did suggests that he followed a different calendar. Whatever the historical events were at the very beginning of the church after the death of Christ, it found expression in this old calendar. The resurrection was celebrated on the old New Year's Day, which was the day of greatest rejoicing in the year. There was also scriptural proof that Jesus had been raised. Hosea said, "After two days he will heal us; on the third day he will raise us" (Hos 6:2). This is probably what Paul meant when he said, "He was raised on the third day, according to the scriptures" (1 Cor 15:4). Historians would count days and observe that there are only two nights and one day between Friday evening and Sunday morning, but these are details about which historians are concerned—not mythologists. Mythologists such as Daniel express their feelings and faith fully and force the historical data to fit; they do not adjust their feelings to suit contrary data.[36]

Pentecost was already there in the calendar being celebrated by Jews in NT times as a day when the Lord's presence was evident, closely related to the pillar of cloud and fire of the tent of meeting. This celebration may have used torches or candles or something like that in its liturgy. The experience described in Acts of the first Christian Pentecost and the reception of the Holy Spirit seems to fit in well with an already traditional celebration. Just as Israelites modified the fast of unleavened bread to fit their needs and justified it according to their own history, so Christians gave expression to their new faith, following the patterns of the old Pentacontad calendar.

---

[35]See also Morgenstern, "Supplementary Studies in the Calendars of Ancient Israel," *HUCA* 10 (1935):1-148, and Morgenstern, *Antecedents,* pp. 16-40.

[36]In addition to the seventy weeks of years in Daniel, E. Wiesenberg, "The Jubilee of Jubilees," *RQ* 3 (1961):3-40, after analyzing the Book of Jubilees, concluded "Evidently, therefore, neither the Jubilee of Jubilees in the *Book of Jubilees* nor its pendant in *Pseudo-Jonathan* arose from sober chronological calculation. It was rather the other way around. The *Book of Jubilees'* ubiquitous chronological trappings are but a contrivance designed to give the air of plausibility to the preconceived notion that the Jubilee of Jubilees was marked by an event of permanent significance" (p. 29). See also TZeb 13:6; JMeg 1; AZ 9b.

The historian will ask whether the resurrection really occurred as a historical event, but he or she cannot answer it because early Jews and Christians were more interested in myth than in history. They explained the historical events mythically when they had religious significance. When they did so, the saga only reflected history as a background for a mythical expression of faith. To be sure, Israelites somehow crossed the Reed Sea, but the mythologist said the water stood up like walls on both sides as they crossed over on dry ground. They actually won a battle against the Philistines, but the mythological poet said, ''The stars in their courses fought against Sisera!'' Judas actually won a very important battle against the Syrian Greeks, but the author of Daniel constructed this event in terms of a judgment scene in the heavenly court when the Son of Man appeared as the plaintiff in the trial and was vindicated. The saga used such terms as clouds of heaven and Son of Man in association with enemy beasts. This is the way religious people wrote saga or myth.

The first seven chapters of this book have tried to distinguish myth from history and show some of the ways in which a historian can responsibly distinguish some of the teachings of the historical Jesus from the later mythological interpretation of the church. These last two chapters have attempted to show how the early church thought when it made its contribution to the gospels. The ''early church'' is the name given here to whatever early Christians there were who contributed to the formation of the gospels following the composition of chreias and parables. No attempt has been made here to identify these leaders by name, date, or geographical location. They can only be known for sure by their scribal activity in the gospels. These early Christians did not write carelessly, maliciously, or deceitfully. Early Christian and Jewish authors had rules, patterns, understandings, and traditions that were taken into account. The readers of their documents understood all of these patterns and this study has been an attempt to introduce these thought-forms to twentieth century Westerners so that readers can pass their own judgments on the data provided.

Apostolic Administration. One of the reasons the church was able to continue after the crucifixion is that there was already an administration functioning. The apostles who had been trained to act as ''fishers of men'' had been selected from the upper classes and were well-trained in administrative skills. It was they who used and preserved the teachings of Jesus in the form of parables and chreias. How extensive this organization was can only be conjectured from small bits of evidence. No later than A.D. 37

the church was already functioning in Damascus, Syria, because that is probably where Paul was converted (Gal 1:17) at least three years (Gal 1:18) before Aretas (9 B.C.—A.D. 40) ceased being ruler of Syria (2 Cor 11:32-33). About fourteen years later (Gal 2:1; 2 Cor 12:2) Paul was making plans to finish a collection and go to Spain (Rom 15:22-33) and he corresponded with a Christian church that was already organized in Rome. By the time of the council in Jerusalem (no later than A.D. 52), Paul needed to negotiate with Peter, James, and John.

At the time of the council Peter seemed to be responsible for the territory in the North because he was in close association with Paul at Antioch (Gal 2:11-12). James was then administering church programs from Jerusalem (Gal 2:9, 12) and John seemed to be in charge of Samaria.[37] Because Jesus had recruited these wealthy tax collectors and businessmen he left not only intelligent and capable leadership but most likely a strongly financed program as well. All of these are factors that are necessary for the continuance of any program. These were men who had been so firmly committed to the program Jesus was leading that they had given all their possessions and skills to the movement. Although they had been expecting to participate in a military revolution, they had been well enough trained in the various aspects of conquest theology to be prepared to reevaluate the signs and reinterpret the scriptures when they were faced with a problem that frustrated their first design. These were some of the human factors that contributed to the organization of the church.

Although much more emphasis has been placed on data than conclusions, more upon interpreting customs than forcing decisions, this has not been completely aimless wandering. There are a few basic conclusions at least tentatively reached as we went along chapter to chapter, and these will be reviewed here.

Summary

Chapter one, "The Kingdom of Heaven," consisted of an examination of this term in relationship to contexts in the OT, Targumim, Rabbinic literature, and the NT. This was discovered to be a code word used to mean the promised land under Jewish control. It was a political term that rightly belonged in a context with other terms applied to Jesus, all of which were titles for a king. This kingdom was compared for Westerners to Khomeini's

---

[37]See further GWB, "The Samaritan Origin of the Gospel of John," pp. 149-75.

government in Iran in an effort to enable people who do not normally think in terms of Near Eastern concepts to understand the thought-forms of the gospels.

Chapter two was a technical chapter, "Rhetoricians, Philosophers, and Literary Forms." Partially in disagreement with earlier form critics, I attempted to define and evaluate the form of the chreias, to show the extent of its use, to examine the reliability with which it was preserved, and to relate it to the teaching methods that produced it, whether they were used by pre-Christian philosophers, rhetoricians, rabbis, church fathers, Greek commentators, or gospel writers. Methods of writing history and homily were studied and the reliability of early Greek historians was appraised. The chreia was found to be a basically trustworthy form for use by historians and it has been used confidently by historians for centuries, not as a means of preserving the exact words of any leader, but of preserving some basic idea or teaching that has been put into capsule form.

Chapter three applied the insights from chreia study to an understanding of the historical Jesus. "Campaigning under Pressure" presented many chreias with one basic emphasis. These were accompanied by corresponding parables with the same major thrust. Jesus was here seen as a man in a hurry under tremendous commitment, urgency, and demand. The coherence of the parables and chreias brought together here fit in well with the historical situation in Palestine before A.D. 70.

Chapter four, "Liberty and Law," was composed around a collection of chreias and parables that showed Jesus in conflict with the Pharisees, defending his program of admitting repentant tax collectors and other "liberal" Jews who had mingled with Romans. He and the apostles had obviously encountered these Pharisees frequently because they had developed many good stock answers and illustrations to use in arguments.

Chapter five was a slight digression, "Monasticism and the Economic Classes." Because chapters three and four indicated that Jesus was associating rather comfortably in an upper class environment while making monastic demands, this special study provided further evidence for supposing that Jesus may once have been very wealthy before giving all of his money to a group that called itself "the poor" and observing monastic principles.

Chapter six, "The Mystery of the Kingdom of Heaven," was also based on chreias and parables that showed evidence of coded messages that had been communicated to groups where there might have been Romans or Roman collaborators as well as Jews. Some of the parables and other messages were designed to give hidden clues to those familiar with scripture and Jewish tradition. This pictures communication taking place in a revolutionary society under political unrest.

Chapter seven, "The Royal Treasury," got its name from the treasury of merits as a metaphor patterned after the nation's treasury. In this chapter were brought together those chreias and parables that deal with either providence or forgiveness. Here were found literary units that discussed such geographical locations as the temple area and the Tower of Siloam at the border of Jerusalem and incidents that took place in the time of Pontius Pilate. They were made to people who understood the events cited without further explanation. Therefore, they must have been written with the locale of Jerusalem and the time of Pontius Pilate to be understood without explanation. Some of the summary conclusions about the study up to that point noted that chreias and parables were so coherent in the gospels and so closely related to personalities like Pilate and Herod and presumed the existence of the temple that it would take a great deal of imagination and credulity to accept the claim that the later church, from many periods and places, composed all of these without betraying their own localities or times.[38]

It would be strange indeed for the later church to compose prophetic statements after the fall of Jerusalem when these hopes, which predicted that the Kingdom of Heaven would come soon, had clearly failed and then attribute them to Jesus! Why would the church want to give an erroneous picture of Jesus as a false prophet? If they had not been very faithful in preserving the accurate teachings of Jesus the normal expectation is that they would have destroyed these.[39] The direction of the church after A.D. 70, and

---

[38]R. Augstein, *Jesus,* p. 237, said "One would like to know what criteria moved J. Jeremias to the statement that anyone who concerns himself with the parables of the first three gospels is standing on 'particularly strong historical ground'; they belong to the 'bedrock of tradition.' " In the preceding chapters of this manuscript some of the criteria Jeremias overlooked have been provided.

[39]Contra Perrin, *Rediscovering,* "So far as we can tell today, there is no single pericope anywhere in the gospels, the present purpose of which is to preserve a historical reminiscence of the earthly Jesus . . ." p. 16. Kähler's argument (M. Kähler, *Der sogenannte historische Jesus und der geschichtliche biblische Christus* [Munich, 1956]) that gospels are only passion narratives with lengthy introductions will no longer hold. The material of the gospels is of different kinds which can be sorted out, distinguishing historical material from mythological or exegetical additions.

especially after A.D. 135, was to disassociate itself from the militarism and sabotage associated with Judaism at the time of Jesus. These chapters encourage the historian to think that the evidence left in writing about Jesus provides a good basis for reconstructing a picture of the historical Jesus during the time of his campaign. The two final chapters show the methodology, thought-form, and performance of the early church in composing the gospels.

Chapter eight, "Cycles of Time and their Signs," like chapter two, is a technical chapter, dealing with methodology, showing how Jews of Jesus' time thought—their concepts of time and how it was fulfilled, their use of scripture to foretell the future and deduce the unknown past, their understanding of typology, and their composition of myths. This was done to prepare the reader for the last chapter.

Chapter nine examined four units or types of literature in the gospels that are not parables and chreias: (1) birth and childhood narratives, (2) a literary unit expanded homiletically to explain an unknown event in the life of Jesus, (3) the relationship of miracles to expectations, prophecy, and typology, and (4) the use of scripture to determine the events at the cross. None of these seemed reliable methods of determining history, but the church followed a long Jewish tradition of using scripture and typology in the way it did to compare myths around conjectured historical events. It was accepted procedure at that time and was well understood by the original readers.

Conclusions

The historical Jesus does not come to us "as one unknown." Those who want to know what is available to know of the historical Jesus must search and this quest involves a study of literature. Nearly all of the available data about the historical Jesus is now recorded in literature. To learn about the social, political, economic, and geographical world in which Jesus lived, the quester must read the literature surrounding the period—the OT, Philo, Josephus, the apocrypha, pseudepigrapha, Dead Sea Scrolls, rabbinic literature, Greek history, philosophy, and rhetoric. This, of course, may be supplemented by an acquaintance with modern geography, customs, language, and politics of the Near East, but most of this information dealing with events of two thousand years ago comes from literature written two thousand years ago. Direct information about the historical Jesus also comes from the literature of the NT. Therefore a study of the historical Jesus requires as much understanding as possible of the literature from which this information must be acquired.

The project undertaken here involved a careful study of such literary forms as chreias, parables, poetry, midrash, and saga. From the chreias and parables we were able to learn some historical factors of the life of Jesus. Here he was shown as a very dedicated man who was pretending to the throne of Israel. In secretive ways he organized a highly committed following and trained leaders to extend his program. He was a devoted Jew who was committed to the principles of conquest theology which he believed to be central to the covenant faith. His program grew, both in numbers and in effectiveness, because of his recruitment success among the wealthy "Reform Jews," namely, the tax collectors and other liberal businessmen. Because of this he and his apostles were constantly in conflict with the Pharisees who objected to Jesus' readmission of these people into the faithful community. He had a secure faith in God and his will for his chosen people and was patiently waiting for a sign from heaven to tell him where and when to act at the time he was captured by the Romans and crucified for insurrection. The most reasonable conjecture from the literature is that Jesus had trained these apostles in recruiting and taught them stock parables and other important teachings necessary for their task.[40] The nonparabolic teachings they organized into chreia form for easy memorization and ready use. This literature was either appropriated or originally composed especially for campaign purposes and it represents only that period of Jesus' life.

After the crucifixion, the apostles and their successors added to the chreias and parables in various ways. Sometimes they prepared homilies that they based either on OT texts or on one of the chreias they had learned. In the homilies they sometimes inserted other chreias or parables as illustrations. The homilies they prepared are also called midrash. Based on their understanding of God, the universe, the scripture, tradition, cycles of time, and typology, they composed sagas or myths which reflect their theological beliefs in the ways God functions in history. Two of these sagas are the in-

---

[40]J. G. Gager, "The Gospels and Jesus: Some Doubts about Method," *Journal of Religion,* 54 (1971):254-55, has argued that even ear and eye witnesses cannot be counted on to report an event accurately. He was assuming that there would be different reporters for each event and that the skill at reporting would be completely accidental. The picture would be different if a group of apostles were jointly obtaining information to use in their future discussions. This provides an opportunity for such corrective measures as checking the exact wording and taking careful notes before memorizing.

fancy and childhood narratives in the gospels and another is the Matthaean account of the events around the cross. Related to the same point of view by which sagas are composed, the miracles were probably written, although no one can know for sure, but miracles are not to be treated by the historian the same way as chreias or parables.

Although the parables reflect historical situations, they also sometimes include either mythological or parabolical language. These are not the same. Parabolical language is a kind of coded speech which permits certain listeners who know the scripture, mythology, and tradition to understand meanings that are not obvious on the surface. Sometimes the coded material in a parable is an allusion to some traditional or scriptural myth or saga that is familiar to those whom the speaker intended to understand his real message. Chreias could also contain coded or mythological language if that was the message the literary unit was designed to preserve.

Although there is a great deal of overlapping among various types of literature that can be used to reconstruct the period of history in Palestine during which Jesus lived and his function within it, it is important, analytically, to distinguish the chreias from parables, maxims, reminiscences, poetry, and other narratives. It is also important to isolate the parables from miracles, distinguish saga from history, and midrash from poetry. These are all legitimate forms of literature and each has a specially designed function. They are all native to the place and period of the historical Jesus, so it is not surprising that they are all included in the same literary gospels. Nonetheless, the reader cannot expect to be successful in his or her quest while confusing these various forms of literature because they have different intentions and possibilities.

After the literature is properly understood, it is still important to learn the history and customs of that period and area. The researcher cannot expect success by applying twentieth century ethics and practices to first century events. Neither is it possible to determine accurately the meaning of Near Eastern practices on the basis of Western ideologies. Once we base our thinking on the literature and practices of Jesus' time, it seems surprising how well the literature related to Jesus reflects his own time and geography and how well he fits into the role he was expected to fulfill.

In addition to the factors listed above, good logic and plain common sense are required to judge what is more and what is less probable. This is the demand that is made, not only upon the author, but also upon the reader. Although suggestive possibilities have been given, enough material is also provided to inspire the reader to consider the data for himself or herself and accept only those conclusions that make sense to her or him. This requires a little courage, sometimes, to realize that a person's own mind is a very useful and dependable instrument, sometimes capable of entertaining better analyses than have been previously considered. After reading the book, some readers may want to review again the data *only* of each chapter and then try to reach their own conclusions independent of the suggested conclusions provided. Then the quest becomes also the project of the reader and not just that of the author. This brings author and readers into a partnership relationship that is highly desired.

Concluding Note

Although thousands of scholars have set about to untangle the many facets of the historical Jesus during the last two centuries, in recent years there has been a great deal of skepticism about the possibility of anyone ever being able to reconstruct anything that would make sense out of the data available for this task. These moans of pessimism did not seem justified to me, so I set out to see if any more could be done than had already been undertaken. I am not laboring under the delusion that skeptical scholars are completely wrong or that I have here solved all of the mysteries.

Most of the things I have attempted have been attempted before. After listening carefully to the critics, I have tried to avoid some previous pitfalls and cover a little neglected ground. Some of the contributions to previous research may be the following: (1) I may have added some new dimensions to the understanding of Jewish thought-forms and customs; (2) I think I have given more attention to the literary forms involved than previous scholars have done; (3) I have attempted to reach objective conclusions on the basis of the data available, regardless of my personal wishes; (4) I have taken into consideration the relationship of the historical Jesus to the cause of his death and the survival of the church after the crucifixion. If this work has been moderately well done, in the future others who are capable of writing better books than this will be stimulated and research in this field will not come to a halt.

I am glad for the opportunity to share these views more widely than is possible without publication and I will be happy to hear the words of those who have been kind enough to read these words of mine.

• INDEXES •

General Index

Author Index

Ancient Authors
and Personalities

Reference Index

MUP Jesus
The King and His Kingdom

Designed by Haywood Ellis and Edd Rowell

Composition by MUP Composition Department

Production Specifications:
    text paper—60-pound Warren's Olde Style
    endpapers—80-pound Legendry, Clay
    cover—(on .088 boards) Joanna Oxford 32300
    dust jacket—80-pound Legendry, Clay
        printed PMS 168

Printing (offset lithography) by Omnipress of Macon, Inc.,
    Macon, Georgia
Binding by John H. Dekker and Sons, Inc.,
    Grand Rapids, Michigan